THE LIFE OF JOSIAH WEDGWOOD FROM HIS PERSONAL CORRESPONDENCE AND FAMILY PAPERS IN THE POSSESSION OF JOSEPH MAYER ... [ET AL] AND OTHER ORIGINAL SOURCES • VOLUME 1 • ELIZA METEYARD

Publisher's Note

The book descriptions we ask book-sellers to display prominently warn that this is an historic book with numerous typos or missing text; it is not indexed or illustrated.

The book was created using optical character recognition software. The software is 99 percent accurate if the book is in good condition. However, we do understand that even one percent can be an annoying number of typos! And sometimes all or part of a page may be missing from our copy of the book. Or the paper may be so discolored from age that it is difficult to read. We apologize and gratefully acknowledge Google's assistance.

After we re-typeset and design a book, the page numbers change so the old index and table of contents no longer work. Therefore, we often remove them; otherwise, please ignore them.

We carefully proof read any book that will sell enough copies to pay for the proof reader; unfortunately, many don't. For those we try to let customers download a free copy of the original typo-free book. Simply enter the bar-code number from the back cover of the paperback in the Free Book form at www.RareBooksClub.com. You may also qualify for a free trial membership in our book club to download up to four books for free. Simply enter the barcode number from the back cover onto the membership form on our home page. The book club entitles you to select from more than a million books at no additional charge. Simply enter the title or subject onto the search form to find the books.

If you have any questions, could you please be so kind as to consult our Frequently Asked Questions page at www.RareBooksClub.com/faqs.cfm? You are also welcome to contact us there.
General Books LLC™, Memphis, USA, 2012.

※ ※ ※ ※ ※ ※ ※ ※

AT length I lay the close of my long and responsible task before the public. Its appearance at an earlier date was impossible, as many of the most important documents did not reach me till a late season. Since then, nothing but steady and persistent industry could have mastered their infinite details, shaped these into sequence, and drawn thence that brevity of facts which narrative, to be vital and picturesque, requires.

Nothing has been spared, either by my publishers, Messrs. Hurst and Blackett, or myself, to make.the present edition acceptable to the public——as the volumes themselves will show.

I have been indebted to no sources whatsoever for the materials on which the work is based, except such as I have honestly indicated. With the exception of Mrs. Howitt's valuable note on Copestake, every line has been written by myself, and every illustration has been selected and placed by my own hand. Amongst the papers intrusted to me is Leslie's Life of Wedgwood;

Vi PREFACE TO an ill-written, incorrect, prosy pamphlet of 105 pages quarto MS. Several copies of this, I understand, have been made at various periods, and one I believe is still extant in the Potteries. The original in my hands has served me in no way beyond affording two, or at most three, cursory facts. It is in Leslie's MS. that we have the account of the deposit of the three Etruscan painted vases beneath the foundations of Etruria Hall.

It would be wearisome to catalogue the names of strangers and friends from whom I have received many marks of courtesy during the progress of this volume. I cannot, however, refrain from specifying those of the Right Hon. V. E. Gladstone, Mr. Smiles, Dr. Hooker, Mr. Bohn, the Rev. Lawford T. Dale, Mr. Roger Acton, Mr. Falcke, Mr. Tulk, Mr. Barlow, and Mrs. Howitt. Mr. Falcke, amongst other kindnesses, has contributed the cost of the engraving of his fine bas-relief, 'Priam begging the body of Hector,' and to Mr. Barlow I owe the engraving of the busts of Horace and Virgil, as well as other specimens. This volume will show how much I have been indebted to the choice and-varied collection of the latter gentleman for its adornment. In

'other ways his fine artistic taste has been useful to me, and will serve me still more, I hope, in subsequent labours devoted to the same end. I have to thank the Committee of the Wedgwood Memorial Institute for various courtesies, and especially the honorary secretary, Mr. Woodafl, to whose energetic able, and disinterested labours, the movement in behalf of Wedgwood's memory owes so much. I have also been obliged in several

THE SECOND VOLUME. vii necessary inquiries by the friendly kindness of Mr. J. A. Bacon, the head-master of the School of Design, Stokeupon-Trent.

My staff of artists has been the same as that employed for the previous volume. Mr. Pearson has been my most kind and able assistant throughout; visiting each collection with me, and carrying out my wishes and arrangements with earnest fidelity. All the illustrations in this volume, as those in the preceding, have been engraved by him. Mr. Justyne's beautiful pencil has also effected some masterpieces; and the exquisite rendering of the bas-reliefs will, I hope, draw public attention to Mr.

Tomlinson's skill in this delicate and difiicult department of figure drawing. I have also been most fortunate in my staff of printers. Without their practised and skilful aid, it would have been impossible to carry this long and arduous task to a satisfactory close; and Messrs. Spottiswoode will, I trust, add to their fame by the preparation of these richly illustrated volumes. In conclusion, I must not forget to refer to the courtesy with which my publisher, Mr. Blackett, has waited my time in respect to this work. But he has been well aware of the lateness at which many of the documents reached my hand, and he also knows that it is impossible for me to work, unless in a spirit of conscicntiousness and truth.

I shall be obliged to those who have collections of Wedgwood ware by any account of the same, or by permission to view them; particularly if such collections contain choice specimens of encaustic painted or black has-relief vases. I should also be obliged to possessors viii PREFACE TO THE SECOND 'OLU.lE.

of fine specimens of en-amelled useful ware by two-inch sketches of the border edgings of the same. Coloured slips, either on the curve or the straight, as the _case may be, would reach me through the courtesy of my publishers.

I now lay down my pen for a brief season. The success of this crowning work of my long public services will stimulate me to fresh labours in the same direction. I shall also feel that my long and self-denying labour has not been wholly barren of results, either as regards the improvement of public taste, or the culture necessary to a true advance in useful and ornamental art.

WEDGWOOD had now reached a very important stage in his career; and with the year 1768 a new one opened to him.. Hitherto the fruits had been hardly commensurate with the toil bestowed; but now, conjointly with much anxious preparative work, the realism tion of what had been hitherto mere dreams of the creative fancy, brought to him an exquisite zest of its own. He had prepared himself to create, and the world now saw the impress of the master-hand. The highest ideality in form—the painter's magic touch in colouring and effect. Of these preliminary labours the narrative must be briefly carried on. We have seen that his friend Mr. Vigor, of Manchester, had, as early as 1766, procured him some specimens of porcelain clay from South

Carolina, and to these had been subsequently added several varieties of the steatites peculiar to that country. The latter were probably calcareous and of little value, but the trials of the former having turned out Well, 'and the clay exhibiting probably some peculiarities of its own, Mr. Wedgwood was desirous of ensuring a definite supply. The place from which it was procured was called Ayorcc,1

' In his letter, Mr. Wedgwood spells the word Ilyorec. But it stands as in the text in the patent of 1763!.

4 CHEROKEE CLAY. Can. I. in the country of the Cherokees, lying about 300 miles from Charlestown. Whilst in London, during the spring of 1767, he ascertained the correct name and situation of this place from the map in the House of Commons, and proceeded, with his usual active vigour, to learn the best means of communicating with that distant country, and of securing a right in its rich alluvial deposits.

But many difficulties arose. If he applied for a Parliamentary grant, he found that it must pass through the hands of the Lords of Trades and Plantations, two of whom were respectively members for Derby and Bristol, and would naturally resist a monopoly in an article of use to such of their constituents as were potters. A patent was equally objectionable, as, from the publicity annexed, the advantages of such a discovery would soon appear, and give rise to endless petitions and difiiculties; and in case the patent were not allowed, a swarm of competitors would be the result. At this stage of the difiiculty, Mr. Wedgwood consulted his unvarying friend Earl Grower. Just then, the latter had many personal but no political friends in the Administration, and could render him no assistance until a change took place. There was necessarily danger in delay, for several persons had seen the clay, and an eager competition to secure it might arise at any moment. His Lordship therefore advised Wedgwood to send out an agent to South Carolina, promising to accredit him in every possible way to the Attorney-General and the Governor; the former

being Lord Gower's personal friend, and under obligation to him, as through his Lordship's interest he had secured his post. The Duke of Bridgewater's advice was also to the same effect. 'I have had,' he writes to Bentley, 'the honour of a long conference with his Grace of Bridge

CBAP. I. AN AGENT FOR SOUTH CAROLINA. 5 water on the subject of Cherokee. I laid the whole case before him without any reserve, & found the confidence I placed in his honour and advice not disagreeable. He does not think a Patent will stand for an exclusive right to the Cherokees, and upon the whole advises to send a Person over immediately without applying for a grant, Patent, or anything Else. Chas. Townshend, he says, as Chancellor of the Excheq', might be apply'd to grant it me Duty free & to lay a duty upon all imported by others, but that must be a Parliam' affair, and must be done another sessions, & very probably wod not pass, but wod inevitably lay the whole affair open. Besides, he says Mr. Townshend is a fr'I of Garb-ts,1 so is L' Shelbourne, & if it is mentid to the L" of Trade, his Grace says he knows G t, who is a Potter in Scotland, is sure to be advis'd of it. So he gives his advice as above, & I have some thoughts of following it.' 2

Curiously enough, Griffiths the reviewer had at this date a brother staying with him at Turnham Green, who had just returned from South Carolina after some years' absence. He was well acquainted with the country, and seasoned to the climate, as he had held a third share

' Mr. Garbett, of Birmingham.

" Wedgwood to Bentley, dated from London, May 23, 1767. From the same letter we learn that Mr. Wedgwood had had a revious interview with the Duke, ut that Brown, the famous landscape gardener, being present, little in reference to his immediate business could be said. 'The D——' he adds, 'rece" & convers'd with me just in the same afiiable, familiar manner as usual, when he first began to know us, by om'sel:.es in Propria Persona, and not from his go be-

tweerw. I intend to attempt another 0 portunity of taking his H——-'s a vice. Mr.

Brown has promised me the honour of a visit at Burslem, says he has often intended it merel from the character the Ladys h given him of me. I told him that in life was devoted to the service of the Ladys, as his was to that of the noblemen S; gentle" He assured me that they were not ungratefull, and intimated that I was nearly as famous amongst the Ladys, as he was amongst the Gen'.— we had a good deal of chatt on various subjects, & are to have another interview in town. He ma be of much service to me, & I sharl not neglect to cultivate what chance has thrown in my way.' in 3,000 acres of land, and had attempted the manufacture of maple sugar, after the manner of the Indians. From want of capital, however, he had to relinquish his partnership, though still retaining an interest in the land-and he now offered his services to Mr. Wedgwood. But there were difficulties even here. An agent entrusted with another mau's capital might convert it to his own use, ' for I have known instances,' explained Mr. Wedgwood to Bentley, ' of persons changing their sentiments & principles with the climate, & totally forgetting their connections with the friend they have left behind them. Suppose I sho' have his Bror bound for him, I shod hardly take the forfeiture if made. ' But thwe preliminary difficulties were finally overcome by fixing a credit in Charlestown with a merchant there, who would also act as a check upon any proceedings of Griffiths, which might be disadvantageous to Mr. Wedgwood's interests. Provided with letters from Lord Gower, which placed him under the protection of the Attorney-General of South Carolina, and with an allowance of 501. per annum and his maintenance, Mr. Griffiths sailed for North America in July or August. At the close of the year, Mr. Wedgwood heard of him through the agency of the AttorneyGeneral. He had then set out for the Cherokee country, accredited to the Indians, and attached to the escort of a native woman, who, years before, had been stolen from her nation, but, now redeemed, was returning to them. We are not told how Mr. Grifiiths succeeded in his mission, or if he was faithful to the trust reposed. The earliest arrival of a cargo of Carolina clay of which we have notice is in October, 1708, but from its being warehoused for a time in Liverpool, it is probable that it was only supplementary to others.

CHA P. I..' DR. FOTHERGILL. 7

For some time previous to this date, a literary correspondence had sprung up between Dr. Fothergill, the celebrated Quaker physician, and Mr. Wedgwood. The Doctor, who took great interest in scientific subjects, seems to have advised with him on this matter of foreign clays, and to have thought, as did merchants and many others who had already imported them in small quantities, that unless they were restricted to the manufacture of highly-prized porcelain, the difiiculties and expense 8 FOREIGN AND NATIVE CLAYS. CRAP. I.

connected with their transit from so remote a region would render them too dear to be available, to any remunerative extent, to either the importer or potter. It was not then very clearly, if at all, understood, that the natural law of supply and demand and the exchanges of commerce would settle this question in a far better way than patents, agents, or monopolies could do; and this, in fact, seems to have been the case, for in the year following Mr. Griffiths' departure, both the Cherokee and Pensacola clays had evidently become, if as yet in comparatively small quantities, an object of general traffic with merchants trading with North America. The war with our colonies for a time interrupted this, as it did almost all the other branches of import and export trade; but after the Declaration of Independence, the import of foreign clay was resumed, and with a considerable increase, though comparatively small compared with the consumption of native clays. Internal navigation had by this time fully proved its capabilities; more was known of the Cornish clays; the roads were being sedulously improved in all the more populated districts of the country, and the spirit of industry animated the body of the people with a power hitherto unknown. As soon as clay ranked with other goods as an article of ordinary import, the potter had the ability to choose that which was best fitted to his peculiar use. Mr. Wedgwood seems to have preferred the clay of Florida to that of South Carolina, and he thus wrote to Bentley respecting it. ' It must be I got as clean from soil, or any heterogenous matter, as if it was to be eat & put into good casks or boxes, & if they were to get several parcels at different depths, & put them in separate casks, properly number'd, I could by that means easily ascertain what depth of thc_mine is best

CHAP. I. TERRA PONDEROSA. 9

for our purpose, as it is very probable that there is a great difierence in that respect, if the stratum be a thick one.'1 '

Coincident with the steps thus taken to secure clay of a superior quality from the regions of the Far West, was a research of infinitely greater account; and one which, after a series of long 'extended experiments, resulted in Mr. Wedgwood's finest discovery, his crowning feat, as a philosophic chemist, that of the use of the Terra ponderosa, the Spath fusible of the French chemists, or the carbonate of baryta, and ultimately its sulphate, in the body of pottery. There can be no doubt that many prior attempts had been made in this direction, and that others were contemporary with his own. It was even rumoured that the T erra ponderosa was one of the ingredients used by the Count de Lauraguais in the composition of his porcelain, and Wedgwood, as we shall see presently, was very uneasy until he saw the Count's patent,2 lest it should restrict his use of the same material; but as he found that no process was given, or material to be used specified, he proceeded with his experiments, and the results were, at no late date, the vehicles of an artistic perfection, hitherto supposed impossible.

It would naturally occur, even to an uneducated mind, that those earthy substances, which were at once semiopaque and densely hard, would be serviceable to the potter; but, beyond its occasional use in glazes, we have no direct evidence that spar, in any of its available 1 "Yedgwood to Bentley, Novelnfarlned Vofod:'all, 1'tlhe prin(t3el:', in tlhe ber 21, 1768. co umns 0 t e ' ornmg ronic e ' = The patent bears the am of 1 June 24 and 29,1713. For this 112 June 10 1766. No specification was had to make a ublic apology which enrolled: On the question of his wpeared in t e 'Evening' Post, patent, the Count de Lauraguais de-. ovember 26, 1773.

10 THE LEAD MINES OF LANCASHIRE. Cn.u. I. formulas, had yet been introduced as a body ingredient. A few years later, we know very well that certain German porcelain manufacturers obtained supplies of this fusible spar in a scant and even surreptitious manner from the debris lying around the neglected, yet once celebrated, lead mines of Anglezark in Lancashire. They employed a' small farmer, who lived amidst the moorland wastes around the mines, to gather the spar which had been long before thrown out of the shafts as refuse, break it in pieces, pack it in boxes, convey it to Chorley, the nearest town, and thence dispatch it to Liverpool to be shipped. In order to carry out their operations with the greater secresy, the man and his wife made their gatherings only on moonlight nights. But at length their movements raised the curiosity of persons passing across the waste; rumours got abroad and reached the ear of Sir Frank Standish, the lord of the manor, and a stop was put to their proceedings. To enquiries, the man remained silent; and it was only some years later when, upon his death-bed, he told a neighbour that, long prior to discovery, he had carried on the sale of this spar, that it was exported to some porcelain works in Germany, and that he had sold it for five guineas per ton.

But beyond his general knowledge of various analyses, as those of the French chemists, of Pott in his Lithogconosia, and his practical acquaintance with felspar as an ingredient in glazes, Mr. Wedgwood had no guide for his own experiments. The results of Scheele's researches into the nature of the T erra ponderosa were not published till 1774, and Dr. Withering's experiments and discovery were of a still later date. The great merit therefore. undoubtcdly belongs to Wedgwood, of introducing, through the discovery of chemical affinities existing in nature,

CRAP. I. THE RESEARCH OF FRIENDS. 11 but previously unknown, of a new porcelaneoussubstance of exquisite adaptability and beauty. Of the successive stages of his analyses and experiments we necessarily know nothing, as the results were written in cypher, and confided to none but his wife, to Darwin, or to Bentley.

But all Wedgwood's confidential friends were aware of these experiments, and assisted, more or less, in supplying the necessary substances. Dr. Darwin, Dr. Fothergill, Mr. Bentley, Mr. Brindley, Mr. Whitehurst of Derby, and Mr. Vigor of Manchester, make up the list; but there can be no doubt, that to Bentley"s' untiring zeal is due the great merit of first supplying his friend with a spar which was not calcareous, and in sufiicient quantities for his experiments.'

We have already seen that, early in 1766, Wedgwood was experimentalising on various kinds of spar, but all the specimens supplied turned out calcareous. Undaunted by failure, he applied to his friend, Mr. Whitehurst of Derby,:1 very ingenious man, who combined the trades of a watehmaker and an engineer, and whose treatise, at a later day, on the 'Theory of the Earth,' was well considered. He worked the Derbyshire lead mines on an extensive scale, and Wedgwood naturally thought that these would prove legitimatc sources of supply; as ultimately they did, although Whitehurst seems to have looked somewhat sceptically on his friend's experiments. 'Mr. Whitehurst & I have settled a sort of correspondence,' he writes to Bentley; 'He hath set his miners to work to put by various samples of earths & clays, & I am to furnish him with all the curious pro

' Although, as we shall see, nearer home. It occui-s_in the beds

"edgwood drew his ultimate sup-of fine clay at Sheltun,1s abundant lies of Stlllhlltfl of barytn from ' at Mole Cup, and is found in the lilt-rl_vr=hire, tilm slnhstance lay much smldstune at Stoke-upon-Trent.

12 POTTS' LITHOGEONOSIA. Can. I. ductions or facts I can pick up from the cuting of the Canal.' ' A little later he proposed to Bentley a visit to the lead mines, but a slight return of previous indisposition made fiilfilment impossible. 'I have for some days past been threatened with a return of my bilious complaint. If it shod go off, I have some thoughts of meeting you at Derby, if you can let me know certainly when you will be there, and that you can stay a few days there; or, if you will return with me to Burslem, I will bring a spare Horse with me, & we can make Matlock in our way, and visit the Lead mines, which I want much to do, being in the midst of a course of Experiments which I expect must be perfected by the Spath Fusible, a substance I cannot at present meet with, but I will bring Putt2 along with me, who will direct us in the pursuit of it, and I am very certain we shod neither lose nor repent our—labour I will not call it, for it wod be the highest entertainment to us both.' But, as a chemical guide, Mr. Wedgwood found Pott's work of little use. ' I am making experiments from Pott, but am sorry to find the heat his experiments were made in was much more intense than can be made use of for Pottmaking. His results, therefore, _& mine are widely different, & I labour under great disadvantage in not being able to read his reasoning upon the subjects of his experim"; however, I have made several interesting ones if I had leisure, or could make it prudent, to pursue them, but my present business is too good to be neglected for uncertainties, & I must, so long as that is the case, be content without arriving at those improvements in my manufacture which a little application W0'1 bring within my reach; however, 1 Vedgwood to Bentley, February ' " Meaning the Lithogeonosia a 13, 1767. book of which Pott was the author.

Cnsr. I. ANTICIPATED IMPROVE-

MENTS. 13

I have improved bodys enough for vases, & ornaments are really an inexhaustible field for us to range in.'1 Yet even these prudential doubts soon passed away. A month later, we find Bentley with his own hand translating Pott's somewhat barbarous and involved Latin for his friend, and searching his French chemical dictionary2 for what the experimentalists of that country had to say on the Spath fusible. Thus assisted, VVedgwood carried on his labours with renewed heart, ' Many of my experiments,' he writes, ' turn out to my wishes, & convince me more & more of the extensive capability of our manufacture for further improvement. It is, at present, comparatively in a rude, uncultivated state, & may easily be polish'1 & bro" to much greater perfection. Such a revolution I believe is at hand, & you must assist in (and) proffitt by it. '3 In the following month, Whitehurst spent a week at Burslem, for the purpose of making experiments with his friend. At the same time Brindley and his wife were taking their brief holiday in the Peak, and on his return the great engineer gave such an account of the refuse thrown from the lead mines into the adjacent brooks, where, being soon washed free from dirt-, ' a great variety of ponderous bodys' were left behind, as to make Mr. Wedgwood wish he were ' fossiling amongst them.' But his experiments were succeeding, and his laboratory in a quiet nook of the ' Brick House Works ' had still greater charms than even the crystal brooks and wild hills of Derbyshire. ' My tryals,' he writes to Bentley, ' turn out admirably, and will enable us to do such things as never were done before, let Solomon or IV/cite/zurst say what 1T:37?Vedgwnod to Bentley, July 6, ;);'te8é)(;:ly v'vas':'ery ably trans" This was without doubt Mac-' 3 /edgwood to Bentley, August qucr's Dictionary, which at this date. 5, 1767.

I4 WEDGWOOD AS AN ANALYST. CRAP. I.

they may.' From this it is evident, that Whitehurst had little of the patient faith of the genuine analyst; and that having 'been witness of some of Wedgwood's failures, he had made short-sighted predictions which genius, as it ever does, held of no account. His knowledge seems to have been more superficial than profound; for though constantly dealing with ponderous and other earthy bodies, he mistook the nature of some clay he forwarded to Dr. Darwin for experiment.1 _

Any dread from the Count dc Lauraguais' patent dis posedof, by reason of the absence of all specification of materials employed, Wedgwood went onwards with his important work. The trial pieces still remaining, show how slow were the advances made; how, defeated today, he renewed his efforts on the morrow; undeterred, un doubting, full of the faith of genius in the ultimate elaboration of the true 'means to the countless purposes of those visions of ideal grace and beauty which filled his mind. The approach to success, the establishment of a criterion.by which he should insure in future an absolute certainty as to the true variety of the mineral employed, is thus heralded to Bentley. 'I have try'd all the Fossils you sent me, which had the appearance or distinguishing quality of S. P.2 & they all prove to be S. P. in reality, and most of them very good, some of them you may remember had the appearance & not the quality of S. P., & those have not the effects of S. P. in my experiments. So that I apprehend that we have a criterion by which this substance may be distinguished from other ap parently similar substances, when it can be met with. ' 3 It may seem surprising that Bentley, amidst his multi

CHAP. I. BENTLEY'S VARIED KNOWLEDGE. 15 farious occupations, could find time to enter so far into these experiments with his friend as to seek for, and be the first to obtain, the requisite mineral, which, so like other sparry andponderous bodies in many of its characteristics, was only distinguishable through the means of an elaborate chemical disintegration. But no branch of science or knowledge appears to have come amiss to this remarkable man. Mining was somewhat a hobby of his;

and he rivalled Dr. Darwin in his enthusiasm for moss drainage. In the previous year we find him with an interest in a mine of peculiarly fine cannel-coal, and he suggests to Wedgwood that a specimen basket of chips be kept at the pattern rooms in Charles Street for the nobility to see; but the project fell to the ground; not so much, as it would seem, from the incongruity of the two objects, coal and exquisite specimens of pottery, as from the fact that Cox was far too busy in selling cream-colour dinner services, and marbled and gilt vases, to attend to the matter. A little later he had entered into some nego tiations respecting foreign tanning, and Mr. Wedgwood, in his usual vein of pleasantry, said he might do as he pleased respecting them, except absent himself from the kingdom. But the drainage of swamps and the cultivation of moor land were Bentley's true hobby. He was an ardent and most unselfish patriot. He thought the best method of reforming the Government of the period was by increasing the productive wealth. of the country, and improving the condition of the people. He saw with concern thousands of acres lying waste, whilst. large masses of the population were unemployed, and corn at a. famine price. He wrote an admirable pamphlet on this subject; 1 as well as contributed

' Like the pamphlets on Canal Navigation, it appeared without the name of the author.

16 DR. TURNER OF LIVERPOOL. ' CRAP. I. several papers of a like character to the meagre and unsatisfactory periodicals of the day. Some short time previously to his leaving Liverpool he bought a little land on the borders of Chat Moss, inclusive of some acres of the waste itself. Here he tried his plan of drainage on a small scale; and with such marvellous success, that there can be no manner of doubt that, had he lived long enough to realise his share in the splendid fruits of his own and his partner's industry, he would have taken in hand, as a recreation, the improvement of this and other dreary swamps contiguous to Liverpool; and changed them, through the magic of cultivation, into fruitful

fields. As it was, he left the traces of the hand of a master on his small estate. Much of it, through neglect, ultimately returned to swamp; but enough remained, when the great Stephenson made his surveys for the Liverpool and Manchester Railway, to show how Bentley had anticipated in his methods of operation, this section of the principles of modern scientific agriculture.

Silently too, in his busy Liverpool surgery, Dr. Turner was compounding varnishes, fumigations, bronze powders, and other chemical appliances for his friend at Burslem. He appears to have excelled in a profound knowledge of the chemistry of colours, and more especially their application to fusible bodies. ' Dr. Turner's varnish came safe to hand, and is too cheap,' writes his generous friend to Bentley. 'One of the Fumigations is a. most excellent Enamel Colour; so fine a yellow, that I have some hopes of the Great Work being perfected, and that we shall be able to turn even the dirt under our feet into Gold.' '

So far for some few of the materials necessary to.

Mr. Wedgwood's advances in his art, whilst. hand-in

' 'edgwood to Bentley.

CHAP. I. IMPROVEMENTS IN THE LATHE. 17 hand, went _ onwards improvements in the lathe, as respected fresh adjustments and eounterpoises of pulleys and weights, ovals, tudicles, and rosets. His turner's experience in the bearing of the tool upon their work, soon did full justice to Plumier's anticipation of the slide-rest; though two-thirds of another century was to elapse before this most valuable mechanical invention was to lend a. new hand, as it were, to the arts. Mr. WedgWood's delicate manipulations in the line of ornamental variation also required tools of exquisite construction and fineness; as punches, spatula-like instruments, and gravers.' ' Of these he invariably drew the outlines with his own hand, and then consigned the necessary fabrication to the workmen of his friend Mr. Wyke of Liverpool, and occasionally to those of Mr. Stamford of Derby. Indeed, there is reason to think, that the more delicate of these little instruments were perfected by Mr. Wyke himself.

We have already seen something of this Liverpool worthy as a member of the Octagon Chapel, and a man of rare ability in his business of a watchmaker. At this date, 1767-8, his means were ample, for be manufactured watches on a great scale both for home and export trade; and having lately erected for himself a substantial house and workshops in a pleasant garden-court ofl' Dale Street, he married his second wife, and more than heretofore foundleisure for friendly duties, and for association with the keen and vigorous intelligence around him. A neighbour and intimate friend of Bentley,2 he was, as a matter

' The Roman potters appear to M. Tudot refer to the variety of the have used a. great variety of these tters' tools found on Iomanolittle instruments in their art. aulish sites.

Many of the most exquisite effects in 1 Mr. Vyke was ten years older the Anetine ware were in part pro-than Bentley, having been born In duced by very small spoon-like in-1720.
strumenta. Both M. Brongniart and 1

VOL. II. C 18 TOOL IVORK. CHAP. I.
of course, Mr. Wedgwood's friend also, and he seems to have spared no pains in fulfilling the commissions that so often came to him through the former.

Mr. 'Wedgwood in his letters to Bentley frequently mentions Mr. Wyke. On one occasion he says pleasantly, in referring to his wife, she 'hath sent you a watch by way of a love token I suppose, she says it is a little out of order, but one Dr. Wyke of your Town perfectly understands its constitution & complaints, & wo' set it to rights again if you will be kind enough to send it to him.'

Very frequently Wyke's men were too fully employed to undertake Wedgwood's commissions; and when that was the case a Mr. Finney was applied to. We find him making what Mr. Wedgwood calls 'punches of the leafage / sort,' and he stamps the pattern thus on

Mr. Stamford of Derby, another great friend of Mr. Bentley, also came in for a share of this business. ' I have this day,' Mr. VVedgwood tells his friend, ' recd some tools from Mr. Stamford to whom I am under great obligations on that & many other accounts, they are much better done than the last, & I apprehend his man will make them very well, Mr Wyke too has been here, & he promises to set about the patterns I sent him before, and some others I have given him, wtn some patt" for runners to be sunk with frieses, &c., as he says he has a hand for that purpose, so that if you have not employed a Tool

CRAP. I. BORDERS AND FRIEZES. 19 maker, I think it will be better to postpone that business for a little.'1 A month later Wedgwood again recurs to this subject. ' Instead of Gadroon edges which are now grown both old and common, I have got some runners made at Liverpool to make such borders as I have sketch'd out below, and other patterns in the same way..... now I think you might find out a dyesinker or seal Engraver to do things of that sort, those I have got done were by an old seal engraver in Liverpool; but they are sadly executed. However, such as they are, I have made sufficient tryals with them to know that runners of that sort well executed will answer my expectations. Neat little friezes may be done the same way, and a variety of ornaments which I will explain to you may be made by means of them. The Lathe is turn'd round only once..... ' 2 Elsewhere he adds, ' Of N o. 1 & 2 I compose beads8 for various things, they are the best I have, & she'1 be glad to have diff' sizes of them for diff' sized vessels, but N o. 2 is not quite hollowed enough in the runner, the leaves are bad, there is no drawing or likeness of a leaf in them, they are too shallow, & the strokes in the leaves are so like the threads which they cover or bind, that the whole effect wants that distinctness which makes so essential a part of the beaut2_'/"ull. My idea of a perfect runner of this sort is, that the ground work sho'1 consist at a, the divisions between the twigs pretty acute or sharp,

but not deep, so far will be done upon the lathe.
1 Vedgwood to Bentley, October the vases of black basaltes are so 24, 1767. very exguisite as to rival anything of ' VVedgwood to Bentley, Novem-the kin in ceramic or metallic art. ber 21, 1767. Examples are to be found in almost 3 Some of the bead mouldings on every collection. 20 TVVIGS AND LEAVES. CRAP. I.

Then leaves must be cut (not punch'd) throI1 this ground work, at proper and equal distances, to have the appearance of binding the three twiggs together, but these leaves sho'I not have lines running lengthways as in No. 1, but shod first be cut plain and then fibred agreeable to nature with a main one, & the rest branching from that, but if these fibres could be left rais'd in the runners, I believe they wo'1 have a better effect, but am not certain of that, N o. 10 shows something of the manner of the leaf but not the ground work.'

Even in these minutest forms of ornamentation, we find that constant reference to the truth of nature, and the adaptability of the ornament to the purpose in view, which were amongst the primary sources of Wedgwood's marvellous success in these and other departments of his art. With the exception of No. 10, thus, these exquisite little sketches have been torn away and lost, but enough is preserved to us to prove the wonderful fertility of his inventive faculties. His mechanical ability was equally great. If a need arose, he could at once sketch out a tool for its accomplishment; and such needs were always arising. Here is his own description of a mechanical necessity, and the 'instrument with which he proposes to supply it. ' It often happens that a frieze is wanted when it cannot be imprinted with a runner, in that case suppose I wanted to put No. 7 there,1 I wod 1 One of the reference sketches which are lost.

CIIAP. I. MECHANICAL DEFECTS. 21 have it cut upon a brass runner, which shod be a groove by means of the projecting sides as a & a, so that running it upon a batt of clay, it she(1 make the impression & cut the frieze out at the same time, which it wo"l leave behind festoons & ornaments will be made in the same way, so that here is a wide field for a dye sinker if you can find a proper one/1

In spite of all which had yet been effected in regard to the lathe, it was comparatively a rude and imperfect machine, with many difficulties annexed to its use; as those relative to mechanical adjustment, the means and forms employed to produce variations of effects, and the connection between the tool-bearing hand and its relative work. With respect to this last difficulty, even Plumier's anticipative idea of the slide-rest gave little aid. Extraordinary as it may seem, Bentley, besides translating a large portion of Plumier's book for his friend, helped him to a practical solution of many difficulties; as this in connection with the tool-bearing force upon the work. We learn this from Mr. Wedgwood himself. ' I thank you for your judicious hints & instructions relative to the tremulous motion I told you we were often embarrassed with. I believe a weight would in general be preferable to a spring, & your ingenious method of adjusting it is a great improvement, & a very simple one, as real improvements & valuable inventions generally are. My workmen have found out by practice what you say, you are certain of the reason why it is so. The utility of
' Miscellaneous Papers.
22 A BUSINESS JOURNEY. CRAP. I. having the rest as near as possible to the work; & if you consider the tool as a lever, the rest as its centre, & the work bearing against, or rather upon, the end of the tool as a weight, the reason I think will be very obvious. But this is a very sad way of conversing on these subjects, one half day's conversation face to face, with the work before us, wo'l be more effectual to the purposes we are aiming at, than an age spent in writing, & I greatly long for such an interview on many accounts.' Mr. Wedgwood then suggests that they should meet at Knutsford any day Bentley will appoint, and adds, ' I propose this as a journey of business to myself, from which I have views of pecuniary

advantage from the art you are to instruct & perfect me in, & therefore I shall expect that you will permit me to act agreeable to my situation & expectations in that respect, therefore the first preliminary in settling this interview is, that it be no expense to you. You must be convinced of the reasonableness of this proposal, & I shall almost think you did not wish to see me if you object to it.... We shall want the book on Engine Turning with us, & if you have found anything curious in the Pottery branch in the 'Antiquitys,'1 if you brought a volume or two of them along with you they wo'l serve as a diversion from the subject at proper intervals. But this luggage requires that you sho' bring a ser' & cloak-bag along with you, or take a chaise & prevail upon your good sister to fill the other seat. The last will certainly be most agreeable to us both, if you can prevail upon Miss Oats to take an airing with you, as you will have the benefit of such good company, & I shall have the pleasure of waiting upon two of my worthy 1 The work by the Count de Caylus.

CRAP. I. DISCUSSIONS. 23 friends instead of one. Very true. I had forgot the Plans.1 They must be talked over & settled upon, & that work cannot possibly be done without the assistance of a Lady. But what must become of Miss Oats whilst we are poreing over our turning & trumpery? I have a wife & sister at her service, & a good & worthy fr'1 at Knutsford, Doct' Colthurst, to whom we owe a visit. The Doc' has a sister housekeeper, who is seldom from home if the Doct' sho'1 be out.' 2

Visits like the one proposed were not unfrequent. The good people of the quiet country town doubtless little dreamt that the strangers arriving with their cloak-bags full of papers and books were amongst the worthiest and wisest of their countrymen; or that their discussions over pipes and ale in the best parlour of the best inn, or around the hospitable hearth of their good doctor, related to improvements destined to advance the artistic condition of an important manufacture, and largely increase its export to foreign countries. But so

it was; and through a subsequent period of many months, the friends were busy with these discussions both personally and by letter. These referred to the rose and crown motion, both separately and combined; the use of weights instead of springs; the shake of the rose against the pulley or tudicle; the double counterpoise; the slope or ramping machine, by which ovals were turned; and many other mechanical adjustments and movements of the engine lathe which it is unnecessary to enter upon. From the ninth chapter of Plumier's treatise Wedgwood seems to have derived 1 Of his own and Mr. Bentley's thing can now be learned beyond the house at Etruria. facts that he was a man of eminence
' "edgwood toBentley,Februarv, in his profession and a predecessor 1767. En uiries have been made of the able and well known Peter respecting r. Conlthnrst, but no-Holland.
24 COLUMNAR FORMS. Can. I. much valuable assistance in relation to the turning of columnar forms, in their three variations of plain, fluted, and twisted. ' The twisted columns,' he says in one of his letters, ' are very apropos to what I am now attempting, an elegant pillar or column candlestick, in which the twisting would, I apprehend, have an excellent efl'ect, & I sho'1 be glad to know on this subject, first, whether you apprehend my lathes can have the apparatus for twisting fixed to them, or the whole lathe must be formed for the purpose? How far the mandarin may be, or requires to be, thrown from the right to theleft, and vice versa for this purpose I What sort of Rosettes, or Crowns, or Tudicles are made use of, and how & when are they fixed? Does it require the lathe to be turned backward and forward alternately, or will the twisted work be made with the Lathe being turned one way only? When I tell you that every motion will be new to me in the Art of Engine Turning, besides those produced by the Rosettes & Crowns used separately & not compounded, you will have a tolerable idea of what I do not know in this art. What I wish to know is every other improvement which may be applied to Pott-Turn, 'Si-_/_--t ing.' The

subsequent use Wedgwood (F,-g_,_, m. ,E,,c,_,,,w,m_ forms, is attested by the exceeding "Y" """"-beauty of many articles in which these effects have a chief prominence, as in the annexed example of a columnar-fluted 'candlestick.

Can. I. SOHO. 25

These improvements in the engine-lathe introduce us anew to Matthew Boulton of Soho. Our first glimpse of him was in connection with the affairs of the Trent and Mersey N avigation,,0f which he was one of the committee, though he appears to have rarely attended any but gene

' ral meetings; his interest connecting itself more with the

Birmingham branch than with the canal generally considered. But the affairs of the navigation, whether special or general, necessarily led to a frequent correspondence with VVedgwood in his ofiicial capacity of treasurer; and business transactions of a more private character soon led to most friendly intercourse.

Soho had by this time become a great speciality in the manufacturing World. The solitary rabbit warren of 1757 had given place in 1765 to a noble range of manufactories, constructed at a cost of 9,000l., and consisting of four squares, with connecting workshops sufliciently extensive for the accommodation of 1,000 workmen. Everything within was in keeping with this fine exterior. All the best machines and newest mechanical contrivances to save labour and perfect workmanship, which were then extant, had been introduced. Amongst these was a steam-engine on Savery's principle, and engine lathes of varying construction to suit the exigencies of metallic Work. England, as yet, had never possessed upon her soil such a splendid instance of organised industry, in which the minutest details were made subservient to one great end—the perfection and accomplishment of work. Taken as a whole, it was an industrial machine on a vast scale; organised by one mind, guided by one hand; in fact, the noble germ, out of which in that day grew Etruria, and in our own, the Saltaires, the Silvertowns, and a thou-

sand other splendidly organised centres of 26 PRODUCTS OF SOHO. CRAP. I.

industry. Organisation was necessary, as the multifarious character of the works produced show. They were far more varied than would now be considered profitable to the capitalist, who secures the best effects of power, whether it be mental or mechanical, through directing it to uniform and special ends. Till the advent of the philosophic Watt, and the concentration of the working force at Soho upon the construction and improvement of the steam-engine, the character of' the articles produced were allied more or less with various branches of the fine arts. Bronzing, enam-clling, inlaying of steel, the fabrication of silver as well as plated goods, button, snuff-box, and buckle making, and the production of ormolu in the shape of vases, candelabra, tripods, and minuter articles of exquisite form and detail, were all carried on in these wellgoverned workshops. Even pottery entered speculatively into the list of productions; and it is not improbable that but for his partnership with Watt, and the concentration of his ardent mind upon the difliculties connected with the improvement and construction of the steam-engine, Wedgwood would have found a formidable rival in his friend Matthew Boulton. Not that the latter could have ever excelled, or even approached, the former in his own special walk. Nature had made Wedgwood a great artist. His was a poet's conception and interpretation of his art. What his hand touched, what his eye vitalised through form and colour, thereon was at once seen the impress of nature herself in delicacy and perfection of truth. The long advancing labours of his fathers had culminated at length in that absolute perfection of vision and touch, by which great artists give tangibility to their conceptions. At this date, 1767-8, Mr. Boulton had taken for his partner a Mr. Fothergill, who generally assisted him in

CHAP. I. BOULTON'S LATHES. 27 all the working details of his great establishment. They opened a corre-

spondence in the chief cities of Europe, imported thence works of art, sought clever workmen both at home and abroad, and perfected them in both design and modelling in a school of their own within the walls of Soho. The result of this was the attainment of a degree of perfection in the manufacture of metal ornaments hitherto unknown in this country; and instead of importing articles of this character as heretofore, the balance of the scale changed hands.

The various improvements in the engine-lathe naturally bore reference to the character of the work it was called upon to execute; and the machine of the potter diflered from that which would be found applicable to the pewterer, the cabinet-maker, or the worker in hardened metals. Thus Wedgwood found that the lathes in use at Soho were somewhat different to his own. ' At Birmingham,' he tells Bentley, 'I saw a lathe executed upon the plan of that w" is full of Rosettes, & every Rosette had a projection from the edge so &c. for a Crown motion; the whole was most completely finished, & the person for whom it was made hath at present no use for it. I am to spend a day or two with him Boulton) and intend to ask him if he we" like to part with it. He. is, I believe, the first or most complete manufacturer in England in metal. He is very ingenious, philosophical, & agreeable. You must be acquainted with him; he has promised to come to Burslem, & wod attend our Congress1 (we are to 1 This was the term applied to Wedgwood was generally present, the frequent and happy meetings ' and they were varionsl enlivened between Mr. VVedgwood and his by Dr. Darwin, Mr. Vhitehurst, friend. Each one was indeed a con-Brindley, Captain Keir, and others. gress in the fullest sense: for Mrs. = 28 LATHES FOR ETRURIA. Cnsr. I.

have one immediately on my return, remember, on many ace"), but this year he is too much immers'd in business to indulge, he says, in anything else. There is a. vast difference betwixt the spirit of this man & the great Taylor, though both of them have behaved exceeding liberal to me, in offering me every improvement they could furnish me with/1

By the spring of 1768 Wedgwood, advised by Bentley, and assisted by the suggestions of his own workmen, had brought his improvements of the engine-lathe, considering them as referable to the potter's art, to a considerable degree of perfection. Combining these under one effective generalisation, he employed a skilful hand to prepare some new lathes for the furnishing of the ornamental works then fast progressing at Etruria. Writing to Bentley on February 22, 1768, he says, 'I wrote to you by the last post, but forgot to desire you would send the Engine Turning book by Daniel, which I now want to look at, as I believe we shall have a lathe or two made here, & can do it better than at Liverpool. We have an ingenious & indefatigable smith amongst us, who, ever since Engine Lathes were first introduced here, has been constantly employed in that business, & he promises me faithfully that whatever improvements I may instruct him in, he will make them for no one else; but that you know is a superfluous engagement, as we have renounced those narrow selfish views, & are to let our improvements take a free course for the benefit of our Brethren and Country.' From this date till the close of the century, when Maudslay's invention of the slide-rest was introduced, but few further improvements in the 1 Wedgwood to Bentley, May 23, 1-761.

Can. I. DR. DARWIN'S VVINDMILL. 29 engine-lathe, as applicable to the potter, in all probability took place; and imperfect as the machine thus necessarily was, the greater credit is due to those who effected the exquisite and often absolutely perfect work to be seen in the vases and other ornamental ware of that period.

Another friend of Wedgwood's was at this date busy 1n his behalf. Dr. Darwin was constructing for him the model of a windmill 'to grind colours (if it shod happen to grind anything,' he confides to Bentley a little archly) ' for our intended ornamental works at Hetruria. ' But a personal inspection of the doctor's labours begot more respect. ' I left home,' he writes to Bentley, ' on Wednesday, & got to Lichfield that eving, where I spent the next day in settling matters with Mr. Pickford & surveying the Doct" Windmill, which I think a very ingenious invention, & have some hopes that it will answer our expectations. If you can understand anything of it by the accurate drawing below, well.

If not, I believe you must come & see it. The middle part a, a, is drawn too small, & sho'I be bro' with a dome to the sails. Eolus, too, is mistaken in the direction of his blast, which sho"I have come horizontal to the directing 30 MODEL OF THE WINDMILL. Can. I. boards, b, b, & rebound from thence to the sails, but all these blunders you will easily set to rights.' 1 At a somewhat earlier date, we have a more philosophical account from the Doctor himself of his intended windmill. 'I think,' he says, 'it is peculiarly adapted to your kind of Business, where the motion is slow & horizontal. If the mixture of Clay or Flint and Water should grow stiff by the wind ceasing, I think it may be so contrived with ease as to be put into Motion again gradually, not suddenly: of this I can not judge quite distinctly, without seeing the consistence this mass will acquire by a few Hours rest. I will make you the model if you require it immediately, which I can do for the expense of 3 or 4 guineas, so as to evince it's Effects. The advantages are, 1. It's Power may be extended much farther than the common Wind-mill. 2. It has fewer moving Parts. 3. In your Business no Tooth and Pinion-work will be necessary. Plain Countries are preferable to hilly ones for windmils, because the wind acquires eddies in the latter.'2 A lengthened correspondence followed on this subject of the windmill; the model was made, and met, as we have seen, with Wedgwood's approval; but at this date he was busy with his buildings at Etruria, and we hear nothing fl1I'l'.1lI' of it till 1779, when Watt and Edgworth assisted in perfecting it, and it was set up at Etruria.

Meanwhile a mightier power than a changeable and ungoverned element was about to lend its giant-aid to the industrial arts under improved conditions, which made it virtually a new creation or development of latent force; and Dr. Darwin, generously casting, as it were, his own

' Wedgwood to Bentley, dated date, but referable to the close of from Charles Street, Grosvenor 1767, or the beginning of 1768. uare, London, March 15, 1768. Darwin Correspondence. Darwin to VVedgwood, without CKAP. I. DARVVIN RECOMMENDS STEAM. 31 mechanical labours and speculations aside, advised his friend to look in this direction. Mr. Wedgwood, as a. matter of course, must have seen Savery's steam-engine, or, as it was then called, fire-engine, at work at Soho, when there in the spring of 1767, and he may have heard Mr. Boulton regret its defective condition; but at any rate it is quite evident that, by the same period of the year 1769, the name of Watt and his improvements of the steam-engine were already well known to the philosophers of the midland counties. I/Vhat follows does the utmost credit to Darwin's generosity, candour, and the previsional character of his intellect. ' I should long ago have wrote to you, but waited to learn in what forwardness Mr. Watts' Fire-Engine was in. He has taken a Partner,1 and I can make no conjecture how soon you may be accommodated by Him with a Power so much more convenient than that of Wind. Iwill make packing Boxes & send you my model, yt you may consult the Ingenious. I am of opinion it will be a powerful and a convenient Windmill, but would recommend steam to you if you can wait awhile, as it will on many Ace" be preferable I believe for all Purposes.'2

Whilst this vast amount of preparative labour of so varied a character was slowly progressing, a London warehouse, which should be something more than a patternroom, occupied a good deal of Wedgwood's attention. The chief difficulty connected with this question was the enormous cost of conveying goods from Staflbrdshire to London, it averaging, as we have seen,

98. per ton by land carriage. The prices of the ware could not be raised in proportion; and WC(lgWOOL1 calculated that if he 82 A LONDON WAREHOUSE. Can. I: paid the carriage without altering the prices, it would make a difference of nearly 500l. per annum in his profits. He was also aware that, if he entered upon the plan of selling his goods at delivered prices, many of his customers would expect them to be delivered free, whether the distance were twenty or three hundred miles.

Undeterred, however, by this prospect of serious pecuniary loss, his resolution to open a London warehouse was sufliciently matured by the spring of 1767 as to induce him to look out for fitting premises. The room in Charles Street, Grosvenor Square, was rapidly becoming too small, and would be wholly so when vases were added to his collection. The first place which offered itself was a very large room in Pall Mall, with others attached; and which, lately used as an auction room, was now occupied as an' Artists' Exhibition Room. But Mr. Bentley strongly objected to hiring premises which had been made a public resort. His reasons were at once accepted by Wedgwood, and indeed strengthened by an observation of his own. 'At present,' he tells his friend, 'the nobility & gentry recommend one another to my rooms, & they never meet with any other Company there, but every body wod be apt to stroll into an Auction Room—one that they had ever had free access into—& that wod be the most effectual method I could take to keep my present sett of Customers out of it. For you well know that they will not mix with the rest of the World any further than their amusements or conveniencys make it necessary. I find I did not sufliciently explain to you my reasons for wanting a Large Boom. It was not to show or have a large stock of Ware in Town, but to enable me to shew various Table and desert services completely set out on two ranges of Tables, six or eight at least; such services are absolutely iieeessary 'to-be shewn, in order to do "the naedfu'll with the Ladys in the neatest, genteelest, and best

method. The same, or indeed a much greater variety of setts of Vases shod de corate the Walls, and both these articles may, every few days, be so alter'd, revers'd, & transfor1n'd as to render the whole a new scene, even to the same Company, every VOL. II. D -3- L _ ARRANGEQIENT OF VASES. CRAP. 1.
time they shall bring their friends to visit us. I need not tell you the very good effects this must produce, when business & amusement can be made to go hand in hand._ Every new show, Exhibition, or rarity soon grows stale in London, 8.: is no longer regarded after the first sight, unless utility, or some such variety as I have hinted at above, continue to recommend it to their notice. A Lady or Gent" may, out of Complaisance to their friends, come with them a few times to see a shew w'h w" they themselves are satiated, but of this they will soon grow weary unless they likewise share in the entertainm', & will much sooner carry their friends to a scene which is new to them all, than to one vhere their eyes have allways met with the same objects & the same arrangment of them. This may be avoided by us with very little address when we have a Room proper for the purpose. I have done something of the sort since I came to Town, & find the immediate good Effects of it. The two first days after the alteration, we sold three complete setts of Vases, at 2 & 3 Guineas a sett, besides many pairs of them, which Vases had been in my Rooms 6, b', and some of them 12 mcinths, & wanted nothing but arrangment to sell them. And besides room for my Ware, I must have more room for my Ladys, for they sometimes come in very large shoals together, and one party are often obliged to wait till another have done their business.' '

These remarks evince that Wedgwood's power in reading the foibles as well as the virtues of mankind had no mean share in his commercial success. As yet few, if an'y,'0f his chef d'1euvres in ornamental art had appeared;

' Vedgwood to Bentley, written mat-

ters mentioned clearly referable at the Baptist Head (lofiee House, to May, 1767. but without date, though from the foras he himself said, his ' vases were still in a rude state,' and seem to have been principally confined to those of marbled and cream-coloured bodies, varied by gilding, and occasionally by necks coloured to resemble lapis lazuli; and yet we find that through a little good management they were eagerly bought up, even where they had been seen under other arrangement by the same customers for many previous months. As to the cream ware table services, their sale by this date was something most extraordinary, although, as we shall presently see, comparatively simple in their decoration; line borderings, and landscapes printed upon the glaze, being the most customary ornaments of a body so beautiful in colour, and so transcenda-nt in the fineness of the glaze and the perfection of its many varied forms, as to be, like nature, fairest when unadorned.

Previously to leaving London on this occasion, Wedgwood entered into negotiations relative to another house at the corner of Scotland Yard, and opposite to the Admiralty; but from some unassigned reason, the project fell to the ground; and we hear nothing further of the London warehousetill the spring of the year following. Again in London, and writing to Bentley from Charles Street, he refers to seeking after a house, or rather warehouse, ' in which I have at last succeeded to my wishes, & quite beyond my most sanguine expectations. I have a lease assign'd over to me for forty years of a house near the bottom of St. Martin's Lane, Charing Cross, which will be quite convenient for VVestminster, & within a 12" ride from St. Paul's Ch. Y'. I have abo' 20 feet to the Street by 150 deep, in wh" I can have, if necessary, besides a house & shop to the Street, two rooms, each 120 feet long by 16, & another 70 P by 18, with a passage between the two buildings,1 but as we shall 'not 'want so many long rooms, I think of making habitations for a Colony of Artists, Modelers, Carvers, &c. I have ah'eady agreed with one very usefull Tennant. A Master Enameler & China piecer,_he joins old valuable pieces of China, not with Rivots, but a white glass, & burns them till the glass vitrifys, & they are as sound as ever they were. I have long had connections with this Man,2 who is sober & steady; he is just come out of Yorkshire to settle here, & was engaged, or rather perswaded, by two China Men here not to advertise or make his business known, & they wo'1 find him constant employment; however, he is dis-'satisfyed with them, & I have secured him, he paints flowers and Landscapes very prettily, prepares a pretty good powder gold, & has a tolerable notion of Colours. He has an Apprentice and another hand. I have set him to' work upon Table & desert ware, & shall get his rooms ready in St. Martin's Lane immediately; The having such a Man as this under the same roof with the warehouse to do Crests, or any other patt" by 0rd', to take sketches, is the most convenient thing imaginable, & nobody but ourselves will know what he

'is doing. A Modeler in the same y" too will be very clever, to send to any La.dy's favourite Antique for a coppy. ' In a week from this date, Wedgwood had seen another house in the same neighbourhood still more suited to his purpose. His own account of it is interesting. ' I have met with 'another house,' he tells Bentley, ' which pleases me better for situation than that I have 1 A plan of these remises is i ' His name was David Rhodes, amongst Mr. Maye1"s M S. But as ' and he proved a very valuable and Mr." edglwood never occupied them, i faithful servant. Much will appear the skew in this instance has no I in relation tohis duties. special interest.'-. 1 ' taken. 'It is at 'the top of Martin's Lane, a_ Corner; house, 60 feet long, the streets wide which lye to it, carriages may come to it either from VVestminster or the City without being incommoded with drays full of Timber, Goals, &c. which are allways pouring in from the various wharfs,' & making stops in the Strand, verypdis; agreeable & sometimes dangerous. The_ rent pf gthislast

'mentd is 100 Guineas a year. My friends in Town tell me it is the best situation in all London for my rooms, I am quite at a loss what to determine, & you can hardly help me out, without seeing the place.'1 Upon receiving further particulars as to the advantages of_ the one house over the other, Bentley probably advised his friend to take it, as in a letter to William Cox from Burslem, dated April 30, VVedgwood says, ' I hope you are doing something towards my geting clear of the house at the bottom of St. Martin's Lane. Every week I keep it on my hands is near 20' loss. I shall be content to part with it, not being a loser. Mr. Pickford (my Architect) will be in Town in about ten days, & will call upon you & advise both about parting with the one & fitting up the other.... I inclose you my agreem' with Fairbone, & wish you wo"_get him to let you see and have the lease exam", that I may know what I have to trust to.' Soon after this workmen were put in to fit up and prepare the show rooms and premises generally; the

Royal Arms over the door of the house in Charles Street, '

Grosvenor Square, were sent to be regilt; and some time in August, 1768, the warehouse was opened.

After transacting a vast amount of business besides this just referred to, and which under its artistic relations will come presently to view, Wedgwood returned to Burslem at the close of March, intending to be in London again in a fortnight, but a vexatious matter arose in connection with the canal at Etruria. Some of his neighbours, who were proprietors, considering that he had too pleasant and valuable a situation by the side of the canal, reported to the Committee that the cutting ought to take a shorter course along the-meadows. A select party of the Committee made a survey, and were convinced in favour of the line laid down; but the matter was referred to Brindley, who again went over the ground, and made the necessary calculations. 'I am in no fear for the event,' wrote VVedgwood to his friend; 'I know my conscience is good, & I feel

myself a match for them all. I an1 preparing a little ammunition for the battle, & I know you will come in full time to assist me to give it full force. Mr. Bri_ndley's brother is at the head of this affair, but this circumstance does not alarm me at all, as I know Brindley the Great to be an honest man, and that he Wlll give in a true state of the case, let the event be what it may.'1 The result proved that Wedgwood's confidence C was well founded. At a meeting of the Navigation Committee held at Trentham on April 28, Brindley made his report, and the point was decided in favour of Mr. Wedgwood.

But the fatigue and anxiety incurred were too much for mind and body. Only two days later in the letter to Cox already referred to, he speaks of having ' over-walked and over-worked his leg. ' The pain in his knee was intense, and to relieve it, his surgeon, Mr. Bent of Newcastle, ordered him a vomit. It gave immediate relief 1 'edgwood to Bentley, April 10, 176.

to the affected part, ' but whether the absorption was too sudden, the matter absorb'd too much, or too much vitiatedl know not,' wrote Mr. Wedgwood at a later date to-his friend, in referring to a case somewhat similar to his own, ' but the pain had no sooner left my knee than I was very ill in other respects, attended with great heat & difficulty of Breathing, insomuch that I was glad to feel the 'pain return again into the knee, & as the Pain retum'd into that part, the other symptoms left me.'1

As there was thus no relieving the pain without imperiling the patient's life, another surgeon was called in, with probably Dr. Darwin in consultation, and amputation of the limb was agreed to; indeed suggested by Wedgwood himself, who had long looked forward to this necessity with philosophic cheerfulness. His leg was like a dead branch on a vigorous tree, an incumbrance and a hindrance in every way; and even apart from this illness, which hastened the crisis, he had mentally resolved to have it removed prior to opening the works at Etruria.2 A master-potter is incessantly ascending and descending ladders and stairs to his various shops and rooms; and if Wedgwood had felt pain, difficulty, and fatigue in doing this in old fashioned buildings of no altitude, such as those _ of the ' Brick-House Works,' how much more was he likely to suffer in traversing the ascents and descents of a vast manufactory. He knew full well that a true master's eye is everywhere, and must be everywhere if justice is to be done to his commands; and even into this question of physical suffering and danger, his calculations had entered, so that he might give force to the genius which prompted 1 Vedgwoodto Bentley. llisoel-I eeived this information personally laneoug pa 11;, i from Mr. Vedgwood. ' Mrs..Iu_ver, of i'evt-astlc, re-; him, and the duties which lay before him. It is an extraordinary instance of moral courage and decision of character, in connection with a power to gather in and make subservient every effect, necessary to a given end.

The amputation took place on May 28, 1768,1 two surgeons and Bentley, as is evident, being with him at the time. ' He would not be assisted, or have the operation hidden from his view; but seated in his chair, bore the unavoidable pain without a shrink or a groan. This power of endurance is the more remarkable, as there existed at that date none of our modern chemical agents for producing a temporary state of coma, and, consequently, an oblivion of physical suffering; and, what was more, operative surgery was still carried on with much of the barbarism of the Middle Ages.

The announcement of this event to the ' house ' in London by Peter Swift is, for its prosaicness, about the most extraordinary ever penned. To think of one human being writing of another in such a fashion; and this in relation to a master much beloved, and whilst his life hung on a thread I The note is addressed to Cox, and is appended to an invoice of cream ware, 'piggins, cream pots, salts,' and a long &c. &c. 'Burslem, 28th May, 1768. Sir,——Your favour of the 26th is just come to hand, but can make no reply to the contents. Mrl VVedgwood has this day had his leg taken of (sic), & is as well as can be expected after such

an execution. The rev'1 Mr. Horne's Goods are packed, and one Crate for the warehouse, the particulars of which I shall insert at foot, or as much as time will pemiitt. Mr. Chester's Goods will be

' According to Vedgwood him-Amputation Day,' thus doubtless self, the operation took place three referring to the anniversary of that days later, for writing to Bentley I event. on May 31, 1770, he styles it 'St. ' delivered on Thursday next. '1 am, &c.—Peter Swift.' 1 Seven days later good Peter is again busy with his wooden pen;, although this time the hand which wields it vibrates with son1e touches from the heart within. ' To Mr. Cox. Sir,—I have now the pleasure to acquaint you that Mr. Wedgwood Continues in a good way, his Leg was opened on Thursday for the first time, & both the Surgeons said it could not possibly be better, & he has every good Symptom, so that we have the greatest hopes of a perfect cure. Poor Master Dicky, after being violently sized (sic) with a Complaint in his Bowels for some time past, expired on Thursday morning, & was Inter'd Last Evening. Indeed, I think Mrs. Wedgwood has had severe tryals of late, but the great hopes of Mr. Weclgwood's perfect recovery seems to" keep her Spirits up in a tollerable degree.'2 The merits of this good wife went far beyond the knowledge of prosaic Peter Swift. Vveary with tending her dying babe, and full of grief that it was taken from her, she yet, as far as possible, concealed the signs of weariness and sorrow. She dressed her husband's wound, administered his medicines, wrote his letters, warded off from him every possible business care, was his right hand in everything, and through her serene cheerfulness greatly hastened his recovery. Mr. Bentley returned to Liverpool as soon as all danger was past, for much business necessitated his presence there; but VVedg_wood's own words hand down to us what this incomparable friend had been to him in his hour of-trial, what also were the services of his wife, and the cour; tesies and solicitude of the surrounding gen-

try. For the
' Mayer MSS. ' old, instead of surviving, as generally
"' Mayer MSS. This was Mr. 1 recorded, till 1782. The Richard 'edgwo0d's son Richard, who died l 'edgwood who died in that year was whilst an infant of about ten months, probably Mrs. 'edgr'ood's father.

42 l'L'Bl.IC SYMPATHY AND INTEREST. CRAP. I. interest excited by Wedgwood's situation was extreme. In London, Lord Cathcart the Russian Ambassador, Lord Bessborough, the Duke of Bedford, the Duke of Marlborough, the Hon. Mrs. Chetwynd at Buckingham House, Sir VVilliam Meredith, Sir George Saville, and many others, called or sent daily to the rooms in Charles Street, to hear if that day's post had brought good news from Staffordshire. From Trentham came a daily messenger; the Duke of Bridgewater had his reports from Gilbert or Brindley as to Wedgwood's progress; and, as soon as he could possibly see company, the local gentry made their calls. Whenever possible Dr. Darwin's chaise made its way to Burslem. With what difficulty these visits were often paid we have the Doctor's own words. ' I am heartily vex'd that I could not get to this Place1 soon enough to day to have come to spend the Evening with you. But I hear you go on well, & yt gives me, I assure you, much Satisfaction, &I have an engagement to morrow near Coleshil, which is on the other side of Lichfield, which prevents me of calling of you tomorrow morning. Mr. Boulton is gone to Buxton for his Health, and talk'd of coming by Newcastle on his Return to call of you and console you, and,' adds the philosophic Doctor, who must have a word on science for the friend who loves it so well, ' Mr. Boulton has got a new metal which rivals Silver both in Lustre, Whiteness, & endures y' Air with as little Tarnish. Capt. Keir is endeavouring to unravel this metal. Mr. Edgeworth, a philosophical Friend of mine in Oxfordshire, writes me word He has nearly completed a Waggon drawn by Fire, and a walking Table which will carry 40 men. This is all the

news
' Newcastle.
CRAP. I. BENTLEYS LETTERS. 43
I can think of to amuse you with in the philosophical Arts.' 1

The day preceding this, viz. June 13, Mr. Wedgwood was so far recovered as to be able to add a brief postscript to a letter Mr. Bentley had written for him to Cox. ' This is the first time I have set pen to paper, except to sign myename, since the Surgeons laid their hands on me, but I hope I shall be able to continue writlg a little now I have begun again; my surgeon has given me an invitation to dine with him at N. Castle this day fortnight, which I hope to be able to accept.' 2

Bentley returned to Liverpool some time between this date and June 20; but though absentin body, he was not in spirit. Every post brought to the sick' chamber one of those letters which were above all price to his friend; and which, as an expression of a manly breadth of thought, combined with a tenderness which–was almost womanly, have never been excelled.3 The testimony to 1 Dr. Darwin to Vedgwood, things. The verv feel of them, even

June Hi, 1768.» Darwin Correspondence.
' Bentley and Vedgwood to Cox, June 13, 1768. Mayer MSS.
3 The following extracts will show what consolation and sterling ' pleasure lfI_r. Ve;1dgwpod élerilved at all times mm is rien 's etters.
Such nragraphs are constantly occurring. e took the greatest care of the letters, sewed each month's accumulation together, and preserved them in a cover. for manydreasons, thaltl they favg not reache our time. en so gi te
as Bentley are rare; and such a friendship as that which existed between him and Mr. Vedgw still rarer. ' Well now I have read your lettert il.H _0tl18l't0tiIl1110 pr two,f I
am more a ensure an you or it, and to tell mv dear friend that I
like these aoiibié l01le"s of his of iiu, ood is' before the seal is broke, cheats my heart & does me good, & I am as eager in hunting out a comer to hide

myself in that I may devour iny delicious morsel without bei molested as–– hem!-ho!—now have it—as an Alderman of —wo" be to find out a vacant seat at a. Turtle feast..... Sei'iously&sincerely my good friend, I do from the bottom of my heart thank you
' for your last friendly and enter.It is a great pity, _ ' fault to find with it. The subset taining epistle. I have only one matter is good—the Type is tolera. le. But a pl-_r/ue of all little paper say I. I think your stationer does not use you well. If you are disposed to change him I can direct you where you may buy your paper as large sin, and two of those sheets well fi l'd wod be It Princely meal, and fit to meet a Patagonian Appetite, such an one as I have got for everything which falls from your pen. '— Wedgwood to Bentley, August 10, 1767. 'How much I am indebted to my dear friend for his afi'ectionate & sympathising epistles, 8: the interest I know he takes in all that concerns me, 44 RECOVERY. Can. 1'.

this is worthy of their incomparable friendship. 'I did intend writing to my dear friend by this post to tell him how thankfull I am for his last most aflectionate letter, & how great—but that is impossible to measure, the oblige»tions he has laid me und'—–is a task I cannot perform, but I am perfectly easy under them, knowing a grateful heart is the most acceptable return I can make him. I say I purposed to write this morn', but L' & Lady Vernon & their Son & Daughter, with Mr. & Mrs. Sneyd & Miss Sneyd, W" other matters & things have prevent' me, & I must send this to Talk 0' th' Hill just to let my good frd know that I proceed in the good way he left me. Have been at the Workhouse, & had two Airings in a Chaise—have left off my Laudanum and do better without it. The skin on the upper part of the wound is healed & got down to the bone,-which I tell you to confute all those who deny the present to be an Age of Miracles.' 1 In another letter of later date, in which are still more ardent expressions of profound gratitude and affection, and in which he begs his friend not to'be distressed if he does not hear

so fre; quently as heretofore, as much necessary correspondence than I shall ever be able to pay, un less he will, as usual, accept of a ' _1/rrltefull heart to ballance all deficiencies. But notwithstanding I owe so much, would you believe me so void of shame, grace, or discretion, that I am every day wishing to owe more. 1 W0" scarcely believe it of niyself, but the s_'mp_toms are too more—-much more— ' 1 few things day.'——Wedgwood to Bentley, Feb strong upon me to deny the charge,
for every post day I catch myself greedily runing over the direction of my letters, and if a well known hand does not a pear, Sally is ready to ask what he so suddenly alter'd my countenance. I am too pettiah
(for you know I am subject to be cholei-ick on a disappointment) to give her any answer, but. read my letters, and unless a good order, or some such circumstanceintervenes,
go right with me that
ruary 14,1767.
' 'edgwood to llcntley, J um:
20, 1-768.

begins' to weigh heavily upon him, he thus cheerfully paints his rapid progress towards convalescence, and just lifts the veil for us to see the wisdom and affection of his faithful wife. 'At present I am well, even beyond most sanguine expectations. My leg is almost healed, the. wound is not quite 2 inches by one & I measur'd it with the compasses this morn' when I dress'd it. Yes! when I dress'd it, for I have turn'd my surgeon adrift, & Sally and I are sole managers now, only we give him leave toipeep at it now &'then, when he lifts up his hands & eyes & will scarcely believe it to be the wound he dress'd before. I have many things to say to you from the good folks at Newcastle &c., & something of the enclos'd Nav" C', but Sally says ' give over, J oss, and tell our frd B. that I command it.' So I have done, only I must just add that if Mr. Hastlet is well assur'd of his estimate 8: a 200,()00l. subscrip" I shod vote for the larger boats.' We see by this how, whether ill or well, Navigation affairs had necessarily to occupy his mind; and how, under such judicious control as this of his wife, his convalescence was more rapidly insured than it otherwise would have been. By the end of June he was enabled to visit Etruria; and we find him 'going thither in his chaise with his father-inlaw, Mr. Richard Wedgwood of Spen Green, who had come to Burslem to spend some days with his daughter on this happy occasion of her husband's advancing recovery.

Meanwhile, many other changes had taken place. &metin1e during the autumn of 1768, there is reason to think Mr. Wedgwood's aged mother died. But if buried at Burslem, the parish register gives no certain informal tion on the point; as not a year is without one or more entries of the name of Mary Vedgwood, and this without 46 KATHERINE WILLET. CRAP. I.

specification of age, condition, or place of residence.1 The original branches of the Wedgwood family had spread in every direction in Burslem and its surrounding neighbourhood; so that to choose the precise ' Mary,' ' John,' or ' Thomas,' is sometimes wholly impossible out of parish registers so loosely kept as were those of the eighteenth century. There is reason to think that Josiah Wedgwood's mother passed the remnant of her days at the Bank-house, Newcastle, with her daughter Katherine Willet; died and was buried there. With his mother's relations, the Stringers, Mr. Wedgwood long kept up a pleasant intimacy. One of her nephews, a Dr. Stringer, had settled at Wattleton, near Oxford; and on their way to and fro to London, Mr. and Mrs. Wedgwood occasionally rested at his house. His young daughters in return paid visits to Burslem; and in 1769 we find cheery letters and presents of cream ware sent on their way into pleasant Oxfordshire.

Mr. Vedgvood's favourite sister was Katherine Villet. They had been companions in childhood, and her aftermarriage with a man of superior attainments was in itself an education, and raised her general understanding more on' a level with that of her gifted brother. She was the constant companion of his wife, and we find the ladies paying visits to-gether to Mr. Bentley and Miss Oates in Liverpool at various periods between 1766 and 1768; and so soon as the warehouse in Newport Street was opened, Mrs. Willet occupied part of Mr. and Wedgwood's chaise to London, and shared with them all that was 1 The constant recurrence of the (giats. The VVedgwood descent exsame Christian names in lines of ' emplifies this to the full, as in many descent without the addition of age, ' cases it is wholly im ible to dis lace, occupation, and often date, has tinguish one indivi ual from among been a cause of grave com-_ other of the same name. plaint with our jurists and genealo worth seeing there in those days. This must have been agreat treat to the country lady, who, unlike Mrs. VVedgwood, had been no frequent visitor to London; and the pleasure thus afforded was frequently renewed. Mr. Villet at this period was a comparatively young man, though seventy years of age. His mind retained much of its early vigour; and he still occasionally published pamphlets on controversial points of theology,I and gave much of his time to scientific pursuits. The honour had been his of first inspiring the illustrious Priestley with a taste for philosophical investigation. He 11ad supplied, as we have seen, mental food through books and instruction to the untilled field of his young kinsman's vigorous mind when the latter lay confined for months by weary illness at-Stoke; and they were now more than ever congenial and attached friends. Throughout the long struggle connected with the Trent and Mersey Navigation, Mr. Willet received and dispatched VVedgwood's most private letters; if the latter was weary or benighted there at ' sister Willet's,' he had a bed and a home. Very, very often in his letters to Bentley Wedgwood says, ' we spent yesterday at Newcastle;' and when. his little children were stricken down with contagious disorders such as come in childhood, they were sent to Newcastle to be nursed. Early in 1767 he had the two eldest inoculated for the small-pox; they were very ill, so much so that he half repented the step" which hadbeen taken; but presently they were sentaway for change of air and nursing to their good aunt Willet, and health returned. It is interesting to catch glimpses of the .-'I Mr. -'edgwood refers to a re-' was still contributing the pages cently published pamphlet in 17651, I of the Theological llo-posltory. Ind three _vem's later Mr. 'illet 1 48 A TENDER FATHER. CRAP. I.

tender father shining through the graver aspect of the concise, determined, and austere man of business. The heavy duties of the day over, the occasionally long vigils of the night in chemical experiments, modelling, or letterwriting not begun, he rides away to see these little babes. How dearly he loves them! How throughout his life he loves his children! How in years to come we shall see him taking pride in the handsome presence and polished manners of his son Josiah, and in the great intellectual gifts of his son Tom; indeed, in all his children, for he had no favourites; and yet for the little maid 'Sukey,' his firstborn, there is a something not expressed in words, and yet apparent to us, that she was gathered up in the innermost folds of his deep affections. As after life showed, there was something very much akin in their respective natures, though gentleness and consideration for others were perhaps intensified in their feminine expression.

Though never very intimate, for their natures were so different, it is yet pleasant to observe, that as years wore by, kind and friendly relations were still maintained between Josiah Wedgwood and his eldest brother at the Overhouse, or as it was sometimes called the Upperhouse. In an old bill headed ' Bror Josiah Wedgwood Bou' of Tho' Wedgwood,' and of which the items run through the years 1766, 1767, and 1768,' we find the former buying oats, 'straw, and ware of his elder brother; and there are 'various charges for the 'lay of a horse,' and for ' the carriage of coals from Snead.' 1 The description of the ware, principally consisting of 'plates, baking-dishes, mugs, and bowls,' proves that Thomas Wedgwood still kept true to his old maxim of non

77l0ll'6; and whilst his

CRAP. I. THOMAS WEDGWOOD. 49 brother-potters were outvying each other in the race 'of improvement, and the least observant mind must have been conscious that great social changes were taking place in respect to productive labour, he went on in the way of his fathers-making the common white ware of thirty years previously, with occasionally an ovenful of ' flint ware,' as this distinction is given in the bill. He probably farmed as much as he potted; although he still carried on the 'Churchyard Works,' and had added to those about the Overhouse; which from this reason and _ the rapid growth of the surrounding town, was fast losing its ancient character of a country house amidst fields and gardens. Thomas Wedgwood had married a second time, but neither added, as we shall see, to his peace or prosperity thereby. And now in 1768-9, he was a man of broken health and hopes, only too glad to. occasionally consult the brother he had so weakly despised.

Otherwise mindful of his kinsmen, for he had found in his cousin Thomas Wedgwood a most able coadjutor and friend, Josiah Wedgwood, about 1768, took into his employ Joseph Wedgwood, a young man descended from one of the elder branches of the Wedgwood family. In his relation's service Joseph remained for some years. The 'Churchyard Works' being then to let, Josiah assisted him to take them, and employed him in the fabrication of a certain class of goods which were chiefly consumed for the export trade at Etruria. From some cause or another he was not a prosperous man, and ultimately became bankrupt. With another of his relations Wedgwood was not more fortunate. The ' new books ' had not induced young Byerley to settle down for long. The roving impetus was strong within him; and without such an outlet for fiery passions as the Byerleys of the northern

VOL. II. E 50 THOMAS BYERLEY. CHAP. I.

shires had had, in heading troopers, or defending manorhouses in the Civil Wars, he ran off to play soldier or citizen on the Dublin stage; but he was encountered at Chester and brought back. Again he disappeared, and joined a company of strolling players. A little practical experience sickened him of the stage. He soon quitted it ' from a conviction of his inability to succeed in any tolerable degree.' He then besought his uncle to ' get him a writer's place, or some place in the service of the East India Company.' 1 Mr. Bentley as usual gave good advice; and counselled leniency towards follies, which nothing but sharp encounter with the stern realities of life could cure. Eventually it was settled that young Byerley should be sent out to Philadelphia; and we find Mr. Vedgwood in the summer of 1768 arranging a credit of 70l. for the young man to receive when he reached that place; and through the introduction of Dr. Fothergill, commending him by letter to the good oflices of a resident, Mr. Logan. ' If he has a mind to take a few pieces, or 3 or 4 pounds worth of my ware with him,' adds Mr. VVedgwood to Bentley, 'you may let him have so much on his own ace', & pray advise him to ship himself in the cheapest way for America, as he may there come to want a crown, or even a shilling, & know not where to have it/2 'But Mr. Bentley described the objections to a cheap passage so forcibly that it was not insisted on.' ' I am very glad Tom does not go in the steerage,' was Mr. Wedgwood's reply, ' I had no idea of its being so disagreeable a berth, & tho" the difference, according to the Captain's letter, as 5l. to 20!. I suppose Tom will have sailed before this reaches you. I have a very sensible

' VVedgwood to Bentley, March I _' Vedgwood to Bentley, June, 2, 1767. 1463

CRAP. I. GOES TO AMERICA. 51 letter from him, in which he expresses his obligations to you with that Warmth wch he ought to do, & must retain as long as he has a spark of gratitude left; he promises to be very good, & I hope for his own sake, as well as his friends, that he will at last perform his repeated promises. My best wishes attend him, & that is all I can now do for him. ' 1

Young Byerley liked America greatly, but for all that he did not settle down; and the succeeding year brought tidings of a renewal of his old follies and wanderings. The generous uncle kept the relation of these from his mother; and very wisely, for her life had been one of care, and she was only now beginning to reap some of the peaceful fruits of her industry and good management. Her business had grown; she journeyed to London to buy goods and to select fashions for her customers; her daughters aided her; and when her boy had suffered, and thus learnt that folly in any shape can have no other reward than pain and misery, he was to come back to her to be a dutiful son, and to repay his generous uncle through long and faithful service.

CHAPTER II. ART IN ITS SPRING.

ROM the beginning of the year 1768 a regular series of invoices furnish an elaborate and authentic history of the successive stages of improvement, and of creative effects in ornamental ware. In the useful ware, so far as related to the cream-colour body and its brilliant glaze, further perfection was impossible; and beyond occasional changes in form, variations in engine work, as in the edges, and after the establishment of the works at Chelsea of a preponderance of enamelling over printing, and of borderings chiefly derived from the antique for dinner and dessert services of the best quality, the cream ware continued much the same through along subsequent period; although, as we shall see, a whiter ware was brought into the market about 1778. Its sale was always increasing. It was exported to France and Germany, to Russia, Holland, Spain, the West India islands, the East Indies; and, in spite of interruptions occasioned by war, to the ports of North America. In the trade with Russia, Boulton and Fothergill began at this date to take a cOn siderable share.1 They bought largely from Etruria, and exported the ware on their own account to their consignees 1 Invoices of cream-colour ware, June 1, 1768, and subsequent dates. Mayer MSS.

56 CREAM-WARE UNIVERSALLY USED. C11.u.lI. at Cadiz, and in the ports of the Baltic. Of this universal taste for cream-ware, we have Mr. Wedgwood's own most interesting testimony. ' The demand for the s" Creamcolour, alias Queerfs Ware, alias Ivory, still increases,' he tells his friend. 'It is really amazing how rapidly the use has spread allmost over the whole globe, & how universally it is liked. How much of this general use & estimation is owing to the mode of its introduction, & how much to its real utility and beauty, are questions in which we may be a good deal interested for the Governm' of our future conduct. The reasons are too obvious to be longer dwelt upon. For instance, if a Royal or Noble introduction be as necessary to the sales of an article of Luxury as real Elegance & beauty, then the Manufacturer, if he consults his own inter", will bestow as muchpains & expence too, if necessary, in gaining the favour of these advantages as he wo'l in bestowing the latter. I had with me yesterday an East Indian Captain, & another Gent" & Lady from those parts, who ordered a good deal of my ware, some of it printed and gilt, to take with them for presents to their fr", & for their own use. They told 1ne it was allready in use there, & in much higher estimation than the present Porcellain, the Capt" said he had dined off a very complete service just before he left India. Don't you think we shall have some Chinese Missionaries come here soon to learn the art of making creamcolour? " A little consideration would have shown Mr. Wedgwood the fallacy of the question he thus asks Bentley. Some portion of this far-reaching favour was undoubtedly due to a Royal name; but it rested on the foundation of his own intrinsic merits in having met, through the results of

' Vedgwood to Bentley, some date during 1767.

CRAP. II. CRITICISM OF SQUIRES AND HOUSEKEEPERS. 57 patient labour and great natural genius, a universal want of the day for moderate priced, cleanly looking, and tasteful table ware. Without these conditions

had been first fulfilled, Royal favour would have been bestowed in vain. This universal cry for cream-colour had, however, its shady points of view as most other things. It was not always possible to obtain the same exact creamy tint or hue. A thousand trifling contingencies, which the potter cannot govern, make these shades of difference. But old dowagers, rubicund squires, and their fat housekeepers, who knew nothing of the varying qualities of clay, differences of temperature, or the results of momentary errors in firing, made occasionally loud lament. 'Sur,' writes the fat housekeeper, sometimes addressing Mr. Wedgwood as ' Mr. Wegwood,' or 'Mr. Wagwood, at the house of Mr. a shoomaker, Charles Street,' 'the yellow pye-dyshes ain't likes the last, sur—they are more yallower.' The politer dowager informs Mr. Wedg-i wood that the cream cups, or compotiers in the crate just sent have not the true tint; and the red-nosed squire, whose writing has been chiefly confined to signing commitments for vagrancy or poaching, growls forth in an ill-spelt epistle his opinions respecting his last punch bowl or venison dishes. In answer to these sort of complaints, Mr. Wedgvood's equable temper is a little stirred sometimes. 'With respect to the colour of my ware,' he writes to Cox in the postscript of an invoice, ' I endeavour to make it as pale as possible to continue it creamcolour, & find my customers in general, though not every individual of them, think the alteration I have made in that respect a great improvem', but it is impossible that any one colour, even though it were to come down from Heaven, sl1od please every taste; & I cannot regularly make two creamcolours, a deep and light shade, without having two works for that purpose. Nor have I any clay to make with certainty a very light colour for Teaware.' '

Mr. Wedgwood had availed himself from an early date, as already seen, of the printer's art for the ornamentation of his cream-colour body. Each week Daniel Morriss, the Lawton carrier, conveyed a cargo of ware to Sadler's

works in Liverpool; whence it was returned a fortnight after to Burslem, and at a later date to Etruria, to be finished. If the ware was for export from Liverpool, the engravings were burnt in on Sadler's premises, and dispatched thence; but the great majority was returned to Mr. Wedgwood's works, impressed principally with small landscapes, of a historical or Watteau-like character, domestic scenes, others slightly comic, or with simple groups of foliage and flowers. The colour used at first was chiefly black; but as Mr. Sadler's experience increased, he enlarged the number of his decorative agents, and we find him employing brown, red, yellow, and a dull green in addition to black, with excellent effect. The annexed representation of a tile (fig. 7) engraved for him by Richard Walker of the Harrington Street Pottery, shows one of these early attempts to introduce a variety of colours; as the ruins to the right are tinted ruddy brown, the wall or rock beyond a gray white, the foliage a dull red, whilst in the distance is the blue of the sea.

Sadler's engravings were all remarkable for their depth and clearness; thus standing out in marked distinction to the blotty, half-effaced impressions that afterwards became so general on all the ordinary descriptions of ware.

' Invoice of cream-colour ware, Burslem, January 27, 1769. Mayor M-SS.

CRAP. II. EXCELLENCE OF THE ENGRAVIBTGS. 59

As his business and that of his partner Guy Green increased, they employed a large number of excellent workmen, some of whom were trained by Mr. Sadlcr himself; whilst others were procured from London, York, and Newcastle-upon-Tyne; the two latter places being at this time famous for their engravers. To these northern towns we owe Bewick and Robert Pollard, the latter so largely employed, as we shall see, by Mr. Wedgwood at a subsequent date; and whose facility of touch and taste in combining outlines, secured him such renown as a die-sinker and letter engraver. Probably for cheapness-sake, some of Sad1er's early decorations were copied from designs in use in other pottery and porcelain works, as those of Worceste1'. The originals of these were painted enamels, made at York House, Battersea, by a Frenchman named Roquet.1 The 60 PASTORAL DESIGNS. Gun. II.

works there, which seemed to have been carried on more as the recreation of a wealthy amateur than for purposes of profit, were the property of Sir Stephen Theodore

Jansen, Bart, Lord Mayor of London in 1754. He was a man of much erudition andiartistic taste; but he became bankrupt in the succeeding year, and everything connected with his Battersea manufactory was disposed of

Engravers and enamellers thus became possessors of the engraved plates, and used them as originally designed.

CHAP. II. POPULAR SUBJECTS. 61

But Sadler and. Green, in the spirit of superior artists, reengraved many of those which fell into their possession; and made them, as in the case of this scene of a shepherd watching his flock (fig. 8), pictures more worthy of Boucher than the first designers of them had conceived. They used these and similar engravings very largely for the ornamentation of tea-ware; and their keenness in choosing popular subjects, in order to in crease their business, is shown on the accompanying teapot (fig. 9), on which we have Wesley preaching. A scene in which appeared a milkmaid and her swain, or a group of cows feeding, as in this little print coloured green (fig. 10), generally ornamented the butter jar or pot; and a gentleman kissing a lady's hand was a favourite pattern for bread-and-butter plates. For export, and to suit the maritime tastes of their townsmen, they ongraved ships and sea scenes; and as they enlarged their 62 IMPROVED CHARACTER OF ENGRAVINGS. CRAP. II.

range of colours, they seem to have ventured upon subjects that were Oriental in their type, as scenes decorated with Chinese pagodas, or umbrella-carrying mandarins.

At the beginning of his business with Sadler and Green, Vlfedgwood may have permitted the use of such designs; but he was not one who would long submit to an ornamentation which was hackneyed or commonplace. As the cream-colour body advanced towards perfection, we therefore find him bestowing unwearied pains on this branch of his art; and, instead of permitting Sadler and Green to furnish the necessary designs for the pottery which he sent in to be printed, he incurred a large annual expense for original subjects. The usual rule seems to have been a fresh design for every dozen plates of a dinner service; and distinct ones for each dish, tureen, and centre-piece. Engravings were made from the prints or drawings thus furnished by Mr. Wedgwood, and the printers retained the plates for future use. In this case the designs must have been copyright to the supplier, had rights in this case and many analogous ones been at all considered by the potters of the day; but, unfortunately, a decoration or an ornament no sooner appeared than it was copied or imitated; so that the only safeguard lay in constant variation or production of new effects. Heavy as was the expense thus incurred, Mr. Wedgwood cheerfully_ met it; and nothing is more striking than his incessant energy to make the decoration of his ware like nature, fresh and unhackneyed; and at the same time to create and foster a wider and better public taste for those essentials of pure and true art simplicity of effects and chastity in colour. Many of the charming prints, coloured and otherwise, of flowers, shells, fruits, birds, butterflies, and country scenes, so generously sent by Sir Willilil Meredith and other

CHAP. II. WEDGWOOD'S ORIGIN.-XLITY OF TASTE. 63 friends, supplied, there can be little doubt, not only Mr. WedgWood's enamellers, but also Sadler's engravers, with a wide field for copy,as well as composition; and between 1765 and 1767 are various indications that Mr. Wedgwood never visited London without a search in the print shops. Amongst the bills of 1768

is a receipt for 13l., signed by ' Celeste Taylor,' ' for prints and all demands/1

Sadler did not escape a hint now and then from Mr. Wedgwood as to eflorts for further improvement; and like a wise man he seems to have bestirred himself accordingly. After a brief visit to Liverpool, at a date when Bentley had become a resident in London, Mr. Wedgwood thus wrote. ' I have had a good deal of talk with Mr. Sadler, & find him very willing to do anything to improve his patterns. He has just completed a sett of Landskips for the inside of dishes &c., with childish, scrawling sprigs of flowers for the rims, all which he thinks very clever, but they will not do for us. He is trying the purple, and thinks he shall manage it, & is willing to have a sett of the red chalk stile, or Mezotinto flowers, but thinks they can do them at Liverpool best. I am afraid of trusting too much to their taste, but they have promis'd to otftrace & coppy any prints 1 shall send them without attempting to mend or alter them. I have promis'd to send him the red chalk plates & a few prints of flowers immediately, & beg you will send him the plates, & pick out some prints of different size flowers to send along with them by the coach to Liverpool.'2 As specimens of Sadler and Green's early and later printed ware we give this canister (fig. 11) 3 from the J ermyn Street Museum; and the others from Mr. Mayer's

' Dated October 1, 1768. Mayer 3 The tea-drinking scene upon it MSS. is from one of Jansen's printed ' Vedgwood to Bentley, May 12, enamels. 1770. unique collection. The last (fig. 13) belongs to afar later day, and is from a design by Stothard, who in his youth worked for Wedgwood. As already noticed, the earliest vases were chiefly cream-colour, gilt, or otherwise ornamented. Next to these came vases with white or cream-coloured bodies, and necks coloured with cobalt to resemble lapis lazuli; and probably ' commingled were vases in the black Egyptian body, Fi»-'T1!-CAf§fmf;:1§F§;R—

M;:FH;r:E;: Plea modelled after the antique, and ornamented with small medallions or festoons in the same colour. The advance thus made was considerable; but it no way satisfied Mr. Wedgwood's desire for excellence. ' Vasw sell,' he writes to Bentley, ' even in the rude state they are now, for such they appear to me when I take a view of what may be done.' Again, at intervals during the succeeding fortnight, he adds, ' I am picking up every design and improvement for a vase work, and every day more and more convinced that it will answer to our wishes.' 'I am preparing designs, models, (um. 11. CRYSTALLINE JASPER nonrns. 65 moulds, clays, colours, &c. for the vase work, by such means we shall be able to do business effectually 12 months sooner than we could without these preparatory steps, and I have no fear but it will answer our utmost wishes.'1 Shnultaneously with the preparations thus recorded, were various experiments with terracotta bodies, some of which, by the aid of the enameller, were marbles, and modelled after antique forms principally derived from the work of Count de Caylus? Two of the

' W'edgwood, in London, to Benthand of the enameller, who veined ley, May 27, June 1, and June 12, the different coloured bodies in imiITG7. tation of nature. ' I have reserved 2 ''e find from Mr. Ved,qwood's my house at Burslem for Mr. Rhodes letters to Bentley during 1769, that and his men, it is quite ready for his ma:-bled bodies were not pro-him, and when he comes you shall dueed by the old method of mixing, have Mr. Bnkewell, but we must or, as it was technically termed, have some one here to vein & finish ' slapping,' but portionnlly by the ' the vases, & if llnltewell goes before

VOL. II. F 06 MARBLED VASES. Cru r. ll.

first vases produced were forwarded to Bentley. ' To-morrow the Liverpool Coach goes through Newcastle, and takes up there two Antique vases, one is of the Holy Door marble & the other Jaune Antique.... You'l see the polish is not complete, but you will form from them as they are some idea of their capabilitys, and I could not bear that you she' wait another day before you feasted

your eyes with such fine things. But you'l please to remember that none of these can be made for sale for some time. Ergo, no man, woman, or child but your own household, nor scarcely them, shod see these things at present. Pray return them by Dan 1, & return yourself as soon as possible to help me (to) get all things ready to proceed with these It is with the greatest difliculty imaginable that I restrain from indulging my fancy in making more of them, & if I am not indued with the Continence of a Scipio, or you do not come & prevent me in my doings, I shall never hold out another week.' For some time previously to this Mr. Wedgwood had been experimcntalising on marbled bodies in terraeotta, as we find him even as late

VEISQS.

Mr. Rhodes comes, we have nobody, ness & extravaganza in the Pebble, if and that business must stand still the the workman gives the halts a twist while. '—Vedg'wood to Bentley, November 19, 1769. At a later day the crystalline bodies were again produced by the mixture of colour in the mass. Thus the former writes, 'I observe what you sav about Pebble vases in general, 3: take the benefit of them as I proceed in this branch; but the mixtures & colours too, after all the attention we 've them, are liable to so many acci ents and alterations from the wot-kmen's unhandiruas & want of ideas. From the uncertainty in firing &c. &c., which accidents we cannot command, that much will at last depend on the Chapter of Accidents. For instance, when the Clays are perfectly mixt to produce:1 111711 edgewayn, instead of keeping them flatt when he puts them into the mould, a line of stringiness is produced, which shows-the Pott instead of finely variegated. Again '

—If we mean the general com lexion of the pebble to be light, ' they meet with a heavy fire 1n the bislnt oven, the stronger colours & middle tints will be many shades darker than intended, & the light colours in the mixtures rather lighter, which annihilates all the middle tints, and produces a disgusting tawdry harshness. I could mention many more

accidents we poor potters are liable to. '-"ledgwood toBentle_', January 27, 1776.

Crur. II. VAST DEMAND FOR VASES. 67 as January, 1768, sending trial pieces of this nature to Bentley in Liverpool, and, whilst bidding him observe the great variety of effects to be 'derived therefrom, be prepares him for some necessary sacrifice by saying, 'Lord have Mercy on our old stock say I.'l But there was in reality no sacrifice after all. By the end of 1768, throughout 1769,-and several subsequent years, the fashionable admiration for this class of ornamental ware, stimulated by the more exquisite products of the bronzed and Etruscan vases, became such as to include in it almost everything which bore the shape or name of a vase or jar; and to meet this demand, vases of the old stocks were mounted on different plinths——sometimes even wooden ones-stopped, retouched, polished, or changed from cream-colour into marble by various processes of varnishing, veining, and enamelling. The connoisseur has, therefore, in respect to this class of ornamental ware, to heed well whether the body be a true terra-cotta from incorporation in the mass, or has received its surface polish, glaze, or veined effects from subsequent applications. The difference is precisely that which exists between true marble and its enamelled or merely painted imitations. Till somewhere towards the close of 1769, when Mr. Bentley was fairly embarked in the London business with Mr. Wedgwood, the invoices give no distinction between useful and ornamental ware. The whole is consigned to the London warehouse under the one head of ' cream colour,' and thus, without some special signification, it is often diflicult to judge if vases with ' goats' heads, festooned and gilt,' or otherwise ornamented, belong to the older class of bodies, as white glaze-ware or creamcolour; or to

' 'edgwood to Bentley, J mu: 3, 17138. I r '2 68 OXFORD AND CHETWYND VASES. CRAP. II. more recent, and in all respects more exquisite, productions. Thus in an invoice of May 23, 1768, we have an entry under the general head of ' cream colour' of two ' three handled vases, gilt,' at 3.9. each, and six 'least ditto' at 2s. 6d. each. From this all that we can infer is that they were of the ordinary and old class of bodies. In an invoice of March in the same year, we have ' a gilt vase with festoons' specified at the price of 6.52, which had probably the same body as those just referred to, only with a larger amount of gilding. A month later we find ' 1 blue neck bottle festooned, & gilt and shot w"' gold, at 7 /6,' '2 blue neck largest vases with striped necks, heads, & horns, gilt, no fe'stoons, at 6/ each,' and ' 3 largest superb-gilt at 5/ each.' All these were without doubt cream-colour.

As numbers do not seem to have been yet introduced to distinguish one pattern or form from another, the more choice and elaborate of these early vases passed by special names, as the 'Bedford,' the 'Oxford,' the 'Chetwynd,' the 'Pope's,' and some others. These were no vulgar appellations given to flatter a patron, or to insure sales; but simply showed that the vases from which these copies had been modelled were derived from the cabinets of those whose names were thus specified. The ' Chetwynd ' vases may have been an exception to this rule, for Mr. Wedg'ood felt he could never sufficiently honour the Staffordshire lady, who had been his first, as, since then, his most generous ' patroness.'

Towards the close of July, 1768, some black marble vases of extraordinary beauty are set down in an invoice; and with these are four antique vases of two sizes, ' with serpent handles twisted and plinths gilt,' in relation to which Peter Swift has a message from Mr. Wedgwood to

CuAr. II..-XNTIQUE FORMS. 69

Cox. ' In said Crate there are some serpent handled antique vases, part of which have the handles twisted & are finished in a more elegant' manner than the others, these Mr. VVedgwood' begs you'l not let be seen till the others are all sold, 8: then raise the price of them 1/ each for being higher finished.' To

this Mr. Wedgwood himself adds in a foot-note, ' If there is any amongst the above with plinths square they must be 18'1 or 2/ more each, & the black (say Etruscan) vases sent the 27th ult., those charg'd 9/ must be 10/6, and those 7/ 6 be 9/, never mind their being thought dear, do not keep them open in the rooms, shew them only to People of F ashion.'1

We have already seen that for a considerable period Mr. Wedgwood had been modelling from antique forms, either indirectly from casts or prints, or directly, though more rarely, from antique vases themselves. In some few instances the latter had been supplied by a choice but small collection already to be found in the British Museum,2 but more largely in the cabinets of the nobility, who at this period, and through the previous forty years, had greatly advanced artistic taste, and given vitality to classical learning by foreign travel. But books and prints had been Mr. Wedgwood's chief resource. We have seen a copy of the Count de Caylus' great work carried in his or Mr. Bentley's cloak-bag, like so many precious jewels, to and fro between Burslem and Liverpool; and for the loan of this they seem to have been indebted to Lord 1 Invoice sent to Cox, Ne ort am to see at the Museum, &c. &c.'

Street, London, September 3, 1 68. There is every reason to infer that Mayer MSS. both Bentley and his friend were 2 He also referred to books there. well acquainted with the works of Vriting to Bentley on the 3rd of La Chausse, Laurent, Beger MontMarch, 1768, he save, in anticipation faucon, Dempster, Gori, and Wineof a. journey to London, ' I shall kelmann, as well as those of Count expect 'written:'nstruȼ-tions what de Caylus. books I am to buy and what 13'" I i

Cathcart, who, through the introduction of Earl Gower, or the Duke of Bedford, had 'been for some time a most kindly patron.l His services now were to be still more important. His family connections, his frequent residence on the continent, and a great natural taste for the fine arts, led to his extensive

acquaintance with the various discoveries which at this date were lending such aid to a knowledge of antiquity, as also with those who promoted them. He was the friend of Mr. Hamilton, afterwards Sir William, who was appointed envoy to the Court of Naples in 1764, and when the former bought the Porcinari collection of antique vases in the previous year, Lord Cathcart was the first to applaud his friend's excellent taste and judgment. Mr. Hamilton was a man of genius, an enthusiast in his love of antique art, and through judicious purchases and excavations carried on at his own cost, after he became a resident in Italy, on various sites, but more particularly on that of Herculaneum, his collection of vases and other antiquities rapidly increased, and

' Vedgwood's first acquaintance with Lord (lat-hcart may be dated as early as 1766. Afterwards, upon the appointment of that nobleman as Ambassador to the Court of Russia in J anuarv 1768, the former, who had 'ust visited Soho, wrote from Lon on to Boulton thus. 'I have waited upon L'I Cathcart, the Am ness, and I am to get done a late by way of specimen with the tussian

Arms & an edging round the plate, both in gold burnt in, 8'. this I must get done in town. llis L"ship has now ordered a large service, plain, to take with him, and I must now desire you will bv return of post let me know at what other courts in

bassador appointed for Russia, to bring about the plan we settled of introducin my manufacture at the

('onrt of Iinssia. I laid before his Illship the great advantages which we" arise from such an introduction to a manufacture which might be reudered much more important than it had hitherto been thought capable of attaining to. The Ambassador,

but particularly his Lady, came into my nieasuros with the utmost l'('udi-in the best manner I could '

Germany or Europe _vou sh" be most solicitous to have this nianufncture introduced, & I will endeavour to get it done, 8: at the same time it shod be made known to the Introduce!where the rinces of the several states may e supplied with the same goods. I.d Gower will send a large Table and desert service, I believe, to Paris next week.'— 'edgwood to Boulton, March 19, 1768. Buulton ('oi'1'e.'po1dence.

CIIAP. II. HIS COLLECTION OF VASES. 71 was indeed soon unrivalled. With a generosity worthy of his taste and genius, he resolved to make it something more then a. mere cabinet for connoisseurs and savants. In order to open it to the world, to constitute it a fountain of true inspiration to the artist and man of letters, to increase general knowledge as to the extent modern civilisation is indebted to older civilisations, and to show that between the past and present runs a chain of causative effects, which the philosophic thinker cannot overlook, he , employed the finest Italian and French artists to copy the masterpieces in his possession, and consigned the necessary letterpress to a Frenchman of the name of D'Hancarville, who for that period was a sound scholar, and had already written well on antique art. The combined result was masterly. Two volumes in folio were published at Naples in 1766, two others in the following year; and it is much to say, considering what engraving at that date was, that these splendid volumes have never been surpassed. Nothing but that lavish pains and patience which often accompany our idolatries could have achieved so much. Portions of D'Hancarville's treatise are admirable. His explanations of ancient artistic methods are of great value, and he wrote his own language well; but its translation in opposite columns through the two first volumes wanted the correcting pen of an Englishman. Mr. Hamilton could have never read the proofs; and Mr. Wedgwood considered that the merits of the original vases and other antiquities represented were exaggerated in their copies. Allowing this much, these splendid folios stand unrivalled.l That they have been what they were intended to be, there can be no doubt, sources of valuable information to the artist and scholar; and at the period of their publication, when our private

collections of antique.
art were but few and difficult of access, our national one in its infancy, and our manufacturing products needing every facility which should raise them out of absolute barbarism, so far as colour, form, and decoration were concerned, their value was great; and we can scarcely over-estimate the liberality of spirit and breadth of culture which thus anticipated one of the public virtues of our own time.1 '

As proofs of the plates were struck off, Mr. Hamilton seems to have scattered a few amongst his friends. Lord Cathcart was a recipient; and he in turn, during various periods in 1766 and 1767, entrusted some ofthese to Mr. 'Wedgwood. They seem to have inspired him at once with new ideas; and from thenceforward we can trace, not merely a recurrence to antique forms, but an elaborate preparation to copy, if not to rival, the masterpieces of Etruscan and Grecian ceramic art. Early in 1768 Lord Cathcart, who was a lieutenant-general and first Commissioner of Police in Scotland, was appointed Ambassador Extraordinary to the Empress of Russia in the room of Sir George Macartney; and in consequence Mr. Wedgwood was called upon to supply a large order for his lordship's outfit. A portion was to consist of printed as well as enamelled dinner and dessert services, each piece to be marked by a crest. In reference to this and other business, Mr. Wedgwood writes to Mr. Bentley, ' I have spent several hours with L'1 1 Applauding Sir Wnl. Hamilton and the British Museum, and passed Gibbon says, 'He wisely diverted his time in elucidating a country of his correspondence from the Secre-, inestimable value to the naturzilist tary of State to the Royal Society ' and antiquarian.'

Cm. II. PAINTING IN ENCAUSTIC COLOURS. 73

Cathcart, our Ambassador to Russia, & we are to do great things for each other.'1 A few weeks later we come upon a reference to the services in hand, as also to one relative to Mr. Hamilton's work. 'This plate for Ld Cathcart's inspection,

with my duty & thanks to his Ldship for his kind concern for my health, & pray inquire where I may get the Etruscan antiquitys when they are published, if you have not done it already. I do not know the price of the Arms at present till more are done.' Subsequently in July we hear further on this matter. ' A long time ago I wrote to desire you W0" ask L" or Lady Cathcart if I sho'I return the prints I had from them, & to learn how I could be supply'd with the three Volumes of them w"11 are publishing abroad, but as you have not given me any answer, I fear you have forgot, & I suppose his L"shp has not left England. ' At this date the Duke of Northumberland had enriched his cabinet by a purchase of Etruscan vases, procured for him' probably by Mr. Hamilton; and Cox describing them added still more to Mr. Wedgwood's eagerness to begin what he very correctly styled his ' great work.'

Some twenty years previously the Count de Caylus, after many experiments in which he was assisted by the extensive chemical knowledge of M. Magault, a physician, had succeeded in discovering one branch of the ancient method of encaustic painting; that which related to covering canvas, wood, and similar surfaces with wax incorporated with various tints and colours. He published a work on the subject, which there is reason to think Bentley translated for Mr. Wedgvood's use at a time when what the latter had observed relative to the

' Wedgwood to Bentley. March 24, 1763. Lord Cnthcart received his appointment J anuary 24, lT6?1.

74   EXPERIMENTS   WITH COLOURS. Cnsr. I1. ancient vases was leading him to attempt encaustic painting in the direction of his own art; with this difference, that, as D'Hancarvile tells us, the Etruscans, and perhaps the Greeks, undoubtedly painted their vases in fresco, his own experiments would, from the superior qualities of the modern over the ancient ceramic bodies, necessarily relate for the most part, though not in all instances, to ware already fired biscuit. Thus stimulated, if

not taught, by the researches of the illustrious antiquary, Mr. Wedgwood entered upon a long and, to one less an enthusiast in his art, weary experiment. Deriving his various colours from the oxides of iron,1 he grasped, it would seem at the beginning, the true and masterly conception of their use; the one which in fact marked the essential difference between encaustic and other methods of painting; namely, that the vehicles incorporated with these colours to serve as a flux must not be such as would leave an enamel or glassy surface. They must, whilst passing through the enamel kiln, sink into the body to which they were applied, and there incorporate and harden without vitrifying. Coincident with this important class of experiments was another relative to the application of a bronze coating or varnish to earthenware; thus imitating, as also had the ancients, in another body the bronze vases of their own era. Mr. Wedgwood was probably led to undertake this new trial of his artistic and chemical skill from observations made at Soho, where Boulton was now carrying on processes connected with the fabrication of articles in bronze, ormolu, and steel, separate as well as in conjunction,

' ' I remember,' says Dr. Bancroft nearly all the fine diversified colours when treating of iron in his 'Philos0-ap lied to his pottery were produced hy of Permanent Colours,' 'having on _v by the oxides of this metal.' e-en told by Mr. 'cdgvood, that which were creating a revolution in ornamental metallic art; and changing, as we have already seen, our trade in these articles from one of import into export. But Boulton's vases, though good as to polish and metal, seem from the annexed example in outline to have been very far inferior in form to the antique; and thus to Wedgwood's subsequent reproductions.1

It is a remarkable fact that, in ancient as in modern' times, any great advance in ceramic art has been contemporaneous with that in orna mental metals. The bronzes of i the age of Phidias surpassed those of former and subsequent periods; and the same date is assigned to the

masterpieces of the Greek potters. In a like manner, though of course in a far less degree, the advance of one ornamental art in this country ran parallel with others soon after the middle._-£ _@L'——§El_ of the last century. This law, if it be one, probably depends not so much upon any necessary con-i nection between the arts them-mg_"_) mu" 0,, A "S, M selves, as upon the general pro-""""""""""" gress of intelligence, wealth, and competitive industry. In Walpole's letters is a passage which curiously enough shows that the respective arts at Etruria and Soho had already gained sufficient eminence to excite alike public patronage and attention. After speaking of the great

' The outlines are signed with the ment at Soho. The vases are to be name of Francis lla_vne, a manager earthenware, and the plinths, pedesor clerk in the ornamental depart-' tal, and ornaments, steel or omolu.

76 ILLUSTRATED PRICE-LISTS. Crur. I1. increase of luxury and the rage for exhibitions, he says, ' Then we have Etruscan vases made of earthenware from two to five guineas, and ormolu, and never made here before, which succeeds so well, that a tea-kettle which the inventor offered for one hundred guineas sold by auction for one hundred and thirty. In short, we are at the height of extravagance and luxury, for we do improve rapidly in taste as well as in the former.'1

Soon after the business connected with improvements in tools and the engine-lathe was at an end, Boulton and 'Wedgwood entered upon a lengthened correspondence as to the best Way of extending a knowledge of their respective manufactures on the continent; and Boulton advised the method afterwards put so fully into force by Mr. Wedgwood, that of distributing printed sheets containing engraved examples of various articles, to which should be added price lists and other particulars. This correspondence seems to have suggested to Boulton a union of their productions in certain branches, and in reference to this Wedgwood writes thus to Bentley: 'We have a11 order from

Mr. Boulton for some bodys of vases for mounting, Wch I must either comply with or affront him, & set him a-trying to get them elsewhere, & they are so simple, the drawing he has sent me, that he may get them done. He desires you will be so good as to do four things for him, 1st to learn wt quantity of Tortoiseshell is imported into Liverpool, 2'1 if there is now any to be sold, 3"ly w' qu"' & price, & fourthly & lastly, that you will come to see him at Soho.' 2 Wedgwood, who at all times writes as to his own heart to Bentley, appears to indicate by this a feel 1 Valpole's Letters, Cunning-l ' Vedgwood to Bentley, January lnun's edit. 'ol. v. p. 2315.; 21, 1761"'.

CRAP. II. GENEROUS RIVALRY. 77 ing that Boulton is treading beyond his own domain'. But this slight feeling of rivalry, if rivalry it was, was soon over-mastered by more generous emotions, joined to which was a good share of prudence and common sense; although, as we shall see, there arose a far stronger recurrence of the same feeling at a later date. Mr. Wedgwood was conscious that he was a great master of his art, that he had reached excellence through laborious pains and self-denials innumerable; and there was naturally a little soreness, that a friend, great in his own speciality, should enter into a competitive struggle with him on ground which genius and industry had made Wedgw0od's own. But his nature was too frank and generous to harbour enmity against any man. His sterling common sense led him to see that it is from rivalries great efforts spring; and honouring Boulton'for his intelligence and energy of purpose, he confided his little chagrins to the ear that never heard them without that sympathy which heals and dissipates all ordinary cares; and thus it does not seem that there was a day's interruption to the friendship existing between the chiefs of Etruria and Soho. It might have been different, had not Watt appeared and turned anew Boulton"s peculiar talent for metallurgic art into its legitimate channel.

On his wayto London in March, 1768, Mr. Wedgwood paid his friend a visit, and from its relation we gather how short-lived had been the feeling referred to. 'I arriv'd at Soho, & spent that day, Saturday, & half of Sunday with Mr. Boulton, where we settled many important matters, & laid the foundation for improving our manufactures, & extending the sale of it to every corner of Europe; many of our ornamental articles will be finished to great advantage with works of metal, printing upon them with purple & gold, &c. &c., which he will undertake to execute, & shew'd me some specimens of his printing with gold, which are really admirable, upon creamcolour as well as Enamel. He prepares the gold himself, & lays it on without the loss of a grain, in the very mode I recommended to Sadler. This improvem' will certainly be of importance to us, but it shod not be mention'd at present..... Mr. Boulton tells me I she(1 be surprised to know W' a trade has lately been made out of Vases at Paris. The artists have even come over to London, picked up all the old whimsical ugly things they could meet with, Carried them to Paris, where they have mounted & ornamented them with metal, & sold them to the virtuosi of every Nation, &, Particularly to Millords D'Anglaise, for the greatest raritys, & if you remember we saw many' such things at L'1 Bolingbr0ke's, which he bro" over with him from France. Of this sort I have seen two or three old China bowles, for want of better things, stuct rim to rim, which have had no bad effect, but looked whimsical and droll enough. This alone the combination of Clay and Metal is a field, to the further end of which we shall never be able to travel."

From the Patent which Mr. Wedgwood took out in November, 1769, for 'The purpose of ornamenting Earthen and Porcelaine Ware with an Encaustic Gold Bronze, together with a peculiar Species of Encaustic Painting in various Colours, in imitation of the Antient Etruscan and Roman Earthenware,'2 we see in some measure the processes and materials he employed in these two resuscitated branches of ornamental art. N o doubt there were chemical methods

and additions, as well as a manipulative ' 'edgwood to Bentley, dated from Charles _Stree_t, Grosvenor Square,. lul'cl 15, lTUl'$. 2 SPQCHIPM'-10"» N0-93" dexterity required, which made the specification a dead _ letter to all but those well acquainted with potting and ornamental metallic art; and even such must have been greatly bafiled, by their ignorance of a practical minutiae of which the specification made no mention; yet for all this, no sooner were the bronze and Etruscan vases brought into the field than competitors arose; the most formidable of whom was a clever potter of the name of Palmer, of Hanley. His imitations of the Etruscan vases never reached the excellence of those of-Mr. Wedgwood, but they were passable in the market, and led, as we shall subsequently see, to the overthrow of the Patent, not through the verdict of a Court of Law_though there is reason to think that had the matter been brought to trial, the adjudication would have been in favour of Palmer-but by the generous relinquishment of the patentee. As soon as he saw the whole bearings of the question, and that 1'almer's imitations, even though inferior to his own, and suspiciously indicative of processes surreptitiously obtained, evinced the ability and industry of an experienced potter, he resolved to throw up the Patent, very wisely considering that he could hold his own; and still more rightly judging that he, least of all men, who had such true opinions respecting art and its tendencies relative to civilisation, should not attempt to curtail its advance by an impossible monopoly, and stultify, as it were, the growing influence of recovered antiquity. To his lasting honour he ceased to contend, as soon as his strong understanding pointed out to him that contention was unworthy.

The Patent, which in portion we annex, gives in detail the materials and processes employed both relatively to bronzing and encaustic painting. In a letter to Bentley 80 PROCESSES. ('n.P. II.

are some further interesting particulars as to bronzing, the secret of which Mr.

Wedgwood had acquired in London. ' The man,' he says, ' who taught me &. shew'd me the whole operation by doing the Glaz'd Vases here, declar'd he W0" not shew the Artists here so much for ten pounds.' 1 The brown varnish, used prior to the in North America. Caleine this in Dry Bl""'k-_D-one "n¢e N-4, a red heat about half-an-hour.

No. 2. Bronze powder. Dissolve one ounce of pure gold in aqureg', precipitate it with co per, then wash the precipitate with ot water till it is sweet or clean from the acid, dry it, and lay it up for use.

No. 3. Take two ounces of crude antimony livigated, two ounces of tin ashes, and six ounces of white.

lead, mix them well together, and calcine them in a potter's furnace along with gloss cream-coloured ware.

No. 4. Take eight ounces of good smnlts, one ounce of roasted borax, four ounces of red lead, one ounce of nitre; mix the ingredients well together and fire them in a crucible in a potter's bisket oven.

No. 5. Take English copperas or vitriol of iron, calcine it in 9. moderate red heat about two hours, then wash it in hot water till it is sweet, dry it, and lay it up for use.

No. 6. White lead.

No. 7. Flint calcined and ground.

No. 8. Manganese.

No. 9. Zafier.

No. 10. Copper calcined to blackness.

Second Process, or Compmurding and of ('oloura.

Shineing Black.-A. Three ounces No. 8, three ounces No. 9, three ounces No. 10, eleven ounces No. 6, six ounces of the green F.

Red.——B. Two ounces No 1, two ounces No. 3, one ounce No. 5, three ounces No. 6.

Third Process, or Application of the Encaustic Bronze and Colours. Application of the Bronze.

I. "hen the vessels are finished ready for 'burning, and before they are uite dry, ground some of the po(lv er ll'o£% oitri oyl of 1turp;intine, an a v 1 ie vesse s or ures with iipspunge or pencil to inigitate bronze in such manner as your fancy

' directs; polish this powder upon the vessel or figure, and burn it in such a furnace, and to such a degree of heat, as is necessary for the wars. After it is burnt, burnish the bronze u n the vessels to what degree 'ou p ease, and the process is finished.

Another method of appI_/ia_r/ Hie Bronze after the ware is fired Biscuit, as some Firjurcs or Vt-ssela-may be too delicate to bear the Process I.

K. Take four ounces N0. 6, and ounce No. 7, grind them well together, spread this verv thin with a spunge or pencil over the ware to be bronzed, and fire-it till this layer of size is fluxed, which may be done in a potter's furnace; then take the powder No. 2, and apply it to the vessel as before directed; then burn the ware over again. till the pmvder

Can. II.

BRONZE ANTIQUE VASES.
application of the bronze powder, was one supplied by his old friend Dr. Turner.1

The first pair of bronze antique vases, which, from what we shall see hereafter, were certainly not encaustic, were finished and. sent towards the close of August, 1768, as a propitiatory offering to the sister or daughter of Mr. Tarleton, a merchant, and one of the members for Liverpool; it being desirable to use that gentleman's interest with the Corporation in order to adheres to the size; burnish &c. as before.

Appliartion 0 the Sllineing Black 0 Red essela in the manner of t Antique Etruscan Vases.

L. Take the colour A, grind it verv fine with oyl of turpentine, and with it trace the outlines of the design you intend to have upon the vessel, then fill up the vacant spaces very even, and shade the drape &c. Fire the vessels in a heat su cient to flux the black, nndtheyare finished.

M. Another method to produce a different effect with the same colour, in the manner of the Etruscans, is to paint the design with black, laid on as dead colouring upon red bislret ware, and to cut up or finish the designs with red and other colours, for which purpose the

above-mentioned ones are prepared; they must also be ground in oyl of turpentine, and burnt upon the Vessels in a muflle or enamel kiln.

N. Another method to produce in nmore expeditious way nearly the effect of the Process L. Take the red B, or the orange C, and lay in your desi with it, as It dead colour upon blac bisket vessels, and shade it with the black D, with or without the addition of any of the other colours, fireing them upon the vessels as before directed.

' In his letter to Bentley, Mr. Wedgwood gives this further account of the bronzing process. 'Lay Dr. Turner's brown varnish

VOL. II.
on (the wt' is not so good) the same as for gilding, then mix some of yr bronze in a. saucer with a large proportion of Lamp black, both dry, W" the size is of a proper dryness for gilding, lay this powd" on plentifull w"' with a large camel hair, or so 't pencil, the pencil sho' be abo' as urge as the end of y" finger, after this, warm the vases, but they must not be much warmer than a blood best, when dry, rub them well with a hard brush, dry them with a gentle heat, and they are finish'd. This is the fine Antique Bronze, if you W0' have any part seem as if it was rubb'd off to the brass, lay 0. very little of the bronze powder alone upon a prominent part before you lay on the mix'd powder. The powders require no nicety in the mixing, the finger and thumb is sufficient, & it shod not be mix'd too fine... I think you sho'l mix the powders before you give them out. A fire-side is heat suflicient, if vou use the stove they are sure to be made too hot, the man never let them come within a y' or two of the fire. ... The bluish cast in the mixture of No. 3 will be a great addition to their beauty, at least to their antiqueness. Nobody will now buy the single polished vases, they have too much the appearance of a varnish, but so much of the polish as I ap rehend your No. 3 will give, will do them good 8: not have that oily appearance.' 82 PROGRESS IN BUILDING. Cnnr. II. push the scheme of the Runcorn aqueduct. Mr. Wedgwood, in this

case as in many others, making his art an instrument whereby to promote general well-being. 'I believe,' he writes to Bentley, 'Dan1 will have D"y' 12

Crates before you receive this, & along with them a basket containing 2 Etruscan bronze vases, full of my compliments to Miss Tarleton, which you will be kind enough to deliver along with the vases to that ingenious Lady, & beg her acceptance of them as an offering of first fruits. There are 3 other imperfect ones to shew' you a little into the light of our impe1_'/'ect'ions in the manufacturing of these delicate compositions, & the disappointments you must expect to meet with when you become a Potter; so that if you can be picking up a little patience, and storeing it against a time of need, there may be no sort of harm in it. Every Vaze in the last kiln were spoil'd, & that only by such a degree of variation in the fire as scarcely affected our cream-colour bisket at all." Miss Tarleton's vases were of the largest size, finished with satyrs' heads, and sold at 188. a pair. Such would probably now fetch the price of 8!. or 10l.

Wliilst such was the progress of the ornamental ware, the work of building at Etruria was not at a stand-still. By January, 1768, Mr. Bentley's house was tiled, and a portion of the works ready for furnishing. But during the summer and autumn, various hindrances arose from the want of timber, bricks proper for Mr. Wedgwood's house, and the cupidity and shortcomings of the architect Mr. Pickford. In August the Etruscan works were nearly ready for roofing, and in November Mr. Wedgwood writes thus to Bentley, 'The works are covered in, &

CRAP. II. ETRURIA. 83 they are beginning upon the Cellar Arches, & the chamber & ground floors, as soon as any of them are finished I shall order them to be fitted up, & put some men into them to make Saggars, prepare Clay, build ovens, &c. &c., that we may begin to do something in earnest as soon as possible. The Partnership books should be opened on Monday the 14th inst., as some hands (Potters) will begin there at that time, & if you can leave home, Liverpool I wo'1 say, for I must now consider Etruria as your home, I think it will be absolutely necessary for you to be here the preceding Saturday at farthest; & we have put off our journey to the 16"', that we may have a few days to settle matters together before We part, concerning fitting up.the works, employing the hands hired for Etruria, &c. '1

As here intimated, Mr. and Mrs. Wedgwood and Mrs. Willet spent a month in London at this date; and, as regarded Mr. Wedgwood, in a manner most advantageous to his art, as we shall see presently. Meanwhile, Mr. Bentley was his representative at Burslem and Etruria; and we find him performing the same duty during the month of February in the succeeding year, when Mr. Wedgwood was again in town. From thence the latter writes urgent letters relative to the completion of the Etruscan works. In April the slip and clay houses were finished, two mills in progress, ' & your house,' adds Mr. Wedgwood to his friend, 'is going on as fast as the Works. The Joyners have left mine to finish yours, which Mr. Pickford assures me shall be completed in seven weeks at farthest.' In May everything relating to vases was removed from Burslem to Etruria; and 1 Wedgwood to Bentley, November 6, 1768.

84 A COLONY OF ARTISTS. CHAP. II. between June 2 and June 25, when he was again in Liverpool, Mr. Bentley was present at the opening of the Etruscan works.

As a beginning to his long matured scheme of gathering around him a colony of artists, who, perfected by his instruction and inspired by his example, would carry out to the full his splendid visions in relation to ornamental art, Mr. Wedgwood, as we have shown, had, upon the engagement of his London warehouse in Newport Street, entered into an agreement with an enameller named David Rhodes, who for some time previously had been working for him. A few days later we hear of another of these artists, and one who became as famous for his rascality as for his clever-

ness. His name was John Voyez. Writing to Bentley, Mr. Wedgwood says, ' I have hired a modeler for three years, the best I am told in London, he serv'd his time with a silversmith, has work'd several years at a China work, has been two or three years carving in wood & marble for Mr. Adams, the famous Architect, is a perfect Master of the Antique stile in ornaments, vases, &c. &c. , & works with equal facility in Clay, wax, wood, or stone.'1 The first articles which Voyez modelled for Mr. Wedgwood were a candlestick and an antique sauce boat; but the first proved clumsy,2 and it was soon

' Wedgwood to Bentle March 31, 1768. y'

' ' The Box with the Leaf Moulds, &c. is come to hand, & by this Specimen Mr. Vedgwood perceives that Mr. Voyes cannot execute anything that will suit his Business without he had him here to receive particular Instructions, as those sent are of no Use, & are unfortunately all of the same Pattern. YVith respect to the Sauce Boat he does not know what passing Orders you might have for it; but it is so very ugly, that he won'd not choose to sell it, but where it is particularly ordered. Mr. Vedgwood would be glad to know when it would suit Mr. Yo ez to come down, that he mi ht ave a house ready for him.'— 2'. Bentle to Cox, dated Burslem, May 18, 17. This is an extract from one of the few letters extent of Mr. Bentley. It is the more interesting from being written a few days prior to the amputation of Mr. 'edg'wood's leg, and whilst he was in attendance upon his invalided friend. Mayer MSS.

CHA P. II. VOYEZ. 85 seen that to make his services available he must work under his master's eye. It was therefore arranged that he should go into Staflbrdshire; and to facilitate this, as he was greatly in debt, Mr. Wedgwood advanced him 201., and sufficient besides to pay his and his wife's expenses by coach. They left London in July, and in August Voyez himself gives this account to Cox of Mr. Wedgwood's generous kindness. ' I beg leave to inform you of Mr. Wedgwood's Exceed-

ing Genteel behaviour to me, who on my Arrivall here entertain'd us in his own house for some time untill our house was gotten ready, which wos by the usiall Diligence, or rather delays of Joiner Show, kept back longer than it otherwise might have been; however, we are now altogether mighty happy, rather more so than one Would imagine might be for persons usually residing in London. I wou'd have you to know, friend Cox, I Live in the Grandee part of the City of Burslem, even in the new building of Mr. Smith, near honover Square! there's for ye! ' After giving Cox sundry directions as to a few miserable articles of fumiture to be sent by Waggon, 'a pr of black stocking breeches,' for which Mr. Vedgwood is to pay, and the purchase of sundry tools for gilding, Voyez winds up by saying, 'if it suits you to send me a Stone bottle full of Good porter and Charge it as above you cannot oblige me more, for I am just dead for want of it.'1 Sending porter into the land of good ale, was like sending coals to N ewcastlc; but the request probably unfolds to us one of the causes of the fellow's graceless conduct—an idle love of sotting. However, for some months he settled down to work; and under his master's tutelage proved

' John V0 oz to William Cox, Great Newport Street, London, August 19, 1768. ayer MSS.

86 HIS RA SCALITY. CRAP. II. himself an admirable hand, not only in carrying out instructions, but in instructing others. Late in the autumn we find him employed upon some bas-reliefs, the models of which were supplied by Mrs. Landre, a famous hand in her peculiar walk; and when we hear of him again in the spring of the following year, he has just received his sentence at the Stafford Lent Assizesl He is to be whipped with 'a cat-o'-nine-tails,' and imprisoned three months. What his crime was it is impossible now to say. It was probably not theft; and yet it must have been an offence of a grave character to incur a sentence which combined whipping and imprisonment. Whilst he was yet in prison, the partners gravely discussed

their own difiiculties in relation to this man. ' I agree with you in most of your sentiments respecting V, & do not intend to have any thing further to do with him on any acc"',' writes Mr. Wedgwood to his friend; but he still considered that there were points in dealing with him which required some caution, for this was his train of reasoning, ' I have got the start of my Brethren in the article of v-s, farther than I ever did in anything else, and it is by much the most profitable I ever launched into; 'tis a pity to lose it'soon—-there is no danger—true, not of losing the business, but the prices may be lower'd by competition, & if the imitations are tolerable, the demand from us may be diminish'd, for all our buyers are not, though many of them are, qualified to discern nice difierences in forms and ornaments. /Vhat then do our competitors stand in most need of to enable them to rival us the most effectually? Some Person to instruct them to compose good forms, & to ornament them with tolerable propriety. V can do this much more effectually than all the Potters in the Country put together, and without much

CHAP. II. VVORKS FOR PALMER. _ 87

Personal labour, as the ornam" may be bo" or model'd by others.' Mr. Wedgwood then proposes to pay him his wages of 368. per week, for doing nothing for his unexpired term of two years; thus preventing competition for so long by restraining him from taking service elsewhere. ' I know he is vicious, & everything that is bad, &-all my feelings are up in Arms against even so much as naming him. But to live in this world as matters & things are constituted, it is sometimes necessary to make a truce with these sensations, whilst we manage a Rascal, our evil stars have thrown in our way, to prevent repeated injuries which he might otherwise do us. I know too that he is Iazy & fickle, & not likely to stay long in any one place. But revenge may be an antidote to the first, & he may stay long enough w"" a Master to give him a relish for such a business as v— making; & depend upon it, my good friend, who-

ever tastes a little of the sweets of it, will afterwards spare no pains or cost to have a full meal; at least I am sure he must be both very dull and very idle who does.' The result of these deliberations does not appear. In all probability Voyez received his wages, and did just what he would have done without them. In September of this same year he was working both for himself and for Palmer of Hanley, and scattering so far as he could the secrets of Mr. Wedgwood's manufactory. A few weeks later he is in London, and on the track, as it is supposed, of the latest Etruscan vases; and the next fact recorded sums up his villany so far. He is again in Stafibrdshire, and raising reports that the generous master who had paid his debts and sheltered him beneath his roof had become bankrupt, and run away from his creditors! These lies were traced home to the vindictive wretch; but Mr. Wedgwood was too wise and magna 38 FEMALE ARTISTS. Cinr. 11.

nimous to punish so contemptible a rascal; and finally, after working off and on with Palmer' and other masters, he set up in business for himself, and we shall see him at a later date copying Wedgwood and Bentley's seals and iutaglios in a wretched body, and literally forcing them on the Birmingham mounters. Yet, with all his_ sins, Voyez was, without doubt, guiltless of the one usually assigned to him; and that which, false as it is, has handed down his name to our own day. Shaw1 and others insinuate that it was Voyez who betrayed the use of the carbonate of baryta in the jasper body; deriving his knowledge from the perusal of a bill of parcels enclosed _in a pocket-book Mr. Wedgwood had dropped. But in 1769 the asper body was still in its experimental stage; and Voyez had long quitted Mr. Wedgwood's service, when the cameos and other specimens of ornamental ware were displaying, through their exquisite effects, the value of a new porcellaneous mixture, and its adaptability to the highest purposes of the arts. The only known work of Voyez's is the accompanying jug, in the original 91$ inches high. It is modelled after the rus-

tic taste then so much in vogue; and, neither remarkable for its form nor ornament, certainly proves that Voyez was only a true artist when working under the guidance of a master-hand.

Despising no source which might contribute to the beautiful, Mr. Wedgwood entrusted some of his best work to female hands. We shall see presently a group of young and clever women busy enamel-painting in the rooms at Chelsea; and prior to, and at the same date, Mrs. Landre was modelling subjects that afterwards, in

' History of Stafibrdshire Potteries, p. 186.

the black Egyptian and jasper bas-reliefs, became very popular.1 A greater artist still was working for Mr. Wedgwood in 1769. This was John Bacon.

He had already acquired considerable fame by a figure of Peace, modelled after the antique, and exhibited by the Society

London: Jun. 2I,176!).

' Mr. Bentley.

B0'. of Mary Lands.

4 quarters of the Earth History of Apolow. 6 Passions or Vices 4 Groops of Boys. 3 Female Virtues..

Anti ue Baccanalians.

The runl-zen Sylenus

The English Poets...

4 Scripture ieces...

Moses and the Serpents.

Jose h.......

The rd's Supper &C0m-

A ginttle piece

w ww ww—h 110 v--IJ:—'u'.HIr-n-IN!»-in-.' so ooacoaooooofi 3 pieces of Vintage

Apolow & Dafnee,

A Baccus & Boys.

Antique figures.

6Fryers......

Antique heads the 12 Cesers & 6 Empresses.

A large Horse

Sylenus..

A Magdalen.

A packing case

£3.11. 50 100 50 so 60 180 50 so 10 woo _2o 16110 25 Man, 1769, Rec'. the above

Contents in full.

lI/im" LA.vnRi-2. of Arts in 1758; but his circumstances were yet humble, for in one of Mr. Wedgwood's letters is a reference to his living in the George Yard, Holborn. He had just taken work at Coade's Artificial Stone Manufactory in Lambeth, then newly established, and it is not improbable that he was recommended to Mr. Wedgwood by the proprietor, as some project of this sort is on several occasions glanced at in his correspondence with Bentley. The subject or subjects modelled by Bacon are not stated,1 but one may have been, as it was to be a companion to the Sacrifice, a reduced copy of his bas-relief of Aineas bearing Anchises from the burning of Troy, for which, in the December of this year, 1769, he received from the hands of Sir Joshua Reynolds the first gold medal ever given for sculpture by the Royal Academy. Bacon had served his apprenticeship with a porcelain maker, and had been accustomed to model as well as to paint in enamel; he therefore well knew the amount of relief a potter can afford to his designs. He was also a man well qualified to fulfil any mission of this character by his enthusiasm for his art, his honesty of purpose, and his painstaking love of excellence.

An enameller, named Joseph Simon, was at work for Mr. Wedgwood in London in 1767, and so continued for a long period, as we find him amongst those who contributed so ably to the completion of the Russian service in 1774. David Rhodes was, however, Mr. Wedgwood's principal enameller; at first combining his work with that of others, and as this increased taking a partner of the name of Craft or Croft to aid him; but eventually he relinquished all extraneous business, and remained literally 28"-,. 1 Rec'I of Mr. Wedgwood bgvthe Hands of Mr. Cox ninelgldundslliifteen shillings in full, for modelling ork done and all demands. Plm Jn. Bacon. £9 15 Mayer MSS.

Cnar. II. RHODES, CROFT, AND COVVARD. ' 91 his master's right hand in this department till his death, in 1777. ' I have had a letter from Mr. Rhodes,' writes Mr. Wedgwood to

Cox,1 ' acquaint" me he has got a partner who has Enamcl at Paris &c., & does it with great Elegance &c., & wants to begin upon some small plates immediately, w" you'l please to furnish them with.' The work of Rhodes and his partner was very exquisite and comparatively highly paid; no patterns are specified except feather edge and bead edge; and no colours but rose and green. For painting an octagon covered dish, they charge 28. 6d.; sauce boats, Is. each; for a basket and stand, 29. 9d.; for a large dish, 38. 6d.; table plates, 832-d.; and dessert plates, 7§ each; flowerpots according to size, and candlesticks 6d. each. Teapots and sugar dishes are painted for Is. each; a large tray is charged 7s. 6d.; and four pierced sugar bowls, painted black, 1s. 3d. each. Two ' Black Vases, Etruscan Satyr Heads,' are painted for 58. each; and other Etruscan vases, painted ' red, blue, white, and green,' are variously charged from 128. to 68."

John Coward was another of Mr. Wedgwood's modellers in 1768,3 and in the year succeeding he took the head of 1 June 20, 1768. Mayer MSS. and November, 1769—sum total, ' Five bills of D. Rhodes and £97 10;. 85d. Mayer MSS. ('n., for work done between January

' Mr. Vedgwood.
.4' s. d.
For 2 coloured sketches of Candlesticks... 0 5 6
For various Drawings of Vauzes, baskets, Dishes after the Duke of Richmond's, &c. &c.... O 1') 0
For Drawing of Do. after Mon'. De Mello's, &c. 0 16 0
For Drawing of baskets sent to Burslem, &c.. 0 3 6
Remains of a Bill Delivered for Queen's Armes. 2 6 0
£4 10 (S
Rec'. 4"' Nov'. 1768
of Mr. Cox on Ace' this Bill for J n Coward
1769. P" Dawson Cowman.
Mr. Wed ewood
' '0 John Coward.
J anus. 12.
For wo work carveing and modeling

the X Ribbons to a neat small tea tray, &c. in mahogany... 0 17 0
this department at a salary of 2001. per annum; a high premium in those days, and only given to men of undoubted ability. Coward's work appears to have been excellent; and though a coxcomb, and presuming on the kindly deference paid to him by his employers, he remained in their service for some time. In addition to the work thus effected, much else was done by extraneous hands. For the model of his first inkstand, Mr. Wedgwood paid 21. 7s. 3d. , in 1769, to a man of the name of Edward Watson; and Theodore Parker,1 James Tassie,2 and an Italian named Pingo3 were at the same period ' lIess"'.
Vedgwood To
Se " 31, Theod. Parker.
769.
To A Statue of Flora
To Do. Seres
To Do. Spencer...
To 1 Bracket Open Vork.
Oct. 7 To A Statue of Hercules
To Do. Seres Large.
To Do. Juno.
To Do. Prudence
To Do. Milton
To Do. Shake ear.
To A Boy A ouch.
3 Doggs.........
Time from the 7th above in Casting... 1
4 0
£3 3 0
Dechr y' 18"', 1769, Rec.'1 the above Contents in full of all Demands
P. Tmconona Panxan.
0000",,'
wwwmp acme?
_ Nov. 11, 1109.
' Mess". 'Vedgewood & Bentley Bill.
Ib-
To 70 impressions in Sulfer, at 2' a piece... ll 8
Two Enammel impressions.... 2
  T3 8
  Box 4 14 0 Recived the Contents
JA'. Tassm.
1769.
Mesa". Vestwood & Co..4' s. d.
Nov. 25.—1 Co per Model of Pondichen-y & 1 of the
irth of the Prince... 0 8 0 1 Copper Mod-

el of Plassy O 3 0 0 1 0

Dec‘ 20, Rec‘ the Contents in full for Mr. Pingo,
J omv Iaanmn.
Mayer MSS.

CRAP. II. ’ THE REGION OF ARTISTS. 93 contributing their‘ artistic aid. Of Tassie, who was one of the most remarkable artistic characters of the eighteenth century, much which is very interesting will appear, as his labours for Mr. Wedgwood extended over a very long period. »

Newport Street, St. Martin's Lane, Long Acre, and Leicester Square, formed at that period the great centre for artists of every class. Sir Joshua Reynolds was already established in Leicester Square; the old Life Academy had in previous years been held in a house at the top of a. court in St. Martin's Lane; and in Long Acre were congregated the colour makers, gold beaters, artists' tool makers, modellers, and journeymen of every kind. A change subsequently took place; and the streets to the south of the Oxford Road, as it was then called, and the newer ones springing up on its northern boundary, gradually absorbed much of the artist population of a superior class; but at the period we refer to, Leicester Square and its surrounding streets were the true region of artist life. Newport Street and its neighbourhood have since then undergone so great an amount of alteration, as to show at this day few, if any, vestiges of its old condition; but judging by our present ideas, relative to space, light, and accessibility, it must have been a comparatively gloomy and confined situation for such a shrine of the arts, and one so resorted to by the noblest in intellect and rank in the land. The partners soon thought so; for we shall find them looking wistfully to the airier and brighter region of the Adelphi; where the brothers Adams were then building their streets and terrace on a palatial scale.

The new warehouse faced both Newport Street and St. Martin's Lane. The ground floor consisted of two 94 THE SHOVV-ROOMS. CRAP. II. shops and a parlour, below which were kitchens. One of the former was soon let to a linendraper; and the other, -that towards Newport Street, was used by Mr. Wedgwood himself, for the sale of more ordinary goods, as seconds, thirds, and odd pieces. The prices of these were marked, and the public entered in and out the shop at pleasure. But the first floor, which extended over both shops, was another region; to which access was gained by a hall and wide staircase. It consisted of two rooms, and probably an antechamber, lighted by high narrow windows. In these the dinner and dessert services, the tea ware and other small articles were ranged on long centre tables; whilst the shelves round the walls supported vases, tripods, large bas-reliefs, flower and bough pots, and other exquisite specimens of ornamental ware. The background of these was covered with variously-coloured paper. Behind the black Egyptian and Etruscan vases glowed a fine carnation red or ochrous yellow; and sea-green or turquoise blue set off the vessels of fairer tints. A few of the very choicest pieces—-the last modelled Etruscan vases, or elegantly enamelled bough pots-were kept in an antechamber or adjacent closet, to which none but the partners or Cox, the manager, had access; and this repository was never shown except to patrons like the Duke of N orthumberland, the Duke of Marlborough, the Duke of Bedford, Lord Bessborough, Lord Gower, Sir Watkin Williams VVynne, Mr. Foley, Lady Chatham, Miss Chetwynd, Mrs. Montague, or others who had wealth and taste. Upon Mr. Bentley's settlement in London, the beauty of all these arrangements became still more marked; and the finest productions as they arrived from Staflbrdshire were enshrined in glass cases with sliding doors. The second floor was used by Mr. Wedgwood and his family when in

Cnsr. II. LIFE IN TOWN. 95 town; and otherwise partially by Cox and the housekeeper. It seems to have consisted of a drawing-room, a room used occasionally as a kitchen, and three bedrooms. Above this floor stretched a range of garrets, used variously for stowage and sleeping

The first visit Mr. Wedgwood paid to London after the amputation of his leg was in October, 1768, on which occasion he was accompanied by Mr. Bentley. They returned to Burslem together about the middle of November; and here Mr. Bentley took up his residence at the Brick House, in order to act for his partner, whilst he revisited town in company with Mrs. Wedgwood and Mrs. Willet. It is pleasant to catch glimpses of the preparations made for the ladies' comfort. New grates are put up in some of the rooms; new beds and fenders are bought; a glass bookcase is set up in the drawing-room; and a wealth of comfortable bedding comes up by waggon from Stafibrdshire. The little party travel leisurely in their own chariot accompanied by a maidservant, and meet with the usual disagreeables of the winter season_bad roads and poor horses. But they make amends for all these things when they reach Newport Street. Bright fires glow. There are'teaparties, suppers, and rubbers at whist. Mrs. Wedgwood receives Mrs. Griffith of Turnham Green, not the shrew who starved Goldsmith, but the kindlier woman, whom the reviewer made his second wife in the autumn of 1767; Mrs. Hodgson, the wife of the rich Russian merchant of St. Mary's Axe; Mrs. Berry, and many others. There are gentlemen, too, in abundance; and Mr. Wedgwood is the merriest among them, except when he is called away,

' Wedgwood to Cox, October 31, and November 7, 1768. Mayer MSS.

as he too often is, on countless matters of business. Tassie has come out of Leicester Square with a sulphur cast of some exquisite antique gem; Bacon or Theodore Parker has brought home his newest bas-relief or figure; or Rhodes, Crofts, or Coward have to consult him on their day's enamel-painting or carving.1

Mr. Boulton is at this date in London, and we hear from Mr. Wedgwood himself what charming days they occasionally spend together, in what he calls this 'fine city.' 'Mr. Boulton,' he writes to Bentley, 'is still in Town, & has not done half his business, nor shall have time, he says, if he stays a month longer. He has seen so many pretty things that he has sent for his Artist to come up to him, & we have been alltogether, the Ladys & all, at Harraches this afternoon, where we have amongst us spent near twenty pounds. Do you remember what Harrach asked for the Raphael bottles? I think it was 10 Guineas. They now ask twenty-five! Harrach is just return'd from Paris and has bro" a great many fine things with him. I bid £30 for 3 pr of Vases; they asked £32 & wod not abate a penny. There's spirit for you I Must not we act in the same way? Mr. Boulton is picking up Vases, & going to make them in Bronze. You know how old China bowles, jarrs, &c. are mounted in Metal; he proposes an alliance betwixt the Pottery and Metal branches, viz. that we shall make such things as will be suitable for mounting,- & not have a Pott look, & he will 1 'I will not trust towriting in 1 employed, we are-in a constant the evening,enga. gements of my own bustle, I have for m own part got or the Ladies allways filling up those i very little done, & t e Ladies have hours, indeed we are under the business enough cut out for them a necessity of incroaching upon regu-j month longer.... Well now it is lar bedtime to have an hour's rest I evening, & we are favoured with the or enjoyment of ourselves in peace; i company of Mrs. Blake, Mrs. Hodgnotwithstanding every moment is son,&a1-oom full of Ladies.....'

CRAP. II. CURIOSITY HUNTING. 97 finish them 'with the mounts. What do you think of it? Perhaps you we.1 rather he wo'i let them alone. Very true, but he will be doing, so that the question is whether we shall refuse having anything to do with him, & thereby affront him, &_ set him of doing them him-self, or employing his frd Garbett. If we-join with him in this scheme, I apprehend we can allways bind him to us by making him such things as nobody else can, & thereby make it his interest to be good. We can make things for mounting with great. facility &" dispatch, & mounting will enhance their value greatly in the eye of the purchaser. Pebble 'will in this Way scarcely be discover'd to be counterfeit. Bass-reliefs will have a most fine effect too, & will fetch Guineas instead of shillin_gs. These things will do for the East India C., & they give any price for fine things. £20, or 30,000 a piece for Clocks I am told is a common price for them to give. One of this sort we have seen to day, though I believe not of that price, but it is the finest piece of work I ever saw in my life. The maker is to visit me, & I expect to have some traflic with him in the ornament way. Mr. Boulton & I go a curiosity hunting all day tomorrow. VVe begin with a' visit to Ld Shelbourne, & shall then proceed--the Ld knows where, for I cannot yet tell you. Mr. Cox is as mad as a March Hare for Etruscan Vases, pray get a quantity made or we shall disgust our good customers by disappointing them in their expectations. But raise no dust at home though about them, for that will make our antagonists open all their ears, & eyes too, & push them forwarder than they wo" perhaps move at their own natural rate.... Mr. Boulton has not yet sent any of his things to St. James's. He soars higher, & is scheming to be sent for by his Majesty! I wish him VOL. ll. H success;' he has a fine spirit, & I think by going hand in hand we may in many respects be usefull to each other....

'tis a pitty but we could be alltogether in this fine world' here, we want you much to help us on, & enjoy the many fine things we see & are plotting to see every day; but it cannot be, somebody must take care of the Etruscans & prepare vessels of honor at home. And pray do not forgetwto take care of yourself; keep a good & hospitable house, & make much of your friends who have goodness enough to visit you... Our love & respects wait on all our friends and your fellow Labourers,-_Mess" T. Wedgwood, Swift, Unwin, die.'1 In another letter of a date somewhat later Mr. Wedgwood adds, ' I can only thank you for your goodness in writing to us, & to tell you that an epidemical madness reigns for Vases, which must be gratified. I have five or six modelers & carvers at work upon different branches, and a moulder constantly in my house. I have seen the Italian Vases, & like them vastly; have seen at Sir Henry Chairs some better prints of vases than any I have, particularly for Bass-reliefs, & he has promised to lend them to me, & _I am in a fine channel for good things if I could stay here awhile.' We have abundant evidence that Mr. Bentley more than performed the business delegated to his able hands. He was, as his great partner often said, his ' second self;' and the universal cry for the exquisite productions which had already revolutionised the art of pottery in this country, was attended to as far as might be. ' We have,' he writes to Cox,2 ' at length got some Etruscan Vases in great forwardness, & shall send you several sets by the next Carrier. If any

' Ved wood to Bentley, dated wealthy and well known dealer in Ne ort street, November 21,1768. articles of vertu, particularly those " he Cox here referred to was a of porcelain.

of your Friends wonder why you have not more & oftener, please to give them to understand that it is very difficult to make fine and perfect things of any kind. How often does our great Mistress Nature Fail, even in the finest Order of her Productions! The angelic Sex themselves are notall perfectly straight, delicate, & beautiful, no more than our Vases; and you may contrive to edge in the Natural Inference that every good Thing deserves a good Price."

Knowing, as our generation does by the fruits of their labolus, what essentially great men they were, and how by every movement of their hand and impulse of their mind they were doing more for the commercial prosperity of their country, and the 'well-being of the people, than half' the orators and placemen in Parliament, there is many a one amongst us who would like to see Wedgwood and Boulton as they passed from Newport Street westward to my Lord Shelburne's, or eastward to the Duke of Bedford's or Lord Mansfield's mansion, on these bright December mornings just a hundred years ago. Boulton as handsome as any duke himself, and with a bearing that earned for him the title of ' Prince of Soho,' was, we may be sure, richly dressed; not an accessory or a point wanting. He was now forty years of age, and in the prime of life. Mr. Wedgwood two years youngermight look older than his friend, for he had but lately undergone a severe surgical operation, and illness in one shape or another was always sapping the vigour of a naturally fine constitution. But there was that in his face and presence, if his step was halting, and his stature less 1 Bentley, from Burslem, to Cox, original letters of Mr. Bentley's now Newport Street, December 7,1768. extant, this is perhaps the most.la_vor MSS. Of the very few charming.

WEDG WOOD'S DRESS.
100 Can. II. than that of his princely-looking friend, which few could pass unobserved. Keenness, sagacity, and firmness, an exquisite benevolence and tenderness, were all expressed in his manly face; and those who remembered him long after said there was a look in his eyes, the like of which they had never otherwise seen. It was depth and dreamy luminousness combined, as though stretched on the retina were ever multiplying pictures of grace and beauty.

His style of dress we know. He wears ' a Lite Brown Dress Bob-Wig." His coat is a plain blue frock; his waistcoat, scarlet cloth laced richly with gold, and ornamented with gilt basket buttons. His nether garments are of knit black silk.2 He wears a cooked hat, and on dress occasions a sword. Whether he wore a peg or a cork leg we do not exactly know, but which ever it was it served an excellent purpose, and well replaced the poor diseased, long inflicting limb?

Though not so keen a politician as his partner, Mr. Wedgwood took great interest in the more important 1 Mn Vi ag-woiii. to Rich" Dowle.
1768.
March 26.—To a Lite Brown Dress Bog-wig
To 11 Times Shaving and Dressing of your wigs.......

1768.
March 29, Race" the Contents in full.
P" Rrcaaan Dowua.
Mayer MSS.
" Tailor's bill, 131. 6.1. 9d. Mayer MSS.
' 'My first wooden leg was made by Mr. Addison, lay-figure maker, in Hanover Street, Long Acre; this was about 18 years ago, & as I have heard nothing of him since I do not know whether he is alive or dead. An ingenious 'oiner in this neighbourhood is ni ing me a new one, which I belive is nearly finished.

He has made me one or two before, had the care of the old one many years, & it has received so many repairs from him, that it has now become almost like the sailors knife, which had so many new blades 82. so many new hafts: I have spoken to him, & he is willing 8: at liberty to make one for the ntleman you mention/—Wedgwo to Darwin,

I June 27, 1788.
CRAP. II. POLITICAL OPINIONS.
101 questions of the day; and there is reason to think by the eminent ability with which he worked the House of _ Commons on the points connected with Pitt's Irish Revo lutions in 1785, that he had habituated himself, whenever in London and time favoured him, to be present at the debates in Parliament. The period under consideration was one of wild political excitement. The general election in the early part of the year had roused the whole country; and the renewal of the Parliamentary contest with the contemptible demagogue Wilkes marked its close. Mr. Wedgwood refers but once or twice to Wilkes, and then in the most cursory manner; but his opinion on graver questions have great weight and force. He utterly condemned the policy of the Government towards America. He considered this ' policy had a tendency to render the Americans independent a century sooner than they would be in the common order of events,' and thus led to the organisation of a scheme of government which bore within it, as even Washington foresaw, the seeds of future disruption and civil strife. Wedg-

wood condemned the selfish struggle for power between the factions of the oligarchy. After one of these contests in the House of Lords, and a possible change of Ministry, he tells Bentley, ' But this is nothing to you and I, for whoever is in, they will make the most of us they can; so my friend let us unite our forces, & endeavour to do the same by them, but in an honester manner.' When called for by circumstances, his criticism on eminent characters was occasionally severe. Both Lord Mansfield and his nephew Lord Stormont were his patrons; but this did not restrain him from thinking, and expressing too, that the judgments of the former were not always impartial. In reference to a trial in which Bentley had been defeated, Mr. /Vedgwood says, ' I have not the least doubt but that if L'1 M had happened to interest himself in your cause, as he did in your antagonists, you

'o" have come offvictorious with as little trouble as they did. To be hasty, partial, and 0t'erbear2'n_q is perfectly cliaraeteristic of your Judge, at least they are attributes which are alhnost universally given to him, & I am very apt to believe the vow Populi to be just in most cases; this & many other instances I have of late had an opportunity of knowing confirms me in the belief, '& I shall not easily depart from it.' But whatever were his leanings and discrepancies on the judgment-seat, Lord Mansfield had given proof that he was a sterling patriot at heart; and amidst the discreditable wrangles of courts and factions, a power was rising, that of multiplied in ('u.u'. II. THE ARTS OF PEACE. 103 dustry and commercial prosperity, in which lay latent the seeds of true and great reforms. After traveising the ocean of a thousand difiiculties, the constitution of this free country, like a stately weather-beaten ship, righted itself at last; and this was due, not to Parliament and statesmen, but to men like Wedgwood, Boulton, Arkwright, and many others as illustrious, who, through cultivating the great arts of peace, insured the well-being of the people, and aroused them to a sense of their true duties as patriots and as Englishmen.

CHAPTER III.

ORNAMENTAL wane.'

T HE ornamental vases produced at Burslem and Etruria may be divided into seven chief sections. The cream-colour and its variations, as those with blue necks and ornaments variously gilt; the black basaltcs; the terra-cotta pebble and marbled bodies; the bronze antique; the encaustic Etruscan and Grecian; and the jasper." There are variations even of these; as the cane colour, ivory, and others, though they respectively belong to one of the sections indicated. The cream-colour vases may date from about 1763, when Mr. Wedgwood had brought this body to a great degree of perfection; the basaltes follow, and were the results of laborious experiments which enabled him to prepare the protoxide of iron, from the coal mines, in a manner that insured a finer grain, a better colour, and a more perfect incorporation in the mass; the pebble and marbled specimens were, as we have seen, first sent to Bentley late in the autumn of 1767; the bronze antique and encaustic Etruscan followed, and were ultimately perfected in 1769; and our earliest notice of the term 'jasper " occurs in 1:775. Exquisite

' It is perhaps to he regretted-. was also ''en to one variation of that n more distinctive term was 1 the crysta line bodies. Thisispuzznot applied to this exquisite com-I ling tn the uninitiated. But the position. For the name of jasper j difficulty can be obviated by re articles were produced in this new body in the following year; and in 1777-8 absolute certainty in the firing of this delicate composition crowned Mr. Wedgwood's untiring labours. The term antique must be taken in its generic sense as applied to form, rather than to colour and decoration; though after 1769 it seems to have been more specially applied to the black or red bodies, on which were painted, in encaustic colours, designs taken from the vases of antiquity.

From the period Mr. Wedgwood first brought his encaustic colours to some degree of perfection, he seems to have variously used them on a black body; but this application of the term antique

to form rather than to ornament, leaves the date of the earliest attempts uncertain. Some vases, it is evident, had been painted prior to June 1769; but the opening of the Etruscan works at Etruria on the 13th of that month, deprives the point of all vagueness beyond this date. ' The six Etrus can vases three-handled,' Writes Mr. Wedgwood to Bentley, ' sent to you a fortnight ago, were those we threw & turned the first at Etruria, and sho'1 be finish'd as high as you please but not sold. They being firstfruits at Etruria.' 1 A little earlier he has told his friend, ' L'1 Moreton wants the first Etruscan urns. Many have been promised some of the first. Sir Watkins Williams, L'1 Bessborough, Ld Clanbrassil, Mr. Crew, Mrs. Chetwynd, for collecting that in the one form the I cotta. body, into the composition of term was applied to a crystalline l which the carbonate or sulphate of terra-cotta body, which variously baryta entered largely.

imitated jasper, agate, and other 1 Vedgwo0d,Etruria, to Bentley, stones of alike character; whilst the Newport Street. November 19, 1769. later jasper was a fine white terra-_

CRAP. III. ETRUSCAN VASES.

109 their Majestys, the first of every capital improvement.'1 'May you not give L'I Cathcart a hint that we are preparing to paint the Etruscan vases after Mr. Hamilton's book,' 2 and in October he adds, ' The Etruscan vases are arrived. I see how the mechanical part of the glaze and painting is performed, all of which may be faithfully imitated at any time/3

Through the first six months of 1769, Mr. Bentley was constantly passing to and fro between Liverpool and Burslem, the business connected with the buildings at Etruria and the new partnership requiring his presence at the latter place; and his mercantile affairs, and the larger warerooms, to which he and Mr. Boardman had but lately removed their stock, necessitating that he should spend some portion of his time in Liverpool. At the close of May he was again Mr. VVedgwood's guest at the Brick House, and, on June 2, he was

witness to an agreement between John Wood, Junr., and Mr. Wedgwood; 4 the former to serve the latter for five years as a warehouseman 'for the business T. Wedgwood now does. Between this date and June 13, the partners were busy with their preparations at Etruria; and on that day, such portion of the ornamental works as was finished was formally opened.

As though with some foreshadowing of the place his name would occupy on the sacred list of illustrious Englishmen, and of the admiration which, growing with time, would at length give something like an antique

I

' Wedgwood, Etruria, t0Bentley, Ne ort Street, September 27, 1769.

' bid. September 20, 1769.

' Ibid. October 9, 1769.

4 On the following terms. For the first two years John 'Wood is to receive no wages from the said

Josiah VVedgwood, and is to be maintained in clothes, meat, drink, &c. by his father. During the following three years, Josiah Vedgwood doth agree to pay the said John Wood eight shillings per week.

110 OPENING OF THE WORKS. Cnar. III. sacredness to his exquisite works, Mr. Wedgwood'resolved, in conjunction with his partner and friend, to hand down to posterity, through the means of their art, the memory of this first day's labour at Etruria. Its fruit should show future generations that-it was not by the hands of others, but through the dignity of their own, that this hitherto sterile spot of moorland was dedicated to its new purpose of educating communities through the arts whichrefine, and the utilities which civilise and purify. Less liberal men would have been spectators and not potters: but'Wedgwood and Bentley were nobly con-' scious, that worthy work consecrates the hand which does it; and that masters are but leaders and foremost workmen, if they lovethe art or calling to which they dedicate their lives..

It is handed down, that on this bright summer's morning, June 13, 1769, Mr.

and Mrs. Wedgwood, their two children, Mr. Bentley, Mr. Wedgwood of Spen Green, M1-.and Mrs.'Willet from Newcastle, and other relations and friends, 'came riding through the pleasant lanes which then lay between Burslem, Newcastle, and Etruria, and were received, as on a gala day, by a large body of workmen atthe new ' Works.' Of buildings, besides tliis portion of the works, little could be yet seen, as the ' Useful Works ' were scarcely yet begun.1 The painters were finishing Mr. Bentley's house on the opposite bank, but that of Mr. Wedgwood's, on the acclivity beyond the works, was only just roofed in; the canal was but recently begun, and fields and patches of moorland occupied what was so soon to be a populous village.

i ' Throughout the whole of the 'UVo1-ks,' that is useful and ornaWedgwood papers the works are 1 mental. The term 'Black "'01-ks' termed the 'U 'orks,' and the never once occurs.

The throwing room, as seen in the illustration,1 was where the company assembled, and here Mr. VVedgwood, divesting himself of his hat and coat, and probably tying on, to the amusement of his visitors, one of the workmen'sf aprons, but in no other way altering his ordinary dress of a gentleman, sat down betore the thrower's board, whilst Mr. Bentley, handsomely attired we may be sure, turned the wheel. One of the favourite old servants made the

' balls of clay ready to his master's hand, and others stood by to assist. Thus environed, Mr. Wedgwood, well

' The figures in the illustration i is little clinngod from its appearance are the ordinary workmen of the l at the date referred to. present day. But the room itself ' 112 FIRST FRUITS. CIIAP. III. remembering his old mastery in this highest province of the potter's art, threw with great precision six vases, in the black basaltes body, averaging about ten inches each in height, and five and a half in the widest part. This done, there was an adjournment to the turners' room, and here, still assisted by his friend, and cheered by the presence of his visitors, Mr. Wedgwood pared down

inequalities at the lathe, and perfected his work so far as was then possible. This done, a luncheon was spread under the shade of some trees on the upland beyond; and the memorable day did not close till the shades of evening fell.

The six vases were fired at the close of the following month, and early in November they were sent to London, as We have seen, to be painted in encaustic colours by David Rhodes or William Crofts. Of these vases, three are still preserved; 1 and the illustration gives a reduced copy of one. The body, which is of a bluish tinge of black, adding thereby, as Mr. Wedgwood explains in a letter to Bentley, 'a. look of antiqueness,' bears on it, painted in two shades of red, a subject taken from a bas-relief in Hamilton's work,2 or more probably a vase in that of Count de Caylus, ' Hercules and his Companions in the Garden of the Hesperides.' The two borders are from the same source. O11 the reverse side is an inscrip 1 At Barlaston Hall, StaH'ord-the work we have consulted, tlfie shire, the seat of Francis Ved-form of the Barlnston vases is to e wood, Esq, Mr. Vedgwood's grand-found in vol. iv. plates 84 and 85, non, whilst the painting is from a plate

" The plates in many of the copies in vol. ii. The original is greatly of Sir Vm. Hamilton's great work modified in the copy, and in some seem arranged according to the bin-respects, as in the foot, the imitation der's caprice rather than by any is vastly inferior. But those were eneral rule. In a reference by Mr. 1 days of first-fruits. Three or four Vedgwood himself, attached to the years later many of the copies vied Barlnston vases, the original vase is with the originals.

said to be in vol. i. In the copy of l

Cnar. III. THE ARTS REVIVED. 113 tion to the effect that it is the product of the first day's work at Etruria, in Stafibrdshire, by Wedgwood and Bentley, and within the fillet above the foot are inserted the words 'Artcs Etruriae Renascuntur.' Another interesting memorial of this day exists. In a letter written to

Cox, Mr. Wedgwood adds in a post-

script the words as voL. II. 1 114 MR. BENTLEY'S HOUSE. CRAP. III. given in the facsimile, ' 13 June, 1769, our days throwing at Etruria.' The form of these vases are far excelled by many of those produced by Wedgwood and Bentley, and the painting was afterwards much improved, as the hands employed attained greater mastery in their art; bgt so far as the subject of a design can go, nothing more appropriate to the purpose could have been selected from the whole range of the heathen mythology. For it typified that the masters of the new Etruria, like another Hercules, entered, after long probationary labours, the garden of their great art, where fruit, richer than the fabled apples, was to be gathered by them and garnered for posterity.

In July Mr. Bentley's house was dry and fit for habitation; and at the close of the month he was expected again at Burslem, for Mr. Wedgwood wrote, ' I have but just time to thank my dear friend for his last good packet, & to tell him that I shall be exceedingly glad to see him on Monday or Tuesday, when he will find the 'first ovenfull of ware firing at Etruria & the gloss oven nearly built. There are four joiners at Work there, & we shall want a good deal of bricklaying before the scheme of keeping each workshop seperate, which I have much set my heart on, can be effected. But more of this & many other things when I have the pleasure of seeing you face to face.' ' Mr. Bentley undoubtedly paid this visit, but whilst making it, circumstances _arose which changed every plan; and when next we hear ofhim, on August 15, he has left Liverpool finally, has settled for a time at the warehouse in Newport Street, and is in treaty for a house at Chelsea.2 As these circumstances, whatever they were, 1 Vedgwo0d to Bentley, July 29, wood was himself the first occupant, 1769. and afterwards it was let to Mr. 9 He never inhabited his house at Ilenshall, Brindley's brother-in-law. Etruria for a single day. Mr. Wedg

Can. III. HE REMOVES TO LONDON. 115 first arose whilst the partners were together, no letters exist to afford explanation of what they were precise-ly»; but we gather subsequently enough to make it clear that the chief causes which changed every plan so suddenly, was,the increasing and astonishing demand for vases of every kind, and the great extent of certain Russian orders which flowed in together. Lord Cathcart's embassy had literally opened the Russian capital to whatever goods l/ Vedgwood and Bentley might choose to send there; and it was probably the use of the service Mr. Wedgwood had, as we have seen, prepared for his lordship which led to one of these orders for four large services at the instance of Mr. Baxter, the British Consul at St. Peters,burgh, who had returned to this country on business connected with the consulship. These services, if not for royalty, were at least for some of the high nobility. They must not however be confounded with the far larger and more splendid service prepared for the Empress, and which gave an European fame to Wedgwood and Bentley.

Weaned as he must have been from his home and friends at Liverpool, by his frequent journies into Staffordshire, by the multifarious duties of his new partnership, and more than all, by the intensity of that noble aflection which led him to regard Wedgwood as himself, and his affairs as his own, Bentley could not thus suddenly have cut the thread of so many associations without feeling the matter keenly. He was a man of ardent and sensitive character. Had the removal been merely into Staffordshire, as so long oontemplated, a few hours' ride would have taken him back to his old haunts, and to the firesides of his brother ' Octagonians.' But this sudden removal to a place then so comparatively distant as London, abruptly closed 116 A LOSS TO LIVERPOOL. CRAP. III.

his more intimate connections with a town he loved so well; and which had benefited so materially by his commercial and corporate services. Not but what there were many men competent to fill his place, who were as ardent patriots, and as much lovers of literature and the fine arts; but there can be no

question that in one or more points of considerable importance to the town, his removal was disadvantageous. Warrington Academy, which he had helped to establish, was yet in the fulness of its fame, as an institution where enlightened culture could be obtained at a moderate expense by the youth of the middle classes; but the congregation which he had been instrumental in gathering together, and for whose use the Octagon Chapel in Temple Court had been built, begun soon after his departure to decline, and in 1776 ceased finally to exist. This was a source of great mortification to him, although he was again instrumental in founding a church in London 'upon a still more noble and liberal plan.' Writing to Mr. Boardman in 1776, in reference to the sale of the Octagon Chapel, he says, 'I cannot understand the principle upon which that institution has been sacrificed, but I am sure if the gentlemen had not been unnecessarily precipitate, and had thought proper to consult their distant friends upon the subject before they had consented to ruin the noblest institution of the kind that has been established, it need not have been given up.' ' Considering the pains,' he adds, 'I have always taken upon this matter, and the many years, I may say, I have spent upon it, I ought, in decency, to have had some intimation of the state of things before so fatal a determination was made; and especially as I had neither dropped my subscription nor cooled in my affections for that respectable society. But it has been otherwise managed, Cmr. III. THE SLAVE TRADE. 117 and at this distance I cannot be active in the matter; I can only lament the loss of an institution favourable to virtue and social worship.'1

It is also probable, had Mr. Bentley remained in Liverpool, his and Brindley's noble scheme of an aqueduct, or as it was sometimes called a 'bridge,' across the Mersey would not have sunk, as we shall hereafter see, in spite of the exertions of a few leading minds, into the oblivion it slowly did as an important public measure, and the appropriate consummation of the greatest engineer-

ing Work of its day. He would have roused the Corporation from its apathy; and if the final result had been no different to what it was, the proprietors of the Grand Trunk Canal would not certainly have made so easy a coalition of their interests with those of the Duke of Bridgewater. In respect to the abominable traffic in slaves, then so unblushingly avowed and carried on by the majority of the Liverpool merchants, his continuous protest might have so far availed in influencing public opinion, as to have better prepared the way for the labours of the Abolitionists twenty years later; and Clarkson might not have found this noble port-next to Bristol— the very sink of these dealings in human flesh and blood.2 Bentley's philanthropy would not have been always ridiculed; his persuasions to change this traflic in human beings for a legitimate and honest one in ivory,

' Bentleyana, p. 18. This isa small tract issued in 1851 by Mr. James Boardman, the son of Bentley's Liverpool partner. Cunsidering the materials at his disposal, it is greatly to be regretted that Bentleyana is such a me compilation.

' The date when the slave trade was first carried on on a large scale, seems coincident with the remark able increase of population in 1752.

It reached its maximum in 1771, and from that period it declined; the supply to the Vest Indies having so far overtaken the demand as to reduce the selling price of slaves. Sufficient, however, of this abominable trafiic remained at the date of Clarkson's final visit to Liverpool, to render this port, next to Bristol, the opprobriuni of a country inhabited by civilised man. 118 EARLY ENAMELLING. CRAP. III palm-oil, woods, and other African products not in every case ineffectual; for in all moral questions the reflex operation of one noble mind upon another is more potential and more frequent than is generally supposed. His continued residence in Liverpool might, too, have prolonged his life. As we have already seen, the town at that day was intersected by gardens, and surrounded by great strips of moorland. It thus afforded to its inhabitants the advantages of town and country combined, in addition to the fine sea-breezes of the Irish Channel. But neither London nor Turnham Green seems to have suited him. From the period Mr. Bentley quitted Liverpool we find him subject to various disorders; the result probably of incessant occupation, bad air, or uncongenial climate. Indeed, it may be said, that both Mr. Wedgwood and himself achieved most of the masterpieces of their art amidst such frequently recurring hindrances of ill-health, as made literally the last years of their respective lives a slow dying to both; a frequent case where the vital power and its expressions are preeminent in degree.

The earliest enamelling by Rhodes and his partner Crofts for Mr. Wedgwood was done on premises of their own; but subsequently a muffie or enamelling oven appears to have been erected in the yard or cellar of the house in Newport Street. The conveniency of this, and presently its insufficiency as the great Russian and other foreign orders poured in, and the demand for vases increased, was undoubtedly in some degree the cause which led the partners to conceive a plan, and as rapidly carry it out, of having the larger portion of the immense amount of enamelling and decorative work now required effected by their own workmen, in premises self-contained and sufficiently remote from London for

Cnar. III. CHELSEA. 119 the purposes of privacy.1 How necessary this last point was we shall see, when no art was left untried in the ceaseless attempts made to acquire or copy patterns, forms, and ornaments; or to ascertain the mixtures of which the various bodies were composed. Conjointly with this purpose was the other, of securing Mr. Bentley a residence befitting his position as Mr. WedgWood's partner and representative; and this in a situation where accessibility to London, good air, and good neighbourhood would be combined. The house in Newport Street, however suitable for a temporary abode, was quite unfitted for the

requirements of a gentleman who had occupied one of the best residences in the then most fashionable street of Liverpool.

Chelsea must have been well known to both Mr. Wedgwood and his partner; for business and pleasure had often taken them there. It was literally what it was called a century ago, 'a village of palaces; ' and in many of its mansions they had dined, as well as inspected the chef d'ceuvres of cabinets and china-closets. Those best of patrons, Sir William Meredith, Sir Henry Chairs, Sir George Saville, had villas there; as also many of those dowagers and ladies whose chariots stayed about the

' Economy, in respect to the number of hands employed, was one of the inducements which led to the concentration for a time of the enamelling business in London; though the higher rate of wages must in point of fact have neutralised the benefit. Greater dispatch, and undoubtedly a higher class of artistic work, were the chief points effected. 'The rincipal reasons why we conclud to haveboth the enamel works at Chelsea were, that they might both have the assistance of the same Press. Printer, Clerk (Mr. Rhodes),

& Master, & I cannot help thinking still, that these advantages over ballance the extra trouble that will arise from these accounts at Chelsea. "'0 shall certainly find it necessary to keep a clerk there to take an account of the work, the were, &c. &c, & one clerk will do the whole with ease, though we must certainly employ many hands, & according to my present ideas twice the number, upon vases as upon useful ware, the former will pass so slowly through their hands.'—Vedgwood to Bentley, April 29, 1770.
120 ITS PORCELAIN WORKS. CRAP. III. rooms in Newport Street. But it was possibly a circumstance connected with their art which first led the partners to look in this direction for what they required.

A few months previously, in writing to Bentley whilst the latter was yet in Liverpool, Mr. Wedgwood had reported, ' The Chelsea moulds, models, &c.

&c. are to be sold, but I'll inclose you the advertisement—there's an immense amount of fine things.'1 Of these it is evident he intended to become a purchaser of at least a portion, had the classes or articles been sold separately, for he says to Cox, ' Pray enquire of Mr. Thomas whether they are determined to sell less than the whole of the models &c. together, if so, I do not think it would suit me to purchase. I should be glad if you could send me any further particulars of the things at Chelsea.'2 But they were sold in the lot, with the manufactory and other appurtenances; and thus Etruria owed nothing, except in a few imitative instances, to Chelsea.

As already seen, the manufacture of soft porcelain, which at first was little other than opaque glass, had been carried on at Chelsea from the close of the seventeenth century. After 1720, when the survivor of the brothers Elers, from Stafibrdshire, joined the establishment for a short time, the body of the ware was improved; and the subsequent patronage of George II., George III, and other members of the Royal family, raised the productions of Chelsea to a degree of perfection which

Manufactolies and others, there is to &c. Likewise all the Buildings and be Sold at the Chelsea Manufactory, many other Articles. For Further by order of the Proprietor (having I Pm'ticulars Enquire for Mr. Thomas, entirel left off malnn the Same) I at the said manufaetory.'—Vedg

' ' To all Proprietors of Porcelaine 1 large Quantity of Biscuit Work, Szc. everyt ing in general elong-ing to wood to Bentley, April 14, 1769. to it.... asallthe Plaster Moulds, ' Vedgwood to Fox, appended to Models in Vax, Lead and Brass invoice, July 24,1769. Maver MSS. Kilns, Mills, Iron Presses, and a ' '

Gnu. III. M. SPERMONT. 121 rivalled tl1ose of Vincennes and Dresden. 1 This period began about 1750 and lasted till 1765, when M. Spermont, who throughout had managed the business and more than a hundred workmen, some of whom were natives of Brunswick and Saxony, retired with an ample fortune. He remained in England, and seems ultimately to have entered into some sort of business connection with Boulton, at Soho; but whether it was of a permanent or merely temporary character is now unknown. Writing from Burslem to Mr. Bentley in London, Mr. Wedgwood remarked, 'I have no fear at all, even from the combination of Chelsea & Soho, if that she'1 ever happen. We have got and shall keep the lead so long as our lives and health are continued to us.' 2 A little later he added in reply to something Bentley had written to him, ' I she" like to have seen Mr. Spirmont; pray what did he say, how did he look, was Cox with him, or has he been at the rooms? I do not think their imitating us improbable at all, at least so as to make vases a principal article at their works.' 3

The successor of M. Spermont at the Chelsea manufactory was a person named Francis Thomas, who pre-. viously had been a foreman in the establishment. But under his direction the business rapidly declined; and after passing through one or more proprietorships, it was sold in August, 1769, to Mr. Duesbury, the proprietor and founder in 1751 of the Derby porcelain works. After their purchase, he carried on the Chelsea. works, simul

' The finest specimens of Chelsea 1 6001. Mrs. Delany's Letters, vol. i. porcelain was highly riced. A ser-p. 459. vice sent to the Du e of Mecklen-Vedgwood to Bentley, Septemburg in 1763, by George III. and her 1,1769. Queen Charlotte, cost 1,2001.; and a 3 Vedgwood to Bentley, Novemlnstre made for the Duke of Cum— I ber 19, l'/'09. berlantl about 1757 was charged 1 122 THE MANUFACTORY. CRAP. III.

taneously with those at Derby till 1784, with no very great success as it would seem, for at that date the premises, kilns, and other working appurtenances were pulled down, and so much as could be made available was sent to Derby. The rapid decline of the manufactory after the retirement of Spermont; appears not to have been due so much to mismanagement as to causes

beyond control. By the death of the Duke of Cumberland, an able friend and patron had been lost; and the Government were probably, even if inclined, deterred from rendering assistance by the remonstrances, powerfully backed, of rival manufacturers. Other. causes were the absurd prejudice then existing against the employment of foreign workmen; the introduction of so much foreign porcelain by an abuse of privilege, at a merely nominal duty, the goods introduced being the product of manufactories supported by royal

' grants; and what perhaps was a still greater cause of commercial decline, was the vigorous and admirable industry of the Staflordshire potters. Goods, comparatively cheap in price, and excellent both in body and form, were poured into the home markets, and soon supplanted for all ordinary domestic purposes more fragile and costly articles.

The building in which the Chelsea manufactory had been carried on was an aggregation of old timber houses, added one to each other, as the business had grown. It was situated at the corner of Justice Walk, at one time an avenue of stately lime trees leading from Church Street to Laurence Street, and so named from some Justice of the Peace who had had a dwelling hard by. At the beginning of the eighteenth century the immediate neighbourhood consisted chiefly of gardens and fields; but in 1708, a row of substantial houses running south to north,

CHAP. III. LITTLE CHEYNE ROVV. 123 and lying a little to the east of Laurence Street, was erected, and named Cheyne Row, after the surname of the Lord of. the Manor. Large-sized gardens lay at the rear of each; behind these were fields. At the top of the row the lane trended at right angles for a few hundred yards to the east. At this part stood one or two substantial houses looking south, known as Little Cheyne Row, with gardens and fields, divided by a narrow cartway, stretching north to the King's Road.1 From the description given in the agreement, it would appear that Mr. Bentley's house, which

belonged to a person of the' name of Green, was one of those looking south, and that the gardens referred to were very extensive. When workshops were erected, and one or two small tenements in the vicinity were occupied by Mr. Rhodes and some of the other workmen, Mr. Bentley had his country house and manufactory all within a stone's throw. Mr. Wedgwood and himself sub-' sequently lost a considerable sum-by the buildings they erected; but for the time being these served the great purpose of facilitating the completion of the vast orders which poured in for every variety of ornamental ware. From some law proceedings which occurred between

Spermont and Duesbury, it appears that the former had retained a share at least in the property of the porcelain works; and it is not unlikely that he had otherwise invested money in Chelsea or its neighbourhood. But the person named Cox, of whom Mr. Wedgwood speaks as in association with him, was the dealer in articles of vertu already referred to; whilst another person of the same name was a land and house agent, residing in Southampton Buildings, Chanccry Lane, and the representative

' This description is gathered from a contemporary map or survey in the British Museum.
of Mr. Green, the owner of the property Wedgwood and Bentley were in treaty for.

We first hear of the Chelsea premises on Mr. Wedgwood's way back from London, early in September, 1769. Writing from Burslem he says, 'I called at the Bells in Chelsea & told Edcs how the case stood with us respecting Mr. Cox's house. He assured me that he was not mistaken, & that 40 Guineas was the money he was authorised to let the house and one Garden for, & 50 Guineas with the others. I like the house and situation vastly, & wo" have you take it, if you can, at the price agreed upon. Mr. Townsend's house, I think, will not do at all.' Upon reaching Burslem Mr. Wedgwood as usual consulted his wife, and her judgment was in favour of a settlement. ' Mrs. Wedgwood says the house & Grounds at

Chelsea are very cheap at 55 Guineas P. Ann". I think you shod not miss them for a trifle.'1 Accordingly, before the month of September had closed, the subjoined agreement was drawn out, and the premises passed into Messrs. Wedgwood and Bentley's hands.2

' to Mr. Cox,

' Wedgwood to Bentley, dated Burslem, September 4, 1769.

Mr. Bentley presents his comp". & if it be convenient will wait upon him to meet Mr. Green, at Mr. Cox's House tomorrow at 4 o'clock, to treat about the House at Chelsea. In the mean Time Mr. Bentley sends Mr. Cox in list of Particulars which Mr. Green and he have put down as necessary to the finishing of the House, & making it tenantable. Thursday Mom', 21 September.

To paint, paper, & whitewash from top to bottom; the papers to be good, & the Patterns agreeable to the Tennant. Locks, bolts, & Fastneners on all the doors, windows, & window shutters. Dressers,

Shelves, Pump and Sink in the Kitchen.......... Stablefor three Horses, Hay loft over it, 8: a Coach House, & to make the House in ever respect fit for a Tennant. To dbesides the above a China Closet and Butler-'s Pantry under the Stairs or in the Lobby. Pave with Flags the foot Path before the House & within the rails. Drains from the house. Kitchen Hearth paved. Fan lights secured with Bars. Cellar & lace behind the Kitchen paved. ash house in the Yard. A wider Door into the Garden to admit a Carriage to the Stables & Coach House. Yard Paved.... The garden out of which the new Piece of road is taken & the Barley Field to be enter'd upon with the House, or at 6 months' notice; or earlier, paying for the Fire &c., & to y none ut the the Gardens. The Tennant have usual Tennant/s axes. The House Liberty to make other Alterations to be finished in 6 weeks, & the for his Convenience at his Expense. Stable in 3 months, from this 22"" The Parties contractin as Tenants,

Meanwhile Mr. Bcntley's house at Etruria stood untenanted; and as his own was yet a mere skeleton of roofed

walls, it occurred to Mr. Wedgwood to occupy the former for:1 time. ' I go to Etruria every day allmost,' he Writes to Bentley, soon after his return from London in the beginning of September, 'but it will not be suflicient to spend an hour or two there in a morning as I do at present. I intend to go & live there if you will lend me your house, & take Mr. Denby with me, whom I shall not spare you at present; he will be very usefull to me, & will help to keep them in ordr with respect to forms, which I am convinc'd with you is the principal part.'1 We hear nothing further of this intention till after Mr. Wedgwood has paid another visit to London early in November. His first letter to Bentley upon his return then gives us this delightful picture of the ' flitting,' and the manner of its accomplishment. ' We were three days upon the road, though we lost no time, and travel'd a little by moonlight each evening, but at the last stage-.Etruria-I was rewarded for all the.risque & pains I had undergone in a tedious, long, and dirty journey. I found my Sally and family at Etruria! just come there to take possession of the Etruscan plains, & sleep upon them for the first night. Was not this very clever now of my own dear Girl's contriving. She expected her J oss on the

Crop. The Tennant exem t from I ficient Fence between the Road & of Sept. 1769. The Tennant to Josiah Wedgwood& omas Benti l take a Lease for 7, 14, or 21 years, ley.

with mission to quit at the above Sam'. Cox, Esq,

Peri s at the Annual Rent of——. Southsmton Buildings,

Sole right to the Road between the Chancery Lane.

Gardens to the King's road until l ' 'edgwood tc-Bentley, Septem-

Mr. Cox may choose to make u suf-ber 16, 1769.

126 THE FLITTING. CHAP. III.

very evening he arrived; had got the disagreeable business of removing all over, & Iwod not have been another night from home for the Indies. To night we are to sup 120 of our workmen in the Townhall, & shall take up our lodgings

here at Burslem.'1 Writing from his new home a few days later, Mr. Wedgwood adds, ' We have now got thirty hands here, but I have much ado to keep the new ones quiet.... I have been but three or four times to Burslem since my return, though they want me there very much indeed. I have been confined to my rooms several days. Planning, with Mr. Gardner,2 the remainder of my works here, which must all be built, besides a Town for the men to live in, the next summer, for I have notice to leave the Brickhouse Works the next year. My Landlord is married, & will come to them himself. Here's a fine piece of work cut out for me! Where shall I get money, materials, or hands to finish so much building in so short a time. It is work enough for years, if I had not one other Irons in the fire, & must be done in one summer, nothing else stand still the while. Collect-Collect my fr'-set all your hands and heads to work-send me the L'a-rgent and you shall see wonders_3,000l.! 3,000l. _?—aye 3,000l., not a farthing less will satisfy my Architect for the next year's business; so you must collect, or take a place for me in the Gazette.'8

By the beginning of December Mr. Bentley, his relative and housekeeper, Miss Oates, and their servants, had removed to Chelsea; and though thus the depth of winter, activity reigned also at Etruria. The pattern

' Wed ood to Bentley, dated ' ' Mr. Pickford's assistant. from the pper-house, as the Over-3 -'edgwood to Bentley, Novemhouse was sometimes styled, Novem-I ber 19, 1769. ber 11, 1769.

CRAP. III. THE TURNING ROOM.

' 127 room, which had been finished all but painting by the end of September, was now fitting _up, and an oven on a smaller scale was building. ' We find our large ovens,'

Mr. Wedgwood tells Bentley, 'very inconvenient for.

vases. I mean in point of time, as it takes near two months' work to fill the bisket oven. I am therefore building a small one of new construction, which is only to hold two or three basket full, say 100l. worth, of vases. It is to be a very good-natured oven, & either bisket gloss or enamel as occasion requires. '1 In fact, not a department of his new works escaped Mr. Wedgwood's attention. Every room was planned with a view to the future purpose it had to serve; and every machine was fitted thereto with a like rigid exactness. A case in point occurred with respect to the turning-room. ' I have alter'd my opinion,' 'he writes to Bentley, 'about the turning-room, & unless you think of any objection shall fix the Lathes in the corner room, under that we before proposed. Here the lights are high enough, & a ground floor is much better for lathes than a chamber story, the latter are so apt to shake with the motion of the lathe; & as we shall want so very often to be stepping into the latheroom, for there the outline is given, it will be more convenient for me to have it without any steps to it. I have thought of another alteration for the Lathes too, which, though it may not be of much consequence for common things, will I think be a great help to the workmen in turning plain Vases, where a true outline free of any irregular swellings or hollows are of the first consequence. The alteration I propose is to set the Lathes so that the Turner shall have an end light, instead of a front which 128-ETRURIA HALL. CHAP. III. they now have. If you hold a mug both these ways to the light, you will soon see the advantage I propose from this alteration. I have try'd the experiment on Abrams' lathe, & it answer'd to my wishes. On shutting out his front light and leaving the windows on his right hand open, he had much ado to shave a piece of ware even enough to please himself.'1 In this adaptation of means to ends, this concentration of force in a given direction lay a part of the secret of ultimate perfection.. Though much had yet to be done to make Mr. Wedgwood's house habitable, enough had been effected to indicate both its internal arrangement and its appearance when finished. Its general plan had been already heartily eulogised by a clever man. ' Captain Keir,' says Dr. Darwin, in writing to

Mr. Wedgwood towards the close of 1767, ' admires the plan of your House, & says it is fit for a Prince.' Subsequent progress realised this praise. It stood now at the close of 1769 a handsome, substantiallooking country-house, without wings or other appendages; and remained thus till a few years before the close of the life of its first possessor. The principal rooms, opening from a hall which ran the whole length of the house, were large, well proportioned, and lofty. The windows and staircase were ample; and capacity existed everywhere for the decorative effects of stained glass and terracotta bas-reliefs. The oflices and gardens in the rear were excellent; and the foreground, sloping to the canal and works, was already in the hands of the landscape gardener, who was gathering the moorland springs into a lake, breaking the levels here and there with knolls, and planting generously. The situation, bleak, bare, and 1 VVedgwood to Bentley, April 9, 1769. exposed on a moorland ridge, needed the shelter of trees; for in one of his letters to Bentley Mr. Wedgwood says,

' We poor villagers neither escape a blast nor a drop of It is not unlikely that 'capability Brown ' had some hand in laying out the grounds; and for a long time, as interesting little facts will yet show, planting and improvement went on.1

Almost all the young trees ' A person writing tlema.n's Magazine, in 1794, thus speaks of Etruria, and the natural capacity of its site for decorative imrovements. 'VVe proceeded from andley Green to Etruria. Here the inimitable works of Mr "ledgwood produced me a singular drawing, and his magnificent house and grounds arrested my attention and speculation. The hills and valleys are in the Gen-I but owe much to the improvement of Art. VVe see here a colony newly raised in a desert, where clay-built man subsists on clay. The forms into which this material are turned are innumerable, both for use and omament. Nay, even the vases of ancient Etrnria are outdone in this pottery. And we now behold this

exquisite composition not only ornamenting the ceilings and chimney here by Nature beautifully formed,, pieces of Mr. Wcdgwond's own house,

VOL. II.

K 129 130 JOSIAH THE YOUNGER. CRAP. III.

planted first at Etruria came from Brompton Nursery, near London;1 a fact which doubtless indicates how little general attention had yet been turned to the decoration of gardens or tracts of country. About the metropolis the nurseryman could thrive; but, with few exceptions, the provinces probably afforded little or no patronage for the results of his toil.

A short time prior to Mr. Wedgwood's removal from Burslem, his family was increased by the birth of his son Josiah,2 for so it had been concluded to call him before his advent? This made the third surviving child. ' A fine boy,' as Mr. Wedgwood wrote; and who, when time wore on, was to bear to foreign courts one of his father's finest copies of the Barberini vase; and of whom Lord Auckland was to write such praise, of graceful manners, perfect ease, and manly bearing, as filled the household hearts at Etruria with more joy than could be well expressed.

The demand for ornamental ware may be dated from the opening of the warehouse in Newport Street in July or August 1768; and its successive increase was as surprising as were the arts resorted to, to pirate these beautiful productions. Yases were the great objects of admiration and demand. ' I could sell 501. or 100i. worth a day if I had them,' wrote Mr. Wedgwood to Bentley. The kind most in request were, at first, ' jarr-shaped vases with dolphin handles, leafage at bottom, and the largest drapery festoons round the shoulders.' Satyr heads and laurel festoons were also favourite effects. Some of the black vases were decorated with white festoons, others but many others in the county.' 2 Mr. Vedgwood to Cox, August Vol. lxiv. Pt. ii. p. 1078. 7, 1769. Mayor MSS.

' Swift to Mr. Bentley, November 3 Mr. 'edgwood to Bentley, July 18, 1769. Mayer MSS. 17, 1769.

CHAP. III. DEMAND FOR VASES. 131 with black. Highly polished vases were not admired; and towards the close of the year vases with medallion bas-reliefs became popular,' Whilst those with marbled bodies had attained a point of great excellence. At this stage the black basaltes of Etruscan form were, as Mr. Wedgwood said, ' so clever and so perfect ' that he hardly knew how to price them; and as this good taste grew for subdued tones and geometrical forms, the bizarre effects of ' sprinkled blue ' and ' sprinkled gold ' fell into desuetude. In February 1769, during one of Mr. Wedgwood's visits to town, we have this announcement, ' Wanted for warehouse immediately 350 of Dolphin ewers, 445 of the Bedfordi-an Goats' heads Vases, The same quty of the Sacrifice do, with abundance of Sugardish Vases, some extreme large, the tops of a. lower kind wo'1 be better, some of these are extravaganza in that respect, I mean the top of all. However, I thank you, my good friend, for the no-ble treat I have just been enjoying. They do me good to see them, but alass, the whole four packages (those by Pyat I mean) are not a mouthful, not one day's sale; I could sell, I am fully persuaded, 1,000l. worth such vases, if I had them before I come home. Large, very large ones are all the cry, & we must endeav-our to satisfy them. You shod set both the mills to work at grinding,

& with two setts of hands, one for night, and the other for the day, or you will soon be short of stuff; the same shod be observ'd in the dish grinding for the outsides, for they sho'1 all be dipped I think.' 1 At this same date or-ders for cream-ware services for the ta-bles of the gentry increased also. Even the Quakers were becoming cus

' Mr. Wedgwood to his wife and 1769, and is addressed 'Mrs. WedgMr. Bentley, jointly. The letter 18 wood, at the Bnckhouse, Burslem, dated from London, February 15, Statfordshlre.'
132 THE QUAKERS. CRAP. III.
tomers. The pale tint, the fine glaze, and the beauty, yet simplicity of forms, were most consonant to their feelings. Dr. Fothergill and his sister recommended

these exquisite productions everywhere; and the wealthy Barclay became a pa-tron. 'It will be of great importance,' Mr. Wedgwood tells Bentley, ' to have the service for my friend Barclay as neat and fine as possible. The Quakers have for some time past been trying my ware, & verily they find it to answer their wishesin every respect, they have now order'd this full set. As my future rec-ommendation to the brethren must de-pend upon their usage in this sample, a word to the wise is enough.' 1

As the spring advanced, ornaments were more largely used upon the vases; and a catalogue was made of those in hand at Etruria, in order to prevent the purchase of duplicates from Mrs. Lan-dre and other modellers. The sources, too, of original designs rapidly in-creased. ' Vases and all things go off well,' writes Mr. VVedgwood in March, 'and new cabinets are opening to me every day. Sir Watkin W""""'2 left a note for me to wait upon him in the morning to show me some things for the improvement of vases he has brought home from his travels.' A few days previously Mr. Wedgwood had made the acquaintance of Lord Bess-borough. ' A fine old Gentleman,' he writes to Bentley, ' a very fine old Gen-tleman, admires our vases & manufac-ture prodigiously, says he sees we shall exceed the Antients, that friezes & many other things may be made, that I am a very ingenious man (there's for you now, did I not tell you what a fine old Gentman he was), & that he will do me every service in his power. He has given me four Guineas for three Vases, 1 Yyedgwoodto Bentley, February 2 Sir Watkin Williams, otherwise 231 1169-' Sir Vatkin Villiams '_vnne.
CRAP. III. LORD BESSBOR-OUGII. 133 one of them the large blue, w" I merit" Mr. Cox had not sold'one of; the other two Etruscans, at a Guinea. I hope he will set these large blue ones ageing.' Lord Bessborough kept his word, and, as we shall subsequently see, rendered Mr. Wedgwood most essential services, not only by permitting him to have casts taken from a fine cabinet of gems which were afterwards sold to the

Duke of Marlborough, but by introduc-ing the vases amongst the Irish nobility, who became enthusiastic patrons. This ' fine old gentleman ' was a man of many sorrows. The sanitary condition of Lon-don must have been at that day fright-ful, for scarcely a household escaped from the dread visitation of a malignant fever. Twice had it entered Lord Bess-borough's house and carried ofl' its vic-tims. The first time four servants; the next two young and lovely daughters. He then fell ill himself; and his Count-ess in nursing him caught the horrible disease and died. For four days they concealed her death from him; and when at last they broke it out, he piteously asked, when his first great agony was over, ' How many children have I left?' 1 The answer was affirma-tively, for his surviving daughters often accompanied him to the warehouse in Newport Street. In his taste for art, in a patriotic love of country, and in a gen-erous desire to serve others, he found a mitigation for the great griefs which had swept over him. The friendship and artistic intercourse begun at this date with Sir Watkin Williams Vynne was also most enduring. A very large pro-portion of Mr. Vedgw0od's list of in-taglios was derived from Sir Vatkin's gems. Other patrons were equally mu-nificent; and, as this year of wonderful prosperity rolled on, they included all the best names in the peerage.
' Valpole's Letters, ('unninghaufs edition, fol. iii. p. 281.

The fame of the marble and pebble vases increased; and the sale became so great of these and other kinds, that in order to meet the demand, wasters, and others out of fashion, had to be resorted to; and by veining, altering, and mend-ing, they were made passable and sold. With his habitual fertility of resources, Mr. Wedgwood invented an excellent cement, made of whiting, lamp black, and glue, for stopping and forming or-naments, by means of which admirable repairs were effected. Foreign pur-chasers also added to this demand. M. Du Burk, a trader of Amsterdam, bought largely. One of his purchases of 50!. worth cleared off Mr. Oox's remaining stock; and the next dispatch of vases, though to the amount of 136l., was, as Mr. Wedgwood wrote to Bentley, contained in a single crate. ' But they are large ones, and he Cox) is now distressed for the smaller sizes to make up sets. I am making a few of these sorts, but two or three hands make little progress in fine goods, &

' if I take any hands from my other works, such I mean as can do anything at Vases, it will almost put a stop to my completing the orders in hand, or supplying my warehouse, for we are as much at a loss for dessert ware, & the fine articles which employ these hands, as we are for vases, & without these finer articles we cannot sell the other goods. What shall I do in this dilemma? Not a hand loose in the country to be hired, this s'1 cream colour has made the trade so brisk. The hands at Liverpool, if there shod be any loose, Wd I doubt be of no use to us, unless by any great chance you cod find out a presser or finisher of China figures, we shall want a few of them immediately. Our last kiln of blacks turn'd out extremely Well; we had a fine cargo of medallions, W"h Mr. Cox writes me are much wanted. Seven large Urns all

CHAP. III. CROWDS OF PURCHASERS. 135 good. The Bedford Goats' heads the same. We now make them with the same certainty as other goods, & several sorts which I have now in embryo may be made with tolerable dispatch if we had but a modeller to form, & a few hands to execute them. And these must be had somewhere, for such an opportunity as we have now before us must not be lost or trifled with.' 1

In May, M. Du Burk's orders for vases and other ornamental goods were still larger; for the demand he had met with in Holland was of a most surprising character. This was even larger at home; for the season was at its height, and London full of company. Fashion had declared in favour of these beautiful wares; and the desire to obtain them drew every lord and lady to Newport Street. ' Mrs. Byerley,' writes Mr. Wedgwood, 'is just returned from Lon-

don, & brings a strange ace' of their goings on in Newport Street. No geting to the door for coaches, nor into the rooms for Ladies and Gent"; and Vases," she says, " are all the rage. We must endeavour to gratify this universal passion, though we shall be sadly short of hands for a year or two, train'd ones I mean; raw nzaterials I could have plenty for the next year, & I intend to ingage a good quantity to choose out of.' 2 For some time previously, there can be no doubt that Mr. Wedgwood had extended his manufacture to bas-reliefs of various forms and sizes. As yet these were chiefly eñected in the basaltes body; though, from some of the black vases being decorated with festoons in white, we may infer that the white biscuit body had already attained great excellence.8 Bacon's, Mrs. Landre's, and 1 Wedgwood to Bentley, April 9, 5 In the refuse to the Catalogue, I769. 2nd edit. 774, two white bodies 1 "t-dgwood to Bentley, May I. " are indicated. Thus, 'A white bislT6£). cuit ware or Terra—cotta, capable 136 SMA LL BAS-RELIEFS. Cnar. Ill.

Theodore Parker's models were, it is evident, for small bas-reliefs both in the white and black bodies. To the subject of these, we have, at this early stage of production, no further clue than what may be obtained from the modellers' bills already given, and one incidental reference at this date, May, 1769, to the price of Marcyas and young Olympus. This was a round tablet formed in black basaltes, sixteen inches in diameter, and probably, from the subject, the work of Bacon.

Towering high as he did above his contemporaries in the potter's art, by his profound insight into the relation and bearings of chemical afiinities, bylhis exquisite taste, by a high standard of morality, which developed, as it were, every point of his great powers to the full, Wedgwood was surrounded by a host of able men, many of whom, not overburdened with principle, a.nd quick enough to see the profit to be reaped, becam_e unscrupulous imitators. As early as the days of his partnership with Wheildon these crimps were on his

track. They imitated the green glaze; and no sooner had he given, by various improvements, a perfectly new character to the cream ware, than they were on the track of that also; and now the ornamental Ware had come into the market, the keenness of competition, and base acuteness combined, reduced this piracy into a perfect system. The opening of the warehouse in Newport Street redoubled the cunning of these pirates. ' You were mentioning some time since,' writes Mr. Wedgwood to Cox, ' that our blue neck'd Vases weregot into the shops. I can give you the history of all our patt"? geting there, if you can from thence of bearing the same heat as the traits, and Bas-reliefs.' In 1769, the basaltes,' and next, 'A fine white white biscuit ware was probably Terra-cotta of great beauty and de-used in these points of extemal delicacy, proper for ('aim-o.=, l'or-r-oration.

C-HAP. III. PIRACY. 137 tell how to remedy it; & if you cannot, the Bronze Vases sent you last will be down here in a fortnight for copying after. The blue necks were sent here to Palmer's by Carravalla. The Person from whom I have the information was at the opening of the box, & assures me from his own knowledge that Caravalla supplies Mrs. P. with all my patterns as they arrive at my rooms in London; & Fogg does the same for Bagnall & Baker, & these last let any of the other potters have them, paying a share of the expence. You must try if you can recollect any particular Persons repeatedly buying a few pairs, or single articles of y' new patterns as they arrive; very probably it may be some sham Gent" or Lady equip'd for the purpose, with their footman or maid to carry them home to prevent a discovery. That they do get my patt" from you in some such way I am certain, but the further particulars you must endeavour to discover.'1 But no discovery was made. The abominable system was still carried on, and seems to have annoyed Mr. Bentley even more than it did Mr.Wedgwood, who, seeing it was not i possible to wholly put a stop to the practices of these persistent crimps, grew philosophic on the matter.

'Never give yourself any pain about Mr. Watt,' he writes to Bentley, 'or the blue neck vases you apprehend are travelling this way. We are far enough before our rivals, & whenever we apprehend they are treading too near our heels, we can at any time manage them better than Ld B_-te can manage the merch", to compare great things with small.' 2

By the succeeding autumn Mr. Wedgwood's copyists 138 PALMER'S IMITATIONS. Cnar. III. had ventured upon higher flights. Though he was about to take out a patent for the bronze antique and encaustic colours, he saw that to take out one for the black basaltes body, or ' black composition ' as he calls it, would answer no useful purpose, as this body, apart from his own modifications or improvements, had been commonly used by the potters for nearly a century. He therefore conjectured, and rightly, that the black Etruscan shaped vases with medallions would soon be imitated. He had not long to wait. 'I saw one of P. 's black vases yesterday,' he writes to Bentley. ' The body is very good, the shape & composition very well, the bas-reliefs are 6 of the small statues which go round the body, Hercules, Omphale, &c_. The figures you know; they are from excellent originals, but abused in putting upon the originals & hackeyed in all the plaster shops. Upon the whole it was better than I expected. We must proceed, or they will tread on our heels. '2 Attempts had been already made to paint figures in colours upon the same body. Hamilton's Etruscan Antiquities were obtained; and in a few months the results, caricatures of the great originals so far as painting, and in the majority of instances of form, went, were in the market.

As already seen, the first Etruscan bronze vases were produced at the close of August, 1768; but more than a year elapsed before the bronzing, as an application burnt in, and thus made homogeneous with the body, was brought to perfection. The like date also gave success to a series of experiments in connection with the preparation and use of gold powder. These triumphs were thus

heralded to Bentley. ' Say nothing of the

Bronze E/zcaustic to anybody,' wrote Mr. VVedgwood. 'It is accomplished. I bring it with me;1 and it will do your heart good to look at it. Trouble not yourself about the gold powder, that process is accomplished likewise. You shall have satisfaction-in both.'2 Shortly after, Mr. Wedgwood obtained his patent for these processes, as well as for painting in encaustie colours; and as soon as he had secured a body of skilled artists and workmen, trained under his own eye, and many of them by his own hand, his visions in respect to his beautiful art were in a measure realised, so far as this stage of its development could go.

From some cause or another, bronze vases are now of great rarity; even accustomed dealers in YVedgwood-ware know nothing of them. It may be that in the majority of cases the metallic lustre of the bronzing has become effaced. But statuettes, busts, tripods, lamps, candelabra, and medallious are seen by a few specimens in most collections; m,,».-11») B'l'ATUEl'll'2OF3l. RSIXB!10XZE and the bronze medals in his-EWUSMPMYER Cmimilol toric series have a place in every n1edallist's cabinet.

140 MARS AND VENUS. CHAP.Ill.

The statuettes of Mars and Venus (figs. 20, 21), from Mr. Mayer's collection, will, by their exquisite beauty give a true idea of the perfection the great potter attained in this department of his art. They belong, however, to a later period, when a. greater mastery had been obtained in modelling. The statuettes, which form a pair, are, inclusive of their pedestals, nine and three-quarter inches in height. The pose of both are admirable. Strength and rest are expressed in the figure of the one; feminine solicitude and tenderness in the other. The drapery falls round Venus with exceeding grace, Cupid's supplicating attitude is prettily rendered; and in the _ shield, helmet, coat of mail, ' and battle-axe of Mars we have the accessories of heroic (Fla-1- srm'»rrn=v'w--v-=1-' mm valour. The pedestals, which E.'CAIJ:fl'I0.

—LlEYEl cou.=x11ux. _ _ are adorned with medallions, goats' heads, and free festoons, bear the closest ex amination, and show that not a detail missed the great master's eye.

But the bronzing in its encaustic form, or as an after eoating applied to various coloured bodies, was neither extensively used, nor gained the popularity of the black basaltcs. It is in t/tis body, polished or unpolished, that

CHAP. III. SMALL GROUPS. 141 we find many of the masterpieces of Etruria. It was converted into every possible form; from the homely teapot and cream jug, to the vase and bas-relief. Busts, statuettes, sphinxes, tritons, tripods, lamps, pedestals, medallions, intaglios were only a portion of this wonderful variety. The largest busts averaged a height of twenty five inches; and the least statuettes formed pretty accessories to the mantel--piece or drawing-room beaufet. Some few busts were tried thus early; whilst smaller groups and single figures, modelled by Mrs. Landre, or perhaps Theodore Parker, display, as in the instances given (figs. 22, 23), excellences of another and simpler character. These small (P18-'-8-1 flixinzgifgczxvs "mmstatuettes were made oc casionally in a white or other body, but never so coinmonly as in the black basaltes.

142 VASES IN BLACK BASALTES. CRAP. III.

Of this body the vases were the great speciality. Where the forms have a fine geometrical outline, whether derived from the antique or not, they are of exquisite beauty. Far excelling the antique in the material or body, and often rivalling it in chastity of decoration. The three examples subjoined will serve as illustrations. Two are from Mr. Mayer's collection, the third from Jermyn Street, and are all probably of early date. The form of each is beautiful. The fluting and drapery, the fcstoons and satyrs' heads, and the simple bas-relief are charming of their

C-nsr. III. THEIR BEAUTIFUL FORMS. 143 kind. How useless, after examples such as these, is the attempt to depreciate Wedgwood, by saying that neither in form nor in colouring did he approach the excellence of the ancients. The truth is, he was no slavish copyist. Except in the case of the Barberini and some few of the

Etruscan vases in the Hamilton collection, or occasional specimens here and there from other sources, Wedgwood never absolutely copied. He interpreted rather than rendered. A form may have its likeness here; wholly or in part, a bordering there; and in this or that direction we have as a bas-relief or painting exquisite similitude of antique beauty; but this rather proved that modern art was not only fruitful of original conceptions, but could be imitative also. Much of his ornamental art was, Mr. Wedgwood knew, esoteric; art rather for high and special

' 'Iobserve what you say upon form of ours for vases. Memorandn, cultivation, than for the ordinary requirements of modern civilisation. It was a feat of power; not a declaration of inferiority. He knew he had the same external elements of nature to guide him; and that also by revert inrr to the sim lest eometrical outlines as the em' or D 1 3 ("D7 the Egg, you know it is a favourite Vedgwood to Bentley.

CHAP. III.
(JRYSTALLINE TERRA-COTTA. 145 the ellipsis, he was sure of proportion and beauty; and he knew by adapting forms and decorations to their intended purpose, he added other elements to the expression of truth through beauty, and by so doing, reverted only to the same principles which had made art, iii the hands of the ancients, no other than expressions of truth idealised. This is proved in a variety of instances; but more particularly by the extraordinary adaptation of his art to the purposes of modern civilisation. we could reproduce all the causes which belonged to antiquity, it would be impossible to reproduce its art. But so far as this was possible, Wedgwood copied its effects with surprising fidelity; and beyond this he soared into a region especially his own.

The invention of the crystalline terracotta body, which, by slight variations,

imitated natural jasper, agate, marble, lapis lazuli, and, at a somewhat later date than 1768-9, porphyry, seems to have been contemporaneous with the improvements in the black Egyptian. It was princi

Unless pots, and candlesticks; though tea ware and other articles were sometimes formed

VOL. II.

in it. But in vases its varying beauty shone best; and where the form was good, and the ornaments simple and not overdone with gilding, the effects of soft hues and delicate veining are often very striking. The annexed examples (figs. 27—30) are from Mr. Mayer's collection and that of the Kensington Museum. Yet beautiful as many of them were, these vases seem never to' have gained the popularity of those in the black basaltes, or baryta jasper body.

The body used for the Etruscan vases, and later for others more distinctively Grecian in character, was the black basaltes, with, _ _ i such a shade of che'P'is 1» '"""='-'1-'= J-¢'"""' 1"" ""-="R"-mieal difference as gave a tone of blueness to the black. On this groups, figures, borders, and other styles of decoration, were painted chiefly in red. More rarely the vases and other ware had a red body, with the decorative effects in black. VVe give specimens of these variations (figs. 31—33). The three vases are from the Kensington Museum, as also the saucer-shaped plate (fig. 34). The ground of the two first vases is black, (um. 111. SPECIMEXS. 147 the third red.1 Far finer specimens of this class of ware are extant; this principally in the possession of the nobility, in whose families they have remained since their first purchase. The black and red bodies with antique figures and borderings were applied to a great variety of purposes. Tea and breakfast services,'trays, lamps, candlestieks, flower-pots, inkstands, ewers, but more especially teapots and cream jugs. The yases were all more or less modifications or exact copies of geometrical forms, and were thus purely antique in character.

' 'e shall see, under a later date, ' fig-

ures were produced, as wellas sold, that the red vases with black prinlrvl at a cheap rate.

Except where 'the size was large and the painting of the highest class, the prices of encaustic Etruscan and

Grecian vases were not exorbitant. From a scale of outlines and prices in an old order book we find the cost price ranged from ll. 11s. to (is. or 7s. Where the vases were large, and the figures and borderings elaborate, the prices rose gradually from 18.9. to five guineas, according to size, as in our example, of which the handles terminate with swans' heads; and where the painting was fine and elaborate_taking perhaps Crofts, Rhodes, Mr. Denby, or, at a later day, Aaron Steele, a month to complete _-the sale price was often and deservedly thirty guineas, or more. T he noble vases made for Lord Shelburne, Lord Rockingham, Lord March, the Duke of Northumberland, the Duke of Bedford, Lord

Mansfield, Lord Clanbrissil, Lord Gower, Sir William Hamilton, Sir Walter Bagot, Mr. Anson, many others, of Whom a three pages, were all of this high character. Some black Etruscan vases with dolphin handles, 29 inches high and 12% wide, sent to London in July, 1769, are marked in the accompanying invoice at 7l. 15s. each; and Mr. Wedgwood adds in his own hand, ' These vases are by far much the finest you have had.' Others with medal and. lions are priced at 21. 128. 611. each, and grey pebble with goats' heads, 31. 3s. a vase.' marbled with gold, £1 11s 61/. Plain marbled, without linths, Tatid. Marbled body, free estoons, gilt, £1 12. _Etruscan vases with husk festoons, 14 inches high', £2 2:. Etruscan sh: e vases from Count ('aylus, 7a. 61. each. White biscuit vase, with Dolphin handles and without plinths, 24 inches wide, 11 high, £3 3.9. Variegated marble vases, satyrs' heads. ornaments gilt, 10inchcs high,£l ls. Blue ground vases, shell shoulders, 10$. (id. each. llronzodvascs from 122 2:4. to 10x. lid. each. Pebble grouml vase, with satyxs' heads and horns, £2 2». ' wide, £4 4s. Etruscan vases with Etruscan vase, with handles on the, drapery festoons, laurel frieze round shoulders, drapery and covered, 13$ shoulders, £2 12s. 611. Grey marbled inches high, £2 2:1. Ditto leafare and gold, of these the prices varied neck, no handles, drapery, 13 hig, ' from 188. 611. to 12s. Blue vases, £2 2s.,sn1aller,£'1 ls. Etruscan sat_vr's head and laurel festoons, goats' heads and drnper festoons, 15, ornaments gilt, 12 inches high, inches high, £3 3.s.ea. e1vase. Ditto £1 12s. each. Biscuit and blue free festoons and medallion of Sacri-vases, 20 inches high for bronzing, lice, 19 inches high, £2 12»: 611. 1 £3 3;. a. vase. Invoices, 1768 and Etl-usea. nl)olphin handle ewer, £2 2.». 1T69_ 11a_-er 11.' _ '5,

Another speciality in ornamental ware were the lamps, candlesticks, and candelabra; of which the variety was infinite. The lamps were principally modelled from the antique, and books containing designs were sought after. ' There is a bookseller,' writes Mr. Wedgwood to Bentley, ' on the left hand side of the H-aymarket, tow" the bottom as you go down from Piccadilly, but he does not make any show of his business to the street. He is a foreigner, Etruscan vase, 19 inches high, 05 Qven; and when the black ba

& was recommended to me by L" Clanbrassil, I 0rd" from him a book of lamps, publish'd at Rome, & I imagine the same you mention. I wish you could find him out, he has often good things by him in our way.'1 The pendant lamps were often of exceeding beauty, as in the annexed sketch (fig. 35) from the Marryat collection. A shallow dish, oval, round, triangular, or hexagonal, was surrounded by airy foliage, dolphins' heads, winged genii; or the edges were fluted, or wrought with beading or exquisite open tracery. Of candlesticks, at first the forms were very simple, the bodies cream ware, or black Egyptian; but as the enginelathe became improved, fluting, spiral convolutions, drapery, or festoons robbed the column or support of its barrenness, as shown in an instance already saltes and crystalline, or terracotta, bodies came into the market, their characteristics were

charmingly developed in light bearing ornaments. The black, as also the marbled, agate, (File "- ";j(',"L-gLP_no'';f _'P--"""" and crystalline jasper candle sticks, were often masterpieces of classic grace. Dolphins' heads, tritons, sphinxes, or crouching lions supported the plinth, or some figure finely modelled bore the flame aloft. The black Etruscan candlesticks were sometimes bronzed, and then the price was doubled, as

' Wedgwood to Bentley, September 16, 1769.

from 12s. to ll;-is-., for a candlestick 10 inches high._ The vase form was largely applied as a support, and candlesticks of this kind, blue and gilt, were about 15s. a pair. In many cases there was a union of bodies. As in instances of a draped female figure in white biscuit, standing upon a black plinth, and holding gracefully a lotus leaf, a bell-shaped flower, a vase, or an empty flambeau for the light; these accessories being black also. Occasionally both column and plinth were still more elaborate; and fac-similes of the porticoes to temples, or sections of the entrance to the classic atrium or triclinium, were sometimes resorted to as light bearing supports. But simpler forms were generally preferred; and these, whether of terra-cotta, black, encaustic painted, or bronzed, reached often the highest ideal conception of the unity of artistic truth and utility. Gray pebble candlesticks with white medallions were an instance of this. In reference to some of these beautiful objects, Mr. Wedgwood says, by the hand of his wife, to Bentley, ' They are sent you to finish and to convert into gems by colouring the ground with brown enamel, leaving the raised part the colour it is, and gilding the frame with burnt in gold, at the same time burning gold upon any other part you think proper.' 1 Tapers in all these various bodies were moulded into an equal infinity of form. The candelabra were usually still more elaborate, but their description will come in at a future stage, when the union between the manufactures of Etruria and Soho will be referred to.

From the days of his earliest devotion

to ornamental art, Mr. Wedgwood had directed his attention to the

CHAP. III. FLOWER-POTS. 153 _ improvement of every description of article used for the reception of plants and flowers. Here his pure taste wrought unfettered in a field of its own. Here he could bring the richest' capacities of his art to bear upon the finest decorative instinct of modern civilisation; the one which shows its refining presence alike in our gardens, our rooms, our pictures, and our books. Here the great master, of utility and beauty combined, reigns supreme, even at this day; and his achievements in this respect have never been surpassed. Here there need be no invidious comparison made betwixt ancient and modern art by those incapable of perceiving the underlying truth that every stage of civilisation, so far as it has yet advanced, has an artistic expression of its own: one contingent upon manifold producing causes, which can neither go before, come after, nor be recurrent; but which, admirable in themselves, have peculiar and often unapproachable excellencies. Neither is it perceived that these causes and effects, creating one the other in a progressive scale, may at length beget a simplicity, an ideal grace, a perfect applicability to varied purposes hitherto unknown. If the ancients inurned the ashes of their dead, or gave as prizes for dexterity and strength, forms in clay and metal of the utmost grace, they seem to have cultivated flowers but sparingly; and this only for the decorative purposes of their feasts and ceremonies. But modern civilisation brings floral nature closer to us, and in a purer sense; has multiplied its forms, has set it around us more or less, whether we be rich or poor. In this we have an expression of modern art, which, whatever be its present defects, has at least thrown off many of those sensuous trammels which were the degradation of art in older days. Thus as we purify, we shall 15-L THEIR VARIETY. ('llAr. III.

perhaps gather to ourselves all the noblest expressions of ancient art; and this with results at present unsuspected, except here and there by a solitary philosophic thinker. Be this as it may, Wedgwood met this modern taste with extraordinary skill and abundant fertility; and in the mosses, the leaves, the hedgerow berries and floyers, which he used so often as decorative effects, we perhaps see some few of the things the truth-loving eye had garnered up from those days, when, satchel in hand, he went through moorland lanes and fields a schoolboy to the neighbouring town.

The variety of the root-pots, flowerpots, and boughpots in colour, form, body, and decoration, exceeds belief. At first the common red flower-pots, as those also of grey and white stone ware, were taken up and improved. 'l'he first by the addition of colours in various ways; the others by drapery or simple medallions in cobalt blue, or by moulded patterns. The famous green glaze was also applied to flower and boughpots;. and when Mr. Wedgwood had brought his cream ware to perfection, flower-pots in this body were as popular as the dinner-ware. They were fluted or hooped; the hoops and sometimes the cross bands being of various colours, or else perforated or traced at the edges, festooned, diceworked, or enamelled. Many of the patterns popular on the table-ware were represented on the flower, root, and bough-pots; and from his enamelling bills we find that much of Rhodes' exquisite skill was expended in this direction. The husk, the vine, and ivy were favourite patterns. Goats' heads, griffins' heads, masks, and dolphins were used for handles. The basaltes and terraeotta bodies were next tried, and 1nore-classical forms adopted. Bas-reliefs: in white biscuit were applied; and

CRAP. III. PYRAMID FLOWERPOTS. 155 stands, pedestals, plinths, and tripods were variously used as supports.

To supply himself with beautiful forms and decorative effects suited for this purpose, Mr. Wedgwood had drawings made not only from the antique, but also from the_finest specimens of Oriental. Dresden. and French porcelain; and a glance through the enormous mass of invoices for the years 1768 and

1769 shows how rapid was the improvement. In the latter year, beside new pendant flower-pots, dice-worked flower-pots, gilt, husk festoons and griflin—head flower-pots, we read of one with a ' white ground & boys dancing amidst leafage and foliage gilt,' its price 12s. ; and of another ' with faces and red festoons on plinths, 9 inches high & 5 wide,' its price 158. Mr. Wedgwood also visited or consulted those who possessed noted gardens, pursued floriculture as a study, or who had an exquisite native or cultivated taste for the arrangement of flowers. In the summer of 1770 he was busy with a new design, which, from a combination of parts, he called a 'pyramid flower-pot.' After telling Mr. Bentley that its ' price is too great at a guinea and a half,' he adds, ' I wish you would show the pyramid flower-pots to Dr. F othergill's sister, and consult her upon them, & if she approves of them, suppose you present her with one; it might not be lost. The middle part of some of them is made green and mossy, that it may be lost amongst the flowers, & not seen as a support to them. The handles are left creamcolour, as we had not time to gild them. If you have any instructions to give concerning these things, let us know them, as we are making a quantity.' ' A few days later he adds, ' I have had another turn with pyramid flower-pots, & shall

' 'ed;r'ood to Bentley, June 2, 1770. 156 LADY CRITICS. CIIAP. III. manage to make them seperate, & in such a manner, too, that each part will serve as a seperate flower-pot when 11ot used together; & in buying a p'r of Pyramid flowerpots, they will buy 1 p' of elegant vases & 3 pr of good dressing flowerpots, all seperate. When they come to your hands then, show both the sorts to our fair friends at Dr. Fothergill's.' ' But one whose excellent taste and sound judgment had been tested on so many occasions, passed a favourable opinion on the new flower-pots, and Mr. Wedgwood was satisfied. ' The Pyramid flower-pots dress with flowers so excellently that my wife says they must sell when their good qualities are known.'2 For he said now, as he had long before,

and did to the end: ' I speak from experience in Female taste, without which I i should have made but a poor figure amongst my Potts; not one of which of any consequence is finished without the Approbation of my Sally.'3 At a later stage of improvement, Mr. Wedgwood had again recourse to female taste; for various sorts of flowerpots had been made which did not sell. ' I have had,' he writes from Etruria to Bentley, ' a visit from Mr. & Mrs. Southwell. They like our new flower & bough pots. They are both adapts in these matters, & I did not miss the opportunity of profitting from their knowledge in this pleasing Art. The Art of disposing the most beautiful productions of Nature in the most agreeable, picturesque, & striking manner to the eyes of the beholder. We fixed our general principles, & then examin'd every flowerpot We had by those principles, & we found all those which we had hitherto made, & which have not sold, to be very deficient 1 Vedgwood to Bentley, June 8, 1 3 Ibid. vithout date,but referable 177. _ " to the year 1766 or 1767. " lbid.. ugust:20, 1770.

CHAP. III. FLOVVER DRESSING. 157 in some of these first principles. I have now much clearer ideas of bow-pots &c. than before, & believe I can now make them to please your customers. Mrs. Southwell is a charming woman. I am more and more in love with her every time I see her; & having such a Mistress in the science of flower dressing, I hope our future productions will show that I have profited accordingly.' 1 A few days earlier the subject of bough-pots had been .diseusse_d with still older and more illustrious patrons.

' This morning I have had an opportunity of consulting with Lady Gower & Lady Teignham, & their two Lords (who have been at the Works here & b0' some flower-pots), upon the subject of Bough-pots, & find they. prefer these things with the spouts, much as the old Delph ones; they say that sort keep the flowers distinct & clever.' And Mr. Wedgwood adds, ' Vases are furniture for a chimneypiece. Bough-pots for a hearth, under a slab or marble table. Ithink they can never be used one instead of another; & I apprehend one reason why we have not made our dressing flower-pots to please has been by adapting them ' to chimney-pieces.'2 Guided by these principles, the improvement in this class of ornamental ware became still more marked. We read of Etruscan flower-pots, pebble flower-pots, in which variation was made by covering them with gold size, and on this sprinkling powdered colours; fawn-coloured flower-pots with white hoops, and others in black and red with ' flutes, hoops, and Etruscan borders of these two colours to produce a very Etruscanitish effect, & at a moderate price.'3 In this way improvements were carried on, till the final perfection of the

' Vifedgwood to Bentley, July 29, 3 V'edgwood to Bentley, August 1772. » 23, I772. ' Ihid.
158 TRITONS AND SPHINXES. ('n.P. III. jasper body allowed of effects still more exquisite and striking.'

The first production of several kinds of ornamental ware, commenced with the opening of the works at Etruria. A few figures, busts, and statuettes, in basaltes or bronze, had been probably made at the Burslem works before this date; but the tritons, 'sphinxes, grifiins, tripods, altars, and other articles, were first produced at Etruria. A man named Boot, clever and docile when he could be kept from drink, was the earliest modeller of some of these forms. He improved as he went on; but Mr. Wedgwood, who worked at the different models himself, assisted by a Mr. Denby, a young artist of considerable promise, and by Hackwood, whose name first appears in August, 1770, soon ran ahead of Boot in the mastery of these productions. Still, for a period this modeller retained a sort of speciality in tritons and sphinxes. The first usually served the purpose of light-holders, the griffins, or chimerae, the same, as We shall hereafter "see. The earliesttiiton candlesticks were modelled from one lent by Mr. Chambers, afterwards Sir William Chambers, the architect; who, at a later date, supplied Mr. Wedgwood with

some fine lions and sphinxes in metallic bronze for artistic copy. The first pair of triton candlesticks were

I The prices of some of the flower-ditto, I/(5. (iriflin head flower-pot pots were as foIIows:—" Engine turned fiower-ts, gilt, 8/ the air. Green&gold,3 ditto. Upright, iceworked, 2/6 each. Ilooped garden pots & stands, 10 inches wide, 4/6 the pair. Festooned ditto, 13 inches, 10/ ditto. Festooned garden (plots and stands, 10 inches, 8/ pr. 'ilt festoons & tops, 10 inches wide, 2/6 r. Lions' heads & festoons nngi t, rom 1/ 6 to 10". each. Husk festoon flower-pot & stand, 4/6. New pendant ditto, gilt, 5/; dice-worked

' and red festoons on gilt with stand, 13 inches wide, 5/. Blue ground fl0wer-ots, dra ery festoons, raised white utes on ttom of belly, and friezed, 11 inches high, 12/ each. Ditto with faces plinths, & feet marbled with gold,9 inches high, 5 wide, 15/ each. Blue ground flower-pots, with griflins' heads & laurel festoons, 8 inches high and 7 wide, 15/ each/—Inv0i¢-es, 1768-9. Mayer M NS.

C HAP. III. EGYPTIAN LIONS. 159 sent to London for the purpose of presentation to the architect, but they were accidentally seen at the vvarehouse in Newport Street by some noble connoisseur, and so borne off in triumph; and the secret had to be kept till another pair could be supplied. These tritons, each of which took two days to begin and finish, and a month's drying before it could be fired, sold for two guineas apiece when perfection was attained. They were either bronzed or left simply black. If unbronzed, they were cheaper. The sphinxes, which with the tritons were sent to M. Du Burk, at the Hague, as early as I770, were principally used as ornaments to balustrades, or to crown high and massive pieces of furniture; were often, as in the annexed example (fig. 36), very beautiful.1 They varied in 160 'l‘RIPODS AND ALTARS. CI-IAP. III.
size and character, some being from antique, and others from modern specimens, and occasionally they were gilt. Lions and sphinxes were, in some in-

stances, modelled after splendid examples by Michael Angelo; and of these a single model cost thirty guineas, and took three weeks to repair when out of condition. Tripods, of which there was eventually a great variety, were much admired, and some of the earliest made were purchased by Earl Gower and Lord Waldegrave; and altars, which were used for almost every purpose of support, as for vases, busts, figures, flower-pots, and clocks, furnished in their forms, their bas-reliefs, drapery, festoons, or medallions many fine' examples of ornamental art. Occasionally Mr. Wedgwood's imagination took flights, which carried him, as he soon found, beyond the bounds of the ideal. He had some elephants modelled, but nobody admired or bought them. 'I will send you no more such ponderous animals,' he writes to Bentley, ' till you have sold what you have; for, as the Lady said, I find we made a Bull when we made an Elephant.'1

If Bentley's letters were sources of inspiration to him, as Mr. Wedgwood was ever acknowledging they were, he, on the other hand, lost no opportunity of urging on his partner not only the study of, but the resort for, examples to antique art. ' I hope you will have an opportunity soon of getting some figures from the Cabinets of y' noble customers, which have not appeared in the shops. Pray make a push for it where & when you can with decency, & I will endeavour to execute them in Terra Cotta.' A-while later he says, 'I was going to say before I left Etruria, that I liked much your plan of hav'z the Bronze CRAP. III. CASTS FROM THE ANTIQUE. 161 figures from Rome, provided they are fine & have not been hackneyed here.'1 ' I think we sho'1 have some

' casts from antique gems from Rome, as well as the figures, & hope by the means of the gentleman you mention, you will be able to settle a correspondence with some of the ingenious gentlemen or artists at Rome yourself, which I think will be very useful to us/ 2 At this date and after, Mr. Anson, Mr. Wedgwood's neighbour, and Mr. Stuart, whose great work on Athens had already placed his name on the list of illustrious men of the eighteenth century, were lending the partners figures and antiques of various kinds; Sir Watkins Williams Wynne and Mr. Foley, casts from ancient gems; and the Duke of Argyle was urging them to copy some splendid examples of Rafaelle-ware in his possession. With respect to gems Mr. Wedgwood wrote, ' Has Ld Bessborough sold all his casts from Antique Gems, or the Gems themselves, to the Duke of Marlbr? I am, & so are you, much interested to know this, as we had leave from L(1 B. to take casts from all his Casts; but if the D. of M. has b0' them, we shall have that leave to solicit again. Though the gems from Italy may be too small to apply to the vases themselves, they will make very good studys, & we can have larger modeled by them much better than from prints; we can likewise paint after them. Gems are the fountain-head of fine & beautiful composition, & we cannot, you know, employ ourselves too near the fountain-head of taste.'3 It appears that Lord Bessborough had not parted with his gems, for three months later Mr. Wedgwood was making medallions from them, and 1 'V to Bentle Se tem-i ' Wedgwood toBentley September 9, 1755. y' P I ber 30, 1709. ' " lbid. September 10, 1100.

VOL. II. M 162 THE BRITISH MUSEUM. CIIAP. III.

reminding Mr. Bentley that his Lordship was to have the first pair. At the same date he was pointing the way to another source of antique art. ' I hope,' he says to Mr. Bentley, 'you will see Dr. Maty soon, & enter uppon your studys at the Museum; and as I suppose you may have the liberty to take Mr. Rhodes & Mr. Crofts along with you, I shou'd think it would be right to shew them as much as possible the nature of the paintings uppon these Vases, & let them copy the paintings, & take outlines, sections, &c. off the Vases. I immagine you cannot make Dr. Maty a more acceptable present than a tea or Cofiee service, or a little Table service for their own use; these would make more shew,

& be less expensive than a pair of Etruscan Vases.'1 The Hamilton collection of vases was already consigned to the British Museum; although, as yet, the nation by its Parliamentary vote was not actually its possessor. We shall see that Wedgwood desired to place some of his most masterly copies amongst the originals; but at that date, as at present, everything native to the soil, or produced by the races who had lived and died upon it, was repudiated by those who were the rulers of the National Collection.

' 'edgvood to Bentley. Dictated to one of the clerks, December 9, 1769.

TOWARDS the close of the year 1769, Mr. Wedgwood became affected with a disorder in his eyes; and for a considerable period subsequently his suffering and depression on this account were very great. In some degree the disease must have been epidemical, for various persons were so afflicted, and often fatally; but in his case effects, which might arise from atmospheric or other general causes, were increased by the incessant strain upon every mental faculty. The first symptoms of the disorder appeared during a. few days' residence in London, and he spoke of them to Mr. Bentley. Upon his return home he consulted his old surgeon, Mr. Bent of Newcastle, and a. little later a Dr. Elliot, who had rendered himself famous by the cure of many similar cases, amongst others those of the Duke of Norfolk and the Duchess of Bedford. But little good was derived from medicine. Being forbidden to use his eyes by candlelight, Mrs. Wedgwood was at first his amanuensis; but she was called away from his side by the severe illness of her father, who lay stricken with fever in the old farmhouse at Spen Green. Thus lonely, we find his usual courage falter; and dangerous as it was to him to use his eyes, he thus, though briefly, tells his sorrows to him who ever lightened them by generous and precious sympathy. 'Dr. Elliot... told me there was always some danger in these cases (Mice Volanti (Muscae Volitantes) I think he calls the disorder) but he hopes he shall be able to overcome

'them. I am this moment returned from Spen Green where I left my wife and her bantling both well, my father is still very poorly, far the apothecary says from being out of danger, but thinks his fever abated. I am very well in health, but cannot help thinking my eyes in a bad way, & I do not know what to determine about building any more, though I must leave my works at Burslem the next year.' 1

The necessity for Mr. Bentley's residence in London had from the first been a source of great disappointment and occasionally of grief to his friend. It is referred to in innumerable letters, and at this period was doubly felt and _mourned over; this the more that Mr. Bentley, though absent, gave 'every proof of sympathy and afl"ec tion. 'Your friends lament with me the necessity of your very distant situation, & cannot any more than myself be reconciled to a plan which robs us of the pleasure we had long flatter'd ourselves with the enjoyment of in your company. '2 In another place he says: ' I know your friendly and affectionate heart, & that you do sympathise with us most cordially, and this perswasion is not without its comfort, though the distance at which we are fixed robs us of a great deal more. I often stand in need of your advice, assistance, & consolation. The great variety & load of business I am at present ingaged in, with the near prospect of a vast increase if I pursue the plan I am in a manner involved in, & can scarcely

' Vedgwood to Bentley, December 29, 1769. 2 lhid. January 1, 1770.

CRAP. IV. DOUBTS AND DIFFICULTIES. 167 retreat from without giving up business intirely, & at the same time being threatened with a disorder which must totally incapacitate me from doing anything at all, & yet it is absolutely necessary that I shod resolve upon and pursue some one plan immediately. These things altogether, with some other anxietys I have lately felt, have at times put on a temporary suppression of spirits which I am not accustomed to, & which do not naturally belong to my constitution. If I carry on my works I must build the next year. If I build I must lay in the timber & other materials, agree with all sorts of workmen &c. immediately, & perhaps may lose both my eyes (for they are equally affected) before the building is completed. Is not this a terrible dilemma. What shall I do my Good fr". But who can advise what is best to be done, when the better or worse depends upon an event which we can neither foresee nor command. But let me turn from this dark scene & tell you that my good father continues to recover without much interruption, & I hope will be able (to) come down stairs, and spare me my wife again in a short time which will be a great comfort to me, for at present I am sadly forlorn indeed. I hope I shall receive a good letter from you by to-night's post which will do me much good. God bless you & preserve you from every evil. Amen.' 1

Some cases in Mr. Wedgwood's own neighbourhood, which ended fatally, added temporarily to his depressing fears, though he prepared himself to meet the worst with fortitude. Perhaps nothing more affecting was ever penned than this allusion to his lameness and anticipated blindness: 'I am learning to acquiesce... whatever may be

' Vedgwood to Bentley, January 16, 1770.
168 WISHES TO INSTRUCT BENT-LEY. Can. IV. the issue, as I wo' wish to do, in every unavoidable evil. I am often practising to see with my fingers, & I think I sho' make a tolerable proficient in that science for one who "begins so late in life; but shall make a wretched walker in the dark with a single leg.' 1 _

The renowned doctor who had cured Dukes and Duchesses failed in the subtler case of Mr. /Vedgwood. But his old surgeon Mr. Bent, treating it as a disease of the liver, soon gave relief; though it was months before his patient could use his eyes without distress by candlelight, and for weeks a varying degree of hypochondria oppressed very evidently his naturally cheerful temperament. He saw the future darkly, and dreading the worst, thus refers to those precious secrets of his art— which he

had won by anxious days and nights of toil. ' I wod just mention,' he writes to Bentley, ' that when you have settled matters in the best manner you can in London & Chelsea, I could wish you to be at the manufactory awhile to learn the art of Pottmaking, whilst I am able to go thro' that 'branch with you, which I shall do with great pleasure, & hope you will carry on to great perfection those improvements which I have been endeavouring to lay a foundation for, & shall be 'happy in leaving them with you my good and worthy friend, who neither want ability nor spirit to pursue the task—may it be a pleasing and successful one-Indeed I have no doubt but it will, & so long as my eyes and my health will permit I shall gladly assist you in it. Do not think by what I have wrote, that my eyes are worse, but I am sensible of my danger, & the last attack may be sudden & not give me an opportunity of communicating many things which I 1 Wedgwood to Bentley, January 15, 1770.

Gnu. IV. AFFAIRS BRIGHTEN. 169 would not have to die with me-I know how ill you can be spared from the Rooms, but I think it will be better to suffer a little inconvenience for the present, than leave you immers'd in a business, & not master of the principal

But whilst thus, in the strange perversity of disease, he was anticipating the darkest which could befall, the things of daily life were again assuming their old aspect of serenity. The invalid at Spen Green was better, his wife was home, his children were around him. He thanks Bentley for sending him an 'interesting account of the debates in the House of Lords, & a thousand other good things,' and then adds this cheery news, ' I left Spen Green yesterday, & this time have brought my Wife and Child2 along with me—Etruria 'now begins to brighten up, and looks like itself again, five long weeks of absence have hung very heavily upon me, but her aid was much wanted to nurse & comfort an aged and worthy parent; and I was well pleased that she was able (to) pay this debt of duty and affection to him_He is now pretty well recover'd

& sends his best respects & thanks to you/3 By the time the summer was fully come, Mr. Richard Wedgwood could drink his favourite toast of the ' five counties ' and was preparing with the alacrity of a school-boy to accompany his son-in-law to London to see the Russian services. They were now rapidly advancing towards completion. Purple husks bloomed round the edges of the table-ware, and finely enamelled little flowers were scattered 011 dessert-plate and dish, as gracefully as though by Nature's hand!

' Wedgwood toBentley February 1 ' Vedgwood to Bentley January 10, 1770. ' 22, 1770. ' " Josiah Vedgwood the younger.
170 ENAMEL PAINTERS. CHAP. IV.

Even before the opening of the ornamental works at Etruria, or the settlement at Chelsea, Mr. Wedgwood had laid the foundation for a body of superior enamel painters. Messrs. Rhodes and Croft and several assistants were at work in Newport Street; James Bakewell, a Liverpool man, Ralph Unwin, a young lad of considerable ability, and some others, were painters at the Brickhouse Works; but he clearly saw that many others would be wanted, not only for the Etruscan encaustic vases, but for enamelling with antique borders, and more modern floral designs, the cream-ware table-services. At this date, June 1769, the proprietors of the porcelain works at Worcester were discharging a number of good hands, and some also from Derby were seeking employment. Of the latter, Mr. VVedgwood hired a figure-maker, and entered into a treaty with others, and a day later a Worcester china-painter of the name of Wilcox applied to him. He had served his time at Christian's potwork in Liverpool, and in relation to this hand, Mr. VVedgwood continues thus to Bentley. ' This Willcox has a wife who paints & is very ingenious, she is at present finishing some work at Worcester. Wilcox says she is an excellent coppyer of figures& other subjects & a much better hand than himself. He show'd me two heads of her doing in indian ink which are very well done. She is a daughter to that Fry who was famous for doing heads in Metzotints, which you have seen. Willcox is at present employ'd by Twemlows, but not engaged, he wants much he says to be fixed and we" article for any time. I like his appearance much, he seems a sober, solid man, & has nothing flighty or coxcomical in his dress or behaviour, of which most of this class are apt to contract a small tincture. His wife & he have got very good wages he says at Worcester. better he believes than he must ever expect again, they wod now be content he says both of them at 253. p week which is low enough if they will be tolerably dilligent. If we get thesepainters & the figure makers, we shall do pretty well in these branches.'1 Mrs. Wilcox was tried, and proved to be an admirable artist. Her services extended over a considerable period, probably indeed till the date of her death a few years after. Some of the best single figures, groups, and borderings on the painted Etruscan ware between 1769 and 1776 were the result of her skill,2 and she headed, as we shall see, the group of female painters, who were engaged to assist in enamelling the great Russian service. Throughout the remainder of the year 1769, and during the year succeeding, painters were sought for in Liverpool, Birmingham, Worcester, Derby, Bow, and Lambeth, and many were hired. Some of them had painted fans, others were 'light India ' painters, and not a few had an exquisite taste for enamelling flowers. A youth named Denby, who was a native of Derby, and had received his early art education there, was engaged more on the footing of a pupil than an apprentice. After working for Mr. Wedgwood at Burslem and Etruria for some months, he was sent in May, 1770, to help Mr. Bentley at Chelsea, under an agreement of service for five years. ' He applys close to business,' wrote Mr. Wedgwood, ' has a delicate modesty in his manners, & I think will be an agreeable & useful assistant to us in a little time. He has not been much used to a brush (or hair) pencil, but will draw you any subject upon the vases you have not plates for with a black-lead Pencil, & 172 THE CHELSEA HOUSEHOLD. CBAIAIV.

may watch over and correct the drawings of other hands for he is really learned in the Anatomy and drawing of a Human figure.' 1

Mr. Bentley, as befitted his position, settled down handsomely at Chelsea. He bought a chariot and pair, had a horse for an occasional ride, and kept up, as in Liverpool, a generous and yet not wasteful hospitality. His faithful friend and sister-in-law Miss Oates was still the mistress of his family, but years were advancing upon her, her hearing was very impaired, and so amidst the occurrences which made life sopleasant, indications were not wanting that other and brighter influences would soon cheer the widower's home. Mr. Stamford, the smith and engineer of Derby, had a daughter, who, as heretofore in Liverpool, came frequently to see her father's old friends Mr. Bentley and Miss Oates. She was in the prime of life; somewhere, it would seem, about five and twenty. Her person comely, her temper cheerful, her manners vivacious. She helped Miss Oates to receive and amuse her guests, she cut out vases and other forms on paper, and was included in what Mr. Vedgwood calls 'the privy council.' Very gallantly Mr. Bentley consulted it on almost all important occasions. Thus by degrees, though slowly, Mary Stamford won upon the generous and manly heart of Thomas Bentley, and it was soon whispered that she would become his wife. Nor was childhood absent from that pleasant home, with its fine gardens, its environing fields, and the 'great silent highway' flowing near. A little niece of either Miss Oates or Mr. Bentley passed much of her time at Chelsea, and neighbours were accessible and friendly. Amongst these was Joseph Cooper, 1 'edgwood to Bentley, May 23, 1770.

CRAP. IV. NEIGHBOURS AND FRIENDS. 173 a printer in that day of some repute, and the inventor of an improved kind of printing ink. He was a man of talent, and ' abounded,' as one who knew him said, 'in plea/santry and the milk of human kindness,' though he was speculative, over-sanguine, and trusted too much to the fortunes and justice of others. But this introduction to Mr. Bentley and his great partner proved of much more value than temporary hospitality and pleasant neighbouring. In 1773 Mr. Cooper entered into partnership with M. Du Burk in the sale of Wedgwood and Bentley's ware, and resided for a time at Amsterdam. The speculation failed, owing chiefly to-Du Burk's want of principle, and when Mr. Cooper returned to his faithful 'Betsey' and his old Chelsea home, he accepted a post in Greek Street, and died the faithful friend and servant of the Wedgwoods in 1806.1 Away from the city too, in summer weather, when it was an exquisite little trip to take boat at London Bridge and glide up the river, came merchants and their wives, and other old acquaintances of Mr. Bentley. From Pall Mall came Mr. More, the friend of the celebrated Dr. Templeman. More was a man of wealth and taste, and probably dealt in objects of vertu. He seems to have been instrumental in procuring many fine specimens of antique art for Mr. Bentley: through him Mr. Wedgwood obtained from China samples

'of real petunse and kaolin; and for him, as sacred to the memory of More's dear friend Dr. Templeman, Mr. Wedgwood made one of his finest vases. It was in basaltes; serpents twined round it as emblems of eternity, and it stood sacred and honoured the penates of the owner's house.

When in town and engaged on business out of doors,

' ' (1'ent.'s.Iag., vol. lxxviii. p. l, p. 470.

Mr. Bentley always used his chariot and pair. VVhen the supply of ornamental ware exceeded, as it did in 1773, the demand, or large numbers of black and yellow dessert services, prepared long before for foreign markets, lay so much dead stock in the warehouse, we find Mr. VVe(gwood bidding his friend take his chariot and go amongst the Russian merchants. During the contention with Palmer of Hanley about the patent, the vehicle often stayed before the chambers of Lord Mansfield in Lincoln's Inn. It was familiar to the doors of Lansdowrie House, so soon now to have a new attraction to Bentley, in the presence of his friend the illustrious Priestley. It stopped often at Leicester House, rolled beneath the gateway of Northumberland House, and waited for its master still more frequently before the town houses of Earl Gower, Sir Watkin Williams Wyniie, a11d other patrons. Occasionally it was to be seen by Buckingham House, for new things had to be shown, or some order was in hand for His or Her Majesty. Vhen in town, M1'. VVedg'ood

CRAP. IV. BENTLEY'S POPULARITY. 175 usually accompanied his friend. 'Last Monday,' writes Mr. Bentley to his Liverpool partner, 'Mr. Wedgwootl and I had a long audience of their majesties at the Queen's palace, to present some bas-relz'e_/'s her majesty had ordered; and to show some new improvements with which they were well pleased. They expressed in the most obliging and condescending manner, their attention to our manufacture; and entered very freely into conversation on the further improvement of it, and on many other subjects. The King is well acquainted with business, and with the characters of the principal manufactures, merchants, and artists; and seems to have the success of all our manufactures much at heart, and to understand the importance of them. The Queen has more sensibility, true politeness, engaging afiability, and sweetness of temper, than any great lady I ever had the honour of speaking to.' 1 As time wore on, Mr. Bentley's popularity grew. His handsome person, and polished manners, were irresistible to otherwise haughty duchesses and ladies; and whilst he poised a vase, or showed bas-relief or cameo, and related the antique stories its designs sought to express, the ladies listened, smiled, bowed, and what was more to the purpose bought. An aristocrat by nature, he was the most courtly of chaptnen. 'Be so good,' writes Mr. Wedgwood soon after Mr. Bentley's settlement in Newport Street, 'to let us know what is going forward

in the Great World. How many Lords & Dukes visit your rooms, praise your beauties, thin your shelves, & fill your purses; and if you will take the trouble to acquaint us with the daily ravages in your stores, we will endeavour to replenish themfi' 176 VISITORS AT ETRURIA. CHAP. IV.

By degrees this popularity attracted to itself something worthier than the fashion of the hour; and by the close of 1772 Mr. Bentley reckoned amongst his friends, 'Athenian Stuart,' Dr. Solander, Mr. Banks (afterwards Sir Joseph), and others whose names live in the scientific and literary history of their time.

The ' works ' at Etruria, where 'the Herculanean pictures ' for the Queen, or the Etruscan vases for the ducal chamber, were formed, shared in these visitations from the titled great. When guests stayed at Trentham, Keel, Shugborough, or other of the neighbouring halls, Etruria was the attractive point for a morning's ride. A few weeks before he removed from Burslem, Mr. Wedgwood writes: 'Whilst I have been at Etruria here (he was at work there with his modellers) they have had Lady

Gower, Lady Pembroke, Ld Robert Spencer, &c. to breakfast. This is the second time the Trentham family have been there, whilst I have been abroad. Well, it cannot be helped.' In numberless other letters Mr. Wedgwood refers to his titled visitors, and the painters at Chelsea are hastened with the vases they have in hand, in order that the show-room at Etruria may be worthily adorned. A year later he tells Bentley, ' We had in Sir Charles Bingham from Ireland on Tuesday last, with his lady _and daughter. They came from Namptwich hither on purpose to see the works they had heard so much talk about in Ireland, & immediately set off for London where you will see them in a little time. They told me the Duke of Richmond had made a present of a pair of vases No.. to the Duke of Leinster who was in Raptures with them, and that the D. is a Gent" of the 1st virtu in Ireland. That some others had seen our vases & there seem'd a violent Vase madness breaking out amongst them,

and we are sure if we had a room in Dublin, a large quantity might be sold. '1 VVe shall see this suggestion bore fruit..

But gratifying as this increasing patronage was, whether it were metropolitan, distant provincial, Scotch, Irish, continental or from sources even more remote, that of the neighbouring gentry, in a great measure the owners of the soil on which long generations of the Wedgwoods had lived and died, must have been still more so. Mr. W(lgVO0Ll was constantly riding to Trentham. The hall, not then the palatial building it is now, but still, as seen in the illustration, a country mansion of mark, with fine gardens, noble woodlands, and a situation of rare beauty on the 'meadindented' Trent. How often he rode beneath the summer boughs, or through the russet shadows of the fall, to consult the good earl on some point of local business, to urge on him, in connection with his official relation to the Court or Ministry, the removal of the

' 'edgwood to Bentley, August 2, 1770.

ms. n. N export duty 011 earthenware to F ranee; or to confer with the countess on her flower-pots, or her cream-ware dairy tiles.1 Something was always in hand at the ' U ' or ' O ' works for Trentham, and Mr. Gilbert, or Mr. Eaton the clerk of the kitchen, was often settling accounts. The earl was a fine specimen of the old Whig nobility. His face, as thus preserved to us in cameo, makes us feel that he was a scholar and a gentleman, and yet one who perhaps shone more as lord of his county, in promoting canals and highways, in patronising agriculture, in presiding at great public meetings, than even in his ministerial capacity, as Lord Privy Seal, Lord Chamberlain, and Lord President (Fig. =19.) mt r;owl-zu. of the Council, popular as he was, even when in coalition with the Opposition under Lord North. He always met Mr. Wedgwood on the simple footing of man with man, and seems never to have been so happy as when at home amidst his neighbours. His name is constantly appearing in Mr. Wedgwood's letters to Bentley. On one occasion he writes to Cox: 'L" Gower promis'd me if possible to send his Danish Majesty to Y' Rooms, so pray be prepar'd for the honor of such a visit.' The wife of Earl Talbot was a frequent correspondent; and the Earl of Harrowby, Sir William Bagot, Mr. Anson, Mr. Sneyd, and many others lent figures and threw open their cabinets of gems and coins, with the liberality of princes. In one of his letters Mr. Vedgwood tells Bentley, ' I am to wait upon our good friend Sir VVm. Bagot at Blithefield in a few days to take his orders for some large vases to furnish the niches in an elegant room he has just built, and I intend at the same time to wait upon Mr. Anson who wants and says he will have some black vases with white festoons. He has some excellent figures and other antiques very suitable for our purposes, which I intend to signify my longings after.' The next day he adds, as a postscript to the same letter: ' We have had Sir Harry Minwaring here this morning: he came on purpose to order a set of vases for a large room amo £13. 4. all Etruscans. I have take (taken) 6 weeks to complete them in.' 1

By December, 1769, the workrooms, and a mutlle bought at Lambeth, were ready at Chelsea, and from this date hands were consecutively drafted oil' from Etruria. The first sent were Mr. and Mrs. VVilcox. They travelled to London by Waggon and were a week on the road. Starting from Newcastle on the Sunday they did not

I reach London till the following Saturday, when they were met at the inn by some of the servants from Newport Street. A fact like this enables us to realise the social changes which less than a century has produced. We have here a woman, capable of fine figure and border painting, wearily travelling amidst the mob of a stage Waggon, with her pencils and brushes tied in a bundle. But Catherine Wilcox, though thus journeying like Smollett's heroes and heroines, was a woman of great ability. Two months before she and her husband were drafted to London Mr. Wedgwood thus referred to her: 'Mrs. Wilcox is losing time here, as she might as well 180

PAINTERS FOR CHELSEA. CRAP. IV.
paint figures upon vases as upon paper, as I am perswaded you will be convinced from the drawings I sent you. If she does such things of herself, what may not be expected from her under the tuition of a Bentley & a Crofts. Pray let me know when I shall send her & her goodman for whilst they continue here there is 18/ at least per week sunk out of 24/.'1 The Wilcoxes were followed in the next year 1770, by W. Boume, Thomas Hutchins a printer who had worked at Soho, Cooper an excellent flower painter, Ralph Unwin, Mr. Denby, James Bakewell, Simpcock, Barrett, Christopher Taylor, and Thomas Glover; and as the vast demand for enamelled table services and vases increased, other bands were sought for amongst the London fan, coach, and fresco painters. Mr. Rhodes also advertised, and travelled to Bow on several occasions on the same errand. But the difficulty was not to meet with painters, as with those capable of the high class work Wedgwood and Bentley required. They soon found at Etruria, as at 7

Chelsea, that nothing but training in their own workrooms would convert medium workmen into fine artists, and the partners seem respectively to have conceived some plan of an academy or classes to promote this object. 'What has become of yr scheme of taking in girls to paint,' asks Mr. Wedgwood in one of his letters. ' Have you spoke to Mrs. Wright. Mr. Coward too said he would tell you of some Fan painters. You observe very justly that few hands can be got to paint flowers the style we want them. I may add, nor any other work we do, we must make them. There is no other way. We have stepped forw'i beyond the other manufactures 1 Vedg-Wood to Bentley, September 17, 1769.

CHAP. IV. A DRAVVING AND MODELLING SCHOOL. 191 (manufacturers) & we must be content to train up hands to suit our purpose. Where amongst our Potters could I get a complete Vase maker? Nay I could not get a hand through the whole Pottery to make a table plate without training them up

for that purpose, & you must be content to train up such Painters as offer to you, & not turn them adrift because they cannot immediately form their hands to our new style; which if you consider what they have been doing all their life we ought not to expect from them.' 1 On his own account, a few days later, Mr. Wedgwood adds: 'I have a waking notion haunts me very much of late which is the _begining, a regular drawing & modeling school to 'train up artists for ourselves. I wod pick up some likely Boys of about 12 years old & take them apprentice till they are twenty or twenty-one, & set them to drawing, & when they had made some tolerable proficiency they shod practice with outlines of figures upon Vases which I V0d send you to be fill'd up. We would make outlines Wh wo' bear carriage & these might tend to facilitate your doing a quantity of the Patent Vases, & when you wanted any hands we could draft them out of this school. The Paintings upon these vases are from W. & B's school-so it may be sd 1,000 years hence.' 2 Shortly after the business of painting the encaustic Etruscan vases was begun, Crofts struck out a scheme for employing faint white outlines, not only for the figures on the black and red bodies, but also for the borders. It stood to reason, that if this class of vases was to be sold to any remunerative extent, their manufacture must be both rapid and economical. To paint

' Vedgwood to Bentley, May 19, 1770. " Ibid. May 23, 177.

each vase elaborately,' except in occasional instances of fine and costly specimens, would be to raise their price far above ordinary demand. At first the outlines were chalked; but in February, 1770, Thomas Hutchins, a printer from Soho, was engaged; and shortly after this date the outlines of figires on all the smaller vases were printed, and the colours subsequently filled in. The border lines were traced at Etruria. ' We are now beginning upon plain Etruscans for painting, of which we shall have about 20 forms & sizes & I cannot help thinking if we put the lines in '"""'"" for the borders, it wod greatly assist the painters 11:1" 1111: even though they were white, & to be traced over again by the enamellers. We would put the lines in gold to stand for good.'2 Bentley dissented to this mechanical kind of art, and intimated that the work could be done better without this printing, ' Here my good friend,' was the reply, 'I cannot join with you, unless you can engage a score or two of Ciprianas, nor do I think any, or at least, the baulk of the Painters you will employ, ought to or will, object to the assistance of an outline, & especially, if to the most delicate ones, it is oflered rather upon the idea of dispatch, so necessary in a manufacture, than to supply any dq/icieru-y in the artist, and as to have full employment for the Printer that that is not at all necessary, as we can use his pencil you know, as well as the Press.'3 Even with respect to the body of the vases themselves, many mechanical aids were in a short period introduced which greatly facilitated production, after one of each pattern had been brought to perfection.

' One Etruscan vase, painted for 2 'edg'ood to Bentley, Feb. 4, Lord ('arlisle, was)l'iCP(at fifteen I770. guinens. " lhid. April '29, ITTO.

The chief classical subjects of the gems, medallions and bas-reliefs, executed during 1769, were a Sacrifice, Apollo and Daphne, Night and Apollo, Jupiter and Leda, Jupiter and Daphne, God of Day, Goddess of Night, and Olympus and Marcyas. The vases decorated with the medallions of Jupiter and his companions were ultimately dispatched to the West Indies; for, even in that age of somewhat gross tastes, it was foimd that art throve best under its purest expressions.

The bookkeeper and manager William Cox had, as we have seen, been with brief interruptions at the head of the London business, from the date of opening the showrooms in Charles Street till shortly after Mr. Bentley's settlement in town. His character, as Mr. Wedgwood confided sometimes to his friend, was 'an enigma.' Painfully reserved, procrastinating, honest yet dilatory and careless to a fault, he fell at length into the greatest confusion re-

specting the monetary affairs of the firm, and sending in bills repeatedly to those who had already paid them, indignant remonstrances were the natural result. Some of. the most interesting letters in Mr. Mayer's collection relate to this matter. There is one from the celebrated Mrs. Montague, others from Mr. Goring afterwards Sir H. Goring, and Lady Talbot. The Scotch lords and ladies are particularly angry, and not a few of the realm of housekeepers sit down in angry mood with their unclassical pens. The blue-stocking Montague writes as tartly as the rest:_' It W'I be a fine story if people had nothing to do but to pay for whatever goods were charged to them; " and Mr. Goring, who is more dignified, says ' I have most undoubtedly paid the money a great many months ago, nor would I by any means suffer you or any man else that I deal with to be so long kept from what was their just right, thro' any neglect of my own.... I should think your Bookkeeper rather deserves reproof for his negligence, in not crossing the account out of his Books, than I to be upbraided with tardiness in paying my just debts.' '

Mr. Wedg'ood had been long making serious complaints of the state in which Cox managed the monetary business entrusted to him; and at length, whilst the latter was in Statforshire towards the close of 1769, the full extent of his bookkeeper's unpardonable negligence was for the first time made known to him. His indignation was unbounded. 'I am much concerned,' he writes to Bentley 'to find so many more blunders in Mr. Cox's cash acc'., and as I am daily suffering in so tender:1 point as that of my Character for Honesty and all through his neglect, I cou'd not help reproving him very severely for it. I shall send him up to Town immediately and before he sets out I shall tell him that I insist on his doing nothing but assist in clearing up the Books; till that is done, and till this work is finish'd, I beg you will not send out any more bills, unless such as you are certain are not paid, for I had rather hire money at fifty p ct. interest, than he under the suspicions Mr. Cox's extreme neglect has brought

upon me. It must appear as the gent" you mention justly observes, that I must either be wanting in honesty, or have trusted my business to servants, who cou'd not or wou'd not keep any books, and as you know the latter has been the case, I beg they may be told so without reserve, or any way 1 Mr, Harry Goring to (,'o.:, dated from Rowdell, March 16,, I769, hlayer MSS.

mincing the matter though Mr. Cox shoud be present at the time. I acquaint him with what I write to you, and I owe this piece of justice to myself. It is equitible and just that he shoud rather lose his character as a bookkeeper, which he has deserved to do, than that I shou'l lose mine for honesty, which I have never forfeited.'1 By some care and diligence, and the assistance of worthy and methodical Peter Swift, the London accounts were brought into better order, and Cox from this date had little more to do with them.

Amongst the correspondents of 1769 was the great Lord Kames, who paused in his philosophical speculations relative to the origin of mankind, to write to Mr. Wedgwood concerning butter-kits-and as though some mathematical problem presented itself even here, the paper on which his letter is written is cut somewhat in the form of a parallelogram, probably to represent the size or the form of the butter kit? Lady Chatham, Lady Camden, and the newly married wife of Pennant the naturalist, were also correspondents. For Lady Cliatham and Lord Pitt, Mr. I/Vedgwood made some exquisite dessert services; that for the wife of England's greatest statesman being exquisitely painted with flowers. Vithout doubt it was a labour of love to the partners—for both were ardent admirers of the illustrious Chatham-and, at no late date after 1774, they gave his somewhat harsh but striking features in cameo to that multitude of Englishmen and foreigners, who saw in him the unselfish and courageous patriot. Mr. Bentley never missed a speech of Chatham's. He was present at that striking scene in the House of 1 'e-dgwood to Bentley, dictated-dated Blair Drummond, January

3, to Swift, December 16, I769. lT(i9, lln_'or MSS. ' Lord Kames in Mr. Vodgwood,

Lords in January, 1770, when the great minister, after long seclusion, and the very obvious ineompetency of his colleagues to carry on the administration when deprived of his direction, suddenly reappeared, and on the usual motion for the address to the Royal speech, moved an amendment, the purport of which was to answer the con duct of the House of Commons in the affair of VVilkes, and to assert the right of the constituency to make a free choice of their representatives. In this great speech Lord Chatham's censures ranged through the whole field of foreign, colonial and domestic policy. ' Last Tuesday,' wrote Bentley to Boardman in one of his admirable letters, ' was a day of high entertainment to me, though of great fatigue. I stood between eight and nine hours in the House of Lords, to hear the very interesting debates upon the King's Speech;—and though I have often heard the debates in both Houses, I never heard any so noble, so eloquent, so animated and animating as these. My Lord Chatham is quite rejuvinated. He talks like a patriot, and seems determined to shine, and even to blaze again in the public eye. His abilities are certainly transcendant, and his knowledge is almost boundless. I like the style of his eloquence better than' Lord Mansfield's. Lord Mansfield pours forth in one continued uniform torrent, while Lord Chatham's eloquence falls like a gentle stream from the mountain_gathers strength by degrees-swells--meanders——dashes against the interposing rocks--and then rushes forward in a noble torrent to the ocean. Lord Camden is plain, perspicuous, honest, and affecting. His speech was the expression of an honest heart— bold, manly, disinterested. Lord Shelburne, animated in the cause of liberty. Lord Littleton—f'or the same cause—— — learned and earnest; but, alas! I could not hear his oration so as to connect it well together."

Mr. Bentley, upon settling in London, still continued his services to the

Monthly Review. These were probably gratuitous, for, early in 1769, Griffiths the editor had presented him with a massive silver inkstand of so elegant a form, that Mr. Wedgwood had it copied in the black basaltes body. At the date just referred to, Bentley seems to have entered upon the defence of Lord Camden,

' Bentley to Iloardman, January garnered up like precious treasures. 16, 17TO.—Bentleyana, p. 16. From these fragments, in tl little pamphlet. of twenty-three pages, we judge how letters which Bentley sent almost dnily to his friend, and which were
They became, as was remarked to Beutlev, alter the latter had settled
. in Lonllon, 'My.nga1.ines,le'icws, fine must have been manv of the
Chronicles, X: I had allmost said my Bible.' 'edg"oo(l to Bentley, Felltcruber 16'», 1769.
in a series of papers, which, though passing as critical reviews on pamphlets and other political works, were in fact an exposure of the ministerial policy in depriving.

Lord Camden of the Great Seal. The elegant scholar, who passed many of his hours in tempting duchesses and countesses by classic stories relative to vases and antique gems, passed also many of his laborious nights in vindicating the rights of the people against the policy and proceedings of the Government.

The Duke of Argyle, as already stated, possessed some fine specimens of majolica, or, as it was then more commonly called, Rafiaelle ware, and he wished Mr. Wedgwood to copy them both in body and painting. But the latter found that it would be necessary to have a true Delft body on which to lay the thick glaze and strong enamels. This could not be procured of the requisite forms in Liverpool, and in London he found it would be dangerous to make the attempt, as Palmer and many other potters were unscrupulous in their piracy. But the painting was tried upon the cream-ware body, and some exquisite vases and other articles were the result of Mrs. Wilcox's labours in this direction.

Through the course of 1770, Mr. Wedgwood effected by slow degrees a great reform in his manufacture, and one for which it became henceforth celebrated. This related to the lightness of the ware. ' I am giving,' he tells Bentley, in one of 'those letters which the disorder in his eyes rendered it so painful to write, ' my people lessons upon the loss of clay, and with it the loss of credit in making heavy ware, but all will not do. I have be" them half a doz. pair of scales, but there seems one thing want" still, which I propose to have soon, 11 Clerk /if lVer'_q/zts and rlleasures, whose constant business

CHAP. IV. REMOVAL TO ETRURIA HALL. 189 it shall be to weigh the goods as they are got up— he will save me three times his wages in Clay, & ten times as much in Credit. The first clever fellow I can spare shall certainly be set down to this business.' 1 0

The Russian services which had been in progress since the latter part of the summer of 1769, were completed in about a year from that date; and between July 2 and 30, 1770, Mr. Wedgwood and his father-in-law were in London to view them. They seem to have been on show at the warehouse in Newport Street. The four services were all in the cream-colour body, but the decorations were difi"erent. On two were views printed by Sadler, and the others were elaborately enamelled with a purple fruit festoon border, and with small scattered groups of flowers. The services included dessert and tea ware, and many of the pieces, as glaciers for liqueurs, wine, and cream, and dishes for crystallised fruit, had to be modelled separately. This was at all times one of the most costly portion of foreign orders, and involved an expense which fell as a loss on the manufacturer. Ultimately, Mr. Wedgwood declined to take orders of this character, except in peculiar cases, which necessitated much special modelling.

Throughout 1770, Mr. Wedgwood was again busy with his building at Etruria, and in September he removed from Mr. Bentley's house to the Hall, the floorcloths and many other things for the furnishing of which had been selected by the latter in town. Mr. Henshall, who was busy with the canal in that neighbourhood, entered at once upon the occupation of the Bank House, the name by which Mr. Bentley's residence was now

‘ Wedgwood to Bentley, December I, 1769.

known; and henceforth we shall see Mr. Wedgwood the enjoyer, as he had been the creator, of a home more fitted to generous hospitality, to the training of his'children, and to the comfort of her who had now for years been ever beside him-an example amongst wives.

It had been so arranged that the partnership between Vedgwood and Bentley related only to ornamental ware, Mr. Thomas Wedgwood still remaining at the head of the ‘ Useful Works ’ as partner and manager. The difficulties involved in this arrangement were 11ot at first apparent, but they soon became very evident to the partners themselves; for, as soon as teapots and other articles were made in antique forms, and bronzed or painted with Etruscan and Grecian figures, the difficult question arose, Vas this useful or ornamental ware? It was ornamental in the fullest sense when viewed as to form or beauty; but certainly, when referred to its ultimate purpose, useful ware. Here was a problem very difficult to solve; the more difiicnlt to Mr. Wedgwood as he wished to measure out justice with the surest hand, between the cousin and partner who had served his interest with such sterling fidelity, and the partner, the man of genius and the friend whom his heart so loved. There is evidence that, for a brief period, Mr. Bentley was both somewhat angry and disappointed; he felt, as it would seem, that he had quitted the certainty of a great and rapidly increasing mercantile business for the m2certa2'nty of what was truly a higher and nobler class of work, but one whose perfection was abstract in theory, and success more foreshadowed by,»/‘hat had been already done, than positively ensured. Must he who had freighted ships with merchandise for the

rich West Indies, the Spanish Main, or the far-extending shores of the American continent, be called on to nicely weigh the question whether a teapot was a teapot, or calculate the fraction gained by its enamelling? But the little shadow between the friends was as evanescent as the clouds upon an April day, or the early dew upon the flowers. Both possessed strong common sense, reasoning faculties of a high order, and, what was higher still, hearts abounding with the noblest emotions of truth and generosity. “That could divide such men? Certainly nothing that had been done, or was yet to do, in this noble art. Wedgwood's letter on this count is a monument to the man. At the distance of near a century, it can be only read with feelings of veneration for him who weighed justice with such an even hand, and swerved neither to the right nor the left in the duty which was his. After explaining the arrangement that each partner was to share in the profit derived from the Etruscan useful ware, he continues, ‘ With respect to the difference between USEFUL WARE & ORNAMENTAL, I do not find any inclination in myself to be overnice in drawing the line. You know I never had any idea that Ornamental ware she(1 not be of “ some _use.”-_You knew this from all we had done hitherto, from the many conversations we have had upon the subject, & from the list we wrote in your commonplace book of the uses to which ornamental vases might be put; I co‘1 have wish'd therefore that you had not repeated this idea so often, & asked me if my partnership with T. W. wod exclude our making “Stella's”1 ewérs. Tell me, my dear friend, did you ask me this question for information, or were _you realy as angry with me, as the question accompanied with any other

‘ Stella was the name of an artist who published a work of designs for vases. idea would import. I hope you were not, for I she‘1 be very unhappy to think you wod be angry with me lightly, or that I had given you any just occasion for the warmth some parts of your letter seem to express. I say seem, for I hope I am mistaken, & shall rest in that hope

till I have the pleasure of hearing from you again. But as this question has put me upon thinking a little more upon the subject, & the situation I am, or may be in, betwixt two Partnerships, it may not be amiss to enter a little deeper into it, & attempt something like a line in T heorie, though I hope we shall none of us be too rigid in our adherence to it, in practice. And first negatively; I do not think that fineness, or ric/mess, or price, or colour, or enameling, or br0nzez'n _q, or gildilzg, can be a criterion for our purpose, for though we make a Table or desert service ever so fine, rich, or expensive, though they are every piece rich enough to adorn a Cabinet, they are in my opinion, usefull toare still, & I think the same may be said of a Teapot or a Chamberpot. Suppose for instance, that I should make pebble desert ware, and vein or edge it with gold burnt in. This would be as rich as the Vases, but must I apprehend be class'd as useful ware still; & on the other hand, though we make a flowerpot, a Vase, Candlestick, &c., ever so plain, it is still in the class of ornamental ware, & clearly within the partnership of W. and B. only, & I shod think I did wrong in making them at Burslem on any occasion without first asking your consent. If degrees of richness or elegance of form, were to constitute the difference in question, & consequently the making of it be transferred from Burslem to Etruria upon its improvement beyond such a pitch, this wod not only lay a foundation for frequent disputes, but must have the same effect upon my

CRAP. IV. THEIR DEFINITION. 193 usefull works, as the King of France's Edict has upon the Potteries of France, to prevent their rivalling his works at Seve, for T. W. might with reason in that case say I have such or such an improvement to introduce into the desert or Tea, but I shall then lose the Article, or if I improve such a single article any further it is gone! This is no forced or unnatural supposition, but is what must result from such a principle being admitted, & as there seems to me to be a more distinct criterion to distinguish between Useful ware and

Ornaments, & which is clear of these, or any other material objections, I cannot hesitate in rejecting the former. May not usefull ware be comprehended under this simple definition, of such vessels as are made use of at meals? This appears to me to be the most simple & natural line, and though it does not take in Wash-hand basons & bottles, or Ewers, Chamberpots, & a few such articles, they are of little consequence, and speak plain enough for themselves; nor W0d this exclude any superb vessels for sideboards, or vases for deserts, if they could be introduc'd, as these articles wo'I be rather for show than use.

' This appears to me the plainest line, & the least liable to objections of all others, but if you think otherwise & have a different one to propose, I am perfectly open to conviction, & am so far from wishing to limit our undertaking or to render it too trifling for your attention, that I wish to extend it by every means, & that, I can very truly assure you, as much on account of my friend as myself. A friend whom I esteem & love (next to the nearer ties of nature) before all mankind, & cannot bear the thought of haggling with him about trifles. The difference betwixt T. W.'s or T. B.'s share in my proffits in any article is no consideration, nor has any weight with vo1.. 11. 0 194 AN APPEAL. CRAP. IV.

me. ' I may not continue long in business, & my life itself is a very precarious one, & whom have I then to leave my business to, capable of conducting it in the manner you know I shod wish to have it continued, but you two; let us therefore my friend & Brother, live, & act like Brothers, & friends indeed, & not suffer any small matters to put our peace and harmony in jeopardie. All I mean by the above distinctions, is to chalk out a path, that I may walk in securely, by defining the limits of two interests, at present separate, & of which my situation renders me the connecting link, without giving offence to either; for if my friend on one side shocl tell me, in any way that I am too partial to my Burslem work & my Relation, and Partner on the other hand be discontent-

ed, & think I lean too much to the ornamental works, & am throwing every advantageous article in that sca l e. '—— Think my friend, you who can feel for me, the situation I must be in. Do you think I could bear it_no & I am sure you would not wish me to lead a miserable life, continually jarring w';h those I Wish most to be at peace with. Next to my Wt'/e Family my Partners are those with whom I must be at peace.

' You have for some time, or at least it has seem'd so to me, from very many passages in your letters, been doubtful of our undertaking being worth the time & attention you have bestowed upon it; & in your last you intimate its certainly coming to nothing upon the present plan. I should be sorry to think so too, but own I have no apprehensions of that sort.—Ornament is a field, which notwithstanding one year's close attention upon it and 1 Mr. VVedgw0od's preference to tell me I sacrifice all to Etruria and Etruria and his ornamental works, vases.' Wedgwood to Bentley, No had been already asserted, 'Poor vember 19, 1769. Burslem, poor creamcolour. They '

Clmr. IV. FAME AND PROFIT. 195 may many, yet it appears to me, that we are but just stepped or are stepping into it, & I am fully perswaded that the fl 1rther we proceed in it, the richer crop we shall reap both of Fame §-Profit, & I do upon the maturest deliberation give it as my firm opinion that mixing usqfull with ornamental wares W0'I in the end limit us in both (in Fame & Proffit I mean) & I make no doubt of your being of the same opinion too, if you have patience & perseverance to proceed on the same tract a. little longer. But how, or in what respect does this first year's essay, give either you or me any ground for re pining, or such gloomy forebodings? If the first year of a business, pays all expenses, & furnishes any profit at all, I she(1 not call it a bad one, but if beyond this, it likewise gives a profiit of 500l. or 1,000l. in Cash for goods really sold & an increase of stock in manufactured goods ready for sale, of one to two thousand pounds more, surely we ought to be more than barely content. I think

we have reason to rejoice, & are robbing ourselves of what is more valuable than money, if we do not take the satisfaction of a prosperous & very promising business along with us, as a. cordial to support us in every hour of toil & fatigue w" our avocations necessarily require at our hands—I must quit this subject till I have the pleasure of seeing you here, which I hope will be soon. Suppose you made Etruria in your way to Liverpool, came this way back again & then by Derby to London. You W0' by that route see your works here twice, & travel very few miles round for it. Adieu my dear friend, believe me most aflectionately yours at all times, J. Wedgwood.' 1 196 HARMONY RESTORED. CHAP. IV.

This manly and generous appeal to the good sense and affection of his friend, touched Bentley at once to the soul! What petty earthly shadows relative to sordid gain, or quibbles weighed in the balance of the Schoolmen, as to where utility ended or grace began, could for a single moment affect deterioratively natures so constituted, so rich in truth, justice, and fidelity? N 0; he set out as quickly as he could to Staflbrdshire, to answer more powerfully by spoken words than by representing signs this manly letter; and ere he started, with something like a consciousness that all these nobler impulses of our being do not and cannot die, and that a generation would come to whom every fragment of truth, relative to their respective lives, would be sought for as keenly as the precious fruits of their art, he endorsed upon it with his rapid pen these words: ' Mr. B. recd this letter a few days before he set out to Etruria. The difficulty was easily settled: & the Etruscan Tea Pots made by y" Company at Etruria. The Company very much wanted some such constant selling article.'

The question of the patent, which in some degree had given rise to these doubts between the partners, soon appeared under a far more formidable aspect_that in connexion with the piracy it sought to prevent. Even before this satisfactory arrangement with his partners was completed, Mr. Wedgwood had accidentally learnt, through a Mr. Wilbraham of N antwich, a travelled gentleman of fortune who paid a visit to Etruria, that cheap Etruscan painted vases were in the market, which as far as possible were copied from Sir William Hamilton's great work. The bodies were made in Staflbrdshire, the painting effected in town by a man in Vine Street whom Mr. Wedg

CRAP. IV. PALMER OF HANLEY. 197

'wood knew,' and simultaneously with the vases appeared

Etruscan painted teapots and other articles. The pirates, as in the previous case of the black bas-relief vases, were Palmer of Hanley and his London partner Neale, whose shop was in Shoe Lane, or rather it should be said, Mrs. Palmer and Neale, for this bold, unscrupulous, clever woman was the real head of her husband's business, as she hired or dismissed the apprentices and men, superintended their work, and Without doubt brought feminine tact and subtlety to bear upon all the preliminaries necessary to piracy.

Upon Bentley's return to town, after this amicable settlement of the 'partnership question, fresh evidence came before him of this piratical industry. Mr. Wedgwood was written to, and he in turn consulted his solicitor. Acting upon Mr. Sparrow's advice, an injunction was served, as soon as possible, upon Neale and Palmer; and the business was put into the hands of a London attorney experienced in patent cases. The opinion of counsel was taken, and a trial seemed inevitable, though Mr. Wedgwood saw clearly that the plea urged by Palmer, that his vases were copied from the prints in Sir William Hamilton's great work, and not from those made by the patentee, would tell unfavourably upon a jury. Thus matters stood in February, 1771. It was necessary to obtain evidence, and Mr. Bentley was urged to pay a visit to Lord Mansfield, and to seek the aid of various powerful friends amongst the aristocracy. A hint had already been dropped relative to a compromise with

Palmer, through the kind ofiices of Mr. Bent, the surgeon of Newcastle; and in reference to this Mr. Wedgwood writes 198 A COMPROMISE PROPOSED. CHAP. IV.

to Bentley. 'I think Mr. P——'s buy" a share of the Pt is the only ground for a compromise without a submission, that could have been hit upon. They will never do us much harm, & will be a support in any future tryal. I rather feel myself inclined to this measure, but shall be guided by your sentiments. Mr. Bent says he is very certain that'Mr. P. had not any of our Etruscan vases to imitate before they had Mr. Hamilton's book, as Mrs. P. had not the least idea W' they were & told him she could not get any of ye vases. Another of our antagonists' pleas is, that as Mr. Hamilton's book was compiled & sent hither for the benefit particularly of the Potteries in England by his Majesty's envoy at Naples, it would be very hard if one person from the lucky circumstance of first meet8 with this book, shod therefore deprive every other Potter in the Kingdom from reaping that advantage by it which was intended by the public spirited author. Such arguments as these may have their weight with a jury.'1

After a good deal of boasting, shufiling, and procras-1 tination on the part of Palmer, whose wife would not permit him to act till she had made the other partner, Neale, easy on the subject, a compromise was effected; either party sharing in the patent, and dividing its cost, as well as the law charges between them. Mr. Wedgwood chose for his referee, at first Mr. Mills, a potter, but finally, Captain Warburton, so called from some yeomanry or militia exploits, but who, in reality, was one of the best potters of the day, and, unlike the generality p of them, a man of learning, and a true gentleman. He was of opinion, that whatever the Law might determine,

' Vedgwood to Bentley, undated, but referable to the spring of 1771.

C HAP. IV. THE REFEREES. 199

supposing the case were brought to trial, the Country would universally give the invention of Etruscan painting to Mr. Wedgwood. 'He told me at once,' adds

Mr. Wedgwood, 'the advantage our enamel painting has over the common glassy enamel, & does not doubt but it will come to be a valuable branch of business & a great acquisition to the trade-wo' you have expected that he she11 have instantly have told me, that the Glaze of enamel was not in Nature.'

The referee chosen by Mr. Palmer was the Rev. Dr. Middleton, curate of Hanley, a man remarkable in his day. He was learned, eloquent, and widely known for his probity, plain-speaking, and simplicity, and despising riches and ostentation, he was for ever reproving the vanities of his congregation. He was also an excellent chemist, well versed in all the technical details of the potter's art, and some twenty years previously had been, though publicly unacknowledged, in partnership with a. Shelton potter, named Warner Edwards, whose skill as to the components and preparation of enamel colours we have already referred to. Both referees seem to have acted in an admirable manner, though the duty thus confided to them was not only onerous but wearisome, as it extended over several months. They were evidently aware that the black body, apart from Mr. Wedgwood's modifications and improvements, had long been used by the majority of potters; and also that designs taken from works avowedly published for the improvement of art and artists in general, could not with any show of justice be monopolised by one manufacturer alone. It was another, and a far more ethical question—-the nicety of which was likely to escape an ordinary jury—-that Mr. Wedgwood's improvements 200 VEDGVVOOD'S ORIGINALITY. CRAP. IV.

and modifications, by rendering the composition more porcellaneous, constituted it, in fact, a new body, or that the nature of his enamel colours, and his method of burning them in, so as to form an integral part of the unglazed body, formed in fact a new branch of decorative art. The more obvious points were those on which a would be sure to decide, and adversely, as the referees judged, to Wedgwood's patent. They therefore counselled adjustment rather than recourse to law.

Their method of proceeding is not indicated, but they finally drew up an agreement, which Wedgwood and Palmer were to sign upon receiving the assent of their respective partners, Bentley and Neale; but it was with difficulty even then that Palmer could be brought to act in a straightforward manner. Eventually, the parties concerned and their respective evidences repaired to London, where, with the concurrence of Mr. Bentley, an agreement was signed. Generally speaking, the manufacturers were strongly in favour of Mr. Wedgwood's right in his patent; for, as he wrote to Bentley, ' they declare that they are certain whatever the Law may determine the Country will universally give the invention of Etruscan painting to me, & I might have what number of Potters I pleas'd to evidence that they never saw or heard of any such thing before I made it.'1

It was this entire originality of his invention, and the fact, that even if Palmer, and others as unscrupulous, could by aid of the specification prepare the encaustic colours, they had yet neither the taste nor skill to render them available to any high artistic purpose, which secured Mr. Wedgwood's interests far more effectually than any

' Vedgwood to Bentley, without date, 'though endorsed 'Etruria, Sunday Morning.'

CHAP. IV. THE QUESTION OF PATENTS. 201

Patent laws. The result proved thisfor though Palmer was undoubtedly a very skilful potter, nothing of his vases, or other piracies, are known at this day; whilst from what we have already seen in one of Mr. Wedgwood's letters in relation to the black bas-relief vases, they were, through the commonplace and hackneyed character of the figures, and the sameness of their disposal, rather a burlesque upon, than an imitation of, antique art. This is where originality may always safely rest upon itself; it is, if true, inimitable. In that generation it was not so keenly seen as at present, that Patent laws, as well as restrictive laws of all kinds, are at best but con-

cessions to the imperfection of human nature, and to defective education. We have simplified the former, and seek still to improve them; but the principle on which they rest is vicious, and, the sooner they are swept from the statute books, the better for all concerned, not only as to facility of invention, but as a test of private morality and the advance of true culture. It follows with the persistence of a law, that originators should be beset by imitators, just as in the natural world the finest organic forms are most liable to parasitical growth; and we may therefore assume, that every great inventive age will have its Hornblowers and its Palmers, men willing to profit by the exuberant bounty of other men's natural gifts. But statute laws will never effectually restrain evils of the kind. Tie up the pirate's right hand, and he will rob you with his left; as Watt found to his cost, and Wedgwood in his contests with Palmer. It would seem, that when the agreement entered into left the latter at liberty to make Etruscan vases at will, their inferiority both of form and design soon brought them to their true level in the market, and stayed production far more effectually than 202 WEDGWOOD'S MAGNANIMITY. CRAP. IV.

legal restrictions could have done. Yet, still undeterred, Palmer next pirated the seals and intaglios, and securing the services of Voyez, made as large a harvest as he could. He followed his great contemporary into the provincial towns, secured the patronage of rival tradesmen, and on one occasion at Bath, as we shall see, contemplated the hiring of rooms for the sale of his goods, Mr. Wedgwood having just opened show-rooms in Westgate Buildings. Ordinary men would have resented this unblushing and greedy pursuit of gain at their cost with bitter acrimony; but not so Wedgwood. Magnanimity was one of his conspicuous virtues, and even when still more deeply wronged, as in the case of the pecuniary delinquencies of young Mather, we shall see him tempering his just indignation with leniency, and a tender forethought not to bring hopeless ruin on the lad. In this case of Palmer,

though often much annoyed, he kept on speaking terms with him, and was even intimate with his relations, Mrs. Chatterley, and her brother Mr. Hollins. When the latter was ill at Bath, he visited him, rendered him various kindly services, and when the dying man went slowly away to London, it was with an introduction to some skilful physician, whom Mr. Wedgwood knew. Palmer must not be taken as a type of the high class potters of his day. Jacob Warburton, Elijah Mayer, then just settling down in Hanley after his ten years' absence in Holland, John Adams, Josiah Spode, and many others, may be reckoned amongst the wise and honourable men, who by their zealous spirit of improvement and keen industry, did such noble service for the social progress of their country. He was rather a pliant instrument in the hands of an unscrupulous partner and a masculine minded wife, to whom gain was of-more account than principle.

CIIAP. IV. BIRTH OF THOMAS VVEDGWOOD. 203

When this unpleasant business was at length settled, Mr. Wedgwood and Bentley took a few days' tour into the south of England, probably on business connected with supplies of clay and moor-stone; and when the former had returned to Burslem, he wrote thus to his friend, ' I find Mr. Palmer like a true simpleton & something else, gives it out publicly that both you & I were fully convinc'd that we had not the least chance of trying the Patent—that our Council, our Lawyer, & ourselves acknowledg'd it!-What the man can mean by telling such barefaced lies, & which must now operate, if they operate at all, as much to his injury as our own, I cannot conceive, unless it be that a false pride or shame has got the better of truth, interest, & every other principle with him. It will be necessary to know what qu"Y of Etruscan painted vases, &c. We have sold for a given time past, in order to lay some state of the trade Mr. Palmer is to pay for before the Referees, & the sooner you send me that acet the better.' 1

It was during this contest with Palmer

on the question of the patent, that Mr. Wedgwood received an accession to his family in the birth of his fourth and last son, who was born some time in April, 1771, and was named Thomas after his paternal grandfather, uncle, and cousins. He was the fifth Thomas Wedgwood in a direct line. We hear no particulars of his birth or infancy; though from the first he appears to have been a delicate child, and derived probably from both his parents—who, prior to his birth, had suffered greatly from impaired health—those seeds of organic disease, which in an after day rendered life an indescribably weary burden, and deprived the world

' Vedgwood to Bentley, date of postmark, July I0.
204 AN EARLY STUDENT. CHAP. 1V. of the fruit of mental powers which, under happier circumstances, would have rendered the name of Wedgwood as illustrious in philosophy as in art. When we first catch a glimpse of him he was, as we shall see, a merry little fellow, full of drollery and fun, and the life of the household. There were no indications then, that, before he was twenty, he would be poring into the deepest secrets of nature, particularly those relative to space, light, and heat; be the hardest of students, or, conjointly with his father's chemist, Alexander Chisholm, be rendering the laboratory at Etruria a place at which, for scientific reasons, the savans of our own day would cast back their gaze, to penetrate, if possible, into some of the early mysteries of the photographic art effected there. But, from the first, Dr. Darwin thought highly of the boy's mental powers; and happily Josiah Wedgwood had passed away before bodily disease had rendered all but useless this son's extraordinary mental powers, or unnerved the assiduous hand which had served him as devotedly in matters relative to art, as in chemical experiments.

CHAPTER V.
VEDGWOOD'S FRIENDS.
'W'E must again see Mr. Wedgwood amidst his scientific and literary friends. In Nov. 1769, James Keir, the translator of Macquer's Dictionary of Chemistry,

and subsequently the author of other treatises and works, became known to him. i' Dear Wedgewood,' wrote Dr. Darwin, ' I have the Pleasure to introduce to your acquaintance Captain James Keir, an old Friend of mine, a successful cultivator of both Arts and Arms. He begs the Favour of seeing your elegant manufactory & hopes to meet our common Friend, the Philosopher, Mr. Whitehurst at your House. The Civilities you shew Capt. Keir will be received by Dear Sir your afiec" humble Ser', E. Darwin.'1 The hospitality thus sought was generously awarded. Keir saw the manufactory, and was shown the plan of the future Etruria Hall, which, as we have seen, he greatly admired. Some date later Dr. Darwin wrote again. ' Capt. Keir is at present at Birmingham. He desired I would say all the fine Things I could think of to thank Mrs. Wedgwood for the Trouble He gave her; of whom indeed he speaks very highly, & was much entertain'd with your manufactory.' 2 From this date 1 Darwin to Vifedgwood, Novem- I ' Darwin to VVedgwo0d, undated; be: 8, 1767. but referable to a few days later.

208 KEIR, SMALL, AND WATT. CHAD. V. the acquaintance ripened, and both at the house of Dr. Small at Birmingham, and at Soho, Mr. Wedgwood occasionally met Keir, who in the opinion of Watt was 'a mighty chemist and a very agreeable man.' The experimental track Wedgwood was at this time and subsequently engaged upon must have made his occasional intercourse with Keir singularly interesting, as it was from Macquer's dictionary in its French form that he had derived, through Bentley's translation of the necessary passages, some portion of his knowledge relative to the spaith fusible, or term ponderosa. Ever since the publication of Reaumur's analyses by the French Academy of Science in 1727 and 1729, the potters and chemists of France and Germany had been incessant in their endeavours to discover native materials for the fabrication of a true porcelain, and none of their services had been more eminent than in 'thus direct-

ing attention to the earthy carbonates.

Dr. Small, a native of Scotland, had emigrated to America, and, after passing some years there, failing health necessitated his return, and he came to England in 1765. In America he had known Franklin, and when resolving to settle in Birmingham to practise his profession, Franklin, who was then in London, gave him a letter of introduction to Matthew Boulton. The result was worthy of the introducer; for the new physician, whose merit in every way was eminent, soon drew around him a large circle of admiring friends, amongst whom, in addition to Boulton, were Keir, Darwin, Wedgwood, Garbett and others. Just prior to the date Keir had been thus made known to Wedgwood through Darwin's introduction, another illustrious man visited Birmingham for the first time. This was James Watt_who had been

C11AP.V. WATT VISITS SOHO. 209 passing some months in London, on business relative to a canal for uniting the rivers Forth and Clyde. Business with Mr. Garbett, Dr. Roebuck's former partner was doubtless the ostensible purpose which led him to the chief town of the Midland Counties; but it is not improbable that beneath lay some latent motives in relation to the scientific ends he had in view. Once within this magic circle of philosophic culture, and industrial energy, friend begot friend, and Small and Watt were drawn together by instinctive sympathy. Watt had a retiring gentle nature, his scientific difficulties were numerous, and hope to a temperament like his, shone at most times darkly in the future; whilst Small was a man of delicate sympathy, keen perceptions, and suggestive energy.-He was also deeply versed in science, and thus saw intuitively that Vatt's recent great discovery of the separate condenser had solved an essential problem; and that henceforth the difficulties connected with the use of steam, as a motive power, were mechanical rather than scientific. The natures of such men were sure to coalesce; for sympathy even more than interest, is a governing power in the moral world.

Boulton was at this time from home, but Dr. Small, in conjunction with Mr. Fothergill, took Watt over the great manufactory at Soho. Though he may have conceived it, the latter had never yet seen labour under so masterly an organization, machinery so fitting to the ends sought, or metallic productions of so exquisite a character; and the wish was his, if expressed to no other person than to Small, that he could work out all his scientific conceptions relative to his engine in an atmosphere so congenial, and where perfection of constructive detail could be ensured. l'rom Birmingham Watt proceeded to Lichfield, vet. ll. 1' where he made the acquaintance of Dr. Darwin, and to whom he seems to have imparted the plan of his improvements in the steam-engine, under a promise of secrecy. Watt does not appear to have met with Wedgwood on this occasion; but Darwin, without breaking trust, made the latter well-acquainted, by description, with his new friend—and the probabilities ensured of the steam-engine being eventua.lly brought into use as an easily managed motive power; thus superseding water or less governable agencies. In the August of the following year, 1768, VVatt again visited Soho, where he stayed a fortnight. The philosophical friends Keir, Small, Darwin and some others met on this occasion, but Mr. Wedgwood must have been again absent, for he had not as yet sufficiently recovered from the amputation of his leg to travel far from home. It may have been two or three years later—that W'att and Wedgwood first met—but the acquaintanceship thus begun, only ended with the life of the latter. Meanwhile the Lichfield doctor strengthened in his belief, that steam was the motive agent best suited to the necessities of his , friend's manufactory--said less and less of the model windmill——whilst often dropping hints that Watt's great work was not at a standstill, ' Mr. W'att's Fire-Engine I believe goes on, but I don't know at what rate " ' Your VVindmill sleeps at my house, but shall be sent you, if you wish it, but I should advise you to wait the WheelFire-Engine, which goes

on slowly.' 2

During 1770-1771, Darwin frequently consulted Vcdgwood on other mechanical and engineering topics. The Company concerned in tlic Wichnor Iron-works, were

' Darwin to 'e(lgwood, l)cce1uber 'J, 1770. 2 Ibid. October 1771. '

CIIAP. V. I)ARVIN'S PROJECTS. 211 advised by Brindley to set up aimill for grinding flints, but apparently both Wedgwood's and Darwin's opinion ran counter to the scheme, for they considered, that as soon as the whole of the Grand Trunk Canal was completed, that the Potteries would be supplied with flints from Liverpool, Bristol, and Hull. In the succeeding year 1771, a still more important matter occupied the doctor's thoughts, and Wedgwood was his recipient and adviser in all its details. The design of making a navigable canal from the-Grand Trunk at Fradley . Heath to the city of Lichfield had been laid aside, for the estimated expense was far greater than any anticipated profits. Yet some means of easy conveyance for coals, lime, and other heavy goods was the need of the town, and Darwin proposed to make a small canal at his own cost. A considerable correspondence followed on this subject, and Wedgwood as locally patriotic as his friend, seems to have bestirred himself in propitiating Brindley and John Gilbert towards the scheme. It appears however to have dropped to the ground, and ultimately a canal on a larger scale, connected Lichfield with the great artificial water-ways of the kingdom.

We have already seen that in the spring of 1769, Wedgwood during a visit to Soho had settled many important matters with Matthew Boulton, laid the foundation for improving their respective manufactures, and for extending the sales of goods produced, whether these were of pottery, metal, or both combined, to every corner of Europe. In one branch thus newly proposed, that of finishing ornamental articles in pottery with works of metal, and occasionally printing upon them with purple, gold and other colours, they beheld a wide field opening 212 ARTISTIC COMBI-

NATION. Can. V.

before them. But VVedgwood, true to his instincts as an artist, and strong undoubtedly in the faith that there were harmonies and capacities in the materials with which he dealt, for effects not only of the highest and most ideal kind, but sufficient to stand alone, went leisurely on his way, as appears. quite clear in this combination affair, whilst Boulton and Fothergill took it up at once with characteristic energy. A Triton, a figure, or a candelabrum, went at first occasionally from Etruria to Soho, for its metal ornaments; but the demand upon Etruria for unornamented vases soon became very large, and soon far greater than could be possibly supplied. It was at this date Boulton and Fothergill took M.-Spermont of the Chelsea works for a time into their employ, and contemplated the manufacture of vases for themselves. 'I told you,' wrote Wedgwood to Bentley, 'Mr.-Cox came here yesterday. We have had very little time together yet, as Saturday is the busiest of my busy days, however he told me he call'd at Mess" Boulton's & Fothergill's to look at their Manufacture. They shew'd him how to make buttons, & watch chains, but W0" not permitt him to see their vase work, & only shew'd him a few pairs of finish'd ones—I 'find they are affronted at my not complying with their orders for the vases to be mounted, & likewise for a pair for each sort, colour, &c. which Mr. Boulton desir'd I wod send him as I got them up. This they mention'd to Mr. Cox, & told him that though I had refused 'them they had been offer'd the vases for mount" by several Potters, but were now determin'd to make the black Vases (Earthenware vases they took care to tell him) themselves, & were building works for that purpose! If this be true, I expect every day to hear of their offering some of our principal

CRAP. V. RIVALRY. 213 hands two or three hundreds a year to manage the works for them. Mr. Cox thinks farther from what he heard them say, & the hints they gave, that they are to be concerned with Cox of Shoe Lane, they talked to him in the stile and manner of Rivals to us, big in their own conceits, with some mighty blow their uplifted hands were prepared to let fall upon us. So stand firm my friend & let us support this threatened attack like veterans prepar'd for every shock, or change of fortune that can befall us. If we must fall, if Etruria cannot stand its ground, but must give way to Soho, & fall before her, let us not sell the victorie too cheap, but main-. tain our ground like men, & endeavour even in our defeat to share the Laurels with our Conquerors. It doubles my courage to have the first manufacturer in England to incounter with. T he match likes me well . I like the man—I like his spirit—He will not be a mere driveling copyist like the antagonists I have hitherto had, but will venture to step out of the lines upon occasion, & afford us some diversion in the combat. A room is taken in Pell Mell, & there they are to exhibit this winter. If everything we do & produce must first be criticis'd upon so severely by the nobles, & instantly copied by the artists, our rivals—Should we not proceed with some prudent caution, & reserve, & not shew either one, or the other too much at once, to glut the curiosity & spoil the choice of the former, or give the latter so large a field to fight us in. I wo' propose then for the winter sale of vases four species only, viz. Blue Pebble, Variegated Pebble, Black Etruscan, Etruscan E/zcaastic. These with the variations of sizes, forms and ornaments, Gilding, veining, Bassreliefs &c. &c., will produce business enough for all the hands we can possibly get together, & I think 214 PRECAUTIONS. CRAP. V.

variety enough for all our reasonable customers. You shall have plain vases enough, & it is needless for me to say you cannot get too many painted. Mr. Crofts you say must begin at home. If he does get a few done there, pray do not shew them at all in the saleroom, nor shew them to any but thwe you perfectly know, for depend upon it, if you do not take this precaution, they will be here in a week after they are shewn in the rooms. I think you shod make a point of shewing and selling these your-

self only, lock them up, do not let Parker see them, remember Voyez is in T own. & the warehousemcu she'1 not have it in their power to shew a pair of these Vases for sale. They may, without offence tell any customer, that you take that branch of business upon yourself. They will think them the more precious. You can tell them the history of the piece and all about it, & let them know that we do not make good things by chance, or at random. It will baulk the spies for some time at least, who are daily haunting the rooms, & answer many other valuable purposes. I shall be glad to have your thoughts upon this subject, you'l easily observe the foundation of my arguments is money geting. Take that away and they all drop to the ground. Instead of this, if you substitute fame (and my bosom begins, and always does glow with a generous warmth at the idea), I say, if instead of money geting, you substitute Fame & the good of the manufacture at large for our principle of action, then we shod do just the contrary of what I have been recommending. Make all the Good, Fine & New things we can immediately, & so far from being afraid of other People geting our patterns, we should Glory in it, throw out all the hints we can, & if possible have all the Artists in Europe working after our models. This wod be noble, & would suit both our dispositions & sentiments much better than all the narrow mercenary selfish trammels. How do you feel yourself my friend, have you forgot how our hearts burned zvithin us, when we convers'd upon this subject in our way from Liverpool to Prescot? We were then perswaded that this open generous plan would not only be most con-1 genial to our hearts, & best feelings, but in all proba. bility might best answer our wishes in pecuniary advantages, & for the time I well remember we agreed to pursue it. Do you think when our principles were known, the Nobility would not still more make it a point to patronize and encourage Men who acted upon such different principles to the rest of mankind? the tradeing & mercantile part of them at least, When they are wit-

ness to our bestowing so much pains and expence in the improvement of a capital Manufacture, nay in creating a new one, & that not for our particular emolument only, but that we generously lay our works open to be imitated by other Artists and manufacturers for the good of the community at large. This wod certainly procure us the goodwill of our best customers, and place us in a very advantageous light to the Public eye. VVe should no doubt be esteemed as antique, & as great curiositys as any of the vases we fabricate, and perhaps upon the whole, this scheme might bring us as much prqflit as loss-with respect to myself, there is nothing relating to business I so much wish for as being released from these degrading slavish chains, these mean selfish fears of other people copying my works_-how many new and good things has, and still does this principle prevent my bringing to light. Dare you step forth my dear 216 DECIDED NOBLY. CHAD. V. frcl & associate & share the risque & honour of acting on these enlarged principles, or do you think it safer, more prudent and advisable to follow the plan laid down in my first sheet. One of them we must adopt & to be consistent, abide by.' 1

Bentley true to his own nature and that of his friend counselled it would seem, as fearless and as generous a revelation of what their genius and art had effected or were likely to effect as was consistent with ordinary prudence. ' We have now 1 think ' replied Wedgwood to the letter which gave this counsel ' nearly fixed the plan of proceedings for this Winter, & with respect to Rivalship, We will cast all dread of that behind our backs, treat it as a base & vanquished enemy, and not bestow another serious thought upon it.' 2 This was worthy of the chiefs of Etruria; and without doubt was shared in by Matthew Boulton although as we shall see, he occasionally gave an exaggerated colouring to facts, when such related to the vastness of his manufacturing resources, or to the glory of Soho. Here was an essential difference in the temperament and character of the men; and it obviously affected the products of their rmpective arts. In the ornamental wares of Soho, there was mo1'e show, daring innovation in form, and startling contrast of colouring. On the contrary VVedgwood's artistic aim throughout was subordination, and if we may so express it, subjugation of effect to effect. The same principle

'ruled him morally. Occasionally he mounts his hobby, and we have outbursts of enthusiasm as to the possibilities and glories of his art; but in a stricter sense, we never find exaggeration, or an overstepping of the bounds 1 Vedgwo0d to Bentley, September 27, 1769. 2 Ibid. October 1, 1769. ' of modesty and truth. 'Etruria is never landed, and if great work is done, it is always with this proviso, that greater lies behind. Thus the rivalry between Wedgwood and Boulton, stimulated only to noble ends. If Fothergill and Cox, threatened, and hinted, and vaunted like foolish partizans, the friendship of their great masters remained uninterrupted; for like heroes and soldiers; if one advanced a step in the mighty industrial march, the other saw the vantage and followed quickly..The arts in such hands were sure to flourish. Referring to some vases in bad taste, though copied from a book called ' Stella,' and which he had presented to Mrs. Boulton, Wedgwood writes to Bentley 'We are every day suffering more disgrace at Mr. Bolton's from some of my first vases (compar'd, as they must be by all his company) with those of Soho! I could not bear this situation, & the odious comparisons they must give rise to, and the only plausible way of moving them, was to oflbr to replace them, which I did with Etruscan painted ones. I wish you wo' send 4 from London & the sooner the better, for we are suffering daily from the present, which I make no doubt you will feel as strongly as myself.' 1

Boulton's wide spread commercial relations with foreign countries was, as we have seen, of great advantage to Wedgwood; and at this date, June 1770, Mr. Baumgartner a German merchant with whom the former had had previous relations took means to introduce the

metallic ornamented vases of Soho, and the Etruscan painted vases of Etruria into Italy. To show the liberal spirit which animated these men in a mer 218 LIGHT BEARING ORNAMENTS. Cn,P.'. ca-ntile point of view, they both unknown to each other supplied Mr. Baumgartner on the terms that he should have the liberty of returning within a limited time such vases as would not sell.1 The friends were also aiding each other in their respective arts. Boulton was making branches for fluted vases and taps for earthenware cisterns; and Mr. Wedgwood on his way with his father-in-law to London to see the minor Russian services went by Soho, to carry Boulton a Triton and some vases? The Triton was for a light bearing figure, and from this date and long subsequently this class of ornaments contributed to a considerable trade between Etruria and Soho. They were of every form and cha . racter. Tritons, sea-nymphs, Y7-_ 9 naiads, bacchantes, chimaerae, __ draped figures male and female, nucopias variously supported. Boot as we have seen was the earliest modeller of Tritons. Mrs. Landre occasionally modelled a naiad or a sea nymph, but when the candelabra were to be on a large or magnificent scale, the genius of Bacon was appealed 'I, _ _ = to.3 Although not probably co' pied from one of the finest examples, the accompanying illustration (fig. 41.) drawn from an temples, rocky plinths, and cor- _ old order book will give an idea of the character of this class of figures. It is meant to represent leptune or 111S
' lbid. July 17 70.
1' Mems. June 6, 1770.
 ' Vedgwood to Bentley, May 12, 1 1770.
__'-_ attendant Triton, though certainly a cornucopia seems out of place in the arms of a watergod. A shell would have been more in artistic keeping, if we may presume at all, that a deity just emerged from the ocean, a shell newly taken from the sea-shore or the sea-cave, or indeed any object connected with an element the antithesis of light and heat, could be in the truest sense a fitting sup-

port for the appliance of light in any of its forms. Here was an artistic error impossible in an age of high culture; and one into which Wedgwood occasionally fell in spite of his exquisite taste, his sound judgment, and his strong objective faculty for relating an effect to its true cause. The chimaera as also given (fig. 42.) is in far better 7 _ taste because it belongs to an imaginative region of art, in (M 4,) mm_m__,mRm which the fancy plays with ""'""'"" truth without mimicking her too closely. 1

From an early date in his artistic career Wedgwood had been acquainted with James Stuart the author of the Antiquities of Athens. We have seen him lending Wedgwood many choice works of art, and at a later day, had Palmer's infringement of Wedgwood's patent been brought to trial, his opinion was to be appealed to. Stuart in fact knew everybody. He had made a great literary 1 Some ofv the light bearing orna- a tripod and a air of fluted candlements in Mr. Mayer's collection are 1 sticks in black nsnltea. of surpassing beauty. Particularly I reputation by his first volume of the Antiquities of Athens which appeared in 1762, but since then he had slumbered over this great work, and devoted his time and eminent abilities, to designs for public and private buildings in the Grecian style. A false taste; when we re collect that porticoes and open colonnades are but little suited to our humid and northern climate, or that our forefathers had raised ecclesiastical, and in some instances domestic edifices which to this hour are unparalleled for harmonious beauty, or for the alliance of purpose and effect. Vedgwood rarely visited London without seeing 'Athenian Stuart' as he was called. This was particularly the case through the years 1770-1771 whilst the

CnAP.V. VISIT TO OXFORD. 221 brothers Adams were covering a large space on the south side of the Strand, with various buildings, of which the Adelphi formed one range, after designs furnished by Stuart.

The enormous and rapid increase of their trade in ornamental wares, had soon shown Wedgwood and his partner that the rooms in Newport Street were unfitted from size and want of sufficient light for either the reception of a large crowd of visitors, or to the display of goods of a decorative character. It therefore seems that when Stuart, or the Adarnses opened the question of adapting a building or erecting one in the Adelphi, which should fully meet Wedgwood and Bentley's requirements, the idea was entertained. VVe first hear of this in December 1770, when Stuart, who had many aristocratic friends and patrons in Staffordshire-Mr. Anson of Shugborough, and Mr. Sneyd in particular-took part of the chaise, in which Mr. Wedgwood made his return journey from a business visit to town. Of this journey we have a charming glimpse: 'I need not tell you that I had a most agreeable journey home. We breakfasted at Oxford 011 Friday (to gain which we rode 20 miles in the Dark o'n Thursday evening) and had an high feast in looking, over the Collection of Paintings, & drawings at Christ Church. I mean a few of them, for there are an immense number of drawings; enough to take up a summer's week to run them over. This we have leave to do, and to off-trace any of them. I saw but few vases that I had not seen before, but suppose there are many more, & some I saw were new and very good. The next morning we breakfasted at Woodstock. Looked over the fine paintings at Blenheim; with which, accompanied with my cmnpaliioifs learned rciiiarks, I was equally delighted 222 ROOMS IN THE ADELPHI. CRAP. V.

& edifyed. We lay at Warwick that evening, tho' it was late before we got there, & on Sunday we dined at Soho. Mr. Boulton has promis'd to make us some branches, such as I have fixed upon, & amongst other things show'd me some bodys & necks, made of Porcelaine, colour'd green, to be mounted in Or Inoleau for Tea kitchens, but he wish'd we wo" make him some of them in Etruscan painted ware, which I promis'd to do, one of which Mr. Stewart has bespoke for Mrs. Montague, instead of a plated one he was to order for

her. They have 35 Chacers at work, and will have a superb show of vases for the spring, but believe he has not yet determin'd upon the mode of sale. He (Mr. Boulton) has spoke to Mr. Adams for rooms at Adelphi, & professes a good deal of pleasure that we were likely to be such near neighbours, but Mr. Stewart has put us both of till he shews us a ground plan of the houses he mention'd, which is to be in a few days. They are in the front of Adelphi, betwixt & the Strand, the very houses Mr. Adams's want ' to purchase to complete their plan. I was sorry to hear this, as it may have disagreeable consequences betwixt Mr. Stewart or Mr. Adams and us; but this must be left to time & circumstances. Mr. Stewart & I debated the matter at full length, whether it wo'l or W0" not be best for both partys that Boulton & Fothergill & Wedgwood & Bentley shod have their show rooms near to each other, or if this alliance sho'i throw an advantage into either scale which W0" have it. We agreed that those customers who were more fond of show & glitter than fine forms, & the appearance of antiquity, wecl buy Soho vases, and that all who could feel the effects of a fine outline & had any veneration for Antiquity we" be with us. I forgot to tell you that Mr. Boulton was making an immense large

CHAP. V. A MEETING OF FRIENDS. 223

Tripod for Mr. Anson to finish the top of Demosthenes Lanthorn, building there from Mr. Stewart's design. The Legs were cast, & weighed about 5 C" W", but the workmen, stagger'd at the bowl, & did not know which way to set about it; a Council of the workmen was call'd, & every method of performing this wonderfull work can vassed over. They concluded by shaking their heads, & ended where they begun. I then could hold no longer, but told them very gravely they were all wrong, they had totally mistaken their Talents and their metals; such great works should not be attempted in Copper or in Brass. They must call in some able Potter to their assistance, and the work might be completed. Would you think it? they took

me at my word, & I have got a fine jobb upon my hands in consequence of a little _ harmless boasting. Mr. Stewart said he knew Mr. Anson wo'l glory in having the Arts of Soho and Etruria united in his Tripod, & that it W0'l be a feather in our Caps which that good gentleman would delight in taking every opportunity to shew to our advantage. So this matter stands at present, but Mr. Boulton, Dr. Darwin, and I are to dine with Mr. Anson on New-Year's Day & shall talk the matter over again.' 1

This hospitable meeting took place, and over good Christmas cheer, it was arranged that Soho should pro vide the models of the tripod, and a fluted vase to stand upon it, and Mr. Wedgwood superintend their copies in the black basaltes body. A little later 1n the month, Dr. Darwin was made the medium of another invitation to Shugborough of Wedgwood, Boulton, Keir, 'and Bentley, if he is in the country;'2 but Mr.

1 "edgw0od to Bentley, l)ecem-'-' Darwin to 'edgvood, J nnilary her 24 to 26, 1770., 15, 1771. 224 LORD CHETWYND. CRAP. V.

Wedgwood was unable to attend. He had met with a. slight hurt which rendered him unable to move his artificial leg. ' But I am now got well, and go abroad again,' -he wrote to Stuart, 'though I am not fond of doing so in frosty weather, being not so expert a footman as I have been, & a slip or accident to my better Leg, might lay 1ne up for good & all, but I hope we shall have some open weather soon, & intend myself the pleasure of waiting upon you the first opportunity.' Mr. Wedgwood met Stuart subsequently in London, and much business followed, though the details are lost to us.1

One point referred to a monument to Lord Viscount Chetwynd, the father of Deborah Chetwynd, Mr. Wedgwood's 'good patroness.' His lordship, who had only succeeded to the family honours in 1767, died April 3, 1770, at an advanced age; and his daughter, who seems to have been tenderly attached to him, wishe'd naturally to hand down some memorial of him to future genera_tions. To none could she more fittingly apply than to

Athenian Stuart,.whom she was constantly meeting in society, or to the great potter whom she had helped to render famous, and who was at once her friend and country neighbour. He had also known Lord Chetwynd intimately, and more than once speaks of having met his lordship riding with his »daughters into Newcastle; the same gay, handsome, courtly, pleasant gentleman he had ever been., though time had naturally bowed his stately figure, and silvered locks once so celebrated for their raven blackness, and for winning female eyes and hearts in the somewhat lax courts of George I. and George II. Lord Chetwynd was buried in the family vault at

CHAP. V. THE CIIETVVYND MONUMENT. 225

Ashley, a small rural village near Market Drayton, 'in Shropshire, and hither Mr. VVedgwo0d journeys in March, 1772, to measure the walls for the intended monument. In July he commissions Bentley to present his oomph. ments to Mr. Stuart, and to learn as soon as may be, 'the size of the vase for the monument, the height and diameter.'1 Later in the autumn both vase and monument are erected, leave being obtained from the Rev. Mr. Mould, the rector of the church, whose residence is in Leicestershire.

1 Vedgwood to Bentley, July 13, 1772. VOL. II. Q 226 DIANA CHETVVYNUS LETTER. CHAP. V.

Looking at what had been achieved by our race centuries before in the province of monumental sculpture, and in materials often the simplest and coarsest of their kind, the Chetwynd monument, though far from pretentious, does justice neither to Athenian Stuart nor to Wedgwood. Beneath the church wall to which it is fixed, is even at this day a rood-screen of great beauty; ' and Wedgwood, if left to the promptings of his own taste, to his native English insular genius, would have doubtless ' effected something in good keeping with what was around; but overruled by the

classical leanings of his friend, who must drag in his Grecian orders and similitudes, let the accompaniments be ever so heterogeneous, the result is entire failure. The monument, though composed of white and yellow marble veined, is bald without even the grace which accompanies simplicity; and the vase which crowns it, though proportionally well-formed, may assuredly be pronounced the ugliest which ever issued from the ornamental works at Etruria. This was probably the fecling of the ' good patroness,' though the fashion of the day was all in favour of the so-called ' classic.' A term, however, which many of its patrons would have had some difficulty in defining; for, on'

January 19 in the succeeding year, 1773, she wrote briefly as follows to Wedgwood, ' Sir, I beg the Favour of you to let me know the Estimate of the small Monument bespoke in memory of my late Father. When I see you I shall mention some things that I am sure you will not be pleased with in relation to it, but let it rest n t e monumen 18 a an ym-' a e um or ma wesm not scription. Round this, on the fillet see his like again.',

CHAP. V. HER CHARACTER. 227 till we meet. I hope Mrs. VVedgwood has her health better since her Return from Bath. Thank God, mine is much mended. I am,

On the back of this letter Mr. Wedgwood adds, ' By the above My Dear Friend will see that something has happen'd respecting the monument to displease my Good Patroness, at which I am very much concern'd, but have not the least idea what it is, & as she says " let it rest till we meet," I believe you must not mention it to her, unless she tells it to you first.'1

Whatever it was that had displeased the gracious lady, whether it related to the cost, taste, or general management of the monument, it was soon explained away, for her good offices were as unceasing to Wedgwood and Bentley as heretofore. She was probably poor; none of the servants of the thrifty Queen were adequately paid for onerous ser-

vices, and the estimate may have exceeded her means; but she shines throughout, a fine specimen of an aristocratic gentlewoman. Highly bred, dignified, courteous, easily accessible, singularly well educated for a period when the daughters of duehesses wrote ill, and spelt worse than kitchenmaids at the present day, she acted for Royalty in all business matters with great tact and judgment. Doubtless she possessed many of the most beautiful masterpieces of

Vedgwood's art, and we know that she remained his friend till her death in. 1782.

The negociations with respect to a warehouse and show-rooms in the Adelphi were carried on throughout 1771,and a large part of 1772. At first the plans did not satisfy the partners, the estimate of expense was heavy, and when at length some of these objections were removed, and a settlement seemed in prospect, the houses were sold and there the matter ended. But in the interval Boulton had hired rooms temporarily in the Adelphi and opened a show of goods manufactured at Soho. Cox, the dealer in China, followed his example, as did also the proprietors of the porcelain works at Derby and Vllorcester, and thus, in the spring of 1772, the area of the Adelphi-covered as it yet was with building materials, and houses in various stages of progress—bccame for a time the fashionable resort of the day. Referring to the effect of these sales Mr. Wedgwood wrote, ' Under the humble idea that the dazzling profusion of these respective shows will need relief I have some hopes for our black Etruscan and Grecian vases still, & as I expect the golden-9-urfeit will rage with you higher than ever this spring, I shall almost tremble even for a gold listel amongst your Vases, & would advise you by all means to provide a Curtain for your Pebble ware shelves, which you may open or shut, inlarge or diminish the shew of gilding as you find your customers affected. In earnest I believe a Curtain before the shelves of Pebble Vases would be very proper on several accounts. It would moderate the-shew at the first entrance—hide the gilding from those who think it a defect, & prevent the Gold from tarnishing.' ' Vedgwood at this date was 1 'edg'ood tn Bentley, April 11, lTTZ?.

Cs.r. V. VVORKS FOR PATRONS. 2:29 somewhat sensitive on the question of show and glitter, for Sir William Hamilton had used the term ' offensive gilding ' in one of his letters, and remarked upon its utter unlikeness, as a decorative effect, to that subdued harmony of colour which was one of the strong objective truths of antique art.1

The years 1770-1772 abounded in artistic labours of great beauty and importance. Royalty gave abundant orders. A new enamelled dinner service was made for the King; of this the borders were edged with purple husks, and the surfaces strewn with exquisite floral sprigs. It was on show to the public for a month. The Princess Dowager of Wales commissioned a dessert service, and ware of different kinds was sent to Berlin for the King of Prussia. Rockingham vases, thirty-one inches high, were made for various patrons; and the good Lord Bessborough, besides soliciting his Irish friends to patronise Wedgwood, lent him porphyry vases of great beauty to model from. Large vases were in hand for Lord March, and in May, 1770, modellers were at work at the Duke of Richmond's town-house, taking impressions of the handles of vases, as also the handles and spouts of teapots of Oriental porcelain. In this year we find that Greek and Roman heads are modelled from coins and medals, and Dacier's work supplies those of the kings of England. At this date also the Etruscan painted vases were dispatched to Italy through the agency of M. Baumgarten, a German merchant; and Lord Shelburne, who visited Etruria at the close of the year, bought three Etruscan vases as a present for the English envoy at Lisbon; 1 Sir V. Hamiltoxfs criticism on ' tawdry effect of the gilding in conthe gilding of the pebble vases was ' 'unction with the veined and man-bled in good taste. No one can see these odies. vases without being struck with the g having already strongly recom-

mended that gentleman to introduce Wedgwood's and Bentley's ornamental ware at court and amongst the Portuguese nobility, many of whom were already possessols of beautiful articles in cream colour.

Amongst the small bas-reliefs we find the marriage of Cupid and Psyche, and Mr. Wedgwood was again busy with his improvements of the white biscuit body. Writing to Bentley, in June 1770, he says, 'The Duke of Marlborough's Gems will be fine subjects for us, I shall be very glad to see them.'

Coward was at this date engaged upon one of the finest and largest models ever executed for Wedgwood and Bentley. It underwent several improvements, and was seemingly perfected in 1772. It was derived from an antique source,' and its reduced copy, from the De la Rue collection, will give the reader some idea of the size and importance of many of the works in the black basaltes body. The original is 15 inches long, 9% inches high, and the repose of the figure, and the perfection of the modelling, render it equal to the finest sculpture. The beholder can scarcely realise that it is formed of clay, or has passed through. the purgatory of the furnace. Other work of the kind was in hand. ' We have made a Boy (Autumn) from the mould Hoskins sent us,' writes Mr. Wedgwood to Bentley, ' but cannot find any pedestal or ground for it to lye upon, & that sent for the infant Hercules we cannot make it fit. The making of these figures out of such moulds as those sent us is an endless 1 The original was at that date in 264; and in.Iutii =i, Statue Antiche, the collection of the Grand Duke at y plate 151. This last engraving is Florence. References to it are to admirable. be found in Spouses l'ol _vnic1is, p.

CRAP. V. _ ARTISTIC SOURCES. 231 work, for they are all to be model'. d over again, & our Statuaries are not qualified for such a task.' 1

As already observed, Wedgwood and Bentley made literature alike an important source of designs, and their own artistic culture. Lord Cathcart gave Mr. Wedgwood the first volume of Hamil-

ton's 'Etruscan Antiquities;' and the partners paid Cadell six guineas for the second and third volumes? When floral designs of more than ordinary beauty were required, they employed an artist named Chivers; as also resorted to Marianne's noble work on floral decoration, and to that of an English artist named Ranby. Spilsbury, also an artist, and Shaw,:1 first-class gilder, were amongst the decorative hands of this period.

In the spring or summer of 1770 we first hear of Mr. Wedgwood sitting for his likeness. This was to an ingenious Chinese inodeller, who had arrived in this country the previous autumn, and becoming a sort of fashion, received a large share of the capricious patronage of the time. Interested as he was in China and many of its productions, it seems not improbable that Wedgwood, accompanied by Bentley, first sought the artist as much to learn something of his country, as to see his modelling, and that a promise to sit to him naturally followed. We have no intimation if this promise was kept, although it 1 'edgwood Bentley, Aug.24, Fol'.; mid to these were soon after 177. i added lluseum_ Odescaleum, sive

'1 In August, 1770, the books be-_ 'lliesaurus Antiql. Genimarum a longingto the firm are set down by Bartol_o, _,Rome_, 7730; Maflie and.Ir. Vedgwoodasfo_llo_vs:—' Hn.mil-Ago_stini _s Gemnis, I'ol'.; Grnvelot's ton's Etruscan Antiquities; Gemms Antiqu1_t _ies; De §i_lde gamma AnDelin, by Elizabeth Cherron, small tique, 1'/O'3; Agostini, by I,-ro'io'ius; FOR, Smm-fig Athens'; Count Ca-Perrico sbtiitiies; _Fie_oi_'oni' s(ve_uuis; lus's Antiq'. 3 vols.; 'lemple of t e Middleton s Aiitiquiities. _)_ edg_l uses, Felt; Rossi's Statues, 'ol".; wood to Bentley, Aug. 24, ll 40. lconologie Ilistoriquu, Do lu I-'osse, probably was, and the bust thus modelled long remained in the possession of some of_ his family.1

In the autumn of 1771, a show room was opened in Dublin, and in the following spring Bentley journeyed to Bath, for the purpose of seeking out like accommodation there. The Irish business was conducted by a person named

Brock, who sold the goods on commission, and was apparently well known to Wedgwood and Bentley. After the retail business had been declined there, Brock became a clerk in Greek Street, and served the firm many years. The Dublin sales were at first very promising, for they were stimulated by the patronage and recommendation of the Duke of Leinster, Lord Charlemont, Lord Clanbrassil, Lord Bessborough, Sir Charles Bingham, and other members of the Irish aristocracy; and some of the finest of the Etruscan vases, the basreliefs, statues, busts and plaques in the black basaltes and white biscuit bodies, the early cameos, and the enamelled tablets for fireplaces were consigned to, and probably yet exist in, the sister kingdom? But this source of patronage was not limitless. The resident gentry were, as a body, too encumbered by debt, and too much mixed up with the social troubles and party strifes of their country, to have money to spend on luxuries, or leisure to give to any efficient patronage of the arts. The Dublin warehouse was therefore, from time to time, a source of much anxiety to the partners; and that at Bath suffered in a similar way from bad seasons and the caprices of the fashionable world.

1 His name was Chitqua. An in-that at Longton Hall, was not long teresting account of this modeller ago sold at an auction near Dublin will be found in the Gent.'s Ma.ga-for 301. After assing through the zine, vol. xli. pp. 257-258.; hands of sever dealers, it was sold

' A chimney piece, much like ' in London for 3001.

CRAP. V. BURDETT THE LIVERPOOL PAINTER. 238

Burdett, the Liverpool artist, became at this date known to Mr. Wedgwood, whose patronage he sought for a new style of engraving, which, as he said, he had invented. It appears, however, to have been simply a variation of the method in use of eating away certain portions of the copper-plate with aquafortis. But to encourage him, he being a Liverpool man, Mr. Wedgwood commissioned him to paint some pictures of dead game, with the ultimate view of his engraving them after the method indicated. Things went on pretty smoothly for a while, but finding he could not monopolise the whole time and attention of the partners, or get them to take up his eugraving-crotchets so fully as he desired, he became as insolent, violent, and exacting, as before he had been humbly solicitous of their patronage. He wrote several most insulting letters to either partner, endeavoured by the basest insinuations to-sow strife between them, and brought Mr. Wedgwood in largely his debtor. To get rid of him, Mr. Vedgw0o_d paid him a portion of his demand, but retained the sketches of dead game. Ultimately these were rettu'ned to him, after being copied by Ralph Unwin, but the weary controversy extended over several months, and was noticeable for nothing except the dignified forbearance of the partners.

In 1772, Wedgwood's children were beginning to be old enough to take an occasional part in his daily life. Never was a' tenderer father, or a more enlightened instructor, as we shall see. In thisrespect he was, in some of his ideas, far in advance of his age. Bentley, who was regarded by the elder ones as their ' second father,' was no unimportant character in the pretty episodes which varied. the gravity and weight of business. On many occasions a dim light shines out of mouldering invoice and letter that the box which came last by coach or Waggon from Liverpool or London holds a great wooden flaxen-headed doll for ' Sukey,' a cart and horse for master 'Jacky,' something smaller for 'little Joss,' and presently for 'little Tom;' or else a great packet of dried fruit, cakes, and ' goodies.' Peter Swift, when quite assured that his ledgers are right for the day, comes in from the ' Works ' hard by, laden with his precious freight; and reverential and decorous as he is, he loves the little ones too well, not to unbend and return their grateful caresses. And next time 'Papa ' writes to Mr. Bentley, they climb his knee and stop his pen, whilst they tell him the messages he is to send. In the February of this year Wedgwood was in,London, and whilst there he looked about for a barrel organ. He came away without choosing one, but a few days after he tells Bentley to let Burdett do this, as the latter had a good ear, and was just then soliciting the patronage he afterwards so cruelly abused.

The organ which offered proved to be an indifierent instrument; but in the succeeding month one was hired for a time, and sent down into Staflbrdshire. ' The Organ arrived safe 8: a most joyful opening of it we have had,' writes Wedgwood. ' About twenty young sprigs were made as happy as mortals could be, & danced & lilted away; it would have done your heart good to have seen them. I wish we had your little sprightly N eice with us, but give my love to her, and tell her when the organ is sent to town again, which it will be soon, it shall be sent to Chelsea for her amusement a week or two.' '

The great square of the Works at Etruria, which had been set out in the spring of the preceding year—Ap1'il, 286 THE SHOW' ROOM. CRAP. V, 1771_was now in part completed, and the final removal from Burslem, which however extended over several months, took place. In 1773 there was yet a final portion of the works to build, and they were finished in the following year. It formed, as seen in the illustration, a noble pile of buildings, with the canal skirting it, and the green upland on which the hall stood rising beyond. In arrangement it formed then, as now, two distinct works, the ' Useful' and ' Ornamental,' with separate ovens, yards, workshops, and rooms of every character. The show-room, when finished, was an important place. Here were displayed, from time to time, to the chief aristocracy of all countries, as they passed through or paid visits into Staflbrdshire, the finest masterpieces of the potter's art. The enamellers at the works in Chelsea, as afterwards in Greek Street, vied with each other in the several processes of their art, and the results were often returned to Etruria to decorate this room. With these in contrast were the labours of the gem setters of London, Birmingham, and Uttoxeter;

enshrining as rings, buckles, brooches, earrings, or seals, cameo-work after the finest models; and here were to be seen the noblest vases and the most exquisite bas-reliefs. Princes and potent dukes, lords and ladies, might well linger in this room, and tell Wedgwood as they did, that neither Dresden nor Sevres had anything to show which bore comparison with his ornamental ware, either in beauty of form or chastity of design. But the room in which was laid the foundations of these masterpieces has a still greater degree of interest for all real lovers of Wedgwood's art. In the modellingroom——as thus seen in the engraving_-the moulds were made or the modelling done from designs in clay or wax supplied by Bacon, Flaxniau, Tassie, Vebber, Hoskins,

Coward, Mrs. Landre, Theodore Parker, and various other English and Italian artists.-Here Hackwood, the exquisite modeller of small things, passed the chief hours of his long service; and we catch glimpses of Webber, Tebo, Boot, and Massey. If Flaxman ever worked at Etruria for a brief season, this was the place of his labours; and Wedgwood himself passed whole days here amidst his modellers. From hence came the Sleeping Boy, the statuettes in the fine white biscuit body, the life-like busts of the heroes of the old and modern world, the bas-reliefs which reflected the glories of antique art; and the Vase, which, as a masterly reproduction of a great original, spread VVedgwood's fame far wider than any other of his multitudinous labours.

Even at this day, the Works at Etruria are picturesque; they must have been much more so in the days of their still its patches of heathland and pleasant field paths, and mines and iron furnaces had not defaced the soil and filled the atmosphere with smoke. A conspicuous object, on entering the works, is a weather-worn flight of wooden steps, which' lead up to what was Mr. Vedgwood's private oflice or countinghouse.1 Here he probably wrote the nlajority of his letters to Bentley; and here the friends conferred when the latter came on his brief visits to Etruria. These old steps as seen here in their'

' The bridge leading from the, to cross it i1 l great haste, as though oﬁce into the "'01-ks, as seen in anxious to convey to his workmen the illustration, Vedgvood often some sudden and good idea which crossed. Mr. Aaron edgwood in-i had flashed across his mind. formsus that he would be oftcnseen '

"CRAP. V. THE CORPORATION OF I,IVERPO()L. 239

'copy must, so long as they last, be an object of interest to those who can fully understand the part VVedgwood played in the industrial and artistic history of his country. Like all other master potters, he ascended many hundred steps a day to his various workshops and rooms, and the peculiar thud or stump of his wooden leg was a well known and welcome sound. He had always, a kind and cheery word for his people, a sympathising look, an approving nod; and it is handed down that no sound was more welcome through the long day's labour, than that which gave the sign of the good master's approach.1

We have seen that Bentley and Brindley's noble scheme of carrying the Grand Trunk Canal by an aqueduct direct to Liverpool across the Mersey fell to the ground chiefly through the apathy of the merchants, but more particularly of the Corporation of Liverpool, whose members at that date were headed by one Matthew Strong,:1 Justice Shallow, much given to the niystification of common sense, and most probably to good dinners. A further cause lay with the proprietors of the canal, who, in opposition to Brindley's original survey, proceeded upon a large plan with the Preston tunnel, which thus corresponding with the Duke of Bridgewater's cut from Runcorn Gap, took in the river boats, and gave a fair pretext for quietly and finally dropping the far more direct and eﬁicient scheme? This occurred in the autumn of 1769,v and after this Wedgwood's Navigation duties were principally those connected with his treasurership, except, as we have seen, when called upon to defeat little plots of 1 Mr. Mayer has heard many of depended upon the energy of ihe the old workmen,conteniporary with 1 Liverpool people. But they failed Wedgwood, recall to memo this 1 to push the scheme vigorously and peculiar sound about the V0r s. 1, immediately, and thus the oppor 1 Brindley saw clearly that the 1 tunity was lost. realisation of the l?l9(llCli mainly 1 neighbours' enmity in relation to the canal at Etruria and its connection with his property and works, or to aid some of the branches connected with the main line, or small local canals, for mining purposes. We have seen what hearty and eﬁicient championship Brindley aﬀorded him on more than one occasion when his neighbours thought fit to assail him; and he in turn greatly aided Brindley on the committees during the diﬁiculties connected with the Harecastle tunnel.

Even when this decrease of Navigation business led to fewer meetings of a public character, those of friendship were as frequent as ever. Brindley was always on the alert in his various mining and tunnelling operations to secure fossils or mineral specimens for his friend; and Wedgwood did not forget the pleasant home at Turnhurst, in the distribution of those kindly gifts to which he was so prone. In 1768 he bought Mrs. Brindley a handsome carved mahogany teatray in London, and without doubt sent with it a choice tea-service. On various occasions of Brindley's absence on surveys, his wife was a guest at Etruria; and now in 1772, when the great engineer's health declined more rapidly than heretofore, she took counsel with Wedgwood as to her husband's portrait. 'I have been to see Mrs. Brindley this morn

' ing by her desire,' wrote Wedgwood to Bentley, '& she has a particular favour to beg of you; Mr. Parsons, you know, took Mr. Brindley's Portrait which he was to have had, but they had a little fracas about the terms, Mr. Parsons demanded 60 guineas for the piece & frame, Mr. Brindley meant to make Mr. Parsons a handsome present for the picture, but did not like the mode of demanding so much from him, & in short told him he wod not have it. Mrs. Brindley always wish'd to have the

Cnsr. V. BRINDLEY'S LAST ILL-NESS. 241 picture, & she begs you wo'l be so good to see Mr. Parsons & tell him so, & that now she is at liberty, she readily complys with his terms, & hopes he will not refuse her the picture, if it is not already disposed of. She has set her heart much upon having it, so if Mr. Parsons has any new terms to propose, you'l please to send them, & stop Mr. Parsons from disposing of it till you hear from her again.' 1 _ I From this it would appear that Brindley had yielded to his wife's entreaties, and at last given her leave to secure the portrait. Though scarcely admitting it, she was probably aware that his life was drawing to a rapid close, for in eight days after this Wedgwood writes, ' I have been at Turnhurst almost every day this week, & can give you but a melancholy ace" from thence. Poor Mr. Brindley has nearly finish'd his course in this world-He says he must leave us, & indeed I do not expect to find him alive in the morning. His disorder I think I told you before is a Diabetes, & this malady he has had upon him for seven years _past most probably, which occasion'd his constant fever and thirst, though I believe no one of his Doctors found it out till Dr. Darwin discover'd it in the present illness, which I fear will deprive us of a valuable friend, and the world of one of the greatest Genius's who seldom live to see justice done to their singular abilities, but must trust to future ages for that tribute of praise & fair fame they so greatly merit from their fellow mortals. Poor Mrs. Brindley is inconsolable, & will scarcely be prevail'd upon to take either rest or food sufiicient to support nature, but she has promis'd me to exert herself in hearing this afilicting 242 BRINDLEY'S DEATH. CRAP. V.

stroke in her power, for the sake of her Aged Parents & her helpless Children.' 1

On the following noon one of the greatest men of the eighteenth century lay dead in the old country house at Turnhurst, and Wedgwood thus affectingly records his death, ' I told you in my last that Mr. Brindley was extremely ill, & I have the grief to tell you he is now no more. He died the 27"' Inst about 12 at Noon, & died in a sound sleep, for about 3 o'clock in the morn", after giving him something to wet his mouth, he said, 'z't-9 enough I shall need no more, & shut his Eyes, never more to open, he continued to the time of his death (about 9 hours) seemingly in a fine sleep, & yielded up his breath at last without a single groan_He has left two young children behind him, & poor Mrs. Brindley, inoonsolable for the loss of a sensible friend & affectionate Husbandwhat the Public has lost can only be conceiv'd by those who best knew his Character & Talents-Talents to which this Age and Country are indebted for works that will be the most lasting monuments to his Fame, & shew to future Ages how much good may be done by one single Genius, when happily employ'd upon works beneficial to mankind. Mr. Brindley had an excellent constitution, but his mind too ardently intent upon the execution of the works it had plann'd, wore down a body at the age of 55, which originally promised to have lasted a century, & might give him the pleasing expectation of living to see those great works completed for which Millions yet unborn will revere and bless his memory.-Do I need to tell you that he bore his last illness with that fortitude & strength of mind which characterised all his actions—If

CHAP. '. PUBLIC ESTIMATION.
you have so much leizure, perhaps you will send anaccount of this event to some of the papers, with suchaccompaniments as your esteem and friendship for the deceased shall dictate, & if a premm is requir'd from the printers I will gladly pay it. The Duke of Bridgewater might and indeed ought to have a handsome compliment paid him on this occasion, to encourage others to bring

Genius to light and support its first efforts as he has nobly done.' 1

Dr. Darwin shared in this noble opinion of Brindley's incomparable genius and worth, and considered that his fame was worthy of a national monument. ' Your Letter,' he writes to his dear friend Wedgwood, 'gave me most sincere grief about Mr. Brindley, whom I have always esteem'd to be a great Genius, & whose loss is truly a public one. I don't believe he has left his equal. I think the various N avigations should erect him a 'monument iu Westminster Abbey, & hope you will at a proper Time give them this Hint. Mr. Stanier sent me no account of him except of his death, tho' I so much desir'd it-, since if I had understood that he got-worse, nothing should have hinder'd me from seeing Him again. If Mr. Henshaw 2 took any Journal of his-lllness, or other circumstances after I saw Him, I wish you would ask him for it, ¢§' enclose it to me. And any Circumstances that you recollect of his Life should be wrote down, & I will sometime degest them into an Eulogium. These men should not die, this nature denys, but their Memories are above her malice-Enough I ' 3

Three days after Brindley's death, Sept. 30, Wedg

' Vedgwood to Bentley, Sept. 28, 3 Darwin to Vedgwood, Lich1772. field, Sept. 30, 1772. ' It means probably I-Ienshall. » wood followed his honoured and beloved friend to his grave amidst the peaceful fields of N ewchapel. His was not a nature to bury the burden of his friendship with his friend. A'few days later he was assisting Mr. Sparrow,Brindley's' solicitor, in publishing reliable accounts of the great 'engineer's death in the country papers, and before October had waned--he was actively engaged in carrying out his friend's dying wishes with respect to a successor.

His efforts were successful, and Mr. Henshall at the next meeting of the Committee of the Coventry and Oxford Canals—-received the appointment of engineer, a? post he held long after the Trent & Mersey Navigation was completed. Brindley left mourning rings to all his friends, amongst others to Bentley,1 who ever active in all kindly offices, secured the portrait for Brindley's widow; After Parsons had made one or more c0pies,_it was sent down into Staflbrdshire towards the close of 1772, and is still in existence.

At one period the Committee of the Trent and Mersey Navigation were in financial straits; but they wisely kept their dificulties from the ear of the world, knowing full well that entiresuccess only awaited the completion of their great work. Meanwhile the Duke of Bridgewater had built his locks at Runcorn, and of these we get a charming glimpse on the occasion of one of Wedgwood's journeys to Liverpool with his children. 'You know,' he writes to Bentley, ' I have seen a good deal of these matters before, but notwithstanding that, I was,quite astonish'd at the vastness of the plan, & the greatness of stile in the execution. The Walls of the Locks are truly admirable, both for strength and beauty of workmanship. The front Lock next to the sea (for such it seems when the Tide is in) in particular, whose walls are comp0s'd of vast stones from 1 to 12 Tons weight, & yet by the excellent machinery made use of, some of which is still left standing, they had as perfect command of these huge masses of Rock as a common' bricklayer of the brick in his hand. In short, to behold ten of these Locks all at one view, with their Gates, Acqueducts, Cisterns, Sluices, bridges, &c. &c., the whole seems to be the work of the Titans, rather than a production of our Pigmy race of beings, 8: 246.THE DUKE OF BRIDGEWATER. CRAP. V.

I do not wonder that the Duke is so enamour'd of his handiworks, that he is now in the fourth month of his stay at this place, & is expected to divide his time between Runcorn & Trentham for the remainder of the summer. The Duke very courteously invited me to dine with him, which I as readily accepted, & after dinner condescended to show me all his works, which took us a long walk, and some hours, dining and altogether not less than five, so that we had a long tete-a-téte conversation upon Navigations & other matters, for nobody was with us: Mr. Gilbert being engaged amongst his men, who it seems had mutinied but the day before. His Grace has promised to come & see me at Etruria, a place he has never yet seen, notwithstanding Ld Gower has so often brought

his company thither when the Duke had been at Trentham. I shew'd his Grace a couple of polished seals which he admir'd greatly & said they were very fine things. The seal engravers were pitied as men whose business was at an end.' 1

At the close of the year 1773, Wedgwood had another contest with certain members of the Navigation Committee with respect to some land, opposite to his estate at Etruria, he had bought in 1771 of the Burton Company. The latter had raised their price £900 above the original bidding, and this the Committee had agreed to indemnify him. After two years had passed, it was reported by certain members of the Committee that this sum had been paid for nothing, and the Duke of Bridgewater, Lord Gower, Mr. Gilbert and others were led to view the transaction in this light. Gilbert had given Wedgwood due notice of the coming storm, and with his habitual

' Vedgw0od to Bentley, Jan. 21, 1773.

Cimr. V. THE TRUTH MADE CLEAR. 247 courage he at once faced it. He sought Lord Gower and explained away this wrong impression; and a day or so afterwards at a general meeting of the Committee held at Trentham he placed the whole business before them in a masterly manner, and recalled to the memories of many their share in the transaction. ' The Chairman,' wrote Wedgwood to Bentley, ' then sumn1'd up the Evidence by which it appear'd to the entire satisfaction of all present, that the transaction was a fair one in every respect, was just what I had represented it to them, & was unanimously ratified & confirm'd, not to be disturbed again. Every one was, or seem'd to be, perfectly pleased. This & other business kept us at Trentham (where the Committee was held) till it was dark and rainy, so most of us continued there & spent a jovial evening together in perfect harmony & good humour. The next morning I waited upon Mr. Gilbert at the I Hall, & begg'd he W0'l pay my duty to the Duke & tell him how the affairs had turn'd out, & that I had sufl'er'd extremely at his 'leaving the Country

preposses'd with the opinion I knew he must have of this Transaction. Mr. Gilbert promis'd to do me full justice with his Grace & at the same time paid me some handsome comp" on my conduct in this business, which he said had pleased him very much. And thus ended this second stroke at my reputation & property, & if a third is sent after it, I have the increased confidence of an honest man, that it cannot hurt me, but must ultimately recoil upon the malignant sender.'1

Wedgwood, as we thus see, did not escape the usual penalties, well-deserved fame and personal merit have to suffer at the instance of the envious and narrow-minded, 1 Wedgwood to Bentley, Nov. 23, 1773.

248 A NAVIGATION TRIP. CRAP. V. who, incapable of good deeds or generous self abnegation, think no arts too vile or too debased, so that they can lessen or injure the reputations they are themselves too low in the scale of nature to gain or even aspire to. One by one he crushed these petty spites and party hates beneath his brave and manly feet; and so far as the cause of Canal Navigation was concerned, we hear no more of them. The great work was nearly done, and occasional pleasure trips and leisurely surveys diversified a business routine of unexampled prosperity. Of one of these we have a jovial and delightful picture, painted as ever for the eye of his dear friend. ' On Tuesday morning I am leaving home for a week. Our next Committee is to begin in Cheshire, & end in Lancashire, and will last so long. The Gent" of the Committee take a running breakfast with me here on Tuesday morning. We_we then take a voyage into our Tunnel,1 from thence to Sandbatch where we conclude the day, surveying our works in Cheshire as we go along. On Vednesday we proceed to view the course our Canal is to take by Middlewich to N orthwich, & from thence to Preston on the Hill, which track I am told in some places approaches as near to impractibility, as anything can do, which is really to be executed as our Canal is you know. I do not know where we are to

lodge on Wednesday night, but we are to visit Runcorn, and from thence proceed in his Grace's boat to Worsley, & there ends our Long Committee, when every man will be at liberty to make the best of his Way home. You will be so pious to put up a petition for our safety in this perilous Voyage, for I hear we are already waylaid with ambuscades of Venison, &

Cnar. V. THE GRAND TRUNK CANAL. 249 other combustibles, so that no man can say what all these things may end in, but of one thing my Dear Friend may ever be assur'd that wherever, or however dispos'd of, I am most truly & affectionately his.' 1 A few days later we hear how these perils were overcome. ' I return'd home last night and had a very pleasant expedition, the weather favouring us more than we had reason to expect, from the very rainy day preceding our outset, & we were very plentifully provided for at the several stages of our journey. We reviewed our works in Cheshire as far as Sandbach the first day, where we shall finish twenty Locks this year, & there will remain only about seven more for the next which will complete our Navigation. We found the Duke of Bridgewater's boat ready to receive us at Preston on the Hill to where Sir R' Brooke says hitherto ye shall go & no farther.

From this place we went to Runcorn in a boat provided for us, & back to VVarrington the same evening. From Warrington to Manchester the Duke has set up two passage boats, one carries passengers at a shilling each. The other is divided into three rooms, & the rates are 2/6 P head for the best room, 10d. & 12d., and it is the pleasantest and cheapest mode of traveling you can conceive. We next visited Worsley which has the appearance of a considerable Seaport Town. His G has built some hundreds of houses, & is every year adding considerably to their number. Manchester was our next stage, from whence I went to Bolton to see my Boy,2 and came back on Saturday to Dunham where I was to have treated with L.1 Stamford for the Limestone at Breden, but his Lordship was not at home. However, 250 A

NIGHT AT DUNIIAM. Gnu. V.

I found his good Lady there, who promis'd to transact the business for me by letter, & pressed me so much to finish the week at Dunham, that I could not refuse her Ladyship the favour of my company, but slept there that night, after spending a very agreeable piece of a day at her hospitable mansion.'

These were delightful episodes in a life of continuous anxiety and toil, and Wedgwood returned a newer and fresher man from the scenes of nature and the courtesies of gracious ladies.

CHAPTER V1.

THE RUSSIAN SERVICE;

HROUGHOUT the greaterpart of 1772. and 1773 Mrs. Wedgwood was very ill. At first from a severe rheumatic affection; later, from circumstances attending her maternal situation. It was a time of intense anxiety to her husband, who had much else to perplex him as We shall see; and to Dr. Darwin also; who in her later illness knowing on what a thread her life hung, watched her with an assiduity and care that never tired. To these, as much as to Darwin's enlightened skill, Wedgwood owed her preservation. From this date they were more than ever friends. Their children occasionally shared each others' homes; and their intellect, full of originality and strength, soon met on the graver and wider field of philosophical speculation.

Mrs. Wedgwood's first attack of illness arose no doubt from her residence in newly built houses; in that erected for Mr; Bentley, and afterwards at Etruria Hall. These things were not much understood at that day, even by physicians. She sufi'ered intensely; her limbs were cramped, her joints were stiffened; she was confined to her bed and room for weeks, and could neither move hand nor foot. In April she was better, and it was proposed she should visit Buxton; but a few weeks later 254 THE BATH SHOVV-ROOMS. CIIAP. VI. this plan was changed, and her husband having business to transact at Bath she accompanied him there by slow stages. The show-rooms in Westga-te Buildings, Mr. Bentley had chosen early in the year were not yet opened, and such time

therefore as Wedgwood could spare from attending the invalid to the pump rooms or in country drives, was devoted to their preparation, and of this we have some interesting particulars. ' Though the season is now nearly over, yet there seems (to me at least) a good deal of company here; and I wish you would enable us to open our Rooms, as I have found some of my good friends here would bestow some pains in advertising for us. These good folks will stay a week or 10 days here, if you could but send us something worth shewing immediately, but we must not baulk the thing in its first starting-Green Bayze _we shall want a good deal & the lowest we can buy here is 2/4. I have a notion you buy it much cheaper about 18d P. y"... Yellow paper for a back ground for the black Vases, & the colour (we none of us know what it is) we put behind the pebble Vases; we must trouble you to send it as there is none to be got here at any rate... The carpenters are more expeditious than I expected & will have things so forward in another day or two, that we could open the Rooms if we had anything to shew. We have rec'l the packages you mention, but those I understand are only Pebble Vases & painted Deserts, we must have all the Gimcracks in the useful ware, gems, Pictures, flowerpots, &c. &c., in short it is our united opinion that we should not open at all till you enable us to make a very complete shew, for there are tolerably decent shops enow here already— we found Mr. Palmer—& Mrs. Chatterly here. It was currently reported in Stafli)I'(lb'1111'C, that Mr. Palmer was trying

Cnu. VI. BOULTON'S VASES. 256 here to establish a warehouse of his goodsf He is gone home this morning, Mrs. Wedgwood & I took him a few miles on his way, but have not heard anything of this design from him or Mrs. Chatterly, but I think we can know from the latter if there is any truth in it.' 1

This generous and friendly intercourse with the man who had so deeply wronged him, and who was yet to prove still further his sordid and ignoble nature by copying Wedgwood and Bentley seals, and by lending a -hand to Voyez in his nefarious practices, proves what we have already said, that the great potter, like all brave, earnest and thoroughly honest men, was wisely magnanimous in these petty strifes engendered by competition. There are persons so constituted, that they cannot act otherwise than ignobly; whatever they do, must have some sign of baseness in it, and wherever they 'set their foot or hand, there they leave the slimy token of their presence. Wedgwood wisely avoided such characters as much as he could; but when circumstances threw them in his way, he was civil, and in cases even friendly. Palmer, it was found, had no intention of opening show rooms, though he had engaged a toyman to sell ware for him. Boulton also had laid siege in somewhat the same manner to the eye and purse of the fashionable crowd. ' We met with a large assortment of Mr. Boulton's vases in a very rich shop in the market place. The Gentn told me a long tale of Mr. Boulton's having ingaged at several £1000 expence the only mine in the world of the Radix Amethyst, and that nobody else could have any of that material. I heard him patiently, but afterwards took an opportunity of advising him when we were alone in a

' Vedgwood to Bentley, dated from Bath, June 2, 177 2.

256 THE SI1OPKEEPER'S STORY. CHAP. VI.

'corner of his shop, not to tell that story too often, as many Gent" who came to Bath had been in Derbyshire, seen the mine, & knew it to be free and open to all the world, on paying a certain known mine rent to the Land owner. The Glentn star'd, & assur'd me upon his honor that he had not said aword more than Mr. Boulton had assur'd him was true. Well done Boulton says I inwardly. I told the Grentn Mr. Boulton might possibly have ingaged them lately as I had not been in that country since the last summer. But, says he, 'tis three years since he told me this story. I was glad to change the subject, & inquired how they sold, but so-so says he, I am

afraid they will never answer Mr. Boulton's end as a manufacturer. He then told me he had a new shop building for him, & would have shewn me the plan, but some company coming in we parted.1 It would thus seem that Boulton in the magnificence of his purposes and ideas, occasionally ventured into the realms of fiction when he had a purpose to serve, or a. point to gain; a Weakness often allied with great strength of character, and with an otherwise high standard of truth both theoretic and practical. Wedgwood's power of self-repression was stronger; his ideal faculties were purer and more objective; his bounds and marks for truth more rigid and defined than those of his great friend. Boulton in his intense ambition to excel others, mistook some of the laws of his particular art; and happy was it for him that the-time was now so near at hand, when in association with Watt, his powerful genius reverted to its natural course of action, and thus realised effects which had as much an ideal, as a purely scientific, and utilitarian aspect.

' 'edgw0od to Bentley, June 6, 1772.

Bentley's marriage to Miss Stamford had been in contemplation from the beginning of the year, but by perversity of fate business of all sorts and kinds poured in, and the expectant lover could not quit his post. At length it was settled that Mr. and Wedgwood should take Chelsea on their way home from Bath and keep house till Bentley's return, as for some weeks he had been entirely alone, Miss Oates having settled in Chesterfield, on an annuity secured by deed for her life, by the provident hands of her good brother-in-law and Mr. Wedgwood,' But the lover grew impatient and made his complaints to his friend. ' You are tired of living by yourself, & wish to know when we think of returning,' wrote Wedgwood quoting Bentley's mournful epistle, and indulging a little in his accustomed vein of pleasantry. ' Poor Man! he counts the minutes for hours, & thinks Old Time drawls along like a Broad-Wheel'd waggon. How many years do you think it-is since some good Ladies departed into Derbyshire, or can you count over

the months since we left you alone at Chelsea. Be comforted "my Good Friend, the time will come, however tardy he may seem; but everybody tells us Mrs. W. will stay about three weeks longer, in the mean time we drink' your health every night, & wish you could be convey'd here somehow or other to spend your even" with us at Bath, but as that cannot be we pity your solitary condition, & hope you will take care of yourself in the best manner you can till we arrive at Chelsea to set you at liberty for a week that you may be made a-Happy man for life. Our best respects wait upon the good Ladies when you write to them.' 2 But Bentley's patience cannot 1 Wedgwood to Bentley, March 22, 1772. ' Ibid. J une 6, 1772.

VOL. II. S 258 BENTLEY'S MARRIAGE. CKAP. VI.

last three weeks. Eight days later we hear of his setting off into Derbyshire, and his dear friend bids him ' go upon his expedition as thoughtless and as gay as a Boy of fifteen.' 1

The marriage took place on June 22, at the church of All Saints, Derby. The letters extant contain no account of the wedding, but Miss Stamford's father was a man of comparative substance, and without doubt the usual wedding festivities were both elegant and generous, and enjoyed by numerous friends. On the 24th Mr. Wedgwood thus writing, shows that Bentley's holiday had been a brief one. ' By this time I hope my Dear Friend & his Good Lady, after the pleasantest journey they ever made, will be safely arriv'd at their habitation in Chelsea, & I need not tell you that I most sincerely wish you every comfort & every joy that your own good sense & good nature can bestow upon each other, or that a kind Providence can bless you with, & I never made a prayer with a stronger perswasion of its being heard & answer'd than that which I now put up for your mutual happiness & felicity thro every period of your lives.' 2

Whilst Bentley thus went on his way to be married, and enjoy his brief honeymoon, Wedgwood and his wife spent their days pleasantly. ' The season seems completely over here, & the town is scarcely habitable for heat. We take a mouthful of fresh air on the Downs in the morning, drink three or four glasses of scalding hot water from the Pump, & sweat it out in the least hot places we can find out the remainder of the day. ' Wedgwood, with a view to business purposes as we shall see, and to a probable movement amongst the Potters, was at this

' Vedgwood to Bentley, June 13, 14, 1772. ' Ibid. June 24, 1772.

CRAP. '/1. COMPANY AT BATH. ' 259 date reading Borlase's ' History and Antiquities of Comwall,' published in 1769, and we can thus fancy him spending the long noon-day hours beside his invalided wife, busy with the open folio on his knee. Beside the kind attention of a respectable couple named Ward who were to manage the show-rooms and the visits as we have seen of Staflbrdshire neighbours, Mr. Wedgwood and his wife received courtesy and attention from such of the aristocracy as the close of the season yet left at Bath. Amongst these were Lord Shelburne, Sir Harbord Harbord, and Lady Harbord his mother. When the showrooms approached completion, it was thought prudent to defer their opening to the beginning of a new season; but the latter were privileged visitors. 1 I' I must not omit to tell you,' Mr. Wedgwood writes to Bentley, ' that though we have not yet open'd the Rooms, we have nevertheless taken hansell. Sir Harbord Harbord desir'd he might bring Lady Harbord (his mother) to our new Rooms before he left Bath, which he did yesterday morning. She bo' a p' of Green-fluted Flower pots & a painted Etruscan teapot & Sir Harbord bo' a plain purple-edged desert service, but he wants to complete it by 4 Twiggen baskets of the smallest size oval, less than any we have, & Lady Harbord desires to see a Glaucier in three parts, I believe either purple or plain will do.... Sir Harbord has been particularly civil to us here,&,I hopewill be a good friend to the Rooms in Westgate, as he has it in his power to be, he set off for London this morning & says he shall

' Sir H. Harbord was one of the the

date of 1769, is amongst the first who adopted, and thus brought Mayer MSS. Sir H. Harbord was into fashion, the beautiful coat and raised to the peerage by the title of sleeve buttons with metal mounts, Lord Sufiield in 1786. formed of Wedgwood's crystalline ' Vedgwood to Bentley, June 24, jasper body. A bill for these of 1774.

260 A VISIT TO CHELSEA. CRAP. VI.

But the Bath waters were of little benefit to Mrs. Wedgwood, and she pined for her children and Etruria; at the close of June, therefore, she & her husband turned their faces homewards. At first they thought, on account of her weakness and the length of the journey, to avoid London altogether, but necessary business, and the yearning of their generous hearts to see Bentley and his bride, overcame all other considerations. They spent a fortnight of the utmost happiness at Chelsea, and then went by slow stages into Staflbrdshire by way of Birmingham, where they saw Boulton. ' We called upon Mr. Boulton on Friday Eveng,' wrote Wedgwood to his friend, ' & saw his superb Gallery, in which there is a great many good things of his manufacture beside the vases. silver cofleepot from St. Nan, some silver cups——moderate, & silver plated ware of the best forms I have seen. A small specimen of which, 4 Candlesticks you will receive by the Birmm Car', & hope you will_ do me the favour to accept them.' In the same letter he adds ' I have now the pleasure of dating from Etruria once more, & thanking you and your good Lady, in which Mrs. Wedgwood joins with me most cordially, for your goodness to us at Chelsea, & for every mark for that friendship & partiallity in our favour which We have so often expen'enc'd, & which we flatter ourselves will not ceace but with our lives. Mrs. Wedgwood laments _ that good folks cannot live nearer together. We have often you know wisl1'd it, but wi_sh'd in vain to annihilate or at least to lessen the distance between Chelsea and Etruria, but-I am afraid we must submit to these things as they are at present——love one

another wherever we are, & meet together as often as we can.' 1

CRAP. VI. WEDGWOOD'S ANXIETIES. 26

As autilm'n' advanced "Mrs. Wedgwood's "illness was renewed; this time from causes wholly difl'e_rent. Dr. Darwin thought her very ill, and her husband's distress was extreme; this the greater because through it all she endeavoured to conceal her danger and sufferings from him. ' She was,' as he tells Bentley, ' patience and resignation itself.' At length an expected crisis in her maternal situation occurred; but left her in so deplorable' a state of weakness that nothing but the greatestattention in nursing and keeping everything quiet about her could save her life. Dr. Darwin sat up one night with her; and on the morrow Wedgwood in writing hurriedly to him who was intrusted alike with his joys and woes, adds after saying that the good doctor gave some hope of her recovery, ' I trust my Dear Friend will excuse my entering into any particular details of business whilst my mind is in this state of anxiety & distress for the safety of my dear Giirl.'1.At this date Wedgwood was himself in indifferent health; he suffered from constant headaches, and from a renewal of the disorder in his eyes, and an in . credible weight of business and difficulties hung heavily upon him. Amongst the latter was the state of the business and domestic affairs in Newport Street. Since Mr. Bentley's removal to Chelsea, there had been no more fitting head of the family than a young female servant. The ordinary cash accounts were 'controlled by a young clerk named Benjamin Mather, who governed all under him by a haughtydomineering manner, that terrified for a time his inferiors into silence. The result was natural. The housekeeper, instead of minding her duties, was receiving the addresses of a young Staflbrdshire lad named John Wood, who had been sent from Etruria to assist in the 262 YOUNG MATHER. CRAP. VI.

books; and Mather, with much small cash in his possession, spent. his nights in taverns and worse places; treated a train of young fellows whom he passed off as cousins; dressed extravagantly, and by Way of bribing him, occasionally permitted his junior clerk John Wood to share in his revels. Hogarth's ' Idle Apprentices ' were performing their part to the full. But presently the truth came to light. John Wood had been honestly and tenderly reared. His conscience was troubled, and from time to time he wrote home and dropped hints to his father. Soon after, an anonymous letter reached Wedgwood, and Mather's delinquencies were revealed. Wedgwood weighed the whole matter with his usual sedate wisdom. He was lenient, because he saw the evil was in a measure begot by their own indifferent government. 'We have both been long sensible,' he writes to Bentley, ' of our want of a proper head of the family in Newport St., & that our property lies at too great a risque there. What avails all our industry & care, if we must finally lodge all the fruits of it in the hands of unprincipled Boys & Spenthrifts, who we see are debauching & ruining themselves, & perhaps half a score of their acquaintance at our expense.' 1 Much as he had erred, both partners were against the hasty dismissal of the young man. They felt that on the one hand he might for a time, at least, go and collect thousands in their name; on the other, if he had not so irredeemably sinned, it was their duty not to drive him to desperation by setting an irretrievable mark upon his character. They took up their hard duty like noble and delicate-minded men. Under a pretext of business they sent Ben Mather to Bath, and during his

" Vlfedgwood to Bentley, Sept. 1, 1772.

CRAP. VI. OVER-PRODUCTION. 268 absence stock was taken, and his accounts examined. His defalcations were found to be not so serious as' at first supposed. He had been foolish but not vicious; a weak vessel needing a controlling hand; he was therefore upon his return from Bath, sent to Chelsea 0 as a keeper of general accounts and an assistant to Mr. Bentley. Here he did his work with fidelity and zeal; throughout

the difficulties connected with the Russian service, he was ever at his post, and won the praise of his generous friend in Staffordshire. Years after we shall find him in Greek Street, not only busy with his pen, but with delicate and experienced touch making _many of those little repairs so often necessary to some of the finest jasper tablets; a finger here for a god Flaxman had modelled, or a tip to _ a wing or a point to his bow for Cupid. His weaknesses still cleaved to him in a degree, for he loved drink and company; but Wedgwood and Bentley well knew that human nature is not perfect, and with an occasional reprimand bore with the infirmities of their servant. Contests with his workmen troubled Mr. Wedgwood at this date. He had keen foresight, but the splendour and wealth of his creative instincts occasionally set pru dence at defiance. Over-production brought the natural ' results; more fine ornamental ware was in stock than the rich would buy, and the cessation of demand necessarily lessened supply. The only way to obviate this difficulty and retain a body of trained and very able workmen, whose services other manufacturers, Palmer in particular, were eager to secure, was to manufacture a cheaper class of vases to meet the ornamental needs of the less wealthy, and till this could be done, no working over hours was permitted at Etruria. ' Yesterday,' wrote Wedgwood to his friend, ' I stopp'd the men at the ornamental works from working over hours,'till I could find out some other work for them, which I would take the first opportunity.of doing when Mrs. W. was a little 'better, for the fact you know is that we have not work for them the commor -hours. Upon this they told DanI they would all leave us

&' they know Mrs. P. wo'1 take them in, which make: them almost unmanagable upon any terms. She has lately taken one of our Boys apprentice out of the Enginc Lathe Room. Now though our business may be a little over done in qu", I do not think it is in such a desperate way that we should set our best hands adrift to the establishment of our antagonists. I know they wod promise

our hands anything—'mountains of Gold to gain them, but if things go well with us in the house, I must spend as much time as I can this week at the works, '& if you want anything I beg you will let me know it immediately.'1

For many days Mrs. Wedgwood lay nearer life than death. Her llusband's sisters, Catherine Willet, and Margaret Byerley, were with him in 'this hour of great extremity, but none was so good a nurse as, he. ' Doc'r Darwin has left me to act as Physicion in his absence, but I believe I shall not gain much credit in my office amongst the female nurses here, as I have prescribed what they durst not think of for my patient. When nothing could stay upon her stomach Igave her fruit, ripe plumbs, &c., as often as she would eat.... I have given her Cyder that blows the cork up to the Cieling. She relishes it vastly, and it does her good. I hope to continue these good accounts to you.' 2

But convalescence came slowly, and as autumn waned

' Ivedgwood to Bentley, Sept. 8, 1772. '' Ibid. Sept. 10, 1772.

_C1 1ar. VI. _ HOUSEHOLD CONSPIRACY. 265 a terrible relapse took place. Fever-fits' and-ague, accompanied her prostrating disease, and her danger 'was greater than ever. Her husband's distress was extreme, ' for I should in losing her, go near to lose myself also,' he tells Bentley, ' & I fear, though I shudder at writing it, that she has but a poor chance of recovery from her present illness.' As soon as possible Mrs. Wedgwood was removed to Dr. Darwin's house at Lichfield, and there under his constant and enlightened care she grew slowly better, though illness at no distant date again prostrated her. ' ' Wedgwood's own health was at this time in a very precarious state, for he had rest for neither body nor mind. There were troubles abroad and troubles at home. A few days before his wife's terrible relapse he thus confided to Bentley, ' N o sooner is one disagreeable event subsided a little but others succeed to keep my mind and body too upon the fret, though I employ all the Philosophy I am master of to prevent it. We have lately discovered a scene of vilany amongst our servants in the House, who have a long time been robbing us of every thing they could carry off, or dispose of amongst a score of my out of door servants, I mean every eatable & drinkable, for I do not know that they have gone any further, but in these matters they have form'd such a correspondence & proceeded to such a degree as is not easy to imagine, & this will render it necessary to sweep the House of every serv" we have in it Male and Female, some from the field men & others from the Works. My head Farmer is in this list, whom I have turn'd adrift, & given several of my Tennants notice to quit their Houses. Add to this a combination amongst our servants at the works, the usefull works I mean, though it may for aught I know extend to 266 HARASSMENT OF MIND AND BODY. CRAP. V1. the other, to have their own prices, which are most exorbitant ones, or to leave us..... In this situation, it is true, I can convey my body from the works, & from my domestic concerns in the house, but till these matters are in a little better order, my mind will be with them, & the more I absent myself, or my attention from them, the more difficult they will be to manage. I have therefore resolv'd to set myself in earnest to redress these matters, that I may the sooner come at a little peace and comfort. The most distressful part respecting my household aflairs is Mrs. W's being so ill prepared to bear any uneasiness in her family, on which account I had kept the knowledge of these things to myself near two months, & now have taken all upon myself, & charged the servants not to say a word to her upon the subject, for I found them inclin'd to attack their mistress in my absence. We have hired a Housekeeper & two other servants, who can come at a day's notice, & I intend to complete the revolution whilst Mrs. W. is on a visit to her Bror in Cheshire, that she may see & feel as little of it as possible. She knows and consults with me about these matters, but then we do it quietly, which could not be the case betwixt the servants & her if they were

to transact these affairs in propria personal' The housekeeper hired (a Mrs. Massey) was of sedate age, and proved an admirable and confidential helpmate. She had kept house at Findem in Derbyshire, and boarded Bentley whilst he was a boy, attending the Dissenting Academy there, and recollecting him with great affection, an interest was added to her services. But Wedgwood had yet more anxiety to endure for his wife. In the last month of the year she again had a severe

' VedgW0od to Bentley, Oct. 27, 1772.

CRAP. VI. WEDGWOOD'S CHILDREN. 267 relapse, through taking a premature journey to Manchester, and it was not till after many weeks' confinement to her room, and a further lengthened stay at Lichfield, that she was restored to her husband and children. I

In this year, 177 2, Wedgwood's three eldest children first left home for school. His daughter went to Manchester, his sons to Hindley, and his wife being ill, and his sister, Mrs. Willet, unable to go a journey, he was necessitated to be their conductor. From this date, whilst they attended school in Lancashire, whatever might be the pressing nature of his engagements, we find him pleasantly travelling to and 'fro in their company. In the December of this year he speaks thus to Bentley of one of these holiday trips, ' We had a very pleasant journey, the weather fine, & found all our little folks well & happy. I have brought the Boys from Hindley, but Mrs. Holland did not care to part with the Lasses1 till they had finish'd their work, which will be about ten days hence, and to reconcile them to staying behind, as I have almost promis'd to fetch them at the expiration of that time. Mrs. Wedgwood bore her journey very well. My sister Willet made one of the party, & we were all very much delighted with the Ball, and particularly in seeing our own young sprigs perform such wonders there, as you may imagine we all thought they did.'2 But Sukey fell ill from confinement at school, and her parents were advised to try sea-bathing at Liverpool. On her way thither with

her father and little cousins, an accident occurred which nearly proved fatal. ' I began this letter ' at Etruria,' he writes, ' but finish it at this place (Knuts

' Mrs. Willet's daughter, Jane, ' 'Wedgwood to Bentley, Dec. 12, accompanied her cousin to school, 1772. very probably at the expence of the L good uncle.

268 LESSONS IN GEOGRAPHY.. CIIAP. VI. ford), where I am arriv'd with two neices & adaughter, & to morrow we hope to take possession of a Bachelor's house in his absence. We should have slept at Warrington to night but were stopped 6 hours upon the road by an accident which proved nearly fatal to my poor Girl. She was in high spirits, playing her pranks upon a' high horse-block, miss'd her footing, and pitch'd with her head upon a stone, which was sharp enough to make a wound, but I hope no otherharmwill ensue.'1 'A few days later all was well, though, as he told Bentley, her skull" is certainly rather of thethick than paper species, or it had been crush'd to pieces. ' '

As time wore on and his children grew older, we find VVedgwood in the new oflice of a tcacher,—and a very able one he was. His views in respect to their mental, moral, and physical training, derived in some measure probably from Darwin, Edgworth and Bentley, were far in advance of the age; and as they became more his companions the more his influence was operative. On one occasion he wrote thus to Bentley, ' I got safe to this place (Manchester) with my children (John and Josiah) on. Satilrday, &leave it to go to Bolton in the morning, where I have promised 'to spend a day or two with my Pupils. They having made me Professor of Metallurgy to the College, & I cannot do less than stop a day or two with them to examine what progress they have made in the Art. The young Ladies at this School are learning Geography, & are very fond of the Science. I have promised to send them some short acct of what is peculiar to each County, & for this purpose must beg the favour of you to enable me to keep my promise by sending me a Tour through' Great Britain.' 1 In our dayslof good maps,' geographical manuals and school books, we smile at this as puerile-but far less than a century ago——the popular ignorance on all these commonplace points was supreme, and the general method of teaching in schools grossly deficient. In the majority of instances it was ignorance striving with the ignorant. It is thereforeimuch to see a man who had, had to teach' himself--and who 'was absorbed literally night and day in an infinite variety of business, thus unbending to give lessons in rudimental science, and to bring ' the Land we Live in' like a picture before children's eyes. ' i '

It is not known when or where Mr. Wedgwood's brother John died.-He is referred to as ' my late brother John ' in April 1773-7-and it is not improbable that his death took place towards the close of 1771, and that the account of it is lost with the letters of that period. A brother less loved, but with whom he had always been on friendly terms died at this date, February 1773. This was Thomas Wedgwood of the Overhouse, who had been long previously ill, and whose affairs were in a sadly unsettled state. He had been married twice, and by both wives had children.' A few days prior to his brother's death Wedgwood tells'Bentley, 'The Eldest son is a sad Rakish Boy. I am' afraid it will not be an easy matter to bring about a settlement to the satisfact" of all parties, & as my brother is very sensible of the difficulties attending it, I fear he will be very backward to begin. However it is very necessary something should be done, & I am solicited on all sides to attempt it with my Bro'. My sister Wedgwood has been lamenting to me this

' Wedgwood to Bentley, January 30, 1773. _ 270 THOMAS WEDGWOOD. Czar. VI.

morning, that she hears I am going to. leave them,1 & when I am gone nobody else she fears can manage these matters with my Brother, & he will have nobody to consult &'c. &c. I told her I wo'1 stay a few days, & try what I could do in that time. I believe I may have

told you that my Bro' has had vexations & frettings enough for ten years past to have destroyed half a doz. constitutions, & I am afraid it has worn him down scarcely to be recOver'd again.'2 The conjecture was right as to Josiah Wedgwood's influence with the sick man, for he prevailed upon him to make some settlement of 11is affairs on the basis of a will drawn up in 1765; and after his death, he set about the more dificult task of an arrangement of afl'airs between the widow and her step-son. The uncle had great pity for the latter, who had been rendered wild and reckless by this woman's cruelty. ' Since my return from London my mind has been so taken up by a series of disagreeable business, & melancholly events,' he tells Bentley, ' as to unfit me for almost anything. My sister Wedgwood by her extreme narrowness, & something rather worse, makes the trust my _late Brother left with me extremely irksome and diflicult to execute, so as to keep any measures with her at alL One of the boys you may remember was very weak, the shock he received from his Father's Death, & the foolish talk & behaviour of his mother to him made him for some time quite an 1 Wedgwood was about setting oil' on a visit to London, but he dela ed it for some days. His brother ied on the 23rd of the month whilst he was absent. With the exception of the cofiin the articles necessary for the funeral were furnished by Mrs. Byerley, thus showing that her trade was curiously miscellaneous. The bill, which is too long to quote, contains many curious particulars relative to the funerals of that period. Thus the crape and silk hatbands cost more than 201. Buckles and sleeve-links were su plied to some of the attendants. 'Fwo gallons of wine provided was charged 15s., and the l)lBClll1S consumed cost ll. 2:. The account for the funeral is dated February 23, 1773. Mayer MSS. 1_';3Wedgwood to Bentley, Feb. 3, 1.

Gmr. VI. HIS ELDEST SON. 271

Idiot, but he is geting better again, though he will never be qualified to do any business, & what we shall do with him I do not know.1 The mother was

evidently herself of weak intellect, for shortly after her mind gave way, under the constant goading of a guilty conscience; whilst her husband's son, whom she had so deeply injured, soon began to show what worthy influence his uncle had over him. Wedgwood made him his companion, cheered him in every way, and soon wrote of him thus to Bentley. ' The improvement of my Nephew, & his Reformation w"h is daily improving, gives me a very sensible pleasure, & I have great hopes it will be continued to me. But his poor step-mother is now in so deplorable a situation, that her ill-treated & allmost ruin'd step-son cannot refuse a tear to her misery. She confesseth that it was her daily study to set his Father against him, in which, alass, she succeeded too well, that she had wrong'd him every wa, & cheated her own Bror & sisters, & has been the vilest wretch that ever liv'd. That her children cannot prosper for her sake, & that she has ruin'd them & herself too. She has returned Tom about £15 in_ money, & many-other things which she had secreted upon my Brothers death at some of her good Neighbours houses. She says she never dares see me again after my telling her so plainly that she must deliver all up, & she assuring me she had done it. The poor Boy I am taking home to this melancholly scene, who is a sensible thoughtful Lad, & must in a day or two meet a mother deprived of reason, & overwhelmed with guilt and despair; and a Brother as unwilling as he is incapable of being taught or managed

' Vedgwood to Bentley, March 15 and 16, 1773.

'late brother's affairs into his hands. 2 272 SETTLEMENT OF CLAIMS. OKAY. VI.

to any good purpose. My heart bleeds for' this poor

Boy, & I would rather take him any other way, but' his mother must & will see him.'1 _ 'For some considerable time Mr. Wedgwood seems to have retained his He established his nephew in his father's Works, assisted him with loans of money, and so 'far as was possible made a general settlement of all the claims upon his brother's estate, even to payingithe legacies bequeathed by his, Josiah Wedgwood's,' own father in 1749, to his daughters Margaret Byerley and Catherine Willet.

This state of Thomas Wedgwood's affairs at his death, not only shows him to have been an incompetent careless man, but the soundness of his brother's judgment years_ before in turning a deaf ear to his timid counsels and narrow-minded prognostications. Thomas Wedgwood had belonged to the old sleepy race of potters whose days were gone by, and had owned nothing in common with the generation around him, or with the great industrial period then rising into view, and of which his brother was already a foremost leader. » Never were characters more strongly contrasted; or the sons of one father more strikingly different.

Mr. Wedgwood had returned from London at the close wood's 'Vill were his brother Josiah and John Knight. They were im 1 Wedgwood to Bentley, May 30, 1773.
3 The Inventory of the Household Goods of Thomas Wedgwood of Burslem, taken July 30, 1773 is extremely interesting but too on to quote 111 this edition. We learn in it that the house was substantially furnished after the simple fashion of the time. There is also evidence that the step-mother took her share of goods, and left the place free to the heir within two months of her husband's death. '

The Executors to Thomas V'edg powered to raise a sutiicient sum by mortgage to all nece exenses and legapdiiis. The Churc yard orks had been already mort, and recovery was not made til 1480 when Josiah Vedgwood became the mort ee. The house was tenanted _v Aaron Wood, and the works from 1788 to 1793 by Joseph Vedgwood. The legacies Thomas Wedgwood of the Overhouse left his daughters, were a charge u on the Churchyard Estate.—Mayer SS.

Gnu'. Vl. CATHERINE OF RUSSIA. _ 273 of February; and was scarcely settled down again to his multifarious employments—executorship duties in-

cluded _than Bentley wrote to him relative to the Russian service. The Semiramis of the N orth—coarse, licentious, and brutal as she was—had yet enough of the woman in her to be at times influenced by the arts of civilisation, and by the refined taste and judgment of the foreign ambassadors and ministers at her Court. France had been thus instrumental in imparting some degree of taste for arts and letters, but an influence of a far more solid character had connected Russia to England since the days of Peter the Great; and though occasionally interrupted by war, or by periods of internal discord or revolution, had visibly increased since the days of Chatham's splendid foreign administration and Lord Cathca.rt's embassy. French and Saxon porcelain reached Russia by the usual channels of trade, but it was Lord Cathcart who introduced to the Empress's notice Wedgwood's exquisite yet unservile copies of antique art; and she had probably seen at the ambassador's or her nobles' tables, that an English manufacturer had been the first to unite in modern days, obvious utility and simple grace. This unity of artistic truth was accepted the more readily from its meeting an idiosyncrasy of the Russian character, in which we find the Northern love for the practical and objective in connexion with the Oriental taste for-rich and harmonious colouring. Hence perhaps, in a day yet to come, the arts of the North may in originality and adaptiveness vie with those of the South in the antique ages. With these exquisite productionsthus brought to her hand, Catherine H. became a truly royal patron. Through the agency of Lord Cathcart and the merchants of St. Petersburg, she adorned her palaces von. ll. 1' 27-1 EXPORTS TO RUSSIA. Ciur. VI with the finest vases, bas-reliefs, and gems, Wedgwood and Bentley had yet produced; and soon after, as we have seen, she commissioned Mr. Baxter the British Consul to procure the dinner and other services completed and sent to Russia in the autumn of 1770. Many of her nobles vied with her in this patronage. To meet this new demand for English fayence

the great commercial houses became gradually large exporters. The amount of useful ware which passed through the hands, chiefly of Boulton and Fothergill, and Mr. Radcliffe of Manchester, at this date is almost incredible, as we find orders for a hundred dozen, a thousand dozen, and often more, of plates, in addition to other pieces, necessary for sorting out into services, and the merchants of N arva and Revel increased this demand by commissions gathered from a wide area.1

Thus gradually habituated to these necessary luxuries of a civilisation more advanced than that of her country, the Empress at the close of 1773, in imitation probably of those German princes whose favours were lavished upon the porcelain works of Dresden and Berlin, commissioned Mr. Baxter, through one of her nobles, to open negociations with Wedgwood and Bentley, for the 1nanufacture of a vast cream-ware service, for every purpose of the table, and on which should be enamelled views of British scenery. Each piece was to bear a different scene, and as the service was for use at the 'Grenouilliere,' a place so called, and forming part of the palace of Tzarsko-selo near St. Petersburg, a child and frog were to be painted on the under-side as a distinctive mark. The child was subsequently omitted, and the frog alone appeared, painted green within a shield.

' The patterns of these orders for were blue ivy, antique purple border, Xarva, Revel, and others, for e.pm-t- ' laurel border, and green feather edge ation to Leghorn by Mr. Radcliffe, and flower. Mayer MSS.

CRAP. VI. THE GREAT SERVICE. 275

Bentley had the pleasure of announcing this royal order to his friend, and in reply Wedgwood thus wrote on March 23, 1773:_ ' I have a score or two of Executorship letters, to finish and send off to day, & have Mr. Gardner with me, agreeing about the finishing of my works & some other buildings which makes me rather busy, but I must say a few words to you about this s" service for my Great Patroness in the North, which the Consul has been so obliging to bring me. Be so good to make my best compliments & thanks to him, & in the next place, if you please to accept a moiety of the honor & profit in finishing this very supurb commission, for such I truly esteem it, it is very much at your service. I supposeit must be painted upon the Royal pattern, & that there must be a border upon the rims of the dishes & plates &c. of some kind, & the buildings &c. in the middle only. The Child & Frog, if they are to be all in the same attitudes, may perhaps be printed. I have no idea of this service being got up in less than two or three years if the Landskips & buildings are to be tolerably done, so as to do any credit to us, & to be copied from pictures of real buildings and situations, nor of its being afforded for less than £1000, or £1500'; why all the Gardens in England will scarcely furnish subjects sufficient for this sett, every piece having a diflerent subject. I think Mr. Baxter sho'l be spoke to very particularly to know what expense he thinks it would be prudent to lay upon the service, for he cannot but know that any sum almost may be expended upon this comm". What our hands can do in this business I do not know, you will try the likelyest, & get what other help you can, which you think necessary. I suppose this service is order'd upon the idea of the two services geting up by 276 POINTS FOR CONSIDERATION. CRAP. VI.

the King of Prussia which I suppose have taken, or will take many years to complete. One with all the battles between the Russians & the Turks, drawn under his Majesty's inspection, & intended as a present, you know, to the Empress, & the others with all the remarkable views and Landskips in his Dominions, for his own use. Suppose the Empress she" die when the service is nearly completed, as it will be a very expensive business, it may not be amiss to mention something of the kind to the Consul.'1 A few days later, Mr. Wedgwood again recurs to these necessary precautions:—' I think we she' have some assurance that no revolution in the North shod affect the validity of the

Consul's order to us. To paint a number of pictures which can only suit one particular situation, to the amount of one or two thousand pounds without any assurance of their being accepted farther than a verbal order which may be countermanded at pleasure, is rather too great a risque. And as these paintings will enhance the value of the pieces so monstrously beyond the prices Ea-rthen Ware Dishes & plates ought to bear; this alone, if there is not a thorough understanding of this circumstance with the Consul before the execution, may furnish a plausible excuse for rejecting the order when completed. Other causes, many other causes may have the same effect. The Death of the Empress, a revolution in her Government or ideas, a War, or bad understanding with our Government. The Death, or change of the present Consul, or even our offending him (a very possible chance, you know) may cause a countermand of this order, unless it be given in some way to make it binding. One W0d on the other hand avoid giving offence by over-inucli caution.'1

Bentley with hisaccustomed zeal to serve his friend, and his generous disregard of self, offered every necessary aid without desire to share in any profit which might result. To this Wedgwood would not listen. ' I am much oblig'd to my Dear Friend for his kind offers of assistance respecting the Russian service but I do not see how I can do anything in it myself at this distance, & when I can come to you is extremely uncertain, so that the whole burthen must lie upon you, & how can I think of you having all the trouble, and sharing none of _the profit? but if you think it cannot be kept distinct, or have any other objections to its being a Partnership service, we must order it some other way, for I must insist on your sharing it with me in some way or other. You think the subjects must be all from real views & real Buildings, & that it is expected from us to send draftsmen all over the Kingdom to take these views—if so, what time, or what money wod be sufficient to perform' the one or pay for the other. As to our being confin'd to Gothique Buildings on-

ly, why there are not enough I am perswaded in Great Britain to furnish subjects for this service. I think before we begin upon this capital work Mr. Baxter should give-us some idea of the expense he would venture upon in the service as it may be done to any value above £1500 or £2000, but I think not for less to do us any credit.' 2

In addition to this of price many artistic difiiculties presented themselves, as that relative to the impossibility of painting on tableware buildings which required mathematical lines; and it had also to be considered if painting

' VVedg'wood to Bentley, March 27, 1773,' Ibid. March 29, 17795.
278 ESTIMATE OF COST. Can. VI. or printing, or both combined should be resorted to in respect to decoration. In the latter case the ware would have to be sent to Liverpool to be printed, and to Chelsea to be bordered. Bentley had another interview with the Consul, but the perplexity relative to cost was not cleared up. He thought the service might be completed for 400l. or 500l. ' which indeed it may,' replied Wedgwood; ' but not fit for an Empre-ss's table, or to do us any credit at double that sum. The Dishes very moderately painted with real views & buildings cannot surely come at less than 20'/ a dish which will be £200 of the money, and the plates at near half the price will almost make out the £500.'1 In order to give a practical solution to one part of this difficulty Bentley set his enamel painters to work to make some first essays; but Wedgwood foresaw that many new hands would be required, and asks this question, ' Dare you undertake to paint the most embelished views, the most beautifull Landskips, with Gothique Ruins, Grecian Temples, and the most Elegant Buildings with hands who never attempted beyond Huts and Windmills, upon Dutch Tile at three halfpence a doz.? And this too for the first Empress in the World! Well, if you dare attempt and can succeed in this, tell me no more of your Alexanders, no nor of your Promethueses neither, for surely it is more to make Art1'.§ts than mere men.' 2

' VVedgwood to Bentley, April 5, I as Cooper. In Ma, Samuel Arm1773. stron was set to e ging the service,

' As thus indicated, the painting of the Russian service was commenced on A ril 3, 1773. (.)n that day James Ba ewell and Mrs. Wilcox were set to paint landsca s, and Nathaniel Cooper the inside orders. On A ril 10, Joseph Linle _v_began the o-borders, and Mrs. Vllcox's husband took in hand the same work and 111 Se tember and November William ence and Thomas Mills were added to the list of inside borderers. Ralph Unwin began painting landscapes in May. With brief intermissions these painters were at work upon the great service for the rest of the year; at which date, or somewhat earlier, a number of very able enamel Painters were hired. Of paper, ' To Painting the Russian serthese, as we shall see, several were vice, 1773.' Mayer MSS.

CHAP. VI. STRINGER OF KNUTSFORD. 279

'Nhilst these tests were in progress at Chelsea, business took Wedgwood to Hindley near Manchester, and on his way back he made Liverpool and Knutsford. At the former place he consulted Green his printer, and at the latter, a young painter of considerable ability, and who, not improbably, was a distant relative on his mother's side. ' On my late journey,' he writes to Bentley, ' I spent an evening at Knutsford with Mr. Stringer & looked at his Landskips & pictures, & told him something of the business we had in hand which I supposed would amount to 2,000 views. He said it was a very arduous undertaking, & must be a most expensive one if we did tolerable justice to the designs. That there were very few Men in England clever at painting Buildings, & on asking his opinion about the expence of painting each View upon our ware; he said it would be necessary to have each view sketched out from any that were now published by some good draftsmen, in order to adapt it to the piece, to take & leave with skill & judgment, &c. , & that this wod deserve half a Guinea for each design. The painting it upon the ware perhaps as much more; as to

the borders, value of the ware, 810. he could say nothing to them but at a rough guess he supposed it could not be done for less than 3 or £4,000, nor in less time than three or four years. So far Mr. Stringer. I have now your good letter of the 3" before me, & am glad to find you have made a beginning upon the service, by which you will soon find the value of these paintings better than from all the reasoning in the world, & to that tryal I resign all further thoughts about it.'1 young, well-educated women. They ' 'edgwood to Bentley, April 9 all worked by time. Abstract of 1773. 280 FORM AND COLOUR. CIIAP. VI".

The form chosen was the Royal pattern, and the ordinary cream colour toned with a delicate sulphur, so as to lgive effect to the tints of the landscapes and borders; and after much discussion between Wedgwood and Stringer, it was settled, in order to avoid formality, that the views should not end in a circle or line, but break off, as many small landscapes do, without any encircling line at all. Bentley was meanwhile trying these two modes of painting, the free and the bounded, and he seems ultimately to have made choice of the latter.1

Mr. Wedgwood-paid a-visit to Chelsea a few days after this was written, and over their pipes, or in the enamelling rooms, the friends solved this and many other relative-perplexities. It was a pleasant time indeed, for Mrs. Bentley had her sister and brother or father staying with her: other company was invited, and, amidst generous hospitality and natures congenial to his own, Wedgwood was in his glory. Upon his return into Statfordshire he set busily to work to model new forms for compotiers, soup-tureens, glaciers, flower baskets, fruit dishes, and all those other gim-crack articles used then as now in the service of the foreign dinner table. His cousin Thomas Wedgwood was equally occupied. Plates and dishes, cups and bowls, of faultless form and precisely matching, were perfected under his guiding eye, and soon Waggons solely laden with this exquisite ware, which

resembled ivory, began to roll their way to distant London, thence to feed the incessant needs of the Chelsea enamellers. Etruria had greater and yet more artistic days close at hand, but none more busy or full of utility than these.

But the money question yet shackled the hands of

' Wedgwood to Bentley, April 18, 1773.

CRAP. VI. AN APPEAL TO THE EMPRESS. 281 those whose hearts burned within them to do justice to their great task. The Consul knew nothing of art or its cost, and wished Wedgwood and Bentley to bind themselves down to a certain sum for the production of the service; but, as the latter very justly said, ' we cannot tell to a £100 or two what the expense will be, and should therefore have some such latitude in our agreement.'1 It is very evident that the Consul persisted in his limitation, for the Empress herself was eventually appealed to, with a result worthy of her rank, and of the great Englishmen she had commissioned to honour her. At once they were delivered A from their bondage, and a new spirit was theirs. Previously they were at work upon an ordinary dinner service; now they felt and acted like men who had a great work of art to set before the world. Previously they could only hope to make sketches from prints; now they had power to appeal to the (W M mum 0, mm_ freshness of Nature herself. '""'" ""'""'" Henceforth they worked with something like an inspiration. ' I thank you for the good account from St. Petersburg. The Empress has again prov'd herself to be what we had before all the reason in the world to believe she was-a woman of sense, fine taste, & spir-it. I will have some real views taken & send them to you, from Trentham, Keel, Lawton, Booth, Swinnerton, Shutboro, Ingestry,

Etruria, & many other places. The Consul should not ' 1 'elgwood to Bentley, April 18, 1773. 282 A CAMERA OBSCURA. CRAP. VI. talk of doing them as much lower as we can. If his Mistress heard him she wod rap his knuckles. We could do them as much lower as he pleases, but to do them in the manner the Empress wishes to see them; & as we (I mean the Consul and all of us) may receive due honour from the execution of the noblest plan ever yet laid down, or undertaken by any manufacturers in Great Britain, the price agreed upon is cheap beyond comparison with anything I know, & you will I make no doubt of it convince the Consul of it in due time.' 1

Thus with full liberty to do his work as his genius prompted, it occurred to Mr. Wedgwood to call Mr. Stringer to his aid. He lived within a reasonable distance, and his patronage he generously knew would aid a young and clever artist. 'Mr. Stringer,' he tells Bentley, ' has promis'd to get me a few views for the Russian service, but I do not expect more than perhaps halt' a doz. Do you think, it would be worth while to ingage Stringer for a few months to paint and instruct our hands in London? Upon this plan I would bring him up to London, have a Camera Obscura with us, & take 100 views upon the road? There are many pictures from real views of seats in the good houses in London. These must be come at, as many as possible. Suppose a written advertisement asking that favour was put up in our Rooms. A Gent" at L" Gowers gave me a good hint if it could be put into execution, which was to apply to Mr. Brown, tell him what we had to do, & that with respect to fame no man in England was so 1 Wedgwood to Bentley, dated must have made its use familiar to from Trentham, July 30, 1773. him, and this i11 turn undoubtedly

" From this we see how early the led his youngest son, Thomas 'Vedgcamera was in Vedgwood's hands. wood, to his first essays in photollis practical knowledge of optics graphic art.

CRAP. VI. VIEWS AND SKETCHES. 283 much interested as himself in the execution of our plan. He could procure us a great number of designs, tell us who had the views of their pleasure grounds taken, & might lend us a hand to take others, & perhaps do more. I wish you could send me a good Camera

Obscura, not too cumbersome, that I could take to the Neighbouring Gent" seats here, as I find it will be in my power to pay some acceptable compt' in that way to some Gent" in our N eighbourhood.' 1

The camera obscura Bentley procured folded up and took large sized views. In addition to Mr. Stringer, a nephew of Mr. Henshall's was employed, and through September and October they were busy taking views in Cheshire and Staifordshirc. On October 28 they were, as they had been for several previous days, at Trentham; and here Mr. Wedgwood joined them, as he did elsewhere whenever possible. Yet with landscapes thus supplied, and other resources, the enamel printers were often at a standstill. 'If your prints are nearly out,' writes Wedgwood, ' where must the thousands we still want come from?' The answer was obvious; real views must be still further resorted to. In November they were still busy. ' For some time past,' writes Wedgwood in apologising to his friend for delay in answering letters, ' young Stringer has taken up a good deal of my time. He is still with me, and I suppose we shall continue taking views for ten days or a fortnight longer, it being abo' two days' work to fix upon a situation, take a rough sketch, & finish & copy another from that, which is the course he takes. 2

The Staffordshire gentry entered heartily into VVedg

Q84 STAFFORDSHIRE VIEVVS. CRAP. VI.

wood's plan of 'taking sketches of their respective seats, and when 'once it was begun, he 'found it necessary, in compliment to them, to finish this artistic business, prior to taking similar sketches on a more extended scale. This priority in so famous a matter seems to have been highly gratifying. The cry from Chelsea was for views— more views. Bentley was in despair. He wrote that he ' must finish with such things as he had,' and John Wood added, ' that if fresh views were not sent, they must proceed in copying those they had over again. To this Mr. Wedgwood replied,

' We could not send you the views we have taken, for the Gent" here will see not only the views of their own seats, but their neighbours' likewise, to compare them together, so that we must finish our Staffordshire views, at 'least those about us, before we can send you any of them. The Gent" seem highly pleas'd with the compliments, as they are pleased to say I am paying to them, and from what I perceive in the little we have done, I could make it well worth my own while to pursue the same plan all over the kingdom.' After begging Bentley not to be in too great haste to finish the service, anddesiring to have a list, with size of pieces, of the quantity already completed, Mr. Wedgwood adds: ' By the above I shall know what sized landskips to take, for we finish them to the Oval of the dishes; and let me tell you whilst I think of it, that L" Gower & some others of my neighbours, will expect to be shown upon some of the larger dishes, and their views are taken accordingly. With respect to views within 20 or 30 miles of London, if you or your fr" know of any young Artists who have not yet made their way into full business, I am sure you might serve them extremely. The Ladies and Gent" here talk of coming up to London

Gnu. VI.-SHALL THE SERVICE BE SHOWN? 285 on purpose to see the service if we'shew it before it'is sent away. I tell them we will get leave if we can', for I am 11ot yet positive as to the consequences of shewing it at all in England. On one side, it would bring an immense number of People of Fashion to our Rooms, wod fully complete our noteriety to the whole Island, & help us greatly, no doubt, in the sale of our goods, both useful & ornamental. It wod confirm the consequence we have attain'd, & increase it by shewing that we are employ'd in a much higher scale than other manufacturers; we should shew that we have paid many comp" to our Friends and Customers and thereby rivet them more firmly to our interests, but then we must do this pretty universally, or you see the danger. For suppose a Gent" thinks himself neglected, either by the omission of his seat, when his neighbours is taken, or by puting it upon a small piece, or not flattering it sufficiently. He then becomes our ene-my—-Gains some of the Artists to his party, & Damns it with the R" Ambassr & with every one he is able. This is a rock, & a dangerous one too, & I cannot see indeed how we can avoid it, shew, or not shew, for if a Gent" asks if we have taken his seat, we must tell him, & if he further asks to see it, I do not know if we can deny him. These ideas have been floating in my head a long time, twenty on one side & a score on the oth-er, so that I am not able to determine anything, but your opinion thrown in-to either scale will make the other kick the beam, & I shall be very impatient to hear-from you upon the subject.' 1

With the consciousness that all great work perfects itself as it goes on, Wedg-wood still advised delay, and

' Wedgwood to Bentley, Novernber-ilI4, 1773.
286 LANDSCAPES ON DISHES. Cnar. VI. this evidently not without an ulterior ambition, ' for I think,' he says to Bentley, ' by what you mention in your last, & by what I have seen and learn'd lately, we shall do much better in every respect than we have hitherto done, & by the time this service is com-pleted we shall be about prepared to ex-ecute such an order for our own Good K. & Q,., but this is under the Rose. ' Lord Stamford lent many fine views, and his brother, the Honble. Booth Gray, not only recommended Mr. Wedgwood to seek the services of De-vis and Smith, two landscape painters of merit, but eventually aided him in procuring beautiful sketches from paint-ings in the town-houses of the London nobility. ' The line we have thus got in-to,' adds Wedgwood, 'is very promis-ing, & I hope will succeed. We have sent you a doz. Views, & shall send you more and those from Enville, 2, 3 or 4 from Soho soon, I am most afraid of our not having large Dishes & other large pieces enough left to oblige our Friends who shod be put into capital situations.' 1

The antithesis between a dish and a fine landscape is so striking as to make their grave association in one common idea wear something of the ludicrous. But to VVedgwood the views and the dishes were very perplexing things. Though the Empress's order was on a scale worthy of Brobdignag, there was limit even here to dishes and their size; and the point was to give the largest dishes to the greatest folks, or rather the greatest patrons. It proves how little Wedgwood and Bentley leant on pa-tronage, even that of royalty, that they forgot it altogether till the service was half completed; and we have other re-markable instances to give of this ab-sorption

' 'edgwood to Bentley, November 23, 1773.
in the ideal portion of their work. Bent-ley was in this respect even more obliv-ious than his friend; but Wedgwood gen-erally corrected the error before it was too late, for George III. and his kindly Queen had held out a most generous hand to their great potter. ' It is a Pity,' writes Wedgwood to his friend, ' but we had more large Dishes in the service. As it is, it will seem & be in reality, too great a partiality for a Country Esq' though he does happen to be one's neighbour, & a good man, to occupy so Capital a situation as a large Dish when there is but 2 or 4 in the whole Ser-vice. If we can afford one of them to L'1 Grower will be as much as the Bar-gain, for we have in my opinion been guilty of a Capital omission in not wait-ing upon his Majesty to acquaint him with the Comm" we have rec'1 from the Empress & to know his Maj——s plea-sure if he would permit us to take any views from the R--l Palaces or Gardens _but it is better late than never & I am firmly of opinion it ought to be done, & beg leave to submit it to your consider-ation.'1

To one of the large dishes was as-signed a fine view of the Works at Etruria; and on the top of the glaciers or ice-bearing vessels for creams, jel-lies, and such things, were set the fig-ures of three old women, as an emblem of Cold or Winter? Wedgwood himself made the drawings for the form of these

vessels; and probably superintended the modelling of their most appropriate em-blem.

Mr. John Gilbert, Lords Radnor and Talbot, and Mr. Anson, supplied views of their seats and gardens. Most of the finest Stafibrdshire views had been painted by Dere, of Newport Street, for Mr. Anson; and these, through the lib-erality of their owner, Wedgwood and Bentley were permitted to copy.

' Ve(lgwood to Bentley, December 1, 1773. " Ibid. November 27, 1773.
288 TERRA-COTTA ORQIAMENTS. CHAP. VI. -We have already seen that the rooms in Newport Street had be-come much too small for the vast and increasing business carried on there, and that the partners had been for some time looking around them for more suit-able premises. The scheme for awhile entertained, of renting one of the large houses then building in the Adelphi by the brothers Adams, and adapting it to _their purpose, had been given up chiefly because Mr. Wedgwood did not consider that the advantages offered were likely to balance the cost to be in-curred, and he had also a distaste to the Strand. He shared in an opinion then prevalent, that the Strand was a vulgar part of the town; and he considered all the approaches to it bad; a point on which Bentley differed from him. Mr. Wedgwood nevertheless kept up a ge-nial intercourse with the Adamses. He wished to introduce terra-cotta orna-ments both for the internaland external decoration of houses; and he was aware, from the wide range of their employ-ment, they had much power in this re-spect. Individually, as Wedgwood says, the brothers were well inclined, and oc-casionally be prepared them slabs or other pieces with enamelled grounds upon unglazed biscuit; but, as abody, the architects opposed what, in the nar-row dogmatism of their art, they con-sidered an innovation. Even Sir William Chambers, who as the royal architect could have effected so much in this re-spect, passed by unheeded this noble source of architectural ornament, and in one instance especially, that in the building of Lord Melbourne's house,

where full liberty had been given to him to introduce at will any striking yet simple style of decoration. Occasionally a gentleman of wealth and taste, who was not a slave in the hands of his all-wise architect, had recourse to this class of orna ment, as in the case of Sir John Wrottcsley, in a fine

Gus 1'. VI. ARC HITECT URAL ORN AMEN TS. 289 room he added to his seat in the autumn of 1772. Mr. Wedgwood told him of the difficulties thrown in his way, but Sir John replied ' he pleased himself and not the architects.' At a later date we find these ornamental tablets more in request, and Wedgwood busy with fresh designs and new amalgamations of colours, as a white upon a black body; but public taste, and the architectural _ accessories necessary to any truly artistic use of terracotta, were not sufiiciently in advance to give encouragement to the great potter's designs in this respect. Here, as in so many other of his artistic ideas he was far greater than his age. Yet he seems never to have lost faith, that clay as the plastic medium of what was most exquisite in ornament, would yet fill a great void in architectural decoration; and though our own day but sees the faint beginning of these things, and recognises but obscurely the true laws of colour and form in ornament, the first steps have been taken, and there may be yet realized, in an architecture more adapted thereto, some of those conceptions which as a great artist only moved before his ideal vision in phantasmagoric beauty. _

At a later date, one of the brothers Adams appears to have supplied a fresh estimate with respect to a house in the Adelphi, but Mr. Wedgwood declined to re-open the treaty. Other houses in the Strand were offered, Lord Bateman's town house was inspected, but the rent was too high. Newcastle House was almost decided upon, and even the notorious Mrs. Cornelly's house in Soho Square was considered. But another chance offered, and its advantages weighed the balance.

At this date Soho Square and its neighbourhood, though declining as a place of fashion, was to the medical world what Leicester Square was to the artistic. The fashion voL. 11. U 290 GREEK STREET, SOHO. Cusp. V I. able doctors had moved west from Red Lion Square, and settled down in this vicinity; and there necessarily gathered round them, the theatres of anatomy, the'.lecture rooms, and the students who profited by both. Soho became gradually what a portion of the Borough is now; and many of the houses were built or adapted to the demand for a certain class of accommodation.

At the rear, and yet communicating with a spacious house in Greek Street, a large dissecting room had been erected, and in November 1772 both were to let. Bentley reported the matter to Wedgwood, who liked it well; for he had laid it down as a rule not to remove to new rooms till those suitable in every respect could be obtained. The requirements were large both for the purposes of show and of artistic labour; for by this time it had become evident to both partners that Chelsea was too far away, and that much would be gained by having the enamelling works and the wholesale and retail business once more in immediate connection. We first hear of Greek Street in November 1772, ' I like the idea of the dissect' room if a gallery can be had to it, it wod make our Rooms most complete." A few days later Mr. Wedgwood says again, ' I cannot get the Dissecting room you mentioned to me out of my head, that with Mr. Bevers House & a Gallery to the former would be. about the qu" of Shew Room we want, & come much cheaper than the Adelphi buildings. That plan I now look upon as given up, & should therefore be very glad if possible to make some capital addition to our own, or get a better. What has become of Mrs. Cornelley's Rooms? She is I hear to remain in prison, & I cannot think anybody else

' Wedgwood to Bentley, November 14, 1772.
cs... VI. ENAMELLING BUSINESS. 201 will venture to take up her plan. Soho Square is not a bad situation I think, but then you know better than I do." Vile hear nothing further of Greek Street in Mr. Wedgwood's letters for some time; though his negotiations respecting the premises in question commenced early in 1773, and at the close of that year or the beginning of the next, they passed into his occupation, as we find from an attorney's bill.'2 In April 1774 the show rooms though yet incomplete were opened; and in July Mr. and Mrs. Bentley removed their household hither from Chelsea.

Far earlier than this,-we find Bentley and his enamellers at work upon a grand scale. The number of hands, both male and female, have been largely augmented, for the demand for enamelled ware, particularly dinner and dessert services, is steadily increasing, and there is work enough, even without the great labours connected with

'the Russian service. He supplements his partner's labours with untiring zeal. He looks around him everywhere for artists, books, and prints. He goes to Boydell, Major, Cadell and Hooper; employs Pye the engraver; and Mr. Pennant of Lichfield, as well as some others, send presents of prints. In February, Mr. Vedgwood may well write to him thus, 'Yes my Dear Friend I am very Well pleas'd with what you have done, & thank you very cordially for it. That business is now as it should be, & the 7 months will be pretty well advanced by the time the Goods are shipp'd. The money in June will be very acceptable too, for I shall want some about that time for for twenty things too tedious now to mention. We have sent some covers for the R" service by the last 292 FEMALE PAINTERS. CHAP. VI.

Waggon, & I am preparing the Glauciers, the only things now wanting from hence that we know of to complete it.1

From forty-six bills relative to wages paid at Chelsea during 1774, it is seen that on an average twenty-eight enamellers were constantly employed, of whom seven were female hands? Of these Miss Pars and Miss Glisson, evidently belonged to a superior situation in life.. They are almost always indicated by the prefix of ' Miss,' a title not so readily bestowed then as in our own day, and the rate of payment indicates superior ability. Thus, Miss Glisson who painted steadily at the works throughout the year received 128. per week; Miss Pars, who was absent during a portion of the summer, 103. 6d. per week. The latter seems to have lived near at hand, and was, without doubt, sister of William Pars, who in 1764 gained the Society of Arts' twenty-guinea premium for historical painting, and in 1770 was chosen associate of the Royal Academy. He was also appointed draughtsman to the party sent out to Greece by the Dilettanti Society to make researches amongst the ruins of antiquity.

Bentley's opinion had in Mr. Wedgwood's words ' kicked

' Vedgwood to Bentley, Febru ll. 11s. (id. to 100. weekly. The ary 27, 1774.

' As the Russian service holds a high place amongstVedgwood'smost famous works, it is well to record the names of those who assisted so ably in its decoration. The males were David Rhodes master, James Bakewell, John En lefield, Joseph Barret, William Quir, Samuel Armstron,

Villiam Henshaw, Nathaniel YVa- fruit and flower baskets, and Glover lace, William Thomas, John Roberts, George Simons, George Sei und, Nathaniel Coo r, VV111inm Ience, Thomas oseph Linley, Ralph Unwin, Thomas Simcock, Ral h Wilcox, Thomas Hutchens, Jo n Roberts, and Mr. Mather, clerk of works. Their wages averaged from female painters were Miss Pars, Miss

Glisson, Catherine Dent, Catherine VVilcox, Ann Mills, Grace Roberts, and Ann Roberts. Their w a ran ed from 184. to 70. weekly. rs. VVi cox received the highest rate of wages, Bakewell and Unwin painted lundsca s, Cooper the frogs at 2§d. and each. Linley the the tea-ware of the service. The females were chiefl employed in bordering; and all t e larger ieces as the chief dishes, tureens, an oompotiers, were distributed amongst those who had great reputation as landscape painters.

Ci1iiP.VI. THE SERVICE SHEVVN. 293 the beam' in favour of

shewing the Russian service. Accordingly,' early in June, its completion being sufliciently advanced, advertisements were inserted in the chief papers to the effect that the service was on show at the new rooms of Wedgwood and Bentley in Greek Street, Soho, and that admission was by tickets.1 The nobility availed themselves of this privilege in great and increasing numbers; so that before a week was out, the Russian Service was one of the most popular sights in London. Mrs. Delany with her fine taste and artistic eye, was one amongst the earliest of these visitors. On June 7, she thus writes, ' I am just returned from viewing the Wedgwood-ware that is to be sent to the Empress of Russia. It consists I believe of as many pieces as there are days in the year. They are displayed at a house in Greek Street, "Soho " called " Portland House," there are three rooms below and two above filled with it, laid out on tables, everything that can be wanted to serve a dinner; the ground, the common ware pale brimstone, the drawings in purple, the borders a wreath of leaves, the middle of each piece a particular view of all the remarkable places in the King's dominions neatly executed. I suppose it will come to a princely price; it is well for the manufacturer, which I am glad of, as his ingenuity and industry deserve encouragement. Among the views (and the prettiest there, tho' justice has not been done to it), is Thorpe Cloud as it appears at the end of the im prove

' As usual Bentleymade the draft ' House, Greek Street, Soho. The of this advertisement, which was I ublic were at the same time inublished through the month of oi-med 'that at the warehouse in une 1774i1i the St. James's ChroNewport Street is ii considerable nicle, the Gazetteer, and the Public variety of vases and other ornaments Advertiser. Later in the same year, i after the finest antique models, that they again advertised the removal of are not quite perfect, and will therethe principal part of their business fore be sold much lower than the from Newport Street to Portland usual prices.' ments at Ilam; but

my indignation was roused when I read the words "A view of Thorpe Cloud belonging to

Mr. Adderly."

I rectified the mistake with the person who had the charge of them, and hope Ilam will acknowledge its true master1 to her Imperial Majesty.' 2 3 Though the service was thus on view, there was yet a considerable amount of enamelling to be done. Shuter was busy with a sketch of Lord Fortescue's house in Wimpole Street.

Major Book, the well known anti

' John Port Esq., husband of Mrs. Delany's niece.

' Correspondence of.rs. Delany, vol. i. second series.

3 We gather some idea of the fashionable tone of the day relative to the social position of trade and gentility, from these somewhat patronising remarks of Mrs. Delany on Vedgwood. To spend money instead of earning it, or in other words, the difference between active mental and manual industry, and. luxurious idleness, made an almost impassable barrier between class and class. Nor as yet was the business of the potter, or the decoration of pottery ranked as a fine art. or its masters et placed in their true position. Wedgwood was the man who did essential service in this respect. Pottery in his hands became a noble art, worthy of the devotion of princes; and his energy it was, in OOI1 _lllCti0I1 with that of' the other mighty industrial leaders of his time, which increased the productive powers of the nation to an extent before undreamt of, and saved it from some of the natural results of the very idleness which thus affected to praise and patronise. In our generation the danger is on the other side; from the still more intolerable and offensive alliance between riches and ignorance. And we shall have made no advance in the solution of this old and difficult uestion, or advantageously testifie to what consti industry, and moral worth, whether

' in alliance with poverty or riches, tutes true civilisation, till intellect,, rank or humble state, are valued for themselves and all the immeasurable blessings they bestow.

Mrs. Delany has two earlier notices than this of Vedgw0od. In the autumn of 1770, when his rapid improvements in ornamental were left a large amount of what be naturally considered an inferior stock on hand, he wrote thus to Bentley, 'Suppose we have an auction at Cobb's room of Statues, Bassrelief pictures, Tri , candelabrum, lamps.' But nearly all the letters of 1771 are lost, and we have no account of this sale. It appears however from Mrs. 'Delanv's report, to have taken place at

' Chi'istie's auction rooms in April 1771. 'I am this moment going to Christie's,' she wrote 'to see the fine productions of Staffordshire which they say are superb.' To this she added after her visit 'I have seen the fine show at Christie's, and am much pleased with the neatness and elegance of the work, but it bears a price only for those who have super uous money/—Vol. i. second series, pi 434-5. In the following year, ecember 1772, there is another notice of 'Wedgwood, 'I found on my table a profile of Captain Edwaz-.l Hamilton in Wedgwood ware in imitation of the antique, very like.'—Ibid. p. 487. Later still we shall see that Mrs. Delanv visited Mrs. Bentley in Greek §treet on terms of' friendly intimacy.

CBAP. VI. DUPLICATE PIECES. 295 quarian, whose acquaintance Mr. Wedgwood had made by this time, lent amongst other views those of Lord Paget's house and stables; and Mr. Vernon and the Duke of Buccleugh permitted various fine landscapes hung up in their houses in town to be copied. From Lord Carlisle they had a view of Castle Howard, and one of Lord Buckingham's house from Mr. Barret.1

Early in June Mr. Wedgwood was in London; and at Dunstable on his way home he wrote thus to his friend. ' I should be glad to have a few duplicates of the Russian service sent to Etruria next Monday. The Soup Plate of L'1 Gowers, & a. few other good ones, Dishes &c., none of the slight ordinary things, they will not be worth shewing. I think the _/ine painted pieces condemn'd to be set aside whether it be

on account of their being blister'd, duplicates, or any other fault, except poor and bad painting, should be divided between Mr. Baxter.and Etruria, & we may paint more without the Frog, to be shown in Greek Street. Be so good as to let Simpcock examine by the Alphabet Catalogue if Mr. Fitzherbert's House is painted, if not, let it be done upon a plate, or some piece that will hold it. ' Amongst the duplicate pieces thus painted without the frog, was a small tea-service, of which the cup and saucer engraved are specimens. They show the general style of composition and effect, though necessarily far 1 Wedgwood to Bentley, memo-I ness in the verdure of his landscapes. randa without date, but written at In 1764 he gained the 501. premium Barnet. This is without doubt from the Society of Arts, being the George Barret the landscape painter, i first prize given by them for the best and not the Joseph Barret employed 3 landscape. He became subsequentl as an enameller. It is another name a Royal Academician. Thong added to the list of distin ished ' patronised by Burke, Lord Powersartists whose services W' ood court and others, he was always, and Bentleyocca.sionallymade51:ir's. 1 from the extravagance of his habits, He was an excellent ainter, being j a needy man. remarkable for fresh an dewy bright 296 STYLE OF DECORATION. (inn. VI.

lessdecidedly, than one of the fine pieces of the great service itself; say a soup tureen, a compotier or an oval dish. Still as the only specimens, now extant, at least in this country, they are of the highest value, in an artistic, and historic sense.

Both cup and saucer are of somewhat J ohnsonian size, and fitted for a generation who spent hours at the teatable; sipping the beverage as flies do honey, whilst -scandal, politics, or gossip moved their tongues. The body is of a highly toned cream or light safifron colour; and the form, the old oriental. The edge and other lines are the pale black of Indian ink which against the other colours assumes a purple hue, the inner antique border the same; the

wreath or outer border, amaranth or dark mauve, for the flowers, with the leaves green. The result of this mass of pale purplish black is very striking, and imparts to the charming landscapes somewhat that of the effect of an autumnal sunset. The subject of the-landscape on the saucer is that of a castle standing amidst woodland. A river of importance, exquisitely shown, winds about it in sylvan reaches; and in the foreground are two gentlemen or keepers, on their way home from shooting; one shows the game to the dog whilst the other converses, probably with the master of the domain who has approached from a distance. The cup, which though small is extremely elegant, both in itself and the annexation of the handle, is edged with the same purple black border. /Vithin are the oak leaves referred to in the bills, composed of different shades of green. The landscape without the cup' is said to be a scene amidst the Welsh hills; for on the side not shown by the artist, green hills and their blue distances are prominently seen.

From a list still extant of the table and dessert services prior to enamelling, we learn that neither tea nor breakfast ware formed any portion of either.-But Mr. Mayer in becoming possessor of these beautiful specimens learnt that they had formed a portion of certain 298 VISIT FROM THE QUEEN. CHAT'. VI. supplementary pieces, painted as seen in the letter already quoted, at the request of Mr. Wedgwood, for the purpose of gifts or personal use. To these, this cup and saucer belonged.

The Russian Service was on show for nearly two months; a period longer than the partners desired. 'I agree with you that our shew in Greek Street ' writes Wedgwood early in July, ' has been continued open a sulficient time, & am glad to hear you are preparing the Catalogue & making the goods ready for packing. I shall congratulate you most heartily when this tedious business is completed, & I cannot repeat my thanks to you too often for the great & continued attention you have for two years past bestowed upon this elaborate work. ' 1 Prior to its close the shew was honoured by a visit from the Queen and Prince Ernest of Mecklenburg her brother. Mr. Wedgwood was just then unable to be in London, but Bentley was his courtly deputy; and the letter descriptive of the Royal visit must have conveyed a vivid picture, as it is thus referred to. ' I thank my Dear Friend for his two last good letters, & congratulate him upon the high honour he has just receiv'd from our good & gracious Queen, & I hope one of these days to repeat my congratulations upon his receiving the like honour from his Majesty. I am very much oblig'd to you for the particular account you have been so obliging to give me of this visit, & the disposition of the Rooms, which I am sure must have a charming effect, & I not therefore so much wonder at her Majesty, & the Prince her Brother expressing their approbation in pretty strong terms. As I could not have the honour of waiting upon

CHAP. VI. BENTLEY'-S LABOURS. 299 her Majesty at Greek Street in Person, you are very good to make the pleasure approach as near to that as possible, by the very clear and minute description you have given me of this visit: & I thank you most sincerely for this amongst a thousand other polite and kind attentions I am every day receiving from you.' 1 2 Whilst Royal and aristocratic visitors thus paid homage to the genius and untiring labours of M12. Wedgwood and his partner, the latter was fully occupied in improving and arranging the new premises in Greek Street, and in elaborating the Catalogue of the great service. If Wedgwood, far away at Etruria, was still ceaselessly bringing what he called his visions' to practical results, Bentley's energy, exquisite taste, and sound judgment supplemented these labours to the utmost. By their perfect unanimity, by deferring one to the other, where there was cause for doubt, by their entire faith in each other, an amount of work' was accomplished, equal to anything known, under the more organized system of the present generation. There was much to do to 'Portland House,' as it was named; and

' VVedgwood to Bentley, July 15 shew what we can of the R service, and 16, 1774.. & as well as we can, and that must

' In 1769 or 1770, when the minor i do! I shall send you our packer, & Russian services were in progress,,' a Cart. You'l please to order what her Majesty made 9. far less cere-you think proper to be put up of the monious visit to New ort Street., R" service, vases, &c. Mrs. WedgMr. Vi/edgwood, who appened to 1 wood will bring the Carr', & I shall be in London with his wife, got be doing what I can here, & shall some intimation of her Majesty's 1n-l be glad to see you here after dinn'. tention, and tried to put it off or defer i Y" affect-ionately, J. Vedgwood. the visit as butlittle ware was ready, This note is without other date than and the shop not in fitting order, but ' Thursday morning. It is addressed without result. He had therefore to 1 'Mr. Bentley, Chelsea.' Ve know dispatcha messenger with this hasty ' nothing further of this royal visit; note toChelsea. 'Dear Sr. I have Queen Charlotte, as Mr. Charles seen Lady Hold— & I told her all I Knight tells us in his charming could, the result is that she says it is Autobiography, was somewhat given impossible to put it off; the Q to thus ' pop ing in ' without cerewants to see the Shop, & we must. mony, upon er good subjects.

300 PORTLAND HOUSE. Can. VI. the arranging the dissecting room to the needs of the enamellers was no easy task. Eventually it was divided into seven small rooms, in one of which was the kiln or muflle. Another was used for the reception of finished ware, and the rest were used for the purposes of the clerks and enamellers.1 7 Time, fire, and alterations of various kinds have so changed the premises occupied by Wedgwood & Bentley in Greek Street, Soho, that it is impossible now to trace the alterations advised by the one, and doubtless carried out by the other. So much of the original building has perished, that no truthful illustration could be obtained; though till very recently it is said Wedgwood's name was to be seen traced with a diamond upon a window pane. A great

artistic interest isassociated with the' old premises and their immediate neighbourhood, for here it was that Wedgwood's fame culminated in the greatest of his matchless works, the jasper tablets, the medallion portraits and busts, the cameos, and the Barberini Vase.

As the great task of the Russian Service thus drew to a close, the point of cost came necessarily under consideration in a letter already quoted from? Mr. Wedgwood says, after thanking his friend for the attention he has 1.»n enamelling kiln is similar to I in some measure the permanency of a glass blower-'s mufile. The one the gilding is referable to the use of spoken of was moveable. In a charcoal. Amongst Mr. Mayer's bill of sundries dated August 6, 1774, ' papers are many bills for billet is the followin, 'Carriage of the ' wood and charcoal. The latter cost lailn to Lambet to mend 1/6; 2 114. 3d. per-bushel. The consum tion pints of beer to the hricklavers of both during the progress 0 the mendinvthekiln8§d.'— MayerMSS., Russian service was enormous. Be

All 'ed 00d's enamelled ware tween March 7 and August 6, 1774. was fired ter painting with wood one dealer supplied 18,000 billets at or charcoal; the charcoal being used; the cost of 17!. 2a. In June of the for certain colours, or after firings ', same year, 10,000 small billets were which re uired an intenser degree of bought, and in August Mr. Bentley heat. T e carbonaceous gases' act aid one Francis Edgeley 181. 3;. for chemically upon many colours, and ' 2,000billets at 16x.6d. per-thousand. competent judges consider that the Mayer MSS. fineness of the enamelled hues, and 2 That of July 8, 1774.

bestowed upon this elaborate work, 'I hope one other trespass upon your patience and good nature will complete the whole. I mean settling the price of this work with our good Patron, Mr. Baxter—you are much better qualified to do this than myself in many respects, as you have negotiated what has hitherto been done in that matter, & must have clearer ideas what was, & was not included in the estimate you gave of this work than I can. According to my ideas, taken from your letters at the time you were endeavouring to give this estimate, there are many extras to be brought into‘ the accoimt upon our final settlement with Mr. Baxter, which I have no doubt he will readily assent to, & I wish you to consult with him upon the properest mode of making them. I will name some of these extra expenses, though they must occur to you without it. Taking original views, copying Pictures & Drawings, Buying Books & Prints to a large amo. The compartments to the Landscapes, & the Frogs and Shields, I believe did not enter into your estimate. Insurance upon the works at Chelsea, Making, Translating, & Printing the Catalogue. These things, to say nothing of the expenses of my journeys to London, & stay there at different times on account of this service near six months, & what is much more, the taking up so much of your time, & the constant exertion of your taste & Talents for two years. I say not to bring these things to any account, this service has cost several hundred pounds in the extras above recited, which were not included in the estimate at all; and you very well know that with this addition, if you call it 5001. there will not be near the profiit upon this service that we have upon our commonest painted goods.‘1 302 ’ ESTIMATES. cm». vi.

The two services contained 952 pieces, and their cost as plain cream-colour Ware was 511. 8s. 4d. being 36!. 6s. for the dinner service, and 15!. 2s. 4d. for the dessert service. The lowest estimate of decorative cost amounted to the sum of 2,3591. 2s. 1d. and this without calculating many extras. The whole is thus set forth by Mr. Bentley, and partly by his own hand.
35 4. vi.-‘ Table Services........ 51 8 4 1244 Enamel Views 8:. Paintings at 5/ 3, 10/6, 21/, 31/6, & 42/—say at 21/ upon an average.. 1306 4 0 1244 Borders & Compartments including 1244 Green Frogs & Compartments at 5/, 10/, 15/, 20/, & 25/—say 15/ upon an average.... _ A9§3_O 0 £2290 12 4 Original Drawings, Co ying Pictures & Drawings, &

Books of latu History 8: Prints—Suppose half the Expence...... 100 0 0 Insurance of the Service in the works at Chelsea 2 18 6 Translating & Printing the Catalogue 9 14 0 22 Packing Cases & Shipping. 7 5 7 £2410 10 5

The Borders, Compartments, & Frogs & Compartments upon a great many pieces have cost as much as the Pictures; & in general full 3/4“ as much. The above Estimate is made upon the same Principles, & in the same Proportion as upon our Common Enamel’d ware, without any allowance for Journeys & extraordinary attention, & time given up &c. to the amount of some hundred Pounds, or for extraordinary risque of ware damaged in the firing, or otherwise defective; which in common cases may be sold at an Inferior.-Price. And of this in the present case there has been & still remains a very considerable quantity; at least to the amount of £10021

’ The price which the Empress ultimately paid is not precisely known, though stated to be 3,0001. This, as 1 List of» the Russian Service. Mayer MSS.
Cnsr. VI. THE ‘GREAT PATRONESS.’ 303
Mr. Wedgwood well said, afforded them no adequate remuneration for the incessant anxiety and immense labour involved in its production. But it served as a splendid advertisement to the whole continent of Europe, and spread /Vedgwood and Bentley’s fame to the most distant foreign courts. Catherine was fond of using these services at her state dinners; and as she outwardly at least attached herself to the English policy, favoured Englishmen, and dealt in a liberal spirit with all that concerned the commerce of our country, there can be no doubt that in the abstract this generous spirit which looked more to great work than great gain, was richly and amply rewarded.1 Catherine was no niggard. Her vices, her duplicity, her cruelty, her ambition, shed nothing but infamy around her name; but she could do royal and noble acts when she pleased, and she thus differed from many of the other royal tyrants of her

day, in not adding meanness to her sins? Had she known that barren honour was almost the sole reward, it is certain ‘ his Great Patroness’ as Mr. Wedgwood loved to call her, would not have stayed her generous hand. But her Consul, or the Russian officials through whom he acted, kept these things from 1 Mr. Harris, afterwards Lord

Sir,’ he writes to his friend Sir

Malmsbury, who went as English Minister to St. Petersburgh in 1777, was quite aware of Catherine‘s innate duplicity of character. During his residence at her court, he had to struggle inst the implacable hatred of rederick the Great towards England, and to guard against the Empress’s false professions of friendship towards a country which she was rejoiced to see engaged in a hot war with France, whilst she matured her rojects against Turkey.

’ Horace Valpole, who was no Puritan, and tlippantly regarded the vices of his time, had no word of _ charity for Catherine.

‘Hy dear 1 p. 234.

Horace Mann, ‘leave it to Voltaire and the venal learned to apologize for that wretched woman. I am not dazzled with her code of laws, nor her fleets in the Archipelago. La Charlotais in prison or exile is venerable. Catherine will be detestable though she should be crowned in St. Sophia, and act a farce of Christianity there. Pray deny her a place in so pure:1 heart as your own. The proper punishment of mighty criminals is their knowing that they are, and must be for ever despised by the good/—VValpole‘s Letters, Cunningham’s Edit. vol. r.
304 THE RUSSIAN CONSUL. (.‘u.r. VI.

Catherine’s ear. Three years later, it would seem thatBaxter made some curious enquiries with respect to the views painted on the service. But Mr. Wedgwood was as usual cautious. ‘I have just time to say, as a first thought,’ he wrote to Bentley in answer, ‘that I would not let Mr. Baxter into the knowledge of the books from whence we had, or may now have our views, nor sell our originals; but if the Empress, or he chuse to have copies, we may make them out to any price according to the finishing. Must I send you the books you mention, or any part of them?' 1

The pecuniary claims for the Russian services were, after some negotiation, finally and amicably settled, and the partners ready to serve the Consul in other ways. ' I cannot sufliciently thank you,' writes Wedgwood to his friend 'for the trouble you so kindly take upon you in everything relative to the R— n service; I hope Mr. Baxter will make the remaining part easier to you, than we expect at 'present.'2 In another letter he says,' 'I beg you will present my respectfull compliments to Mr. Baxter & if he has any commands for 1ne with Mr. Henshall, (our Engineer), I will gladly execute them, & he will find Mr. Henshall dispos'd to do everything in his power to furnish the Consul with such Plans & models as he may wish to be supplied with.'8 At a later date, Baxter visited Staflbrdshire and the adjacent counties for the purpose of seeing the Grand Trunk Canal, and tracing out some of Brindley's surveys, and this probably in an oflicial sense for the Russian government. Catherine strenuously endeavoured to improve the intercommunication between one part of her kingdom and another, and

Gnu. VI. CATALOGUE OF THE RUSSIAN SERVICE. 305 thus Wedgwood whilst looking only to the perfection of one art, was the indirect means of promoting others of as great efficiency to the ends of civilisation.

Not the least of Bentley's labours in connection with the Russian Service was its Catalogue. He wrote the introduction, which afterwards, with the list of views, was translated into French. It is unknown what number of copies were printed. They are now so utterly lost sight of, that that possessed by Mr. Mayer1 is unique in its kind. A portion, no doubt, was printed in English, and distributed amongst the nobility and gentry, who had so generously contributed to the adornment of the' service; and in the hidden recesses of country halls some few copies may be extant. There was a. patriotic feeling abroad

amongst the higher classes in favour of the service; many regarding with pride the graceful art which conveyed to remote distances facsimiles of the old ancestral homes, where generations of their race had dwelt in honour and peace.

Wedgwood and Bentley's desire to please their Royal Patroness was more than fulfilled; Catherine was warm in her praise. She conveyed her thanks not only through the English Consul, but her own Ambassador. She enshrined the service in the most fantastic, and yet most beautiful of her country retreats, and showed it there to Lord Malmsbury in 1779.2 It was used in those 1 It was translated for this edition i any stranger is used to. She admits but press of matter necessitated its me to all her parties of cards, and a omission. It will appear, with many few daiys ago carried me with only other interestingnotes, subsequently. two 0 her courtiers to a country

' Petersburg, June 3, 1779. 'I palace, where she has placed the have the good fortune,' wrote the ortraits of all the crowned heads of future Lord Malmsbury to his fa-'urope. We discussed much on ther, 'to have made myself not dis-their several merits, and still more agreeable to the Empress. She on the great demerits of the modern notices me much more than any of portrait painters, since in the whole my colleagues; more I believe than collection, except one of our two

VOL. II. X 806 FAME OF THE GREAT SERVICE. CRAP. VI. splendid entertainments she gave from time to time, in the palace of Tzarskoselo, and she preferred it to royal gifts of Berlin and Dresden porcelain. As its fitness and beauty, its simplicity and taste thus came before her eyes, let us hope, if for the moment only, art exerted a portion of its divine prerogative, and inspired in her breast feelings more worthy of woman's nature, than those habitual to her. The great service was in every sense a national work, and its fame was not only national but European. eldest princes done by West, there is not a single picture that has either design, colour, or composition. She calls

this place la Grenoulliere, & it was for it that Wedgwood made some years ago, a very remarkable the different country gardens 8: houses in England. Tl11S also was shown, & this led us to a conversation on English gardening in which the Empress is a great adept.' Lord Malmsbu1'y's Diaries and Corre service of his were on which a green spondence, vol. i. p. 231. frog was painted. It represented

UMIEO, DEEIGNE FOR GERMANY.

CHANGE IN THE PASHIONABLE TASTE FOR CREAM WARE— WEDGVOOD DISINCLINED TO FAVOUR THIS CAPRICE——IMPROVES THE ORDINARY BISCUIT BODY——BEGINS HIS EXPERIMENTS FOR ONE STILL 1'INER— —THE CORNISH CLAYS——FIRST TRIALS OF THE CARBONATE OF BARYTA——I1IS DELIGHT IN CHEMICAL EXPERIMENT—THE TERRA PONDEROSA OB CARBONATE OF BARYTA——ITS PROTEAN CHARACTER—A HINT FROM PRIESTLEY——THE SULPHATE OF BARYTA OR CAIVK— ITS USE AS AN INGREDIENT IN THE NEW BODY——J'OACIIIM SMITH'S PORTRAITS IN WAX— C.AWK FOUND TO BE THE TRUE MATERIAIr—PORTRAITS AND SMALL STATUE BAS-RELIEFS— PROMISE OF

LARGER COMPOSITIONS—THE HIRRA PONDEROSA NOT WVHOLLY

DISCARDED, THOUGH REDUCED TO FRACTIONAL USE— CHANGE IN PROCESSES—CAWK ON MIDDLETON MOOR—PRECAUTION S NECESSARY IN OBTAINING IT—DISGUISED BY POUNDING——WEDGWOOD OVERVORKED——TABLETS FOR CHIMNEY-PIECES—-FLAXMAN— HIS FIRST WORK FOR WEDGWOOD——MODELLERS' BILLS— STAINED RELIEF VORK— CAMEOS——MANUFACTURING PROCESSES——THE TERM JASPER APPLIED TO THE NEW COMPOSITION——ITS. INGREDI-

ENTS——DIFFICULTIES WITH ITS SECRET——TABLETS BY HACK-WOOD—CAMEOS—— A CABINET OF GEMS——A BOOK OF VASES—SUBJECTS IN WHITE BISCUIT AND UNCOLOURED J'ASPER—THE CHOICE OF IIERCULES— PLAQUE OF POMONA—HEAD OF MEDUSA—THAT OF MINERVA——VASE OF EXQUISITE FORM——SACRIFICE TO PAN AND ITS COMPANION ——INCREASE IN ENAMELLED WARE-BORDERS—OTHER PATTERNS——PRINTING—SHELL AND SEA-WEED'PATTERNS——FURTHER IMPROVEMENTS —PROPOSED PRINTING MANUFACTORY ON THE BANKS OF THE GRAND TRUNK CANAL—PRICES—TILES——GREEN'S LENGTHENED SERVICES TO WVEDGWOOD.

CHAPTER VII.

THE NEW COMPOSITION AND ITS RESULTS.

IN spite of its artistic tone of colour, its exquisite glaze and its wide spread popularity, both at home and abroad, there were those, who from caprice of taste, or a restless desire for novelty, wearied in time of the Queen's ware, and through the retail dealers, and often of the manufacturers themselves, began to enquire for a new sort of table-ware which should approach, or indeed exceed stoneware in whiteness. Sir William Meredith was one of those who aimed at change, and reported amongst his friends that WVedgwood would soon adorn their tables with a whiter ware; but the latter, though he entertained the idea for a time, dropped it as it would seem without even making an experiment. ' You know,' he says to Bentley at this date, ' that I have given over the thoughts of making any other colour but Queen's ware. The white ware would be a great deal dearer, & I apprehend not much better liked; & the Queens ware, whilst it continues to sell, is quite as much business as I can manage/1 But the improvements in manufacturing processes are usually in themselves the cause of change. The substitution of Derbyshire chert for boul-

ders of blue granite, in the process of grinding flint, necessarily purified and 1 Wedgwood to Bentley, July 2, 1770. 310 A FINER BODY. Cmr. VII. slightly whitened the ware from the absence of all particles of granite from the ground substance; and with this purer colour, Wedgwood after much consideration, was content for a further period. Three plans floated in his mind; one to continue his manufacture of the cream-colour as heretofore, _a second to deepen the colour ' so as to make it as deep a'straW colour as possible,' and a third to make a ware entirely white. After much correspondence with Bentley on the subject, and elaborate calculations on the cost of manufacture, he decided, and wisely, in improving as far as possible, but not altering the colour of the ware his skill and industry had raised into a staple.

A white biscuit body variously compounded, had long been in use in the Potteries, and Wedgwood, at an early date, turned his attention to its improvement by the use of purer clays and other substances. Writing to Bentley in 1770 he says, ' I shall go about white biskit immediately.'1 He kept his word; and the result was soon apparent in the colour and sharpness of the early cameos, whether the grounds were an ordinary earthenware body, a crystalline jasper, or other variation. But this served only for a time. As artistic excellence increased, it was evident that the medium itself of this expression needed further improvement. Bentley knew that his friend had already made experiments with this view, and he urged their renewal. ' You want a finer body for gems?' replies Wedgwood ' I think a fine China body would not do. I have several times mixed bodies for this purpose, but some of them miscarried, and others have been lost or spoiled for want of my being able to attend to and go ' VVedgwood to Bentley, June 13, 17 70.

CHAD. VII. EXPERIMENTS. 311 on with the experiments. At present I cannot promise to engage in a course of experiments. I feel that close application will not do for me. If I am stronger

in the spring something may be done. '1 Instead of waiting for the spring, he soon afterwards set earnestly to work, and early in February 1773, just prior to a visit to town, he reports, ' I have made some very promising experiments lately upon finer bodies for Gems and other things, some proof of which I shall bring along with me.'2

This experimental business, both relatively to useful as to ornamental ware, brought prominently under Wedgwood's notice the whole question of the southwestern native clays, and the Patent which restricted or monopolised their use. We therefore find him referring to Cookworthy's Patent, in order to see how far he might proceed in his improvements. The Patent restricted him not only with respect to improvements in useful ware but with bodies for ornamental purposes, as moorstone was in some of them a necessary ingredient; although the substances which at this period principally engaged his attention for the improvement of bodies designed for ornamental purposes, were those only used hitherto by the porcelain makers of France and Germany, and occasionally in porcelain glazes by our own potters.3 Wedgwood, as we have seen, had already turned his attention in this direction,4 and the new experiments for a finer body for gems, undoubtedly included some portion, —and as it seems at first a considerable one——of the terraponderosa, or carbonate of baryta. VVriting on January 1, 1 'Vedgwood to Bentley, Febru-lain fusible spar is mentioned as my 6, 1773. one of the ingredients of the glaze. " Ibid. December 31, 1772. Specification of Patent, No. 1096. '' Inthe patent granted to Richard ' Vol. i. pp. 436, 437. Champion in 1775 for making porce 312_ CORNISII STONES AND CLAYS. Gm. VII. 1774 to Bentley he asks, ' By white tablets for chimney-pieces do you mean to have them of the fine white composition or of the cream-colour body, we have sent you some of the latter for painting, but cannot yet make them long & narrow enough for chimney-pieces. It is the narrowness of the tablets in proportion to their length which makes the principal difficulty. I am now trying to make them hard enough for two tablets, and to saw them in two when fired.' He also seems to have tried the carbonate of baryta as an ingredient in other formulas of body; or at least discovered that the porosity inherent in these substances admitted an easy application of colour, for he adds, 'One or two of the greens will make beautiful grounds, & perhaps the green basaltes form busts &c. Figures and vases too may be made in these coloured clays, but I am at some loss how to have the principal ingredient without making a noise.1 I rather think you must get a friend to order it up to town, disguise it there, and send it hither in boxes or casks.' Bentley was widely known amongst scientific men, and there can be no doubt that both the Cornish stones and clays, as well as the specimens of fusible spar first used by Wedgwood, were procured through his agency; the latter from the Lancashire mines.

This class of experiments, as well as others carried on at the same time gave Wedgwood infinite pleasure. ' The main things we want at present to complete our cameos and bas-reliefs, & to add a little variety to our vases, Candlesticks &c. I believe will be managed, & as to the

Blanching of our Ware in general— when that step is 1 The principal ingredient here stone, the use of which was yet alluded to, was probably not the restricted by Co0kworthy's patent. spaith fusible, but Moor or Cornish

Cnnr. VII. DELIGHT IN EXPERIMENTS. 313 absolutely necessary I hope it may be done. I have for some time past been reviewing my experiments, & I find such Roots, such Seeds, as would open and branch out wonderfully, if I could nail myself down to the cultivation of them for a year or two. And the Fox-hunter does not employ more pleasure from the chase, than I do from the prosecution of my experiments when I am fairly enter'd into the field, and the further I go, the wider this field extends before me. The Agate, the Green & other coloured Glazes have had their day, & done pretty well, & are

certain of a resurrection soon, for there are & ever will be a numerous Class of People to purchace shewy & cheap things. The Cream colour is of a superior class & I trust has not yet run its race by many degrees. The Black is sterling & will last for ever. These are a few of the Roots which have been selected, & put into a state of cultivation, & I never look over my Books, but I find many more which I should very gladly bring into action; but the too common fate of schemers is ever before my Eyes, & you have given me many excellent lectures upon the bad policy of hurrying things too fast upon one another. I have not been on Horseback for a week? This morning some business calls me from my Books & Vases & trumpery, & I am very thankfull for it, for I have scarcely power of my own mere motion, to quit my present pursuits for a few hours.1

But these intellectual enjoyments, keen as they Were, had their drawbacks and penalties. No two pieces of fusible spar were found to be alike. Nature, as he well said in a future letter, did not weigh her materials, and here her vagaries were supreme. But he was not disheartened. He was philosopher enough to know that

' Vedgw0od to Bentley, March 7, 1774.

314 VARIABILITY OF MATERIALS. CIIAP. VII. her bounty was infinite; and that he had but to search to find her substitutes and analogies. Writing to his friend no great while after, he says:

It is not possible for me to tell you what can be done with the heads you mention, as large as life, &. as to the price it is more in the ofling still. I have no knowledge, not can any be acquired but from experience, how our white Bodies will stand in such large masses, & provided they will stand ever so well, you know I have no raw materials & do not know when I shall get any. M——-stone, & Spaith fusible are the two articles I want, & the several samples I have of the latter are so diferent in their properties, that no dependence can be had upon them. They have plagued me sadly of late—At one time the body is white & fine as it shod be, the next

we make perhaps, having used a different lump of the Spaith, is a Cinnamon colour—One time it is melted to a Glass, another time as dry as a Tob. Pipe—And this way it has led me a dance ever since I came home without my knowing why, till I tried each seperate lump by itself. I am afraid this said S. Fusible is too Proteous like to make afixed solid basis for a Manufacture, & I have now begun a series of experiments upon Materials easy to be had in sufficient quantities, & of qualities allways the same.'

It was but a natural induction from a simple truth, that if one body possessed certain qualities, another sufliciently alike, for it to be classed under the same category, would possess similar afiinities, even if in a varying degree. Wedgwood therefore sought further amongst the class of spars for what he required; namely, a substance which should possess a porcellaneous texture, intense whiteness, and the ability to give density and hardness to large and compact masses. It was probable that at that day of imperfect chemical knowledge, the distinction between the sulphates and carbonates of a inineral substance, was but little understood, and that the

' Wedgwood to Bentley, July 21, 1774.

CHAP. VII. CAWK OR SULPHATE OF BARYTA. 315 terms were inditferently applied. Wedgwood had rather to conceal, than to publish the processes and results of his chemical experiments; and therefore we have no clue as to whether he made his.discoveries through exhaustive analysis, or by happy but empirical induction. Priestley, there can be little doubt, supplied hints that were valuable; for by a somewhat singular coincidence he was at this time busy with experiments for the second volume of his work, ' Observations on Air' and one of these related to an acid contained in what chemists at that date called jluor, the Derbyshire spar, of which vases and ornaments were made. The air was procured by pouring on the spar oil of vitriol, and receiving the produce in quicksilver.I

But it was to another substance of the same class that Wedgwood's attention was now directed. He had tested the carbonate of baryta, and found, as seen, its characteristics too variable to form any efficient basis of a manufacture; he therefore turned to the sulphate of the same substance. A variety of this, locally called cawk, was abundant in Derbyshire; and this, after repeated tests, was found to answer in a preeminent degree all the purposes required.

At this date, and for some time previously, a modeller of merit named Joachim Smith residing in Berners Street, Oxford Street, had been employed by Wedgwood & Bentley in making portraits in wax of the nobility and gentry; and these had been copied by them, first in the ordinary white biscuit ware, and next from about the middle of the previous year 1773, in the fine white terra. cotta body; which containing some portion of the spaith fusible or term ponderosa, is the one referred to in the

' Rutt's Life of Priestley, vol. i. p. 275. Observations on Air, vol.

316 JOACHIM SMITH. Cnar. VII. first and second editions of the Catalogue, as ' A fine white Terra Cotta of great Beauty and Delicacy; proper for Cameos, Portraits & Bas-reliefs.' Many of these portraits were very popular; and Joachim Smith's sale of them to his customers occasionally large. The heads of Lady Finch and her beautiful daughters were exceedingly admired; and the demand became far greater than the supply, troubled as Mr. Wedgwood was for a time with materials on which he could have no dependence. ' I must go into Derbyshire,' he writes to Bentley at the close of July, 'to search for spaith fusible or No. 19. When I have got this of a right sort, we may be able to go on with Mr. Smith's heads, but I have been teased with unperceived variations in this compound.' The substance, however, when procured was even more Protean than heretofore, and made him again resort to his experiments. These were again successful. 'I believe' he Writes in September after a month's absorbing labour, ' I shall make an excellent white body, & with absolute certainty without the fusible spars.' Two days later he forwards specimens to Bentley.

By To morrow's Coach we shall send you a. pare1 in which will be a sample or two in Gems of the new white composition of less delicate materials which I mentioned to you & of this I believe it will be in my power to make Mr. Smith 10,000 Heads of the same colour, texture &c. &c. If he pleases we will make the whole number of L—s Finches of this composition (It will be little expense now the stamps are made) & this body is so delicate a colour and so fine in every other respect that I hope both the Ladies & he will think it worth while waiting a few weeks for. If you think them too white (is that possible) I can give them the Onyx bluish cast. Pray shew these to Mr. Smith as soon as you can, & tell him I am preparing a quty of this body for his use, & whatever he sends shall now be done immediately.1 1 'Vedg'ood to Bentley, September 5, 1774.

CRAP. VII. PROPERTIES OF THE NEW COMPOSITION. 317

By November, Mr. Wedgwood had succeeded in bolder attempts with this composition.

I have made a few small oval statue bas-reliefs of the same composition as the gems which Mr. Smith brings with him.' Please to try how they will ground, & let me know how you will like them. I shall proceed by degrees to larger & larger bas-reliefs of the same composition & do not at present see any reason to doubt of success in them.'I

It must not be thought that the carbonate of baryta was now wholly discarded in the composition of these beautiful bodies. It formed, as we shall see, a fractional portion of the true jasper, and was variously applied in other mixtures.

VVedgwood soon discovered another property in his new composition. That of porosity, by its ready incorporation of certain metallic oxides; of cobalt especially. Hitherto colours had been applied to these gems, by ground-laying enamel colours; but this fine property revolutionised many of these laborious

processes; and whilst thus lessening the manufacturers' and artists' labour, cheapened the article itself.

I am glad you think the white body of sufiicient fineness & have no reason to doubt of being able to continue it so. The blue body I am likewise absolute in of almost any shade, and have likewise a beautifull Sea-Green, and several other colours for grounds to Cameos, Intaglios &c. & shall be able to make almost any of our Cameos in figures, from the Herculaneum size to the least Marriage of Cupid &c., in heads from Peter the Great to the smallest Gem for Rings, of the blue and other colour'd grounds, with the figures & heads in our fine white composition. Look at our heads of Eminent men, Greeks, Romans, & Moderns, & let me know which way you would have them; whether the heads seperate & color'd grounds for 1 Smith was at this date paying a visit to Etruria.

" Veclgwood to Bentley, November 6, 1774.

318 MANUFACTURDIG PROCESSES. CHAP. VII.

you to polish, which will doubtless with metal frames make the richest cabinet pictures imaginable. And more especially, as the heads will, in this case, be a little under cut in the manner of the finest Gems—-or would you have them in the style they now are, only the relief on fine white with color'd grounds. These improvements may be introduced in part, either now, or may make a most capital change for the next yea.r—I say in part, for as the seperate Heads, if we make any quantity of them, must have new stamps made for them, it will take some time to be fully prepar'd to execute our plan with dispatch.l

This last passage is very important, as it proves that hitherto the grounds and reliefs of the various sized gems, if not the tablets, had been made, generally speaking, from one mould and by one process; or at least if moulded separately, conjoined previously to being fired biscuit.

Many facts of deep interest gleam out in respect to these and other compositions. Scraps of London crown glass were pounded and used, either in glaze, or some of the bodies. Wedgwood also, whilst in Derbyshire in search of No. 19 or spaith fusible, first came upon specimens of cawk, or to use his private sign for it, 74, the substance he required. His father-in-law, Richard Wedgwood, and Bentley were in his company at the time, and he thus recalls the facts to the memory of the latter.

This letter going by the Coach, and not by the Post, I will give you a full description of the substance I want, for I have not a single piece unpounded. It is a white chalky looking substance, in form generally fiatt, about an inch, or from one to two inches thick & often inclosing small lumps of Lead Ore. We found it in great plenty at the first mines we 1 Wedgwood to Bentley, January there for Joachim Smith. He 1, 1775. In the same letter IVeCllr-gathered his information from a man wood states that at this time, he s out of work, who had been employed were made at the Derby chinaworks, twenty eight-years in the factory.

8:. that a number were in progress

Cnar. VH. A MORE RELMBLE INGREDIENT. 819 visited short of Middleton, going from Matlock, where my Father call'd Godbehere to us, & asked him 'i f he knew what we wanted.' He call'd it Cauk, but we were then in search of Spath fusible or No. 19 which he afterwards found for us upon Middleton Moor, & ca.11'd it Wheat Stone, I inclose a little of this Cauk, pounded in a paper A. I apprehend Mr. Stamford has a share in some of the mines which produce this substance. Some Person from BirmIn had a quantity of it lately to try as an Ore, & that will perhaps be the best idea for us to procure it under; but it must not be pounded till it is under our management, or that of our friend, for the Lead Ore must be carefully picked out of it at the time it is pounded & before it is made small. I am not yet certain that some of the 19 may not do as well as this 74 (for that is my No. for this Cauk, & so I shall hereafter call it) but the different specimens of 19 I have had, have possess'd very different qualities one from another, as

they regard my experiments, and the 74 has been all alike; no one piece differing from another, which is of great consequence to us, & would induce me to give the preference to 74, if 19 should be equal 'to it, in every other respects. .. It will be next to impossible, we are such notorious & suspected Folks, to come at the 74 unnoticed, & we must be cautious in our first steps, not to appear in it, if it be possible to avoid it. Godbehere works at the mines near Middleton—we mentioned Mr. Stamford to him, so that if Mr. Stamford is a link in the Chain, we shall be blown at once. But we will let this business lie dormant, if you please, till I have tried the 19 you have sent me, & you have got some quantity of it.'

A few days previously he says, in relation to this necessary precaution in procuring the cawk, and his ability to make all the cameos wanted, not only of a fine white, but likewise with blue and other coloured grounds, and at something less expense than Bentley could have them grounded:

The only difliculty I have is the mode of procuring & conveying in cog the raw material above mention'd. It is some

' Wedgwood to Bentley, January 15, 1775.
320 VVEDGIVOOD INCESSANTLY OCCUPIED. CIIAP. VII. thing round about by way of London, but if it was sent by the West Indies the expence would not be worth naming in comparison with other considerations. I must have some before I can proceed & I dare not have it the nearest way, not undisguised, though I could only wish to have it pounded & put through a coarse hair sieve, but even this I would not have done with your People, nor have them to see it at all. Could not Mr. More set some poor man to work upon it in some of the uninhabited buildings at the Adelphi. Every body knows him to be a conjurer, & this may well pass for an Ore for him to operate upon.l

At this date, as so often afterwards, Wedgwood's engagements were incessant. Business so largely predominated over pleasure, as to tell grievously upon

his already somewhat outworn frame. Apologising to Bentley for delay in answering his letters, he thus writes:

Yesterday I dined with L'1 Stamford & his Bro' & company of Fox hunters at Trentham, & to day I have two of Doct" Darwin's sons to come to stay with me, so that I have but little time for writing, & besides I dare not do much just now, for my business has at this time secur'd itself so firmly in the Capital that it will not give place to sleep, sometimes for whole nights, two out of the last three nights, I could not go to sleep till seven in the morning, & then only for an hour or two, so that I find it absolutely necessary to relax a little.2

Thoroughly aware of the immense importance of his friend's experimental advances with the new white body, and as enthusiastic as himself in the desire to place it in exquisite forms before the world, Bentley pressed upon his attention the desirableness of having tablets made of a. proper size for chimney-pieces, and the consequence it was likely to be in extending their trade in ornamental ware. Wedgwood at once responded by work and words.
1 VVedgwood to Bentley January 5 1775. 1 Ibid. January 5, 1770.' '
CRAP. VII. FLAXMAN. 321
In reference to these suggestions as to chimney-pieces, he says:_

Having tried all the hands I have who were likely to execute them, but in vain, I have taken the business up myself, & am not much afraid of being able to complete it t-o your satisfaction, but stand in need of your directions relative to the blocks & ovals to the Tablets.1

Bentley had already made other attempts to carry out the highest artistic work--he had looked around him for a modeller--that modeller was Flaxman.

Wedgwood's words in response, are memorable. ' I am glad you have met with a Modeller, & that Flaxman is so valuable an Artist. It is but a few years since he was a most supreme Coxcomb, but a little more experience may have cured him of this foible.'2 This must allude to Flaxman's competition for the gold medal of the Royal Academy, and his subsequent disappointment.

Reynolds, who knew comparatively nothing of sculpture, and too often depreciated its merits, showed little judgment in his award of the prize to an inferior artist like Engleheart. Time proved, that Flaxman's certainty of success arose from no overweening conceit of his own merit, but from an intuitive perception, however offensively expressed, of his possession of high artistic power. But, as yet the world saw only an untutored stripling, in whom self reliant genius wore the appearance of vanity. Wedgwood who always visited the Academy's Exhibitions, had probably caught the current story, and bore it as we thus see in his vigorous memory.

In his next reference to the sculptor, Mr. Wedgwood says:—

Perhaps Flaxman can model you a good Tablet for a chimney

' Wedgwood to Bentley, January 14, 1775. ' Ibid. VOL. II. Y pieee—you know we have not one of a proper size. It should be modelled upon a piece of ground glass or marble, & you may allow an inch at 8 for shrinking. I need not tell you that the Figures should be open, & managed properly for a coloured ground. Vhat do you think of Vases of our fine blue body with white laurel festoons, medallions &c. or for Grecian painting? '

Fortunately Flaxman's first hill 2 to Wedgwood is preserved. We learn from it, that two models of vases

A D" of Hope.. 10

An Antique Vase sculptured with figtires. 1 15

A Packing Case..

To J. Flaxman.

1775. £ 8. d.

March 25. A Pair of Vases, one with a Satyr 8: the

other with a Triton handle... 3 3 O

A Basso Relievo of Melpomone... 10 6

A D of Thalia...... 10 6

A D of Terpsichore..... 10 6

A D" of Euterpe...... 10 6

A 1) of Sap ho...... 10 6

A D" of Apo lo...... 10 6

A D" of Hercules and the Lion... 10 6

A D'1 of Hercules and the Boar... 10 6

A D of Hercules and Cerberus... 10 6

A D" of Bacchus..... 7 0

A D of Ariadne...... 7 0

V A Packing Case...... 3 9

April 11. Four Bass Releivos of the Seasons.. 2 2 0

A D" of Jupiter...... 10 6

A D of Juno...... 10 6

A D" of Minerva..... 10 6

A D" of Justice...... 10 6 6 0 6

Moulding & making a from a of Lennneus...... Mending a Vax Medall & making a. Mould from It...... 2 0 M 1 1 2 S t £15 9 8 are 1 7. ta ues.... 2 2 0 6 Cups & Saucers... 8 62 10 6 12 18 9 1775.' J any 3' Received the Contents in full of all Demands. for my father, J onn Bums, J un".

' The figure 5 here is clearly in mistake for that of 6, as work which only closed in the middle of the year could not be paid for in the previous January. This mistake is often made when a new year first sets in.

The vases first mentioned in the bill will be found figured in the next chapter.

Crmr. VII. EARLY PORTRAITS AND BAS-RELIEFS. 823 were supplied, that he worked on account of his father, and we also ascertain what were the subjects of the basreliefs. They were all classical, and prove with what eyes of love he already looked upon antique art. We hear nothing further of his modelling till July, when Wedgwood writes:

—

Sir Tho' Broughton has two boys at School near London & wishes to treat his Lady with their portraits for a pair of bracelets in our blue and white compositions, but desires to know what the expense of modelling will be to have them full or three quarter faces, & if the modeller would alter them if he should not think them good likenesses. I suppose Mr. Flaxman will be more moderate than Mr. Smith. Please let me have an answer as soon as may be. 1

A few days later, Wedgwood suggests further work for Flaxman. ' Suppose you were to employ Mr. Flaxman to model some figures. They would do for Tablets, Vases, inlaying, &c. We have nobody here that can do them.' 2

As the autumn set in, and Bentley prepared to pay a visit with his wife to Etruria, the sculptor is again mentioned, and we learn that he is modelling the portraits of Mr. Banks3 & Dr. Solander.

I have little to say (wrote VVedgwood to-his friend) only I wish you to see Mr. Flaxman before you leave London & if you could prevail upon him to finish Mr. Banks & Dr. Solander, they would be an acquisition to us, & and as we shall now make with tolerable ce1'ta'int_1/ any moderate sized has-reliefs of the composition sent you last in a. Conqueror's Province & companion I submit it to you whether we should not have some of the finest things that can be modelled, & originals which have not been hackney'd in Wax and Plaister for a century past, & if you think we should, would it not be saving time to set Mr. Flaxman upon some business before you leave him? Mr. Grenville you know gave us permission to copy or mould from 1 "'edgWood to Bentley, July 3, ' Ihid. July 11, I775. 1775,-" Afterwards Sir Joseph Banks. 324 MODELS FROM HOSKINS AND GRANT. CIIAP. VII. any of the fine things in his possession. He has a Vase or two in town full of Bas-relief figures which would do for us charmingly. If we had a number of such figures as would compose into Bacchanalian processions, Sacrifices, Births, &c. we could make many wonderful things from them. Mr. Grenville told me that many of his best things were at Stow & invited me to call in my way to or from Town to look at them, & see what would convert to our purpose. This invitation was you know to VV. & B. & I wish you would make Stow to or from Etruria, it is a. very few miles aside & Mr. Grenville will be glad to see you.

From the year 1769, when last referred to, the work of modelling, apart from that carried on at Etruria by Hackwood, Tebo, and others, had not been stationary and from the bills of 1773, 1774 and 1775, we gather many interesting particulars both as to the artists employed, and the subjects of their labour. The annexed bills ' of

' Mr. Wedgwood and Co.

6

To James Hoskins.

Jan' 16.

1773. To 2 Moulds from a heads a M Paisko.

To 2 Mould from a Gem....

To 2 Moulds from:1 Medal of St. Peter.

To 2 from Sulpher Medals.. '..

To 2 from Ivery.....

To 1 from a Seal of Cicero....

To Moulding a "'01: Model of Mr. Bentley

To 2 from Snlpher of Mr. Garrick...

To a mould of Likeness of Mr. Bentley.

.

Dec. 8. To 6 small moulds from Vax & Sulpher..

To 7 Moulds from Sulphers.

oooooooooooom wwwowoowwoo"

soamonaooawfi

O

—-

—I

Q

Receiv'd 24"' July 1774

The Contents in full of all demands,

J AMES Ilosnnms.

Mr. Wedgwood and Bentley to Hoskings and Grant for Plaster Casts Prepaird to Mould from

March 21, 1774.

£ a. d.

To a Busto of Zeno...... 1 1 0

To Ditto Pinder...... 1 1 0

To Ditto F austena...... 1 1 0

To Ditto Germanicus.... 1 1 0

To Ditto Anteninus Pius..... 1 1 0

Carry forward..... £5 5 0

Cm. VII. SUBJECTS.

325

Hoskins and Grant, Mrs. Landre, Richard Parker, and P. Stephan, throw:1. flood of light upon the earlier editions of the Catalogues, and enable us to assign dates

To Ditto i inerva.......

To Ditto Inico Jones and Palladio...

To Ditto Homer......

To Ditto Antenos.....-.

To Ditto Solon.....

To Ditto E icurus......

To Ditto 3 arshus Brutus.....

To Ditto Junus Brutus.....

To Ditto Plato.......

To Ditto Agrepina....

To Ditto Marcus Aurelus...

To 4 Ovels 0 the Elements....

To a. Tablit Syche & Cupid....

To Ditto S hyncks & Lyre....

To 2 Moul s from a. Sulpher Cast of S' Robert

Deducted for Portridgo 8s. Gd.

29 13

August y" 27,

Receiv'd the Contents of this Bill in full for Self & Co.

B. Grant.

Mess" 'Wedgwood & Bentley,

Jan! 1. To Iloskins & Grant.

1775.

n the

First Case

Carry forward... £13

Second Case.

326 EARLY MODELS. C1111'. VII. and artists to many objects in ornamental ware which are now enshrined in the collections of connoisseurs.

None of the modelling bills for 1770, 1771 and 1772 are

Cnsr. VII. SPECIALITY OF THE NEW COMPOSITION. 327 extant, and of even those of the three succeeding years, we have undoubtedly but a small part of the whole. Such as remain are precious relics spared from the wreck of time, as they permit us to individualise objects of a most interesting character.

One of the specialities of the new composition Whether compounded of the sulphate or carbonate of baryta, or as finally with the sulphate in maximum, and if present the carbonate in minimum, was, as already mentioned its ready incorporation of metallic oxides, especially that of cobalt. But much difficulty was at first incurred by the colour of the ground staining during firing through the white relief. Practice and experience ultimately conquered this defect; but for a time it acted deteriovatively upon the modellers' work; as in such portions of London 1st Sept. 1774.

Mess" VVedgwood & Bentley. _

B0' of P. Stephen.

13 a d.

1 Model of Lion for Teapot.. 0 10 6

1 D" of Grayhound for d. 0 10 6

1 D Lap Do for D.. 0 10 6

3 Moulds of t e above.. 0 10 6

£2 2 0

Sept. 2, 1774.

Received the above contents in full.

P. Stephan.

total want of finishing in both the 118088. They are in my opinion far

Wedgwood does not seem to have thought very highly of Stephen. ' I have received' he writes to Bentley, '& examined Mr. Steven's moulds of Hope & the Conquer'd Province, & am glad to find the drawing 8: proportions so well preserved, but in everything else they are infinitely short of the ex uisite originals. The Drapery is h & unfinish'd, & the characters of the Faces are those of common mortals of the lower Class. The armour in the Oonquer'd Province comes out too much a great deal. The face of the figure is crooked, greatly so, and there is a rom being equal to our figures of the same class, & I am afraid we shall not be able to make them so. Mr. Stevens can do it better than us, if he would bestow a. little more attention 8: labour upon them. You perceive I am very explicit, but I am not writing to Mr. Stevens, I wo'd not hurt him; but when you have the naked truth before you, you may cloath herin silk, or ser e as you find it most expedient.' 1 'edgwood to Bentley, August 22. 1774 328 DIFFICULTIES FROM STAINING. 'CRAP. VII their reliefs as required thinness, and even pellucidity, extreme delicacy had to be avoided.1 For a period there seemed no method of obviating this great difliculty, but in firing the 'ground and relief separately, and then fastening them together with cement. But further improvements in the application of colour conquered this and similar difiieulties. What some of these were, Wedgwood himself shows.

I must next say a few words to some proofs sent you in the box. By the proofs in the paper B, you will see that the brown ground fluxes, dissolves, 8: eats away the white compos", & by the proofs in C, you will observe that the blue 8: Green Grounds stain it. These are new and uuforseen difficulties, & how far I shall be able to conquer them I do not at present clearly see, but I will attempt it & let you know the result.

By the proof in D, you'l perceive that this quality of staining does not affect the larger heads, or masses of the white, but the ground of this head being much too easy fired, I will not answer for it when the ground is bro' up to its proper heat, & degree of vitrification; only this I may assert, that the thinner the white relief is, the more liable it will be to be stained. That those heads, and figures which can be made seperately, undercut a little at the edges, then fixed to the ground, & fired biscuit will be less liable to staining still than the Head in paper C. But the Heads & Figures which can be made & fired seperate & fixed on afterwards will be totally free from this inconvenience, & may have the great advantage of a perfectly even & polish'd ground. This will be the ultimate perfection of our Cameos." They will then be absolute. I shall not attempt to proceed any further in improving them, but apply my attention to multiplication only. Let me add, this is the state they must come to at last. I can do it now in a great variety of cameos, & if We do it at once, we shall thereby avoid another dead stock, which would accrue from a third or 4th improvement of our Cameos,

' In every considerable collection " There can be no doubt that all of cameos, this defect is to be ob-the finest of Wedgwood's cameos, served, though at the same time it is the portrait cameos especially, were a proof of early manufacture. executed in this manner.

CHAP. VII. ULTIMATE PERFECTION FORESEEN. 329 when we can carry our improvements to the utmost at this next alteration. There is but one objection to this plan which seems of any considerable importance to me, & that is, If our Antagonists should overtake us at this stage, we cannot again take another step before them to leave them behind again. And to this I would answer, that we shall leave them at so great a distance & they have so many obstacles to surmount before they can come up to us, that I think we have little to apprehend on that account—besides, taking it for granted that they will in time come at our compositions & we

shall still have variety of s"u.bjects—Eacecutio'n, Character, & connections in our favour suflicient to continue us at the head of this business, & lastly we must not forget a good resolution we have long since made of not permitting any apprehension of being robbed of our inventions, prevent our putting them into execution, when we think it proper in other respects. I am afraid you will think me tedious, but I wish'd to say all I had in my mind upon this subject at once & so have done with it. This leads me to the contents of the paper I). The Marr of Cupid &c. by which you will perceive that Groups of Figures as well as heads may be adapted to this mode of execution, & if my imagination does not mislead me, it has very great capabilities, & will take place in a vast variety of works from Rings to Chimney pieces—what can be richer & more beautifull, than a Tablet or Friese of a fine blue, ground true & polish'd, & ornamented with Figures in our fine white, not mere Bass-reliefs, such as one sees at once may be made out of a mould, but under cut, & made free in the manner of this man" of Cupid——I do not apprehend any difiiculty in fixing this, or any other piece, with cement, so as to cut the back of them as flat as the workman pleases, nor in fixing it afterwards to a polished blank with a soft flux by fire, or with a proper glue or cement without fire, which in many cases may be suflicient. The Birm'n manufactures go thro' more tedious & delicate operations, & are sold at a very inconsiderable price at last.'

From this letter, which is valuable alike to the artist, the connoisseur, and the potter, we learn some of the 1 Vedgwood to Bentley, January 15, 1775. 330 APPROACHES TOWARDS PERFECTION. CRAP. VII. most valuable secrets of Wedgwood's art, and the stages by which he brought this branch of it to perfection. Considering what this perfection ultimately was; that in quality and character of body, in beauty of colour, in mastery of minute and most exquisite details, the jasper ware far transcends anything known to us of the works of the potters of antiquity,

every successive efibrt by which Wedgwood gained this mastery has profound interest. It was the enthusiasm of Palissy, conjoined to a sobriety which arose from the consciousness of power, and an accurate judgment of probabilities. It was the artist transferring the finest of visions to clay, whilst the man of severe science steadied and watched the hand that wrought.

But this advance towards perfection was slow. Although in the month succeeding the date of the letter_ last quoted, six modellers were at work at Etruria, the difliculties connected with the grinding of the materials and the firing of these compositions greatly perplexed Wedgwood; often to a degree that would have disheartened less hopeful, accustomed, and resolute men. Writiiig to Bentley in July, he says:

Vhen all the circumstances attending this delicate composition have happened to jump together just right as they should & the firing exactly to suit it, the result is very fine, but we are very far from certainty & ever shall be, though by study & application we may approximate nearer & nearer to that truth & certainty which we can never perfectly attain.

To this truly philosophic idea, that we approach, but never realize-an absolute perfection of results—he adds a few days after: 1

Fate I suppose has decreed that we must go on. We must

O11.-xr. VII. PROSPECTS. 331 have our Hobby Horse, & mount him, & mount him again if he throws us ten times aday. This has been my case & I suppose it is pretty general amongst the fraternity.

The very next lines show how he had ridden and meant to ride his hobby to the end. ''

Count Sthall (how do you spell his name?) did us the honour of a visit yesterday. I attended him through both works, & he express'd the highest satisfaction with what he saw. He told his companion, which the interpreter afterwards told me, that nothing he had seen in England had given him so much pleasure. The manufactures of Dresden &

Berlin Porcelain both of which he had visited were not, he said to be compar'd with ours for taste, Elegance of designs, & fine modeling. If I am not greatly decelv'd in my expectations, your shew will be greatly superior to anything your good Princes & customers have seen. I am going upon a large scale with our models &c. which is one reason why you have so few new things just now, but I hope to bring the whole in compass for your next Winter's shew and ASTONISH THE WORLD ALL AT ones, for I hate piddling you know.'

When first brought into use, the supplies of cawk fell often short. On one occasion, Wedgwood with characteristic energy set off by himself to the mines near Matloek, where it had been hitherto procured. Here he obtained a large quantity, and of excellent colour; his scientific knowledge enabling him to direct the miners rightly in their search. With part of this he filled his chaise and returned home. The rest was sent to London, there to be pounded to a fineness sufiicicnt for disguise, and from thence to be dispatched in casks and boxes, by Waggon or canal into the Potteries.

The first time we hear the new body called by the name of jasper is in November 1775. Considering that Wedgwood already applied this term to one variation of

' Wedgwood to Bentley, August 6, 17 75.

his crystalline bodies, it is to be regretted that another more distinctive had not been found. Onyx would have been a more relative and appropriate name. But except to the student and connoisseur the crystalline jasper is unknown; whilst the latter use of the term is immortalised in a thousand forms of beauty and utility. A few months later we come upon the revelation of the ingredients of the new body. It is quite clear, that Wedgwood prepared it under several formulas. ' You desire ' he writes to Bentley, 'to have a mixture—will you be content to have part of it now, & the remainder another time? It is too precious to reveal all at once,..' The ingredients are then given, though afterwards carefully

struck out with a pen. Bentley however writes them fair on a blank part of the letter, as though for his own use. As written by Wedgwood they are in French thus: ' 17_Cailloux. 22— Argiles des Potiers. 20Albatre, i part. 24-Saphire. 74-6 '1 or in plain words: Flint, potters' clay, carbonate of baryta a quarter part_Zafl're, and sulphate of baryta a sixth part: for by the word albatre is undoubtedly meant, the carbonate of baryta, or terra ponderosa? In a succeeding letter Mr. Wedgwood writes, 'Our Jasper is one of 17-six of 74-three of 22_and a quarter of 20. You can hardly conceive the difiiculty and trouble I have had in mixing two tons of this composition, and leaving everybody as wise as they were.'3

' Wedgwood to Bentley, Februmy 3, 1776.

2 In some of the French dictionnries the word is put thus, Albatre Vitreux sorto de faut albzitre, or spath fusible. -" Vcdgwood to Bentley, February 6, 1776.

Brongniart does not give any for mula for the jasper body. In Knapp and Ronald's Chemical Technology, vol. ii. p. 476, we have two, which show distinct but not conjoint use of the sulphate and carbonate of baryta. Mr. 'Vt-dgwood's composition clearly included both, though in quantitive portions widely diiierent. The modern formulas are as follows:

One of the peculiarities of this mixture when put to ferment in a cellar, was that unlike other bodies it acquired an intense coldness. This was soon observed by Wedgwood, who to test-the degrees of cold, sent to Bentley for a new thermometer.

Continued practice and unwearied patience produced their true result. With occasional failures, almost every firing produced finer and finer things, till by the end of 1776 absolute perfection was nearly attained, except in the case of the largest tablets. The difficulty with them lay in the firing, and to conquer it, Wedgwood in July 1777, built a kiln on purpose. ' Our common Bisquit firing ' he tells Bentley 'will not be brought to suit it, nor will the composition be al-

tered to agree with the fire, and we have now nothing but the firing which stands between us & making the finest thing imaginable.'1 A short

Sul hate of Barytes. 48 or Carbonate of Ba es... 34 Chiiia Clay...... 16 China Clay.... 15 Dorset Clay...... 24 Dorset Clay...... 15 Flint........ 10 Cornish Granite..... 33 Gypsum..... 2 Vhite Lead...... 3 room which was probably his study. The cicerone of modern days says a nursery, but he was too cautious a man to trust his business secrets to children and nursemaids. The trap

These mixtures produce a fine white body for ornaments, and are stained blue by the addition of 1'; er cent. of oxide of cobalt, or green, y ses uioxide of chromium.

0 far Knapp and Ronald. But it is ve certain that modern jasper as a be y is greatly inferior to that prepared by We gwood. The dif erence is not only apparent to the touch, but to the eye; and it is to be hoped that this publication of the great master's secret will be of value to the manufacturer.

At Etruria Hall, the laces are still to be seen in which 'edgwood stored the cawk and other materials, and made his secret mixtures. They are a. range of cellars shut off from the rest by thick partition walls, and heavy doors. Vedgw00d's means of access was a trap—door, and a flight of narrow brick steps leading from a.

door steps ended in a wide passage, and from this opened a door to the outer air, as also the cellar in which the mixtures were made, the bins or troughs still remaining. The outpost of this fortress is equally well guarded. It is ap reached from the rear of the Hall y a double wall screen, forming a sort of winding passage. At the end of this are wide steps, and the door before mentioned. Thus guarded and masked, barrels and boxes could be brought in without the eognizance of anyone, except the immediate agents in the secret.

'77Vedgwood to Bentley, July 17, 17.

334 IMPROVED PROCESS. Crmr. VII. time previous to this another great improvement had been made, that of

washing the grounds of the tablets and cameos, instead of as heretofore mixing the colour with the composition. The improvement grew out of a necessity. Cobalt, from its increased consumption by the potters, had greatly risen in price; and more economical use naturally followed. ' In the box by the coach,' says Wedgwood to his partner, ' are two heads with exquisite blue grounds. I wish we may be able to make you some tablets in this way. They are coloured with the cobalt at 36/ p. 1b., which being too dear to mix with clay of the whole grounds we have washed them over, & I think them by far the finest ground we have ever made.' 1 The new kiln was a great success, and certainty in firing the finest tablets thus ensured. After years of patient toil, Wedgwood thus records his triumph to his friend, and this in connection with a masterpiece. Suppose, (he writes to Bentley) we were to make S' Wm Hamilton a. present of an Etruscan tablet Homer? The expense to us would be trifling in comparison to the value of the present, & the compliment paid to him, which he well deserves at our hands, & it would be the best introduction they could have in the country where he resides... I have now c0nquer'd every difficulty, which have not been a few in the management of the Jaspers, great as well as small, and wish much, very much to difl'use them properly.2

From this date, therefore, till Wedgwood's death——a period of seventeen years, the finest things in the jasper body were pr0duced—both in ornamental as well as useful ware.' 8 ' 1 Wedgwood to Bentley, April 13, wood says, 'I have tried my new 1777. mixing of Jasper, 8: find it very ' Ibid. October 16, 1778. good. Indeed had not much fear " Even before this date, success of it, but it is a satisfaction to be was certain. Writing to Bentley certain, & I am now absolute in this in November 1777, Mr. Wedg-precious article, & can make it with

Cnar. VII. RESULTS OF EXQUIS-ITE CHARACTER. 335

But prior to this many of the smaller cameos and basreliefs were very fine.

Of these a portion were without coloured grounds, as in the case of the Greek heads. Writing at the close of 1775, Wedgwood says:

We have sent a complete set of the Greek heads in white with gilt frames. Some of the same, (but not a complete set) with blue grounds. Some Anthonies & Cleopatrias very fine, & a few has-reliefs, all of which I wish you to look at before they go into the Rooms. The blue grounds are out of the last kiln & the Cleopatrias, both of which are the finest things imaginable. It really hurts me to think of parting with these Gems, the fruit of twenty years' toil for the trifle I fear we must do, to make a business worth our notice of it.1

A little later he says:

We send a. Night & Day. The best we have made of the new white. A Medusa large & very fine—& heads blue grounds——too fine to sell! Reasons for sending this cargo is that you may see our firing of the new white altogether. I think we improve in the science of firing, & that seems to be the only point we are deficient in respecting this very fine body. Hackwood has nearly finished the two tablets of the Birth & Triumph of Bacchus; ' but am afraid we shall not be able to make either of them in one continued Tablet so! 5%,. A E-3 I we could make them to fill a friese very cleverly in separate @)6)§%¢/"" antique. Both the former tablets are in the choice collection of T. 0. Barlow Esq., the eminent engraver. In the Birth of Bacchus the inferiority of Hackwood to Flaxman pieces so as much facility & certainty as black wane. Sell what quantity you please. I would as readily engage to furnish you with this, as any potte

I make. We have only now to pus it forward with the world, keep our secret,' &c. &c.

1 Vedgwood to Bentley, November 6, 1775. 9 Neither of these tablets are in the first and second editions of the Catalogue, and were consequently new models. Of the Birth of Bacchus there was another model from the in style, com osition, and grouping, is prominent y seen. The figures appear to have little

to do with each other; whereas one of the canons of Flaxman's art, both theoretically and practically, was that of a whole; each figure in its relation to the other serving to complete a perfect idea. 336 GEMS FOR CABINETS. Cm. VII. the grounds of the ovals blue, & the figures white & all the pieces together making up one subject would be better to fill a friese than detached statues & figures which have no connection one with another.1

As early as 1772-1773 the head of Shakespeare and those of the English kings from Astle had been modelled. By the beginning of 1774 the medals of the Popes were in hand, and the figures of Morpheus and Autumn. A little later the Continence of Scipio was the subject of a tablet; and the heads of Scavalo and of Hippocrates were considered very-fine. Cameos were multiplied both in size and form; and this not so much for ornamental purposes as for assortment and preservation in cabinets. This was Wedgwood's original idea, and one which was a favourite to the close of his life. In November 1775 he tells Bentley ' We are putting up one set of impressions of Gems in my Cabinet, & putting another at the same time for you, but this business goes on slowly.' This idea of making a collection of his works was no new one to Wedgwood.

VVe are moulding from Mr. Stuart's sulphurs (he informs his friend). We also mould all before us in Sir Wm's gems & I mean some time-to make each of us a complete set of them, & all our good things t-0 be left as a sacred deposit for the use of our children and children's children, which with some acet of what has been done, & what may be done, some hints, & seeds for future discoveries might perhaps be the most valuable treasure we could leave them. But when shall we get time to write? when we have not time to say half we wish to do on the business of the current day.'

In the succeeding year he pursues the same idea, and on the occasion of a visit from his London friend, Mr. More, he tells Bentley,

CHAP.VII.   BAS-RELIEF——CI-

IOICE OF HERCULES. 337

We have had some serious delibera-tions upon a cabinet for _ each of us. Mr. More thinks, which I believe we have talked of before, that we should, each of us have, in our private posses-sion, a specimen of all our fine Bas-reliefs, Cameos, Intaglios, & whatever else of our manufacture we think would be valuable to our Children, or Friends of the next Generation.——I mean not merely by way of a collection of fine things to shew our Friends, or amuse ourselves with, but to serve as a model to form such another Manufacture as our own upon, supposing our other works and warehouses be no more.—— I had often wish'd I had saved a single specimen of all the new articles I had made, & would now give twenty times the original value for such a. collection. For ten years past I have omitted doing this, because I did not begin ten years before. I am now from thinking & talk-ing a little more upon this subject with Mr. More resolved to ntalx: a beg-in-ning & we have sketched out a Cabinet for some of the smaller & finer things, which Mr. More is so kind to promise to see executed for me, if you approve of the plan.'

Previously to this, Ralph Unwin had made coloured '

' Wedgwood to Bentley, Septem-par-ticularlv in the choicest specimens sketches of all the finest of the Etruscan painted vases with some others; and a set when bound was assigned to either partner.

A vast number of cameos and tablets were made in a white body; in fine bis-cuit, or as it is termed in the invoices of ornamental Ware, 'common white ' and in uncoloured jasper. The ' Choice of Hercules ' as here given is in the for-mer body? It is an oval tablet 18 inch-es by 13, and as it is mentioned in the first edition of the Catalogue,8 it cannot be with any probability referred to Flax-man (fig. 52). It may be Tebo's work, as he excelled in large bas-relief figures. Both ground and figures have been formed in a mould together, and not her 3, 1774. _ of the white bodies, both bis-cuit and 2 In the collection of T. O. Bar-

low ' _ _ jasper. Esq. The invoices of 1779 abound 3 Page 20, N0_ 69_ VOL. II. 7.

338 DESCRIPTION OF THE BAS-RE-LIEF. CHAP. VII. by distinct opera-tions, as in the majority of bas-reliefs whether in cameos or tablets. The cen-tral figure of Hercules is well modelled from the antique. On the right hand a beautiful female figure leans on a bank and lures him, but in vain, to a life of pleasure; for he turns away and looks to a rocky steep towards which another

CRAP. VII.-OVAL TABLET. POMONA. 339 figure more chastely clothed, points and leads the willing god. The group is illustrative of a well-known passage in Xenophon. It is ably conceived, and both in style and com-position heads the list of these early works. The second illustration is an oval tablet, likewise white. It is in the Mayer collection, and represents Pomona, the goddess of gardens and fruits (fig. 53). The figure, which is aerial, descends to-wards the earth, bearing in one hand a cluster of fruit, in the other a short wand. The drapery is exquisitely ren-dered; the relief strongly undercut, and the whole emblematic of motion and grace. The figure is said to have been modelled by Flaxman, and certainly 3-LO HEAD OF MEDUSA. CRAP. VII. bears the impress of his hand. Yet, if intended to represent Pomona, it is not named as such in any of the Catalogues. 1 The annexed head of Medusa (fig. 54), and the vase (fig. 55) in which the purity and truth of the elliptical outline are obvious, are likewise in the fine white biscuit body or early jasper. Of the jasper as finally perfected into a por-cellaneous body of exquisite fineness, sharpness, and adaptability to the high-est requirements of the modeller and artist, the examples are endless. They include many of the finest cameos, some intaglios, heads of illustrious an-cients, and figures or small statuettes. The oval cameo of Minerva (fig. 56), from Mr. Barlow's collection, will show to what perfection, body, 1 Mr. Mayerpiirchased this plaque-field. They are in their ori ':11 or tablet in Milan There are two I' gilt frames, and are

said to ave similar though if the writer re-been bought at a. sale at one of the collects' correctly, the ground in these Prebendn houses. cases is blue, in the. Iuseum at Lich

CIIAP. VII. CAMEOS IN THE VII-ITE BODY. 341 modelling, and finish were brought. The French in particular admired and patronised the various works of art in the white bodies. Wedg-wood himself delighted in his cameos and bas-reliefs of a single colour. In one case some cameos were so fine that he bid Bentley hide them in a wrapper for ' they are too good for common show.'

The Sacrifice to Pan and its compan-ion-tablets, were also in the white body, and highly considered by the great mas-ter. In his own words, they are if you can find in yr heart to sell them, set what prices upon them you please, but it will be really a sin & a shame to part with them for 158. a. pair.

This reluctance to sell the precious fruits of his long and weary labours was not only the natural result of a fine artis-tic taste, of' a sense of truth and beauty in their highest forms, but of a keen ap-preciation of the power which creates. True genius loves its work, and (Fig.-56.) HHADOI-'.Il.'1P.RVA. conserves it where it can. Some "mow Couxmol of the greatest sculptors and painters, both ancient and modern, have kept a favourite work beside them whilst they lived, and at their death left it to careful hands. This is not so much the result of egotism, as a worship 342 ENAMEL PATTERNS. CHAP. VII.

of the spirit.' of truth in which they wrought; and an intuitive perception that in working to the height of their ideal, and in regarding only that, they had done justice to themselves and their art. Unlike the sculptor and the painter, Wedgwood could easily multiply his works. Still, with the knowledge experi-ence forced upon him that perfection is rarely gained, he was naturally willing to conserve these precious testimonies of his success in an hitherto untried field.

We have already shown that the enamelling of cream ware table services reached a point of great excellence in the works at Chelsea. But the patterns were still further improved and a great variety added after the removal to Greek Street. The sales which gradually increased for some years,1 were in 1776 very large, and so continued with little variation to the close of Wedgwood's life. The patterns were, many of them, taken from the antique, from the Etruscan and Greek vases, from lamps and paterze, in some few cases from bas-reliefs, mouldings and freizes, or from objects belonging to a later and more debased period of art, the fresco wall-paintings found at Herculaneum. In all these, admirable as many of the patterns are, there is a certain degree of monotony. Even where the artist sought to vary, it was upon the old types of wreaths of ivy, laurel and myrtle, helices or tendrils, as of the vine, the egg and tongue border, spirals, maeanders, waves or the cymation border, and others. As already said,2 Wedgwood does not seem to have had access to, or else his attention directed to the richest and most original source of border 1 VVed ood to Bentley September 18 1776. 1 Vol. 5'; 2e. ' '

.CHAP. VII. THEIR SOURCES AND CHARACTER. 343 patterns, the red lustrous ware of antiquity.1 There we find the poverty of the ancients in this respect_varied by an exquisite grace and fertility, which bear a nearer relation to oriental or the best phases of medizeval art, than to Etruscan or Grecian in its other branches. The patterns Wedgwood copied directly or relatively from the antique were greatly in request by our own nobility and by continental states, as Italy and Germany. He exported largely such patterns as Nos. 3, 13, 14, 27, 29, 30, 32, 35, 37, 39, and 40, in the annexed plates. The colours of some of these patterns were greatly varied, though Nos. 13, 14, 22, 27, 29, 35, 37, 39, and 40 were generally a rich brown red. Pattern 3 is a somewhat complex variation of the egg and tongue border, and in different colours was much prized in this country. Figure 13 was the mzeander pattern, with a slight addition of dots derived likewise from an antique source. Nos. 14 and 22 were amongst the most popular patterns enamelled by

Wedgwood. They were called the red, green, black, blue and purple antique, as they happened to vary in their colour; though the latter pattern was more generally a rich brown red——occasionally this was called Etruscan. Both borders were rather exquisite adaptations than direct copies. The first was derived from an ornamentation peculiar to the fine vases of Nola, and the latter was the adaptation of a pattern originally Egyptian. Nos. 30, 32, and 37 were in common use. Of patterns strongly characteristic of Wedgwood's taste for simple ornament and subdued colouring, Nos. 7, 9, 10, 16, 21, and 23, are examples, and their number

' For men exquisite specimens reader is referred to the plates in of embossed orderings in the red Roman London, by C. R. Smith, lustrous ware, the ceramic artist or F. S. A.

344 FAVOURITE PATTERNS. CHAP. VII. might be greatly multiplied. No. 21 was the pattern of the table ware supplied for Mr. Eden, afterwards Lord Auckland, on the occasion of his embassy to Copenhagen. The grape and ivy-leaf borders, Nos. 24 and 28, were simple, graceful, and beautiful, and thus always in demand. The former pattern in purple and gold was painted on a dessert service for Lord Chatham just prior to his decease. The ivy leaf was the pattern of the dessert service prepared as a marriage gift, in 1778, for young Mr. Davenport, the son of Rousseau's friend.1 It may interest the reader to learn that Nos. 3, 9, 14, and 28, are copied from the original coloured slips appended to an order of M. Rost a German n1erchant.. Nos. 8 and 11 are from an Italian order, and 5, 15, 17, 33, and 36 were patterns sought by the French merchants and dealers. Most of the other borderings are taken from invoices and papers; though we may with certainty assume, that with the exception of Nos. 3, 9, 10, 14, 16, 21, 22, and 24, we have not before us the finest of Wedgwood's border designs. What remain as specimens are now for the most part treasured up as precious relics, and are thus not easily accessible. The invoices, particularly those of the Chelsea

period of enamelling, prove this to be the case; as we have borderings mentioned in these, and similar papers of a later date, which point to designs of a most exquisite character. Edging in various colours was a very popular method of decoration; and feather-edge, No. 28, whether simply embossed on the edge of the ware, or tinted, was extremely so. Of this edging there were several varieties. Sometimes it

' Wedgwood to Bentley, May 4, ' friend. Mr. and Mrs. Davenport are 1778. referred to in Madame D'Arblay's He married a daughter of Mr. I diary. Vols. i. and ii.

Sneyd, Vedgwood's neighbour and 1 CRAP. VII. THEIR INFINITE VARIETY. 845 was placed between gadroons, sometimes it had a serrated edge, at others the serrated edge died away on the plate; but the general rule was for the feathering to fade away into the body colour. The husk border was a favourite pattern with George III. The verinicelli pattern, N o. 23, was chiefly exported.1

Beyond the limit of these received patterns, the range was very wide. Flowers, fruits, shells)' Weeds, plants, arms and crests, were all subjects for the enamellers. The simple hedgerow plants and flowers of our country predominated in such designs over those cultivated in garden and green-house. The borders used with ware having family arms or a crest in the centre, or on the rim, were most varied. Sometimes they were the ordinary patterns; at others a riband of a favourite colour, waved.

Landscapes were occasionally painted, and after the date of the great Russian Service, ware so decorated came much into vogue. Certain patterns also bore names significant of the purpose for which they were intended as the ' Cottage pattern ' or ' Naval pattern'. When form and colouring were alike copies from nature, the name given to the ware was equally expressive, as the 'Autumnal leaf pattern ' and the ' Shell pattern.' From some 1 It may be interesting. to give ders, 2/. Plates with black flowers, some few items as to the prices paid 3/ a doz. Blue antique plates, 3§d.

for enamelling useful ware. Sweetmeat baskets ed (1 with pu le, each 1§d. Soup Izdles, 3d. ardbz. Bowl shaped dishes, 6§d. each. For bordering more was paid. Small plates with blue ivy or laurel, 2 a doz. Sauce boats and stands with the green antique border were 6d. each. The same for flowering royal feather edge compotiers. Plates with husks and green edge, 2/6 a. doz. Dishes with grape border, 1011. each. Dishes with sprigs in the centre, 1, each. Glaciers with antique bor apiece. 10:1. for a teapot, arrow pattern. Grape bordered dessert plates, 2§d. each. Cups and saueers, purple antique border, 1/3 doz. Ditto lue shell edge, 2§d. each. Teapots purple edge, 2d. each. Purple antique bordered plates, 8/ a doz., and 2/ for laurel pattern. 1 tea-tray green anti ue music 1/0. Invoices & bills 177. Mayer MSS.

'' Shell edge bordering made its' first appearance during the summer of 1776. 346 THE COTTAGE PATTERN. CRAP. VII. small plates preserved of the ' Cottage pattern ' in the collection of Dr. Hooker, we give the annexed example (fig..57); and the borderings Nos. 1, 2, 4, 7, 12, and 34 are selected from others in the same set. The plates are small, and in the centre of each are the varied implements of the dairy, the farm, and the garden. The ' Autumnal Leaf' was for dessert. Each plate and dish was an enlarged representation of nature both in colour and form.1 Occasionally the pectons or valves of plants were simulated with wonderful truth to nature. During 1778 and afterwards, Wedgwood made oonchology his study, and formed an admirable collection of shells. From this date may be traced his adaptation of these exquisite natural forms to his art. The flatter or valve-like shells were 1 A beautiful dessert service of ' Autumnal Leaves' is in possession of the writer's friend, Mrs. Todhunter of VVillesden.

Clur. VII. FORMS AND PATTERNS FROM NATURE. 347 copied for plates, whilst the larger and occasionally more convoluted, served as basins, baskets and dishes. This exquisite example (fig. 58) from M. De la Rue's collection, is an absolutely perfect copy of the nautilus, though colouring is needed to convey to the reader's eye the matchless beauty of the pinky and pearl-white tints of the original ware.

For many years previously to his death, in December 1789, John Sadler of Liverpool seems to have retired from the printing business, or at least resigned to his partner, Guy Green, the chief details of its management. The latter was probably a younger man. Thus, from about 1772, we find Green referred to solely by Wedgwood; and from this date a great, if slow, improvement in printed patterns took place. A greater variety of colours were used, and the art of their contrast and assimilation improved upon, so that by the end of 1776 many of the patterns hitherto enamelled were printed in outline and then filled in with the requisite colours. For this latter business Green employed young girls at wages 348 UNION OF PRINTING AND PAINTING. Cnar. VII.

of 1s. 6d. each per week. One of the patterns brought into use at this date was that of shells and sea-weeds.' It was suggested by Wedgwood, and he thus writes to Bentley on the subject:

The shell pattern is a first essay, the borders in particular are so too. I have wrote to Mr. Green that the groups are too large for the plates, that the green is of too common a colour upon some of the weeds & lies too high above the glaze. But that I think them very promising proofs & have desired to have the prices.'

A few days later Wedgwood adds:—

Yes, I make no doubt Painting & Printing may exist together. I hope we_ shall do both in quantities both in Table and Teaware. Many patterns cannot be Printed & these will employ the pencils. I had wrote to Mr. Green upon the first sight of the Shell patterns that they were coloured too high, & must be kept down, especially the gree-n—Shells and weeds may be colour'd as chaste as any subjects whatever, & I hope we shall get into the way of it in time. But this pattern was intended chiefly for abroad, & foreigners in general will bear higher colouring & more forcible contrasts than the English.3

A considerable quantity of the shell and seaweed pattern painted and printed ware is yet in existence, and this dish (fig. 59) from Mr. Mayer's collection, will suflice to convey to the eye of the reader the truth to nature of the details, and the delicacy of eflect attained by their separation and distinctiveness, although so much is lost in the print by the absence of colour.4 From this date Green greatly enlarged his range of colours and subjects.

1 A mere shell border had, how-I great reduction in size. In Mr. ever, been in use for some years, Mayer's Museum, Colquit Street, previously. Liverpool, there is a considerable

' 'Vedgwood to Bentley, Decem-variety of this ware, and Mr. Falcke's bet 5, 1776. collection contains many choice spe

" Ibid. December 15, 1776. cimens of enamelled table ware, and 4 The original dish is nine inches I that in which enamelling and printb_' seven, so that the engraving is a I ing were so efi'ectivel_v combined.

CRAP. VII. SHELLS AND SEA-WEEDS. 349

Most of the crests and coats of arms were thus first printed and then coloured, and even more elaborate patterns were successfully attempted. Wedgwood had long complained of the limit put on the extension of sales, by the cost incurred by the manufacturer in enamelling. '

Some shell plates (he writes) I have just rec'd from Liverpool, convince me of a revolution being at hand, but our Painters may nevertheless be continued, if it is not their own fault. The tawdry appearance is all va.nish'd & I am fully convinc'd that the Ivy and Grape bord" may be done at one third of what I now pay.'

The result fulfilled Wedgwood's expectations, and he soon came to see that the printer at no distant day would make a further step in his art, and free himself altogether from a connection witl1 the enameller. In the spring of the succeeding year, 1777, he proposed to Green to build enamel works upon the banks of the Grand Trunk Canal somewhere between Liverpool and

Etruria, and near enough to some town—Middlewich 1 Wedgwood to Bentley, December 28, 1776.
350 ENAMEL VVORKS PROPOSED. CHAP. VII. was proposed--to employ the children there; but the scheme, after further consideration, fell to the ground, owing, as it would seem, to Green's objection to reside at the proposed works. At first the Liverpool enamellers were exceedingly jealous of this union between painting and printing, and sought to nullify it by charging an exorbitant price for colouring the groups of shells, &c.; but when Green complained of this to Wedgwood, he suggested a true remedy: 'I told him,' he wrote to Bentley, ' he might do the whole without them, at which he shook his head, but I plied him upon the subject till he promised me to try, & I am fully persuaded he will accomplish it.'1 This revolution in the monopoly sought by the enamellers was nearer than expected. From the improvements in the art of printing, and the competition amongst masters, the reduction in the prices paid to enamellers became, as early as the succeeding year 1778, surprising.

Another point brought Green and Wedgwood's business into still closer alliance. With occasional exceptions, as for some noble_ patron or personal friend, the latter gradually declined tile making, and thus when wanted tiles were usually procured from Green. The Staffordshire clay was not so well adapted for tiles as some qualities imported into Liverpool, the potters there were more accustomed to manipulating and firing a coarse body which approximated that of delft, and Green moreover had space and conveniences for the business. ' If I began a new manufacture it would be that of tile making on an improved plan,' wrote Wedgwood about this date; but he was not inclined to build a special manufactory, or turn his thoughts in this direction. If he had, there can be no doubt he would have anticipated some of the

' Wzadgwood to Bentley, April 8,

1777.

Can. VII. TILES. 351 improvements of our own day in encaustic tile work, and perhaps aided in the recovery of the lost arts of the mediaaval tilewrights; as that of the retention of colour and glaze through long periods of atmospheric change. But he was more worthily employed in those higher departments of his art, to which so few aspire, and in which fewer still excel.

Green carried on his interesting labours for Wedgwood till the death of the latter. In 1783, Wedgwood furnished a table and tea-service to the executors of David Garrick, on which Green had printed an edging and the cypher D. G. at the cost of 8l. 6s. Hid. ' The great actor had ordered it, but he died previous to its completion. But before this date, and after, printing upon the glaze was very generally introduced into the Staffordshire Potteries, and at Etruria after the death of its founder. Yet, possessing the blocks of the old patterns, Green still printed matches and occasionally other articles for Wedgwood's successors, till he gave up business in 1799 to enjoy the honest fruits of a long and laborious life.
-trade in pottery was carried on be-i the

' Bill of Guy Green to "'edg-' k-horse days, still conveyed wood, November 7, 1783. Mayer ' ll'-'2dgwood's were to and fro for MSS. l printing in his wagons and carts; it

These hills, which are scattered singular fact, considering that the over a lengthened period, furnish Grand Trunk Canal liadbeen finished many interesting particulars, besides I eighteen years. Probably 'edgthose connected with patterns and i wood found there was less stealage colour. They inform us that in and breakage in the old method of times of peace a considerable export i transport; or it may be explained on ground of the tenacity with tween Liverpool and Holland, in-' which he held by his tried and faithcluding Belgium; and that the sale ' ful servants. lorris's services to was large of a peculiar kind of cofi'ee Vedgwood must have extended over cup, which was made at Etruria of 8. a eriod of full five and thirty ears. thick

white ware, on which was T e bills also show us that 'edg rinted by Green some religious wood's shell patterns in various device or monogram. Ve also earn colours, had a great run, and that that even so late as 1793, Daniel red landscapes and green flower Morris of Lawton, the old carrier of patterns were equally popular.

THE CATALOGUI-IS——'ARIOUS EDITIONS—SUBJECTS IN THE FIRST, SECOND, FOURTH, AND FIFTH EDITIONS——FLAXMANIS WORK—THE 'GENIUS OF SCULPTURE,—HIGH AND LOW RELIEF —THE MUSE8— FLAXMAN'S PORTRAIT IN WAX—— TABLETS FOR CHIMNEY-PIECE8—— LONGTON HALL, SIR WILLIAM BAGOT—NO FIXED AND UNVARIABLE PRICE FOR FINE WORKS——A CHIMNEY-PIECE FOR TRENTHAM—BROWN THE GARDENER AND ARCHITECT——ORTHODOX THEORY IN RELATION TO COLOUR—-OPPOSITION OF THE ARCHITECTS—SIR W'. CHAMBERS PERSUADES THE QUEEN THAT WEDGWOOD'S TABLETS ARE NOT FIT FOR CHIMNEY-PIECES—A BAS-RELIEF FOR SIR W. HAMILTON—HIS LETTER-——WEDGWOOD'S CHIMNEY-PIECES WIDELY, THOUGH SPARSELY SCATTERED—— SLABS FOR ENAMEL I'AINTING—STUBBS—HIS PERSISTENT CHARACTF-R——BLACK B.S-RELIEF V.-SES—THE EARL OF WARWICK—BUSTS—-THE DE WIT'IS—-GREAT MEN OF OTHER COUNTRIES—SEALS —-POLISHIN G—ROBERT POLLARD-—-PIRATES — PALMER AND VOYEZ AGAIN—'OYEZ'S SEALS—TRAVELS ABOUT THE COUNTRY—-FORGES WEDGWOOD AND BENTLEY'S NAMES-—IN TROUBLE AT LAST—— VEDGWOODl8 DIGNIFIED SILENCE—VOYEZ DISAPPEARS FROM THE SCENE—PALIER'S BANKRUPTCY—RESULTS—— TASSIE—HIS MEDALLION PORTRAITS—CAHEOS—CABmETS—COPESTAKE, THE LAP1— DARY

AND JEWELLER AT UTTOX-ETER—SOHO—GROUND-LAYING IN WATER—COLOURS—THE DECORATION OF FURNITURE AND FANCY ARTICLES WITH CAHEOS—BOULTON AND FOTHERGILL'S WARES AT THE RUSSIAN COURT-—KNIFE AND FORK VASES—STORER AND HIS PATENT—ROSSO ANTICO—CANE AND BAMBOO WARES—GOLD BRONZE._INKSTA.NDB—MORTAR MATERIAL INTRODUCED-—IMPROVEHENTS —MORTAR8 AT APOTHECARIES' HALL-—llULTI-FARIOUS WORKS.

VOL. II. ' A A

CHAPTER VIII.

THE CATALOGUES AND THEIR CONTENTS.

N 1773, four years from the commencement of their partnership, when their stock of ornamental ware had accumulated sufficiently for such a purpose, Wedgwood and Bentley published the first edition of their Catalogue. It is an insignificant-looking little pamphlet of sixty pages 1'3mo, printed on very bad paper, and stitched in a' thin marbled cover. Yet considering its contents, the position of the fine arts at that period, the advance therein it shows, and its excessive rarity, this little book is far more precious than many a larger' and costlier volume. A second edition appeared in the following year, 1774, and in this we find in the last sheet a printed reference to Portland House, Greek Street, Soho. Shortly afterward this edition was translated into French, and called, the third. A fourth in English was published in 1777; a fifth in English and a sixth in French in 1779; and a sixth in English in 1787, and this was again translated into French in 1788. The English edition of 1787 was reprinted in Liverpool in 1817 by Mr. Boardman, under the title of ' Museum Etruriae.' Bentley wrote the introduction to the first edition; the various modifications and additions up to 1779 proceeded from his pen, though always with reference to the judgment and corrections of his partner.1 Wedgivood thought highly of this per

' A rough draft of this, written by Bentley on the back of an old letter, is amongst the Mayer MSS. 356 VARIOUS EDITIONS OF THE CATALOGUES. CRAP. VIII formance, for he added, after suggesting some improvements and alterations: ' The whole is extremely well done. I thank you for it, and hope it will bring us both credit and profit.' 1 Again he Writes, in _relation to the second edition, its improvement and added matter: 'The introduction you have been so kind to send for my perusal is very clever and will do honour to the composer, and, I hope, will be attended with the desired effect. I cannot do anything to mend it, and would not willingly make it worse.' 2 The Catalogue was also translated into German and Dutch, if not into Italian. M. Veldhuysen, the successor of Du Burk and Cooper in the Amsterdam branch of Wedgwood and Bentley's business, translated it into Dutch, and published it in that city in the early winter of 1778.3 The edition for Germany was undertaken by M. Rost, a wealthy Leipsic merchant, who translated and dispersed it at his own expense.' For his energy and friendly aid in this matter, the generous Englishmen presented him with some choice pieces of their manufacture. Besides these were Catalogues of intaglios for seals and rings;5 and Lists of useful ware, in almost every continental language, were scattered Wide and far.6

The Catalogues are of singular value in tracing the history of the ornamental bodies and the subjects modelled. With two exceptions, the Rosso Antico or red ware, and the cane colour, this history of material has been given; although it is still curious to trace the simple white

' Vedg'W00d to Bentley, March 1 and the names of their owners are as 15, 1773. follows: 1st Edition. I. F alcke, Esq. Ibid. March 2,1774. 2nd. Library Great Seal Patent ' Wedgwood to Bentley, Nov. 4, Oflice. 4th. Dr. Rimbault. 5th.
1778. J. A. Tulk, Esq. 6th. French and 4 Ibid. June 14, 1779. 6th English. Joseph Mayer, Esq., 5 Several editions were published, Museum Etrurine-the

wr1ter's own. the first in 1773, the last in 1779. In "the Mayer Collection is also the G The editions used by the writer, l Catalogue of Seals, 1779.

CRAP. VIII. FIRST EDITION OF THE CATALOGUE. 357 body of the first edition, confirmed in the second into a fine white terra-cotta through the use of the carbonate of baryta; and this in the fourth edition into the still finer jasper, by the substitution in maximum of the simpler and less Protean sulphate of the same substance. Here was an exquisite material ascension, which, once grasped, reflected itself in the highest provinces of a most beautiful art!

The lists of cameos and intaglios in the first edition of the Catalogue prove how diligently Wedgwood and his able partner had applied themselves to the study of the antique gems. Of these they purchased impressions from Tassie the well-known modeller of gems in sulphur, wax, and awhite paste or plaster composition; or more generally, as at a later date, they modelled from the gems themselves; as from those of the Duke of Marlborough, Lord Bessborough, Lord Clanbrassil, SirWilliam Hamilton, Sir Watkili Wynne, Sir Roger Newdigate, Mr. Anson, Mr. Foley, Athenian Stuart, and various other possessors of these exquisite specimens of antique simplicity and grace in art. Sir W. Wynne was one of Wedgwood's earliest and most munificent patrons. He contributed 172 intaglios and 173 gems or cameos to Wedgwood's first lists.1 Amongst the number are some of the finest subjects of antique art as interpreted by the gem engravers of the Alexandrian, and later of the Augustine age. At the close of the earliest list of cameos we have the Marriage of Cupid and Psyche (fig. 60); thus first obtained from a sulphur cast by Tassie, but afterwards freshly modelled from the original gem, and given to the world in both the fine biscuit and uncoloured jasper, as also in jasper with

' These were largely added to, ' numbers from 2 to 290 in the edition from the same source from time to j of 1787, with the exception of sixtytime. The lists in MSS. are still four varied numbers. extant. The intaglios include the ' 355 MARRIAGE OF CUPID AND PSYCIIE. CHAP. VIIL blue grounds, and in sizes from the largest oval plaque to the minutest ring gem for a lady's finger.1 The accompanying illustration is a reduced copy of a large sized blue and white cameo in Mr. Mayer's collection. Its original may be well called one of the I finest specimens of ancient art. The whole subject, as an allegory upon marriage, is full of delicacy, truth, grace and feeling. It has none of the grossness of a later day of art, when such symbols would have been so differently expressed. It may well be said that purity is an-inherent principle in the highest expressions of art--for it is not to be conceived that a mind looking only at the outer and grosser forms of truth, can represent them under their more subtle and ideal aspect-in a word, psychologically and not sensually. What modesty and grace in the veiled

' This exquisite gem, first engraved by Bartolozzi, is to be found in the 1st vol. of Br_'ant's Ancient Mythology.

Can. VIII. NIOBE'S CHILDREN. 359 face, the downcast looks, the half reluctant, half willing steps of Psyche! What equal truth in the half bold, 11alf sly expression of Cupid's' face, in the cradle filled with fruit, and in the loose fillet_chain of'love_by which the other Cupid, more resolute because less impassioned, leads them onward to that which, another Cupid uncovering, we may presume to be the symbol of the marriage bed! None but a mind of the highest order could have given artistic expression to this allegory of the great passion of human life, and the results, which in causation, constitute the generations of the world.

The tablets in the first edition of the Catalogue are eighty-two in number, and include various fine subjects from the antique, as the Destruction of N iobe's Children, the Feast of the Gods, the Death of a Roman Warrior, the Choice of Hercules, and many others. A reduced copy of Niobe's Children from a cameo of a later day is 'here shown (fig. 61), as also a Centaur with Perseus or Apollo, 360 CENTAUR. CRAP. VI-

II. and the Death of a Roman Warrior. The Centaur (fig. 62), a round tablet and framed, and 16 inches in diameter, is in the black basaltes body, and is an exquisite work of art, showing, that even thus early, great skill had been acquired in inodelling. It is one of the gems of the De La Rue Collection. The Death of a Roman Warrior is another1 (fig. 63). It is a longitudinal tablet in black, 20 inches by 1, and was copied from an ancient sarcophagus at Reine. Its bas-reliefgives all the attributes of the Roman soldier. His shield, his helmet, his sword, and the ensigns he _ 1 By some it is said to represent the death of Julius Caesar, but (.':esar fell pierced with wounds in the senate-house, and not in battle.

CRAP. VIII. DEATH OF A RO-MAN VVARRIOR. 361 carried on his march, or in battle. The drapery on the various figures is finely rendered, and the figure of the Dead Warrior, as it rests inert on the arms of the soldiers, may have served as a study for some of the painters of the Renaissance, as it is not unlike various representations of the dead Saviour.

Heads of illustrious Greeks, Romans, and Moderiis follow. The busts in bronze or black basaltes are twentythree in number, and of these the annexed one of Horace (fig. 64), 19 inches high, modelled from a cast by Hoskins, is a fine specimen of Wedgwood's earliest works in his bronze ware. It was probably modelled by Hackwood, who at that date, and later, employed a large part of his time in this direction. Writing to Bentley shortly after, Wedgwood says, ' We are going on with the busts,1 but we proceed very slowly, it being a fortnight's work to prepare

' The were as follows: Homer Palladio, unknown large head, Inigo large an small, Solon, Pindar, Plato, Jones, Junius Brutus,.Iarcus BruEpicurns, Zeno, Minerva, Venus. his, Airrippina, Seneca, Antoniiius.

362 BUST OF HORACE. CRAP. VIII. and mould one of these heads, & whilst this business continues we have no one to work at the statues.'1 A month later he says 2

We are going on very fast with the busts, having four of our principal hands almost constantly employed on them. You will find our busts much better finished than the plaister casts or models we take them from. Hackwood bestows a.week upon each head in restoring it to wha.t we suppose it was when it came out of the hands of the statuary. Pray do not let our labour be unobserved when they are under your care.'

In the second edition of the Catalogue, 1774, the various classes of artistic work are added to considerably and (Fig. 64.) uus1' or m.@=._.....-M cottmox. We find mention of

Joachim Smith and his portrait models. The cameos and intaglios are many of them superb; and the bas-reliefs, tablets, and medallions, show a small increase. The busts are very numerous. In the fourth edition of the Catalogue, 1777, the intaglios for seals and rings are spoken of as improved by giving a

Faustina, Augustus Caesar, Antoni-long piece of work. Wedgvood to nus Pius, Marcus Aurelius, Ger-Bentlev, June 24,1774. manicus, Cato. These I believe are ' ' Ibid. July 24, 1774. from Hoskins; to make the moulds. " Ibid. August 16, 1774. from these busts will be a great and '

CRAP. VIII. BUST OF VIRGIL. 363 ground of pale blue to the surface of the stone, and by polishing. The jasper and waxen biscuit bodies are also first referred to; and the bas-reliefs, medallions, and tablets exhibit an increase. For two years Flaxman has been more or less at work for Wedgwood, and the fine heads of illustrious Greeks, as also those of Iris, Ariadne, Bacchus, Pan and Syrinx, may be referred to him. The busts are numerous and fine, and those of Virgil and Seneca (figs. 65 and 66) which are thus given, indicate the mastery obtained by Hackwood and his assist-mg 6,) ant modellers.

In 1779 appeared the fifth and last edition of the Catalogue, prior to the death of Bentley-In this we have clearly much more of Flaxman's work, as the Apotheosis of Homer, the Muses with

Apollo, the Dancing Hours, Priam begging the body of Hector from Achilles,1 and one or more of the Sacrifices. It has been questioned whether the Apotheosis of Homer, as that also of Virgil, are Flaxman's work; but a reference to the former (fig. 67), as

' It will be seen in a future page that there was another version of this tablet modelled by I lalmnzzoni.

here given, and to the other in a subsequent page, will, we think, confirm the generally received opinion that both were modelled by him. There is a distinctness in the grouping and figures, and a peculiarity in the graceful folds and flow of the drapery which belong essentially to his style; and to him surely, of all the modellers employed by Wedgwood, would, we think, be assigned the task of copying the deitication of the greatest of the ancient poets; and this from some print or model of the original bas-relief which at that date' formed part of the collection in the Colonna Palace, Home. It now forms part of our tional treasures, having been purchased for the British Museum in 1819.1

In January 1776, we find Flaxm-an at work upon large bas-reliefs for chimney-pieces,2 and a little later a commission is given to him for a few Greek heads.3 It is at na

' The invoices shed great light, future edition. ' upon the history and prices of the j ' Wedgwood to Bentley, January ornamental ware. But extracts must 4. 177. be referred, for want of space. to a E-" Ibid. February 14, 177.

CRAP. VIII. APOTHEOSIS OF HOMER. _ 365 this date that Wedgwood styles him the ' Genius of Sculpture,' and it is probable that Flaxman has raised his terms for modelling, for the former restricts his commissions on account of cost. Wedgwood began now to form his moulds in clay, which, as he said, 'made them everlasting;' but as the firing reduced them a full size, the sculptor had to increase the size of his models in proportion. He had in hand at this date, June 19, 1776, the model for the tablet of Silenus and Boys, the heads of Julius Caasar, Pan, and Syrinx; two

Fauns, the figures of Day and of two Bacchanals. Of one of the first copies of the former, VVedgwood writes_for it had got slightly broken in the fire: ' The Tablet of Silenus, if it had been whole, would have been worth four or five guineas. Nothing so fine can be had for five times the money, if at all, and these things can be had only from us, nor shall we have any competitor in haste.' Later in the summer he is at work upon a draped female figure, holding a cornucopia under her arm; and also upon those of Plenty and of Medea. In relation to one of these, Wedgwood's critical judgment comes into play, bearing out what we have already said, 'that the artist's model was one thing and its transference by the potter's hand into his art another.' '

Mr. Flaxman's model (he says) is too flat in several parts to be made in coloured grounds, & we can sooner finish our own than raise our models. I am aware of the necessity a modeller will plead for making some of the parts so flat in order to keep those parts back, and to give a proper relief to the whole. But you will soon see by turning to our blue & white Jaspers that we cannot admit of such delicate parts, & must be content with such effects in our Figures as can be produced without them. In some things the blue shade which our ground is so apt to east through the thin parts of the white may be of advantage to the subject, as in the Armour by the side of the Conquered Province.-Any parts of drapery which require to be thrown back, or other apendages to the Figures.—But when the naked part of the Figure is penetrated with the colour of the ground, it is generally injurious. See the poor Queen's nose, and many other Cameos.'

We hear nothing further of Flaxman till the summer of the following year, when Wedgwood cautions Bentley not to mention to him their process of making clay moulds. Three months later, Flaxman is commissioned to model six of the nine Muses, he having, as we have 1 Preface to Vol. I. p. xx. ' Vedgwood to Bentley, J uly 9, 1776.

CHAP. VIII. THE NINE MUSES.

367 seen from the bill,1 modelled Melpomene, Thalia, and Terpsichore, with their god Apollo, in the previous year. But the order is shortly eountermanded:

Having (writes VVedgwo0d) laid all our bas-relief Goddesses upon their backs upon a board before me, in order to increase their number, I instantly perceived the six Muses we want might be produced from this lovely Group at half the trouble & expense they could be procur'd from Flaxman, and much better figures. For little more than 58. each we can complete them very well. I hope you have not order'd them to be model'd as I desired you would; but if you have, so be it, it is only so much loss. If he has not begun upon them you might give him as good an order in a Tablet, and all would be well.

Wedgwood's countermand was, happily for the sake of art, too late. Flaxman completed, as he had begun, this lovely group of female figures, and Wedgwood was subsequently as proud of them as Flaxman him self. They formed, with Apollo, a magnificent tablet, both for framing and for chimney-pieces, and, in a reduced form, were used as an encircling group for some of the finest of the jasper vases.

A new set of models of the English poets, taken from the finest prints, and for which he received 10/6 per head, employed F1axma.n during the early winter of 1777, and, later, he was employed upon the Sacrifice to Pan, and the Dancing Hours. The last was intended as a freize or freizes to the Marriage of Cupid and Psyche, which, with two of the Seasons for blocks, made a complete chimney-piece. The Apotheosis of Homer was also formed into a tablet for this purpose, with freizes of Apollo and the nine Muses. In the summer of 1778, Flaxman seems to have visited 3 Ante, p. 322, note.

Stalfordshire, though not as a guest of Wedgwood; for in a letter, dated from'Etruria, the latter says to Bentley: ' Mr. Flaxman called to tell me he was modelling a basrelief of LA Chatham in order to sell copies in Wax. I told him we should be glad of a cast, & he knew what we should make of it. I do not know what he means to charge other people, but we you know are to pay a price below casts & models.' 1 Shortly after, and through various portions of the year 1779, Flaxman was at work upon some of his most interesting models, as the Boys and Goat, the Triumph of Ariadne Homer and Hesiod,3 and an Oflering to Flora. He seems also to have wholly remodelled, or adapted to a chimney-piece tablet, one of the Bacchanalian Sacrifices mentioned in the early Catalogues, although it could not have been formed in the blue and white jasper body before this date, for the firing of such large pieces had only been recently perfected. This tablet, one of the largest known, is 23 inches by 9% _;. It is here given (fig. 68) from the collection of J. J. Bagshawe, Esq., of Sheflield, and is probably an early specimen of the tablets prepared for chimney-pieces.

In the spring of this latter year, Flaxman modelled his own likeness in wax, and a copy in the same material or in plaster was sent down to Etruria for transference into the jasper or basaltes body. None of these copies seem to be known, though specimens may exist amongst the treasures of connoisseurs. The entry relating. to this matter is interesting. ' I shall be very glad,' says Wedgwood to Bentley, ' to see Mr. Flaxman's head at Etruria & will do all the justice I can to it in my power.' 4 1 Wedgwood to Bentley, July 1, VVedgwood to Bentley, N ovem1778. ber 8, 1778. ' Ibid. October 27, 1778. 4 Ibid. March 20, 1779.

VOL. II. B B

Through the kindness of Mr. Falcke, an engraving is here given from one of these original models in wax (fie. 69). The 'Genius of Sculpture' had achieved by this time some portion of his true and noble fame, and had shown the world that the weaknesses and little vanities of beardless boys often foreshadow the strength and capabilities of earnest men.

The first bas-reliefs were modelled by 1-oyez at the close of 1768, and from that date we hear more or less of them in the various ordinary bodies of basaltes,

common biscuit, and terra-cotta. The grounds of the biscuit were generally enamelled. These may be said to form the first cameos or tablets on a large scale, and are as marked for their comparative rudeness and high relief as the tablets of a later day say the Rape of Proserpine,

CIIAP. VIII. HERCULANEUM PICTURES. 371 the Dancing Hours, or Apollo and the Nine Muses, in a finer body—for exquisite delicacy, finish, and low relief. The contrast between the two is as great as between the earliest Etruscan pitcher and the exquisitely-painted vases of the (lays of Phidias.' Besides these tablets in bas-relief, were others called Herculaneum pictures. These were generally elongated slabs in the black basaltes body, or coloured black on the biscuit, on which were painted in encaustic colours mythological scenes, Bacchanalian scenes, or aerial figures. The smaller articles of this character were intended as pictures for dressing-rooms, or for ornamenting writing tables, cabinets, and the walls of apartments; the larger for chimney-pieces. Unwin, Catherine Wilcox, Dovoto, and, at a later day— from April 1784Aaron Steel, were employed in painting these Herculaneum pictures; as also, on a minute scale, in ornamenting teapots and other articles in useful ware with aerial figures of the same character. In the Mayer collection are two sheets of these descending figures, beautifully painted from original copies; and another sheet of original designs by Aaron Steel of a more modern character. There were also what were called ivory Herculaneum pictures-that is, the white biscuit reliefs and ground were covered over with a peculiar glaze or composition, which, upon firing, imparted all the appearance of the finest ivory.

' One of these earlv tablets is in the possession of J. F. Streatfield, Esq., 15 Upper Brook Street. It, measures about 14 by 6Q inches, has I"edgw00d and Bentley's name on the back in capitals, and formed originally the upper part of a marble chimnev-piece of an old house in the city of London. The subject is

a Bacchanalian procession, and the figures are in extraordinarily high relief. i

Some parts of all the figures, the most rominent more particularly, bear a rown tinge. Some consider
' this to be the result of time or fire,
' but it is more probablv the efi'ects of enamel colour laid on;'as both brown and also grey tints are spoken of in reference to these early tablets, the purpose being undoubtedly to convey the embrowned hues of a southern climate.
372 EARLY TABLETS FOR CHIMNEY-PIECES. CHAP. VIII.

Sir Watkin and Lady Wynne were amongst the first to try the black bas-relief tablets in chimney-pieces; as the Adamses, the Adelphi architects, Sir John Wrottisley, and some others, terra cotta ornaments in building, both interiorly and exteriorly. But these examples were little followed, although Sir Watkin's chimney-piece, and another painted in encaustic enamel for a Mr. H. Lutwidge, in the autumn of 1774, were greatly admired.

The early jasper body was first tried in large tablets about the same period, and from this date we find Wedgwood earnestly bent on introducing these fine ornaments more and more as decorations of the domestic hearth. But immense and, for a time as it seemed, insuperable difiiculties stood in the way of success; and it was not till he had hardened the composition, and built, as already seen, a kiln on purpose, that pieces so large and massive could be produced without defects. Meanwhile, however, they were made in the ordinary biscuit body, and then sent to London to receive enamel grounds,1 or in the black basaltes, which required no colouring. Boulton had at this time taken up the trade in chimney-pieces, and, unlike Wedgwood, won the patronage of the builders. The cornish, freize, and jambs were of' wood, decorated with tin ornaments, which when painted as one with the wood, had the effect of fine carving.

But by slow degrees Wedgwood advanced upon the steps of his great purpose. As he mastered the science of firing large masses, this beautiful branch of his art 'The fame of your painted Chimney ieces is not confined to London 0 y, we are asked much after if we do not sell them, but I think the latter is very probable, & I have almost promise this treat to them here; 8.: if you can spare us a good sett to show here this summer, now our season is commenced, it will be a treat at least to our good visitants some of our constant friends and customers here.' Vedgwood to Bentley, July 8, 1775.

CHAP. VIII. CHIMNEY-PIECE, LONGTON HALL. 373 grew more a. possibility, and no sooner had he prepared some ornaments of this character in the jasper body, than fortune favoured him.

Mr. Heathcote, you know he (writes to Bentley) is repairing Longton Hall in our neighbourhood, & he wishes to have one of our chimneypieces, but when I came to talk with Gardner, his architect, I find Mr. Heathcote's idea is to have our jaspers set in a wood freese & tablet. I have convinc'd Mr. G. of the impropriety of this combination, & am to undertake the same with Mr. H. I told Mr. G. we were making some metopes, tablets, oval has-reliefs for frieses, blocks &c. for wood chimneypieces, glass frames &c. & show'd him some samples which he a.pprov'd of very much, & did not doubt but great quant-it-ys would be sold to compose chimney-pieces of 10 to 15 guineas price which, he said, were the chief run in all country gentle (Fig, 70.) cnnr.'E'-PIECE, I/_'L'G'l'0.' HALL. s'r. Pr'onnsnim-'..

men's houses & he would put some of them up in chimneypieces he had now in hand as soon as I could furnish him with them.'

' Vedgwnod to Bentley, Deceniber 17, lTTT.

374 DIFFICULTIES CONQUEREI). Can'. VIII.

We have no further data relative to this chimney-piece, except that it was erected, and most probably at a period somewhat later, as the centre tablet, seen in the engraving (fig. 70), represents the Apotheosis of Virgil-a subject modelled later than the Apotheosis of Homer, and not referred to in the Catalogue of 1779. Wedgwood evidently converted Mr. Heathcote to his opinion, as the freize, jambs, and entablature are alike with the centre ornament in the jasper body. The freize, which merely represents an antique border, and the somewhat unmeaning heading to the trophies on the jambs, show an early stage in this style of decoration, although the Medusa's head at the corner of the jambs, and the tripod altars bearing the sacred flame at the feet, were repeated afterwards in chimney-pieces of higher pretensions.

By the autumn of 1778, every difficulty in firing was conquered, and Wedgwood thus wrote to Bentley:

Do you wish to have any tablets sent? or would you rather sell what you have first? We have a very perfect one from Mr. Fl_axman's model, & have several more in hand of difl"erent subjects. You shall have a. most glorious assortment for the opening of the next season of Tablets, frieses, & blocks, to go together in the composition of a chimneypiece. We can make the frieses of any length & very true & even—I have just mixed half a ton of Jasper, & shall go on with more that we may have a year's composition before-hand, the advantages of which will be very great in many respects; & when we have completed our present suit of tablets & their accompaniments for chimneypieces we will make another attack upon the architects & hope to conquer. One thing I am at least clear in, that our weapons will be superior to any we have hitherto brandish'd before them. Mr. Brown— The Broirn, I mean is almost new building

L'I Gover's house at Trentham, & comes down pretty often..

I intend to shew him a suit for a chimnev piece when I have

CHAP. VIII. SIR WILLIAM BAGO'I"S CHIMNEY-PIECE. 376 them quite complete. I think we have not attempted 'him at present in any way.l _ At this date Sir William Bagot,' of Blithefield, was adding a large room to his house, and his wife, wishing to contribute to its decoration, invited Mr. Wedgwood thither, and ordered one of his finest chininey-pieces. The Apotheosis of Homer, and Apollo and the Nine Muses were the subjects fixed upon. For these and the various other pieces necessary to complete the work, the price named was thirty-two guineas, although as yet no definite prices had been fixed. In relation to this point, Mr. Wedgwood consulted Bentley:— '

I shall be glad to know what price you think they will bear to sell a good quantity. I do not mean what they are worth for they are in every respect more valuable than so much carved marble; but as we can now make them with absolute certainty & success I wish to put them in a train of moving in quantities."

On this visit and one subsequently, Mr. lVedgwood carried some of his finest tablets with him, and making, as it were, a little tour to various neighbouring seats, he found opportunities of showing them to Mr. Anson, Lord 1 Vedgwood to Bentley, August ' pieces as tablets, or such suits as the 9, 1778. Muses rise above a medium I think " Created a Baron in 1780. ' they should be inark'd with a price '" VedgWood to Bentley, Sep-i accordingly. 'hat I mean to offer tember 1, 1778. A little later 'Vedg-' to your consideration upon the subwood says further in relation to price: i ject, is shortly this, That:1 Homer & ' The white Jasper Muses & Tablets _ Hesiod tablet, or a suit of the Muses of Homer & llesiod are worth nny-' should not have a fixed 8'. invariable thing. Please to look at them & if i price like a quart mug, but that on think the should be charged this individual tablet or that suit of ess than the b ue grounds put them the Muses should be so much 8, 10, at what you please. These very or 12 G' according to their comparatine and perfect works should be live merit, 8: if it is necessary to charg'd singly upon inspection with fix a medium price, I would neversome relation to their individual tlieless have some fixed both above merit, 8: when there are defects put, and below that medium if the differsuch pieces at lower prices according ence in the fineness of the pieces to the degrees of their im-

perfections, would bear the distinction. ' Ibid. 8'. when the merit of such large. m'ch 14 and 15. I779.
376 A SPLENDID ROOM. C-HAP. VIII.

Scarsdale, Lord Huntingdon, Mr. Talbot, and Sir Wm. Broughton. A little later he has been on a brief journey to Birmingham, and thus reports to Bentley:

I visited Sir Wm. Bagot on my return home, & am to spend some days with him after Lichfield races. He has a noble collection of pictures & will furnish his grand room with them whilst I am there, & has determined to accept his Lady's present of a. chimney piece for it, & is pleased to say that the tablet & freizes Homer & 'Co. & the Muses—are the finest things he ever saw anywhere, & they will be placed in very good company Guido, Titian, & a long &c. of the worthy Knights of the pencil. l

In the spring of the subsequent year this chimneypiece was set up, and during the summer Mr. Wedgwood had the pleasure of seeing it.

Upon leaving Lichfield I made Blithefield in my way, & had a. high treat there upon more dishes than one. Sir William's new room is hung round with Correggios, Raphaels, Guerchinos (Guercino), Bassans & many more great masters which I shall not attempt to describe to you, but upon the whole it is one of the first rooms in the Kingdom. Amongst other great works of art Sir W" particularly pointed out the chimneypiece to my attention, assuring me, at the same time, that he esteem'd it the best piece in his room, & shews it as such to all his company. You know the pieces—Homer & Hesiod for the tablet, & the iIuses for the frise. The statuary has done them justice, & they look charmingly, & do more than merely support themselves in the very fine company into which he has introduc'd them. One circumstance I cannot omit, though I have perhaps said too much already, as it shews in the strongest manner the propriety of the resolution we came to of having the Edges of our has-reliefs polished & that this finish should

be extended to our largest works—-In looking at the tablet I was lamenting:1. little chip off the edge, which misfortune I suppose had befalan it in the hands of the workmen. Misfortune do you call it crys 3" W"'? We esteem it a very happy accident»——It

Crmr. VIII. LIBRARY AT TRENTHAM. 877 shews the merit—the fine texture of the composition which otherwise might have pass'd for a painted surface.'

The attempt to win the 'good will of Lord Gower and his architect Brown for the tablets was eminently successful. Both Lord and Lady Gower were greatly charmed, and fixed upon a tablet and two friezes for their library-the subject of the friezes being Apollo and the Nine Muses. A few days later Wedgwood saw Brown himself:_

I had an hour's conversation with him (he writes to Bentley) upon the subject of tablets &c. when amongst many encomiums upon what he had seen, he assur'd me he did not mean to speak as a courtier when he express'd his strongest approbation & even admiration of what he had seen. He preferred them greatly to sculpture in marble, would make use of them himself as an architect when he had an opportunity & recommend them everywhere. He assur'd me of his real attachment to our interest from the merit of our productions & desir'd we would call upon him in town at any time when we thought he could be of any use to us with his advice or anything else in his power. We had nothing to fear he said from the opposition of the architects, for such things as those must come into use when seen. Mr. B. & Ld Grower objected to the blue ground unless it _could be made in Lapis Lazuli. I shewed them a sea. green & some other colours to which Mr. Brown said they were pretty colours & he should not object to those for the ground of a room, but they did not come up to his idea of the ground of a tablet, nor would any other colour, unless it was a copy of some natural & valuable stone. All other eolor'd grounds give ideas of color'd paper, painting, compositions, casting, moulding &c. & if we could not make

our color'd grounds imitate marble or natural stones, he advises us to make the whole white, as like to statuary marble as he could — This is certainly orthodox doctrine & we must endeavour to profit by it. This gentleman, if there is any confidence to be placed in the greatest apparent sincerity 1 Wedgwood to Bentley, July-'50, 1775!.
378 VHITE POLISHED TABLETS. Clur. VIII.

& earnestness, means really to serve us, & he gives for his reas0n—because we deserve it.1

VVedgwood and his partner too were Won over to this rightly called orthodox doctrine, for all the finest chimneypieces extant are in this purest and loveliest of N ature's colours.

In my opinion (wrote Wedgwood a few days after this interview) white polish'd tablets will he liked better for chimneypieces than any colour'd grounds we can make, for they will be to other stones. What you think of making the figures only in our fine white jasper & let the statuaries put them upon their own grounds. The figures must be contriv'd for the purpose & in a. large style & high relief, & so they are when carv'd in marble & laid upon the Sienna grounds. And these figures might be shown to the architects only. I believe we could make them & think it merits some consideration on several accounts: If we can bring over the architects in one good article, some of the others will follow of course.'

But the architects were not to be persuaded, though Bentley's efforts were unceasing. Men of cultivation and taste like Stuart were to be won over to things, heterodox simply because they were new in the truest sense; but the architects, with a few honourable exceptions, and headed by Sir VVm. Chambers, talked them down_and with result. The latter persuaded the Queen that Wedgwood and Bentley's tablets were not fit for chimney-pieces. Well might Wedgwood write when he heard of this:—

Fashion is infinitely superior to merit in many respects; & it is plain from a thousand instances, that if you have a favorite child you wish the public to fondle & take notice of you have only to make choice of proper sponsors. If you are lucky in them no matter what the brat is, black, brown, or fair, its fortune is made. V'e were really unfortunate in the introduc

' 'edgwood to Bentle_v, (ilctober 6, 1778.

" lbid. (lctober 27. 1778.

Can. VIII. OPPOSITION OF THE ARCHITECTS. 379 tion of our jaspers into public notice, that we could not prevail upon the architects to be godfathers t-0 our child. Instead of taking it by the hand & giving it their benediction, they cursed the poor infant by bell, book & candle, & it must have a hard struggle to support itself, & rise from under their maledictions.'

True, the Queen patronised the pearl-white tea-ware then newly introduced, though she was persuaded to look askance upon Apollo and his lovely train, or the deification of him-old, poor, and blind—who immortalised the wars of Troy. But, after all, were not platters and teacups things more akin to the endowments of a royal lady whose favourite mental nutriment was sermons fitted for the days of Sacheverell, who could smile graciously at doggerel lines on her ' great coat,' tolerate Mrs. Schwellenberg and her frogs, and whose only knowledge of the external world around her was such as it had been interpreted to her in the petrifying atmosphere of a small German Court? Certainly! as the tree is fashioned and nurtured, so are the qualities of the fruit it bears. But Genius was invincible in her eternal faith; Wedgwood felt that other generations were to come, other men to behold his works, other eyes to see 'that he had exalted his art by the only means it is to be exalted—namely, by patience and truth. ' My tablets,' he says in one of his letters, ' only want age and scarcity to make them worth any price.' He was a true prophet, and till some one as great as himself shall arise, their value will go on increasing in the sight of all those who measure Art by the breadth and height of their own culture.

But there were sources awaiting him where the highest artistic cultivation, the truest natural taste, ensured both appreciation and keen sympathy. The one whom he

' 'edgwood to Bentley, J uly 19, 1779.

880 SIR WILLIAM HAMILTON. CRAP. VIII. first thought of when the tablets were thus perfected was Sir William Hamilton; the zealous friend of so many years, and with whom he and Bentley were constantly corresponding on various matters relative to their productions. After expressing a previous wish to Bentley that one of the finest tablets should be sent to Sir William, Wedgwood thus wrote again:_

I believe they do not use Tablets in chimneypieces in Italy & did not mean the one I mention'd sending to Sir Wm Hamilton for that purpose, but rather as a picture or a cabinet piece of art & thought it might be agreeable to Sir Vm to shew his friends in Italy the use which had been made of his collection of vases in England & not a bad mode of shewing our productions there, if he should chuse to put it in a chimneypiece in England he can easily bring it over with the rest of his furniture. After this explanation do what you please & I shall be satisfied. If it goes it should have a fine mahogany box, lined with a. suitable coloured silk. I am almost superstitious in the efi'ects of such accompaniments.'

This wish was obeyed, and during the summer of the succeeding year Sir Wm. Hamilton received his present, and thus gracefully acknowledged its safe arrival:—

Nams, June 22, 1779. Sirs. I have had the pleasure of receiving safe your de-light ful Basrelief of the Apotheosis of Homer, or some celebrated Poet indeed it is far superior to my most sanguine expectation, I was sure that your industry would produce in time something excellent in the way of Basreliefs from the specimens I saw before I left England but I realy am surprised & delighted to the highest degree with this proof of the hasty strides you

' Wedgwood to Bentley, October 1

You remember Tim Bobbin's reason 27, 1778. On this latter omt Vedg-' for covering his Baudehewit. It will wood had written a few ays earlier: hold we well know, in other things ' I am eting some boxes made ' & we shouldkuse every means our2 neatl & ined with silk or some fine ower to ma e our customers e ieve stuifzo keep &shew the tablets in; I illey are not Tm; V.R:.' Ibid. some singly and others to contain October 16, 1778. jnspers for a whole cliini-iiey-piece.,

CIIAP. VIII. HIS GREAT LIBER-ALITY. 381 have made towards perfection in your art, I only wish you may continue to meet with the encouragement you so richly deserve, but I fear that Luxury of every kind & the expensive War we are at present engaged in will in a short time so drain us that we shall nothing left to please our fancy. In the mean time however I return you my sincere thanks of this fresh mark of your attention to me. If you want new subjects for other Basreliefs I recommended these, of P, 43 vol. 3, only the group of three Women with an Umbrella, of Plates 73, 76 (118 Thetis with armour of Achilles) and the right hand side of (Pl 123 the Hesperides feeding the serpent) and 130 all of the 3'1 vol 71, & 81, of the 4th vol, are likewise charming subjects. Notwithstanding the Times are hard I have made some charming additions to my collection which shall one day be added to those already in the British Museum. I cannot refrain when anything excellent comes in my way, which is not often, for excellence was always & ever will be rare. Your Basrelief astonishes all the Artists here, it is more pure and in a truer _antique Taste than any of their performances tho' they have so many fine models before them.

His Majesty's envoy at Naples well deserved this attention from Wedgwood and Bentley. He had presented them with a set of Etruscan vases, in addition to a part, at least, of his work on Antiquities. He had from time to time sent them over cases filled with casts from basreliefs and other antique subjects.1 He had lent them cameos and gems, and had been instrumental in opening many choice collections to their use. He had commis

' Two cases on board theship Abraham, June 30, 1775. Freight of one October 5, 1775. Mayer MSS.
382 CONTINUOUS PATRO.'AGE. CRAP. VIII. . sioned them to make busts for the entablature of a bridge in his pleasure grounds at Naples, and he was the purchaser of the earliest of the black bas-relief vases; he wore their cameos and seals, and distributed others as gifts amongst his friends. Specimens of every improvement or addition to both the useful and ornamental manufactures were at his desire habitually consigned to him, and he ,CHAP. VIII. CHIMNEY-PIECES STILL EXTANT. 38-"? even offered to take a number of fine enamelled dinner and dessert services, and endeavour to sell them wherever he could, but this latter proposition Wedgwood declined.1. In short, this admirable patron and friend received no more than his due in this gift of a masterpiece in white ' jasper-the Apotheosis of Homer.

Wedgwood's bas-relief chimney-pieces were widely, if sparsely, scattered all over Great Britain and Ireland. In London a few new-built houses of the nobility and gentry were decorated with them. An attempt was made to win over the architect of Mrs. Montague's new house in Portman Square, but it is unknown if successfully. At a. somewhat later date, when Wedgwood added friezes for ceilings to his other ornaments in jasper on a large scale, a fine one was executed for a room in the house of the Countess of Cork, in Grosvenor Square. In Derbyshire a splendid chimney-place still exists, which Wedgwood executed at this period for Lord Scarsdale. In Ireland the taste for these fine ornaments was even more general than in England. Many of them are still 'extant in town and country houses, and, if sold, find ready purchasers if consigned to this country. The splendid chimney-piece, with its tablet of the Apotheosis of Homer, lately shown at Alton Towers, and the property of D. C. Marjoribanks, M.P., came originally from thence, where it had

beautified some noble room for many years.2

From October 1777, Wedgwood was occupied with another class of tablets, or rather pallets, of large size, for Stubbs, the animal painter. Cosway had been the first

' Wedgwood to Bentley, Novem-chimney-piece was not engraved. It ber 20, 1775. I' will, however, probably have a place

' By an oversight which could not in a subsequent edition. be rectified till too late, this fine i 384 STUBBS THE ANIMAL PAINTER. CRAP. VIII._ to direct Stubbs's attention to enamel painting, but the difficulty of procuring sheets of copper sufiiciently large for any full-size picture came in the way, as also others connected with the requisite colours. Finding none to his purpose, be set to to make a 'complete set for himself, and after incredible pains, labour, and expense, extending over two years, and which occupied every spare moment of his time, he succeeded in his object to the full, by producing nineteen distinct tints in enamel colours. Stubbs had already shown great perseverance and determination of character. He had taught himself engraving, and in a great measure painting. He had shut himself up for eighteen months in a lonely farm-house amidst the swamps of Lincolnshire, in order to master by dissection the Anatomy of the Horse, and prepare the plates of his great and well-known work on that subj ect—and he was now, at the age of fifty-three, the most noted animal painter in the kingdom. He painted horses on the canvasses of Sir Joshua Reynolds, and others that had won on the race-course and in the hunting field. He had painted homely favourites and homely scenes. The Farmer's Wife and Raven, from Gay's Fables, and Lord Torrington's Bricklayers and Labourers, and engraved them in a masterly manner as well.

Wedgwood readily undertook Stubbs's commission. The first dificulty lay with the clay or earth;1 ordinary white ware or cream ware would not do. The next with the firing. However, progress was made, and tablets ,were

produced of 22 by 17 inches. But these did not reach the needed size. Fresh trials were made, extending over a further period.

' Some peculiar earth was tried from an estate of the Duke of Athol. Vedgwood to Bentley, November 26, 1777.
CRAP. VIII. TABLETS FOR ENAMEL PAINTING. 385
When you see Mr. Stubs (Writes Wedgwood to his friend) pray tell him how hard I have been labouring to furnish him with the means of adding immortality to his very excellent pencil. I mean only to arrogate to myself the honor of being his canvas malzr. But alass this honor is at present denied to my endeavours though you may a.ssure him that I will succeed if I live awhile longer undisturbed by the French as I only want an inclin'd plane that will stand our fire. My first attempt has fail'd & I cannot well succeed in my attempts till we lay by work for Xmas when our kilns will be at liberty for my trials.l

In the May succeeding this, Wedgwood's experiments had resulted in tablets of 30 inches, and he hoped ultimately to bring them to 36 inches by 24 inches._

But that is at present in the offing (he tells Bentley) & I would not mention to Mr. Stubbs beyond 30 at present. If Hr. Stubbs succeeds he will be followed by others to which he does not seem to have the least objection, but rather wishes for it; & if the oil painters too should use them, they may becomea considerable object. 'At present I think we should give Mr. Stubbs every encouragement to proceed & establish the fashion. He wishes you know to do something for us by way of setting off against the tablets. My picture & Mrs. Wedgwood in enamel will do something. Perhaps he may take your Governess in by the same means. I should have no objection to a family piece, or rather two perhaps in oil, if he should visit 'us this summer at Etruria. These things will go much beyond his present trifling debt to us. Now I wish you to see Mr. Stubs & if the idea meets your approbation, to tell him that if it is convenient for him to pay in money for what he has hitherto had, it will pay something towards the kilns & alterations in kilns we have made & the other expenses we have been at in our essays & the next £100 or £150 in tablets, perhaps more, shall be work & work, we will take payment» in paintings.'

Of this proposal we shall see the results in our next chapter.

386 BLACK BAS-RELIEF VASES. Cnsr. VIII.

In the summer of 1776, Wedgwood improved his black vases by surrounding them by fine bas-reliefs from the antique. Hitherto tl1is class of vases had been ornamented with little more than plinth mouldings, medallions, single figures, and festoons, and by Satyrs' heads or snakes for the handles. These fine vases were first made public in the season of 1777; but earlier than this they had been shown to Sir William Hamilton, who was then in London; and they met with the special approbation of the Earl of Warwick. Wedgwood was at this time suffering from an accident to his amputated limb, had to move on crutches, and to be carried to the works in his carriage. Of this he says: '— ' '

L'VWarwick & his Lady have been here from Trentharn this morning & I sat in the pattern room in state to receive them; They were both exceedingly polite & afiable & order'd several things to be sent to Warwick Castle. Flowerpots & tripods, a large head of the Medusa such as he had before, & would have order'd a set of the new Basrelief Vases,. _ which be praised pro(Flg. 12.) m..cK nas-ur..n-:1-vase on PUP. _, I»: M lws v1-1-lwuort digiously & said we got forward amazingly, but I advis'd his Lordship to wait till spring when we should have a greater variety. So he is to come & chuse them at the Rooms. /q-.-in-1-i..-,5"-w I

...,,

1 Vedgw00d to Bentley, Septem-' dernble additional risk in their being ber12,1776. 'The prices ofbas-relief I good, as all large pieces in figures, vases,' says Vedg-wood in a subse-_ & laid upon a plain ground, are very quent letter, 'should be equal at least liable to

crack. Vedgwood to Bentto the Greek painted ones, for there isa ley, October, 1776. It wasthese black great expense in the models 8: moulds has-relief vases which firstsiiggested or the Figures, besides a very consi-the more splendid ones in Jasper.

A specimen of these basrelief vases is here given (fig. 72), and another is shown in vol. i. p. 481. Neither specimen can be pronounced of the highest order of workmanship, as Wedgwood refers to vases adorned with the Dancing Hours, and others from Flaxman's models, as well as from exquisite bas-reliefs in the possession of Sir Roger N ewdigate. Lord /Varwick's vases were? probably of this high character. The two succeeding examples of pitcher vases (figs. 73 and 74) are of much interest. Both, as his first bill has shown, were modelled by Flaxman. Vases, at this date, were also made in the black body and left unfirecl. Lord Warwick and Sir William Hamilton particularly admired the colour thus obtained, and vases of this character were sent to Italy for the latter. The busts in the black body, bronzed or otherwise, became, as we have already seen, the finest things imaginable. Some of peculiar interest were modelled life-size in 1779, from medals or prints supplied, through M. Veldhuysen, by the Lord Burgomaster 'of Amsterdam. They included the two De Witts, and subsequently Gro tius, Boerhaave, and Michel de Ruyter. The illustration (fig. 75) gives one of the De Witts, though whether John or Cornelius is unknown. The bust is 25 inches high, and from its size and exquisite modelling, forms one of the gems of the De la Rue collection, which is particularly rich in this respect. The Dutch, proud of their patriots and great men, purchased these busts in such large numbers, as to lead to a vast increase in Ve1dhuysen's sales. Stimulated by this patronage, Wedgwood undertook the busts of the great men of other countries; but except in our own and in Germany, the sales seem never to have been large. In too many of them, at that date, tyranny had crushed out the love of liberty and the love of country as well. Af-

ter the death of Bentley another class of portraiture came greatly into request. These were oval bas-relief medallions of from 4 to 5 and 6 inches in height, in the basaltes body, with frames of the same. Many of these are of great beauty, and of the highest class of workmanship.1

The fabrication of seals had occupied Wedgwood's attention from an early date. They progressed, like the vases, from the black to the red and crystalline bodies, then to laminated grounds, and next to jasper, which, from its hardness, formed the finest surface for the impressions of the dies.-Y These were-taken from the rarest works of antiquity—fr0m those of 'the Renaissance

' Mr. Carruthers, of Norwood, has a particularly fine collection of these portrait medallions.

Modelling bills of 1779.

Mesa". Wedgvood 8: Bentley

To J. Flaxman.

1779..

Aug. 21. £ 5. (I.

The portrait of Mr. Banks modelled in Clay 2 2 0

Received in full of all demands by Jonrv FLAXMAN, J un'.

Mr. Vood D'.

To Jn Cheese. £ 8 d.

'l'o four busts of Shakespeare, Plato, and Aristotle, 10,6 each 2 2 0

To a case.......... 0 5 6

£32'? _G

Feb' y' 24 1774 received y' Contents in full per me

Jn (.'m:nsF..

Sculptor in Cenient.

Note by Mr. Mayer.

.ln_'cr.lS-'.

391 SEAL POLISHING. ('HAP. VIII.

and of a later day. Cyphers and initial letters were another and a favourite class of decoration, and one which Wedgwood was greatly instrumental in promoting. His object was to check the feudal passion for heraldic ornament, and, by introducing truly classic subjects, to lead artists in this department to a higher and a better style. He, however, only partially succeeded; for the passion depended on causes which only the slow progress of civilisation can eiface.

Half his letters are filled with business relative to seals-their improvement, polishing, setting, and dispersion. The polishing was done at Birmingham, afterwards at Etruria, and finally in London. Here his polishing was done, as also much engraving, by Robert Pollard, a man of remarkable ability, a native of Newcastle-upon-Tyne, and a friend of Thomas Bewick, whom 1779.

Mess". Vedgwood & Bentley
'10 Hoskins 8: Grant. £ a. d.
May 5 To a large Bust of Bacchus.. 2 2 0
TouDitt0....ofAriadne 111 (F
To a Vase...... 1 11 6
To a Large Antique Bust of Mercury 1 1 0
To a ditto of Alexandre... 2 2 0
To 2 Busts of Shakespeare & Garrick. 1 16 0
To 6 Basreleve Figures... 3 3 0
To 2 Figures Zingara 8: Chrispagnia. 2 2 0
To Cases for Ditto.... 1 9 1
June 28 To a Cast of an Oval Pshyche & Cupid. 2 12 6
To a Cast of the Aurora & n smale Tablet. 1 1 0
To a setting Figure of Venus.. 2 2 0
To a Mould of Sterne.... 2 2 0
To a Setting Figure of Mercury.. 2 2 0
To Cases for Ditto.... 1 7 1§
£:.8 4 9
A Bust of Julius Caesar.. O 14 0
-8 18 9
Deduct for packing cases as above. 2 16 3
26 2 6
Disc'. 10 per C'.. 2 12 'I
23 10 3
packing cases 2 16 3
.1326 G (5

Received the contents in full of all Demands

Bs.'J". GRANT. Mayer MSS.

CRAP. VIII. ROBERT POLLARD. 391 he befriended and obtained work for, when the afterwards famous engraver on wood came up to London at the close of his apprenticeship in 1776. Pollard had all the virtues of his north-country race. Wedgwood greatly respected him, and employed him for a lengthened period in work of a most ex-

quisite character, that of polishing his finest gems and bas-reliefs.

The black seals were easily imitated. Undeterred by the restraints imposed upon him by the arrangements made in reference to Wedgwood's Patent for encaustic painting, Palmer carried on his piracies in a most unblushing manner; and then, by means of underselling his forged and trashy wares, he glutted the market, and injured Wedgwood's sales. He took in, if possible, every hand discharged from Etruria; and by this means, towards the close of 1772, succeeded in imitating Wedgwood's improvements in black tea-pots, which, finely formed and delicately wrought by tools, or upon the engine-lathe, were models of their kind. He next temporarily allied

"himself with Burdett till he had learnt all that weak and foolish man could teach; and soon after he commenced seal-making. These were sold in Birmingham to the setters, from some of whom Wedgwood got tidings of the piracy. 'We may safely take it for granted,' he writes to Bentley, 'they will not let us enjoy this business unrivalled, how then shall we distinguish ours from theirs? Wedgwood & Bentley is rather too much to put on the backs of our seals with the No. besides, the small ones especially, & I do not know whether we can put any sirzgle mar/c upon them which our neighbours dare not copy.'1 In another letter he says: 'I lament

' "edgwood to Bentley, June 7, 1773 we have not a Patent, it would be worth £10,000 to us, and I think the ground was perfectly clear for one, as intaglios for seals had-never been made.'2 Their sales were, however, very considerable, and every means was taken to disperse these fine intaglios on the continent and even in America.,

Voyez, who for a time had flitted like an evil spirit between London and the Potteries, had now settled down somewhere in Burslem, occasionally working for Palmer, and otherwise in seal-making for himself. These, as Wedgwood said, ' were sad trash.' Yet he managed to dispose of them amongst

merchants and setters by propagating a tale that Wedgwood and Bentley's seals were only to be obtained from particular persons. He next published a catalogue, containing 11early 200 names, which Wedgwood obtained and sent to Bentley for his amusement in a leisure moment. 'This man's seals are wretched things,' added Wedgwood; ' but by mere dint of application to the buyers,- I do not know whether he does not sell more than us, but I suppose after Monday his career will be cut short in Birmingham.' 3 Temporarily it probably was, for he was always in the last shifts of a needy vagabond. His next plan was to have a sale by auction of his seals, at which he had no bidder; and making, a few months after, a still further descent in rascality, he prepared a fresh stock, on which he forged Wedgwood and Bentley's name. 'I am now certain,' writes l/Vedgwood, ' that Voyez puts our names full length upon his seals. A servant who work'd for Voyez is now with Mr. Hales, & says if we desire it, he will take oath to fact, 8: says that Voyez is now gone on a journey to

CHAP. VIII. HIS FORGERY OF NAMES. 393

Worcester, Gloucester, Bristol & the West of England with a quantity of these to dispose of them as our seals.' 1 This was more than the _equanimity of Wedgwood could bear. He consulted his partner and his attorney Sparrow; but, as in the case of the Patent, they found little could be done in establishing the facts of piracy before either a country or a London jury. Next, they thought of advertising the rogue in all the provincial papers; but, advised by Sparrow, they let this idea 'drop. Emboldened by this leniency, the fellow carried on his nefarious trade with the utmost impudence for many months. He travelled about in a vehicle with an assistant, or else a woman who was not his.wife. "Then he reached a place, he scattered handbills, soon drew an amazing crowd, and sometimes sold as many as: 10 worth of seals in a day. When he is asked (adds Wedgwood) by any Gent" whilst he is selling his seals, why he puts Wedgwood & Bentley upon them, ' I borrow & lend with them ' he says ' when I am out of any particular sorts, or they want any that I have we borrow & lend with each other' so you see we are upon very friendly terms, & it might be a pity to interrupt this mutual exchange of good offices by an Action of Trespass. What do you think of it? I do not know how far this kind of Forgery is punish able by law, but it is not very pleasing & should in some way or other he contradicted.2

V oyez at this date had made one of his reappearances in Statfordshire, and it was then found that, though the partners could not sustain an action with any hope of success on their own behalf, he was yet punishable on other and more criminal grounds, that of _robbing Wedgwood's informant, a young man who had been his servant. Finding himself at length in the toil of the law, he wrote Wedg 394 VOYEZ DISAPPEARS. Can. VIII.

wood an impudent penitential letter. ' I have not given any answer,' wrote Wedgwood, ' nor do I intend it, as I neither like the letter or the writer. The lad told me, they had not put their names upon our seals for some time——so it may perhaps be as well to let the Thief alone. I hate any sort of contest if it can be decently avoided with a dirty fellow it being almost impossible to keep oneself unmir'd.' 1 In this spirit of silent dignity, wood dropped the matter. A few months later, we hear our last of this fellow and his piracies. ' Voyez _has given up making clay intaglios & has sold all his goods & chattels here to go & make paste seals in London where I believe he now is, for I met him, his wife, and his Child & a good deal of luggage in a chaise upon the London road a few days since. So Mr. Tassie must take care of him.'

Thus Voyez fades from our view; nor did Palmer gain much by his unwearied piracies. His domineering wife, who years before had gone disguised into Newport Street to buy blue neck and encaustic painted vases, and later to Soho to get cameos and seals, died, and in due season the potter married again. Of this event and what followed, Wedg-

wood tells us:

We have two houses failed or failing with us, but the times cannot be charged with their fall. They owe their fate to extravagance & inattention in the extreme. The parties are Mess"' Beeches brothers to Mr. Beech partner with Mr. Bent surgeon of Newcastle & our friend Mr. Palmer. Mr. Neale is come down to settle the affairs of the latter who it is said owes £10,000—-£500 of which sum Mr. Neale is in for. The other creditors hope he will take all & pay the debts. Mr. P. married a young wife lately & settled pretty largely upon her, which threw his family affairs into disorder, & alarmed his creditors. He keeps house at present 8: it is imagined his afi'airs are irretrevable.1

Through the agency of Neale, Palmer's business was re-established under the title of Neale and Palmer; but this change in no way lessened the old and discreditable system. The tempting of workmen away from their allegiance, the copying in a cheap and debased form the encaustic painted vases, the imitation of everything new which appeared, characterised the partnership as much under its new as its old form. Occasionally they boasted, as did others, that they had discovered the secret of the jasper body. 'They might as well boast,' wrote Wedgwood triumphantly, ' that they had discovered the philo-. sopher's stone.' 2 But it did become known at last through the treachery of some workman, clerk, or servant, who found particulars relating to.the body in a pocket-book his master had dropped; but the real facts of the story, though true in itself, are unknown. Tradition has long pointed out to Voyez as the guilty knave; but from what we have stated, he seems innocent at least in this respect.

Tassie was, as we have seen, a far more formidable rival than Voyez to Wedgwood; not only in the seal trade but in that of the cameos, prior to the perfection of the jasper body. But then he was an admirable artist and an honourable man, ' whom,' as Wedgwood said, ' it is a credit to emulate,' ' although his seals are not so good as

mine.' To the close of Wedgwood's life, as after it, Tassie's small models and casts often found their way to Etruria. Originally a country stonemason, born and reared in the neighbourhood of Glasgow, it was the accidental sight of a collection of paintings which raised in

' Vedgw00d to Bentley, March 14, 1775. Ibid. July 1776.
396 TASSIE. CRAP. VIII. him the ambition to become an artist; and he acquired a knowledge of drawing whilst earning his daily bread as a. common mason. Repairing to Dublin in search of work, he became acquainted with Dr. Quin of that city, who amused his leisure hours in endeavouring to imitate the precious stones in coloured pastes, and in taking accurate impressions of the engravings that were on them, and from him Tassie learnt these beautiful arts. In 1766 he removed to London, and after conquering innumerable difficulties, he established a great fame for fine and perfect work; his cameos as well as intaglios cast in coloured pastes, white enamel, and sulphur, being eagerly sought for by artists and collectors. The best cabinets both here and on the continent were opened to him; and his collection of imitated gems became at length extraordinary both for beauty, number, and variety.1 But Tassie's most original work were his portraits in wax, which he afterwards moulded and cast in paste. Many of the eminent personages of his time sat to him, and of these portraits a considerable number were copied by Wedgwood?

Wedgwood's great object in multiplying his cameos was for their preservation in a collected form, in exquisite little cabinets of many drawers. Here should rest gems 1 Tassie issued two Catalo es— ' sittings in one day, if he have some a small edition in 1775, and a arger, hours betwixt to work at it by himin two vols. quarto, in 1791. This self. It is the same to him whether last was edited by an artist named he goes out to you, or you to him,

Rasple. _ only the hours from about 12 to 4 2 he celebrated Thomas Walker 7 he is occupied in attending his shop. of Manchester, at the request of Lord

During the sitting you mav be occuD-eer, sat to Tessie for his medallion pied at almost whatyo11wil'l—eati11g-, likeness. His method Valker dewriting, &c.. as he only needs a few scribes as follows: 'He takes three minutes' sitting at finishing partisittings. The two first about an ' cular parts.'—-Valker's Let-ters and hour each; the third not half an Papers in the possession of Dr. Vi1hour. If preferred, he can take two.' kinson of Maiichester. of the purest white, or with the reliefs on coloured grounds; the size to vary from the cameo fitted for the smallest ring, to a picture large enough for the lid of a snuflbox or the case of a watch; nay, some even larger. We have traced Wedgwvool's unceasing efibrts towards improvement from 1772, when cameos are first mentioned, till they cul-minated in such masterpieces of ab-solutely perfect work as the Antonies and Cleopatras, the Pan and Syrinx, in white jasper. But this did not content him. As early as the close of 1777 he wrote:

I shall not sit down content with bracelet and ring cameos till I can make most of them with color'd grounds, pol-ish'd & without staining; & if I succeed, that branch alone, I am fully persuaded, would be a capital business. But oh! time! time! time! There is no time to bring to maturity a thousandth part of the possibilitys of our enjoying & pro-lific business. I see at a single glance immensely further than I shall ever be able to travel; & whether any of my young men will have perseverance sut-ficient to carry them to the heights from whence alone such prospects can be viewed, I have much more doubt than expectatio_n. But whither am I carried? I return to my memorandums again.' When he had in a measure attained his object he Wrote again:

By-the little Cupid you will see how small we can make them -with colour'd grounds. Several hundreds of the suit of gems may be made, if we should make little cabinets. I have just been looking over them for that purpose, but it-would furnish a world of modelling. Pray con-sider of this plan. It appears to me of consequence, they would be so much superior to anything ever made of the kind. They appear so distinct, & are so pleasant to look at with colour'd grounds that I cannot help thinking some great folks might be found liable to temptation from them. We should give them a little nurled gilt frame, l 'edgwood to Bentley, December 20, 1777.

2398 GEM SETTING. CRAP. VIII. which would look very well with the blue ground. The whole assemblage of white, blue, gold, & black drawers would have a. striking effect, & be very pleasing.'

A large number of these gems were set as rings, earrings, chatelaines, bracelets, and other such adornments. At first, when gold was employed as the setting, the work was done in London by Nodes, the goldsmith already men-tioned. For steel work, and later, when Nodes's prices were found too high, for gold work too, the gems were sent to Birmingham; though from 1773, and for some years subsequently, all the finer portion of these gold settings were the work of Thomas Copestake, a jeweller of Uttoxeter in Staiffordshire. Copestake was a man renowned throughout all the midland counties as a lapidary, an en-graver, and a goldsmith. He exported jewellery, principally to Russia, and employed from one to two hundred hands in the various branches of his trade. His house and workshops are said to have been picturesque in the extreme; the former being an old timbered hall lying just without the town; the latter, where the lapidaries had their wheels, being ranged round a square treeshaded court or yard, whilst above were the shops for the smiths and setters. Copes-take, who was a great admirer of Wedg-wood's work, was first employed by him to set seals, and from these he ad-vanced to necklaces, bracelets, and oth-er ornaments. He also bought gems of Vedgwood to set on his own account, so that for some years the dealings be-tween them were considerable; yet in spite of skill and immense trade, Copes-take from some unexplained cause was not a prosperous man. He eventually borrowed money of Wedgwood, and died

' Vedgwood to Bentley, November 13, 1778.

towards the close of the century in such reduced circumstances as to necessitate an unmarried daughter to set up frames for lacework in order to procure the means to live. The ancient house and workshops fell into decay, were en-croached upon by the town, were finally swept away, and their site is now cov-ered by some portion of a railway.'

' The following very interesting par-ticulars of Thomas Copestake's resi-dence, and of his daughter Grace, have been furnished to the writer by her friend Mrs Howitt, a native of,

Uttoxeter. She says:

Copestake must have been dead before my time, which begins with the last year in the last century; but the house in which he lived, the traditions of the prosperity which his lapidary work ad given to the town, are amongst my ear-liest remmiscences.

those times as " the good old times;" and I remember perfectly well sundry old men of apeculinrly quiet manner, neat appearance, and slow gait, who were given to angling and similar con-teniplativeoccupations,allancient lapi-daries, and who probably after the lapi-daries' shops were closed had never tak-en to any very active or laborious mode of gaining their living.

Some of them were thought lazy,

but I do not think it was other than the natural effects of years spent at the lap-idary-wheel or bench cutting and mani ulating delicate stones.

'The opestnkes' house, called

"The Hall," was a hrge irregular brick mansion by the roadside at the entrance of the town from Tutbury and Derby. It stood a little apart from the road, with a grass-grown court before it, intersected by paved walks, or perhaps the whole court had been paved, and was then completely overgrown with grass ex-cept where kept bare b goin to and from the house. t sto on the brow of a pleasant slope overlooking the verdant meadows of the Dove,

with the wooded ascent of Needwood Forest to the right, and to the left

Doveridge and Sudbury, the seats of ' Thomas '

People talked about ' the Ivaterparks and Vernons, and the ruins of Tutbury Castle. The situation was fine, and the house, though much dilapidated in those days, and now for many years entirely ulled down, must originally have een a place of some little consideration, as it was one of the most important mansions near the town.

' On the town side of the old Hall extended a large court, inclosed from the road bv an old red-brick wall, as old no doubt as the house itself, and entered by a weatherbeaten door. Round the three inner sides of this court were erected worksho s for the lapidaries, two storeys hig as it seems to me, or perhaps raised to the hei ht of a second storey for better ht, as outside flights of steps 1 up to them. These shops were lighted by long, or rather broad, casemented windows for the free admission of light, like the shops of silk-weavers and stockingers. At this time they were falling, or rather had fallen, into decay. The court was 'overgrown with as, tall rank weeds seeded there, the outside flights of steps, which probably were ofwood, were dila idated, the glass in the windows was roken, and the whole had a strange air of desolation about it.

' Now and then however it was turned to ncount as aplace of amusement. A troop of horse-riders would hire it temporarily, and no doubt a better place for the exhibition of their feats could hardly have been chosen. The old deserted shops with their outside flight of steps and their large windows affording tiers of boxes and seats as in a theatre.

'The only descendant of Thomas Copestake that I ever knew was his' 400 Birmingham, far more than London, was the centre of

SOHO AND ETRURIA.

Cnar. VIII.

Wedgwood's trade in seals and cameos. As early as the summer of 1772 Wedgwood showed buttons from Soho in his rooms; and Boulton, on theother hand, sent specimens of Wedgwood's seals to his foreign correspondents, and

procured customers, in Russia especially, for unsaleable stocks of black and yellow painted as also printed ware. In the spring of the succeeding year he undertook seal setting on a small scale, and bought at Wedgwood's suggestion cameos to set in vases, lockets, bracelets and daughter Grace.

been middle aged at that time; a tall thin lady dressed in the narrow skirted classical style of those days which made her look still thinner.

Her features were good and her countenance remarkable for an expression

was not an independent lady; was not the representative of an old line living simply on the scanty remnant of the family fortune in the decayed home of her ancestors. She was something much more interesting than this, thou h the people amongst whom she live could not understand it. They constantly spoke of her as

" oor Miss Grace,' and in all probasaility this ex ression of pity was the result of the alf-wonder1ngc0m—

passion with which the narrowminded dwellers in a small town regard any deviation from the regular course of conventional life. She

was alady who strove to maintain ' herself; and was certainly one of the earliest of that race of independent women, which has given a. marked characteristic to the present century. She introduced the "lace work" as it was called into the town, and one if not more of the la rooms in the desolate hall were filled with frames for this purpose. These resembled quiltin frames, and supported on tressels eld the plain piece of lace as it came from the maker in Nottingham, and which was unroll ed from one side of the frame, and rolled

She must have ' up on the other, as the work of sprigging, of which the pattern was stamped in blue ink upon the lace, was completed. Young women did this work seated at the frames and working with blunted needles. Lace

' of all widths, and often of verv deli of decision and firmness. Miss Grace.' cats and elaborate patterns, veils and

' shawls were worked in this wav. . masons.-Some

After the decline of the lapidai-y work this might be said to have become the staple trade of the little town, for not only was it done at the Hall, but in almost every small house the space beneath the windows was occu ied by a lace frame at which the aughtersor woman of the house, and even little boys worked.

' At length Miss Copestake retired from the scene, either because her lace working establishment was not sufficiently remunerative, or for other, and let us hope more comfortable years after the house (1 into other hands, was pulled own and the materials sold. On this occasion our father was the purchaser of a quantity of handsome dark wainscoting which he put up in two rooms of a house belon ' g to himself, and where I believe it still remains.

'One of his daughters married I believea Mr. Holy,:1 Sheffield manufacturer, a man of substance and consideration. But whether Thomas Copestake had other children than these two daughters I know not.'

CHAP. VIII. ETRURIA AN D SOHO. 401 other ornaments. The first trials of this ornamental setting were in tortoiseshell. Cameo buttons were suggested by Fothergill and tried next. They were for foreign countries, and provided they were cheap, would sell in large quantities. Boulton and Fothergill had already manufactured this kind of button.

They set them all under crystals (writeswedgwood to Bentley), & would be therefore content with them of white bisket, without polish or col0ur'd grounds, as they could do the latter in water colours. They have done some cameos for vases in that way, & they look much better than our burnt-in grounds; & being cover'd with a. glass, are sufliciently durable..... Mr. Fothergill mentioned our setting some of their articles in our rooms. They show other people's articles, china a,1't'icles, in their show rooms. I told him I thought we could with propriety show anything in which our manufacture had a. place, but wod write to you upon the subject. They will do the same for us; & as our season begins when the Soho season ends, I t-hink we may be of use to each other in that way.'

This question of plain cameos to be ground-laid with water-colours brought about one of those little, and not at this date unfrequent, differences between the masters of_

Etruria and Soho.

I do not know how to manage with Mr. Boulton (confides VVedgwood to his partner) abot grounding cameos in Water colours, for he is one of those high spirits who likes to do things his own way, & if crossed-in that will perhaps do nothing at all, or worse. I willattempt to confine the water colouring to cameo buttons, but if he will order plain white cameos it will be dangerous to refuse him... B. & F. have concerns with the VVOrcester people. If we refuse to let them have the cameos in white, they may set these gentry to work.... At present I am of opinion it would be worth while to try the experiment. We have no models to buy. We can make any quantity, & with certainty.'

' Wedgwood to Bentle, November 23, 1773.
' Ibid. December 12, 1 73.
VOL. II. D D

The difficulty of the point was, that Boulton by his cheap processes could, when once furnished with the cameos, undersell Wedgwood in his own market. However, the latter seems to have acquiesced; but soon, by means the most legitimate, that of improving the body, so that it would incorporate colour in the mass, or receive it readily as a dip or wash, thus doing away with enamelling altogether—he placed his work beyond the reach of any competition to injure it in the market. Boulton was no mere imitator. Wedgwood's exquisite, and ultimately cheap, productions gained the ascendency; mere imitations faded before them, and Boulton as much as any man aided in their dispersion and sale.

It is at this date we first hear of Egginton, who was engaged at Soho, in his business of printing in colours. Early in the succeeding year, 1774, a few of the cabinetmakers of Birming-

ham and other Midland towns were using cameos and encaustic paintings in the decoration of furniture. Of the latter VVedgwood suggested to have drawings and catalogues made; but it does not appear if the plan-was tried. This style of decoration was also popular at Soho, and the demand there for cameos considerable.

During 1775 and the early part of 1776, Boulton seems to have been too occupied in his negotiations with Watt, and with business relative to the steam-engine, to take any very active part in his ornamental manufactory. But a man named Clay, a most ingenious cabinet-maker of Birmingham, was at this time doing much for Wedgwood's fame, by inserting the cameos in tea-caddies, writing-desks, dressing-cases, and similar articles; and so much were these admired, that he soon began to make small drcssinr and other box lids entirely of one cameo.

These signs of Clay's exceeding taste and ingenuity induced Boulton to suggest a partnership, but Clay for some reason declined, ' and afterwards Mr. Boulton says,' confides Wedgwood to Bentley, 'talked with his servant Egginton in such a way as has very much offended Mr. B., and obliged him to enter into partnership with his servant in that branch, to keep him easy and in his service in other branches where he cannot very well do without him. So Mr. B. and Mr. C. do not see each other.
' 1 At this date Boulton and Fothergill were sending over a young man to St. Petersburgh to attend the Court there, introduce their fine things, and take orders, and by this means ' they hoped to supplant the French as well in the plate as gilt, both of which are very considerable.' After saying that they had ofl'ered to him the services of their intended representative at the Russian Court, Wedgwood adds, ' I had no conception of the quantity of D' Or Moulu they have sold chiefly abroad. You remember a poor Venus weeping over the Tomb of Adonis—a Timepiece. How many could you imagine they have sold of this Group? 200 at 25 guineas each including the watch! They now sell as

much of the manufacture in Tripods, Vases, Groups, &c., as they can get up.'
'

After this difference with Clay, Boulton added the business of cabinetmaking to the already multifarious works at Soho, and introduced painted cartoons and cameos into various kinds of decorative furniture. Another of his suggestions was vases for holding knives and forks at the dinner-table, and I/Vedgwood and he were for some time busy working out this 'idea jointly. The
' 'ed,frwood to Bentley, July 14, 17745.
latter made a drawing and sent it to Bentley, from which we see that the pedestal was composed of drawers for the knives and forks, above was a vase of earthenware or metal, whilst around were twined metal ornaments. Boulton also pursued Wedgwood's idea of inlaying his timepieces and the altars which supported groups of figures with ' statues, &c., with blue grounds;' and subjects proper for Russia and other countries were modelled and prepared at Etruria. Wedgwood often visited Birmingham at this date; but for the gaieties at Soho he had little taste; and frequently declining them, repaired to his inn to smoke his pipe, and hold, through his pen, quiet communion with Bentley.

A year later, and the great idea at Soho was, as already seen, the manufacture of chimney-pieces, panels for doors, &c., principally formed in wood with tin ornaments. ' But Boulton, Fothergill, and Egginton,' confidesWedgwood to his friend, have simply 'taken up the trade we laid down at Chelsea, only instead of casting, they make their ornaments in dies, by which the work is perfectly sharp.' This was true. In 1775, whilst their business was at Chelsea, Wedgwood and Bentley had entered into negotiations with a view to partnership with a person named William Storer, who the year previously had taken out a patent for 'Making, Chasing, or Imbossing in Lead all sorts of Girandoles, Frames for Pier-Glasses, Tablets, Friezes, and Brackets for Chimney Pieces and Rooms, and of Hardening the same, so that such Ornaments are rendered as Durable as if made in Copper or other Metal." Their object was to combine pottery and metal for ornamental purposes, and so far had matters proceeded that

' Specification of Patent, No. 1068, August 10, 1774.

CIIAP. VIII. STORER'S PATENT.

4-05 articles of partnership were already sketched out. But enquiries, and Storer's own conduct after being in their service some few weeks, proved to them he was a man in needy if not desperate circumstances, and that he had wilfully deceived them in many essential particulars. Fortunately for them he had, after borrowing considerable sums of money, to fly from his creditors to Dunkirk, and Wedgwood and Bentley washed their hands of the affair. They had probably to effect this object by some sort of compromise, as Wedgwood thought it necessary to draw up a paper in which he stated in a masterly manner his ' Reasons for breaking with Mr. Storer.' The latter, however, appears to have reestablished himself in business, and to have taken a more honest and worthy course, as we find Wedgwood speaking kindly of the man and hopefully of his business in after years. 1

In one way or another, butI especially in this of chimney-pieces, the business relations between Etruria and Soho became extensive, though eventually personal and table ornaments gave place to most other articles. The chimney-pieces in wood with tin ornaments of Soho were the toys of an hour; but the cameos, the vases, the tripods, and the light bearing articles of Etruria were sterling, and could outlive competition. More and more Boulton became absorbed in the steam engine and his partnership business with Watt; till at length as Wedgwood wrote to Bentley, ' Certain steam engines have lifted a good friend of ours above his watch-chain & sleevebutton business.'

Red ware, as already seen in those beautiful specimens of the Elers' workmanship, had long been made in the 1 Heads of Partnership. Reasons for Breaking with Mr. Storer. Mayer MSS.

406 ROSSO A NTICU.

Cmr. VIII.

Potteries, and some of Wetlgwoo(1's earliest portrait me dallions and bas-reliefs were in this body. He made the former at Bentley's suggestion, but he wrote—' My objection to it is the extreme vulgarity of red wares. If it had never been made in Tpots & the commonest wares, my objection w'i not have existed. But as it will be necessary they shd be sold cheap, and we shd give some obvious reasons for that cheapness, this alone may render it proper to make them of the red clay. I will send you a few to look at soon.'1 The results were not satisfactory, and Bentley urged him to try for the beautiful red tint of antiquity; but from some unexplained cause it could not be hit. In this dilemma Wedgwood said, 'I wish you to fix upon one of the Bronze like

CHAP. YIII. ROSSO ANTICO. 40? colours for heads for the cheap cabinets, as we shall never be able to make the Ros-so Antico, otherwise than to put you in mind of a red Pot Teapot.'1 Subsequently, at the suggestion of Sir William Hamilton, some vases were made of red slightly tinged with yellow, but even this tint failed to bring the colour to the fineness of that of antiquity. Moclern attempts have been in a certain degree more successful. But the secret of the marvellous glaze is still a. desideratum.

The first trials for cane and bamboo colours were made towards the close 1 Ved wood toBentle_v, March 3, 1776. any specimens of Vedgv0od's red Ware of this date are in

Mr. Ma_ver's collection. But the have all, as VVe(lgwood said, muc the look of a red teapot or gardenpot. ' Vedgwood to Bentley, September, 1776.

as flowerpots and teapots soon became popular. But the body had many defects, and when it was tried as a material for busts, as it was for those of Voltaire and Rousseau in October 1779, Wedgwood found that these were irremediable. He therefore tried the cane colour in an entirely new body, and with the utmost success; and during the period which

elapsed between this date and his death, many most beautiful articles were produced in this ware, and its variation in the bamboo tints. The four annexed specimens (figs. 76, 77, 78 and 79) are all very choice.

The copper glaze or gold bronze ware took its rise from a receipt given to Wedgwood by Dr. F othergill in 1776. It was first tried by Bentley with great success. Upon hearing this, Wedgwood wrote ' The Dr.'s idea was to apply it to frames, but I trust some more profitable purpose may be secured by this discovery.'1 He took the matter in hand, made experiments, and the results were shown in nuinberless articles of great beauty. The annexed example of the gold bronze Ware (fig. 80) is a pitcher-shaped vase of exceeding beauty in Mr. Bohn's collection, although from the absence of the exquisite metallic tinge in the engraving half the beauty of the original is lost.

Inkpots were made in every kind of ware, from the earliest period of Wedgwood's labours as a potter. As he improved his wares and his forms, they improved also; as countless examples still show. A third of his correspondence with Bentley is filled with matter relative to the dispersion of seals and inkpots. They formed together two great staples of his trade; and after 1779, when Mr. Byerley began to travel for the firm, the inkstands were to be found in almost every toy and bookseller's shop in the kingdom. They are first referred to in the Catalogue of the same year, and it is curious to observe from the diagram given with the letterpress therein, how much Wedgwood's mechanical genius was made subservient to the purposes of his art. The annexed (fig. 81) is a charming specimen of an inkstand in black, with red floral relief. Its form has only to be observed, to prove the exceeding pains which was taken to beautify the commonest objects of utility. Many most exquisite specimens in other bodies could have been given did space permit.1

C'/rucibles, retorts, evaporating baths, and many other vessels, for the laboratory had been supplied by Wedgwood to Priestley even before the latter left Leeds in 1773. From this date we frequently hear of them as in demand by the philosophers and chemists of this and foreign

IThis inkstand was the foundation 'I asked 4d. for it, and this sum he stone of Mr. Barlow's very choice 1 gave. Its original price was probably collection. He bought it at an old about 71;. 611. It is now valued at £5. rag and iron shop in Salford, Man-1 That sum for it has been offered and cheater. The owner of the shop _ refused.

410 MORTAR MATERIAL.' can». VI-II. countries. The introduction of the mortar material is of a considerably later date. Its resistive force seems in some measure to lie in the components of Cornish clay; and till this could be obtained in sufficient quantities through the triumph of the potters over Champion's monopolising patent, it is probable, if even his experiments in this direction had proved successful at an earlier period, little could have been do11e. We first hear of mortars in March 1779; though yet so far imperfect as to be uncertain if they would stand the necessary fire. The next faults were those of imbibition and blistering.

To cure this body of the malady of blistering (writes Wedgwood) it should be hid under ground for half a. century; but as the body pol-z't'ic, as Well as our own pa'rt'icula1' bodies, are in too fluctuating a state to think of applying so long winded a remedy, I am endeavouring to make a new one (composition) without such freaks as render the other imperfect. In the former body I employed a substance containing much fixed air. I now substitute one which I believe contains none, or very little if any. This occasions an unavoidable interruption in your supply of mortars, but perfection being our a.im in all things, we must not stop too far short of it, even in mortars.'

This difficulty conquered, the next was with their form.

Mr. More's remark (he tells Bentley) of the necessity of the mortar and pestle being sections of the same circle, is a very good one as far as it goes, & I had

from the beginning ordered our people to make them so; but they did not know how, & I had not bestowed suflicient attention to the subject to put them in a way of doing it, or indeed to learn the art myself. It requires a. set of tools both for the mortars & pest-les, as nothing-must be left to the random hand of the workman; for if I am right in my theory, there is only one amongst the infinite variety of

CIIAP. VIII. MORTARS AT APOTIIECARIES' HALL. 411 curves that will give the qualities desired to these machines. Qu. Which is that curve?'

He discovered it, and shortly after the mortars and pestles were introduced at Apothecaries' Hall, and from the test they withstood there, soon acquired a fame which has lasted to the present day.

In relation to these manifold experiments and their results, Wedgwood might well write

You can scarcely conceive the dificiulty we have arising merely from making & drying so many different kinds and colours of clay, as they each require different cisterns, tools, kilns, &c., to say nothing of inventing & after that experimenting them into perfection. And when the clays are made black, white, blue, green, red, yellow, compact, open, &c., &c. To work these multifarious compositions upon the same wheels, lathes, & moulds, & at the same time prevent their mixing with each other, & after all to give them their different & proper workings, dryings, firings, glazings, & a. 100 more &c.'s, makes me crazy almost to think upon so complex a. subject to manage, & not a little t-imorous in increasing another wheel or spring in this already too complex a machine.2

LITERARY AND SCIENTIFIC FRIENDS—HIS LABOURS AS A POLITICIAN AND REVIEWI-'.R—AMERICAN AFFAIRS—USELESS-NESS OF THE CHAPTER IX.
GREEK STREET AND BENTLEY.

HE houses Nos. 12 and 13 Greek Street, Soho, were separated by an archway from each other; but communicat-

ed by means of a chamber above it. This archway led into a large yard in the rear, in which were the enamelling rooms already referred to, as also a warehouse and other offices. No. 13 was hired soon after the settlement of the business relative to the larger house No. 12, and here it was that Bentley and his wife took up their residence in the summer of 1774; and remained there till the summer of 1777, when, as we shall see, they removed to Turnham Green. The house was comparatively small, and of this accommodation two or three rooms were taken for business purposes; but enough remained for elegant and bounteous hospitality. When Wedgwood and his wife came to town, sleeping accommodation was hired hard by; but for the rest they lived with their friends as one family. The ladies spent their mornings in shopping, sight-seeing, or in paying or receiving visits; their husbands were immersed in business in their showrooms, or out amongst artists, modellers, or connoisseurs; but evening come, they met round the tea or supper table, where, if alone, the partners discussed the real or ideal position, of their vast and complicated 416 BENTLEY'S AUTIIORSHIP. Crmr. IX.

trade; or, if guests were there, politics, and the social wrongs of those sad and momentous days, or scientific topics pleased and lured away the hours; for Bentley's acquaintances were many. He touched upon the bounds of science through the tastes of his partner and friend; his club was another source of introduction to men of real eminence; his relationship to Sir Richard J ebb, the well-known physician, yet another; and his constant communication, not only with the ministry, but with members of either House of Parliament, on subjects principally relative to the commercial interests of the Staffordshire Potters, brought him into frequent contact with men of many classes and opinions. On his own account he was at home with authors, and those few politicians who honestly loved their country, and sighed for its well-being; for his patriotism was ardent, and his love for literary labour the greatest love of all. If his taste in the fine arts was exquisite, his taste for letters was supreme. In character it was prompt and versatile. It spent itself in political pamphlets, newspaper articles, dashing squibs, and satirical songs; 1 and when he reviewed—as he was ever doing in the Monthly Review, politics and the controversies of theology were the marks for his pen. For literary labour which required preparation, care, and thought, he had, if not less aptitude, at least less time; as it was not till after repeated incitations from Wedgwood, who had been, in conjunction with Henshall, at great pains to procure a large amount of information, that be completed his article on Brindley for the Biogra-phia Britannica. ' None can do it so well as yourself,' wrote Wedgwood, ' & unless you can bestow a little time upon it, we shall

' In one of his letters to Boulton, Vedgwood complains of Bentley wasting his time in writing political songs. Soho MSS.

CHAD. IX. AMERICAN AFFAIRS. 417 have a bare & deficient account of a man who has deserved to be remembered by posterity.' 1 But months elapsed before it was completed.

There is to be traced throughout Wedgwood's letters a knowledge of political movements and affairs, especially those relative to America, which were evidently derived from Bentley, who appears to have had various private sources of information. Mr. Hodgson, a merchant of Coleman Street, trading with America, and an intimate friend of Dr. Franklin's, was one of these; and from him he learnt those remonstrances of the colonists, and those aggressions on the part of the mother country, which, reported to Wedgwood in letters, had roused his indignation often hours before any report had appeared in the public prints. None knew better than Wedgwood, from his trading relations with America, the sacrifice the mother country was making in this senseless struggle. In 1774, before the strife began, Great Britain exported to North America nearly the whole of the surplus products of her industry; and since 1704 the American trade had grown from half

a million sterling a year to six millions and a half. His and Bentley's feelings were therefore from the first strongly opposed to those of the great majority of their countrymen, who looked upon the Americans as rebels, and only worthy the fate of such. But time brought a change. As the uselessness of the contest showed itself, the public began slowly to perceive how much more was lost than gained.

I agree with my dear friend most heartily & intirely (wrote Vedgwood) that some one should be made to say distinctly what has been the object of this wicked & preposterous war with our brethren & best friends... I have not yet seen a paper in the

' Vvedgwood to Bentley, August 14, 1778. VOL. II. E E 418 DR. FRANKLIN. CRAP. IX.
public prints, nor a speech in the House that has handled the recantation to my satisfaction, nor made that use of it to express the absurdity, folly, & wickedness of our whole proceedings with America which the ministers' concessions and confessions have given ample room for... The people are quite chapfallen & dismayed, & nothing but half a score Highland, Manchestrian, & Liverpool regiments amongst us will revive their malignant spirit again, or enable them to look any man who has not been as mad as themselves in the face.'

A few days later, he adds:

I am glad that America is free, & rejoice most sincerely that it is so, and the pleasing idea of a refuge being provided for those who choose rather to flee from, than submit to the iron hand of tyranny has raised so much hilarity in my mind, that I do not at present feel for our own situation as I may do the next rainy day. We must have war, & perhaps continue to be beat. To what degree is in the womb of time. If our drubbing keeps pace with our deserts, the L'! have mercy upon us.'

During the latter part of our contest with America, Mr. Hodgson was exposed to much calumny through his friendship for Franklin. But this in no way lessened his good oflices to either Americans, or to those who sympa-

thised in their cause. He raised funds for the sufferers in the war, to which Wedgwood and Bentley contributed; and he procured the prints from which was modelled the annexed medallion of the illustrious Franklin. (fig. 82).

Bentley belonged to a club which met every Wednesday night at Young Slaughter's coffee-house in St. Martin's Lane. It bore no distinctive title, though frequented by men of real science and distinguished merit. John Hunter, the great anatomist, was at one time its chairman. Sir Joseph Banks, Solander, Sir C. Blagden, Dr. George Fordyce, Milne, Maskelyne, Captain Cook, Sir G. Shuck Wedgwood to Bentley, March 3, ms. 1 Ibid. March 19, 1778.

CRAP. IX. BENTLEY'S CLUB. 419 burgh, Lord Mulgrave, Smeaton, Bamsden, Griflith the publisher, and many others were, or had been, members. Edgeworth and Wedgwood generally attended its meetings as guests when in town. Researches and discoveries were discussed; and lengthened arguments, differences and agreements, were always crowned by a supper which after January 3, 1775, was eaten off a special service of cream ware, supplied by Wedgwood, and probably a Here it was, if not at Lichfield or Etruria, that Bentley made the acquaintance of Edgeworth. They became warm friends; and visits at a somewhat later period were often made reciprocally to New Church and to Turnham Green. Not unfrequently on other nights, members of the club supped in Greek Street; and Mrs. Bentley seems 420 HOSPITALITY IN GREEK STREET. CRAP. IX.
to have zealously aided her husband in the entertainment of his literary and scientific friends. In this respect and others, his marriage seems to have been a most happy one. Mrs. Bentley had evidently not the force of character of Mrs. Wedgwood; she could not judge and decide, and this with results that almost always proved correct; but she was amiable and kindly, and as much secured her husband's affection as the kindly regard of 11 wide circle of friends.' With Mrs. Wedgwood, her relations were even sisterly. Never once in all that

lengthened correspondence do we find even a semblance of coldness or difference. The meetings in Greek Street and at Etruria were as much anticipated, and as much a source of happiness to the ladies as to their husbands. In this Bentley was most fortunate, for he loved women with all the strength of his generous and chivalrous nature; and, as Wedgwood well said, was never so happy as when amongst them. But this felicity had its side of shadow. He had from time to time the hope, but not the irealisation, of having children of his own. His wife's health was not good; his own indifl'erent. Severe attacks of the gout', and the results of an overworked brain, occasionally prostrated him. Greek Street did not agree with either ruler or ruled. The clerks, the enamellers, the servants, were always falling ill. ' I cannot think,' wrote Wedgwood, ' what makes my young men drop off so.' The causes were not so patent to that generation as to our own. Bentley removed to Turnham Green, but he was ill even there; for though Wedgwood earnestly and frequently entreated him to take rest, he rarely did; but went on and on with his incessant labours, till his end 1 Mrs. Delany s aka of making a morning call on Mrs. Bentley in Greek Street, March 177. Correspondence, 2nd series, vol. ii. p. 202.

CHAP. IX. CHAMPIONS PATENT. 421 came suddenly in the prime of his days. But he made contentment in his childless heart by his love for

» Wedgwood's little daughter; and if overfilled with duties, his hours seem to have been most happy ones. Wedgwoocl, as we have seen, whilst attending his sick wife at Bath in 1772, was studying Borlase's ' History of Cornwall,' and from that date we find him more or less occupied in the business relative to the supplies of native clay. Cookworthy's Patent, which had been taken out in 1768, virtually confined the China. clay and China stone of Cornwall to one monopolist, or to such as the monopolist might license to use them; and this fell hard upon the general body of manufacturers, all of whom were more or less interested in improving

their wares; and upon Wedgwood in especial, who just at this date was engaged with his jasper composition, as also in making experiments for a whiter ware, and to him therefore finer and whiter clays were a desideratum The fashionable world were getting tired of cream colour, and enquiring for other; and

Wedgwood, though much against his inclination, saw that" he must ultimately obey. In 1774 Cookworthy assigned over his patent to Champion of Bristol, who soon after applied to Parliament for its extension for a further period of fourteen years, when the original term should have expired. This desire of a further monopoly excited the warmest opposition; and we find Wedgwood as early as March 1775 bidding Bentley ' mount his chariot' and wait upon the county members and others who, in addition to Earl Gower, were likely to use their influence in behalf of the Potters. An explanatory pamphlet from Wedgwood's pen was also published and widely dispersed; and two

' I11 his ultimate trials he found the Growan or china clay mix best with the 74 or cnwk.

422 WEDGWOOD IN CORNWALL. Cmr. IX. months later we find him and his friend Mr. Turner, the eminent potter of Lane End, on their way to Cornwall to view for themselves its mineral treasures. They were accompanied by a Mr. Tolcher and by Thomas Griifiths, Wedgwood's former clay agent in Carolina, by a guide and two servants, and for several days they explored the clay-producing districts. This appears to have been VVedgwood's first visit to the southern shore of our island, and he was singularly delighted with its beautiful scenery. He kept a journal of his tour for Bentley, and therefore wrote briefly. But he says in a letter dated from Plymouth_-' We were upon the water several hours yesterday afternoon. Have you seen Mount Edgecombe? If you have not seen Mount Edgecombe you have seen nothing. Ve sailed twice past this terrestrial paradise, and such a sun setting I never beheld.'1 The result of this visit was, that Turner and Wedg-

wood became joint lessees of certain clay mines at St. Stephen's, a place between St. Austle and Redruth, and that Griffiths remained as their agent.

'We are to have a meeting of our Potters (he wrote to Bentley as soon as he reached home), after which you shall hear from me again.... Mr. Turner & I have concluded to set about washing some clay for ourselves and for others as soon as we can, if they chuse to have it, but at the same time to leave the raw clay open to all who chuse rather to prepare it for themselves, for I am firmly persuaded that an exclusive Company, or rather an exclusive right in the Clay in any Company or under any regulations whatever, would soon degenerate into a pernicious monopoly.'2 1 IVedg'wo0d to Bentley, dated I hehadneitherprofessionalknowledge, romPl month, June 2, 1775. i sufficient capital, nor scarcely anv real

" We gwood, inallusion toCham-' acquaintance with the materials he pion's Patent, calls it a 'cunning. was working upon. I suppose we a ecification,' as it notoriously was. might buv some G-rowan stone and e gained nothing by his monopo-Growan clay now upon easy terms, lising spirit, for he failed in August for they have prepared a large quan1778. 'Poor Champion, you ma tity this last year.'—Vedgwood to have heard, is quite demolished. t Bentley, August 24. 1778. was never likely to be otherwise, as

Gnu. IX. EXPERIMENTAL VORK PROPOSED. 423

It is evident from this, that in the interval between March and June the opposition of the Potters to Champion's Bill in the House of Lords had been so far successful as to secure to the petitioner a sole right to its use onlyin transparent ware, whether termed porcelain or not; whilst it left open to the general trade the free use of Cornish stone and clay in opaque pottery and glazes of every kind. This was a great point gained; although the Patent sadly trammeled Wedgwood in relation to his experiments for a whiter ware; as Champion only waited for him to produce a body or glaze which might be judged to approximate porcelain to involve him in all the difliculties of a legal contest.

Wedgwood's proposal of an Experimental Work in which should be tested clays and other substances used in bodies as also in glazes, in which when certainty of fitness should be obtained new descriptions of ware should be wrought, and by which without monopoly clay should be procured on a large scale, was well received by the Potters; though Bentley saw in the scheme inherent defects which were sure to nullify practical results. However, the Potters met again and again. Just as they needed a clerk to draw up proposals and undertake the necessary business of their embryo association, one presented himself. This was no less than young Byerley, who, capable and energetic, was willing to do any work which lay before him. The proposed company came to nothing. It lingered in nubibus from June to November, and then died a natural death, upon the question being put at a General Meeting ' whether the partners in Company should pay separately or jointly.' There was no settling this point, and so the matter ended. From this time the Potters took their own course with respect to the materials of their manufacture; 424 BYERLEY'S RETURN. CHAD. IX.

and Wedgwood, in many respects often conjointly with his friend Turner, his.

From 1769 till now in 1775 he returned to his native country, Thomas Byerley had undergone many vicissitudes. For a large portion of this time he had led a wandering life through many parts of New England. Sometimes a player, sometimes a schoolmaster, at others a reckless lad only intent upon the lawless promptings of the hour. Of these days many tales reached England through Wedgwood's correspondents. But at length the wild oats were sown, and he settled down in New York to the peaceful calling of a schoolmaster. During this period be improved himself in French and Latin, procured scholars, fought a steady and faithful fight-for bread; and when in time more pleasing accounts reached his uncle, they were as promptly related to his mother as the

foregone ill reports had been sedulously concealed. Forty pounds was sent to rid him of certain small encumbrances; and at length, in April 1774, Wedgwood commissioned Bentley 'to buy Tom a fine pair of globes' for the better instruction of his scholars. But hostilities broke out; he

'was too much an Englishman to take part against his country, so he gave up his school and came home; to the infinite joy of his mother and sisters, whose brighter days lost half their pleasure till the prodigal came to share them.

The Experimental Company at an end, Byerley did any work which stood ready. He translated French letters-for his uncle, collected debts, undertook business relative to the supply of flints; and in these matters, as in others, proved himself capable and earnest. At length his possession of business qualities of a very superior kind were too obvious to be overlooked. In the summer of 1777

CRAP. IX. A TIMOROUS TRAVELLER. 425 .it became apparent to both Wedgwood and Bentley, that if their seals, inkstands, portrait cameos, medallions and similar articles of ornamental ware were to have remunerative sales, they must be made known throughout the country by personal agency. Their first plan was that of employing their collector, a young man named Brownbill, to show goods and solicit orders in the metropolis and its neighbourhood; their next to despatch him on a tour through the west and south-western counties of England, mounted on a horse with his goods stored in boxes, and these in saddlebags. Devonshire and Cornwall were omitted from the counties visited, for the reason that they were supplied by three great dealers who derived a large part of their wares from Etruria. These men, though wealthy, lived in villages and obscure places, for the sake of cheap warehouse-room and pastureage for their horses; for their method of dispersing their goods over this wide region was as yet by packhorse and pannier.

After a few somewhat unsatisfactory journeys, the saddlebags and boxes

were given up for a light chaise. But Brownbill, timorous before, was a coward now. In fact he could not drive, and the approach of cart or coach was too much for him. He tried the road a few miles; and then, overcome with terror, returned whence he came. So ended his travels, and he was employed no more. The loss was gain. He had shown no tact in the soliciting orders or disposing of goods; and he had highly offended his masters by carrying about specimens of brown ware for Peter Swift, who, having saved perhaps a little money, had invested it in a small potwork for brown goods, and also taken the Leopard Inn in Burslem, though still cashier at Etruria. Petcr's ambition was 426 BYERLEY'S BUSINESS CAPABILITIES. Cm. IX.

short lived. He neither succeeded as a landlord nor a potter. In a few months he was in difiiculties. Wedgwood, who knew the man, had prophesied as much; and when the reality became known to him he called his clerk aside. He told him it was almost impossible for a man to be in his situation and remain honest, and that he must either give up his extraneous callings or leave Etruria; at the same time offering to free him from embarrassments. Peter was a worthy man, and faithfully attached to his master. He gladly accepted these conditions. Less than a hundred pounds made him again free; and thenceforth he kept to his pen and his ledgers, and ended his faithful service only with his life.

In the interval Byerley had shown the greatest aptitude for commercial business. He had prudence, tact, and sound judgment. Every short journey he made proved by its results that he had found his true place and Work; and thus in January 1779 he commenced those widespread journeys over Great Britain and Ireland of which his letters give such graphic record. He penetrated into every nook and corner of the land; and Wedgwood's useful as well as choicest productions became still more famous, for they were to be bought and seen everywhere.

During these passing years there had been, as ever in the roll of human fate, birth and death. Three daughters, —his last children,——were successively born to Wedgwood —Catherine in November 1774, Sarah in September 17 76, and Mary Ann in August 1778. These events were always followed by a christening feast. A splendid dinner was given, and neighbours were invited. Upon the birth of Catherine, a neighbouring clergyman named Sneyd wrote some verses on the event, and Wedgwood, in thanking him, asked him to stand godfather; telling him he was

Cm. IX. CHRISTENING FESTIVALS. 427

' not over rigid in vows and promises; only now and then a. hint in rhyme when she stands in need of it, and a couplet at her marriage, is all we shall expect." The christening of his last born child Mary Ann was on a. still grander scale.

I receiv'd a fine haunch of venison from this gentleman (Sir Thomas Broughton) for my christening (he tells Bentley) with a note that he should come and partake of it, which he did yesterday. VVe had Mr. Sneyd and sons, Mr. Davenport, half a score of our neighbours, & spent a very agreeable afternoon together. We had but little conversation upon politics, the company being so much divided in their opinions upon that subject, it might have broke in upon our harmony. '

From the period of his daughter's marriage Richard Wedgwood had led his usual retired life in the old farmhouse at Spen Green: Wedgwood and his wife often visiting him, and he in turn taking exceeding interest in all which concerned his famous son-in-law. It is not very clear if he and his only son John Wedgwood lived together, as the latter is always spoken of as of Smallwood, the former of Spen Green; but these places may have been named thus inditferently. The son had taken up his father's business of a cheese-factor on a large scale; and for some years had led an active, if not a prudent life. But in the early winter of 1774 he was stricken down by illness, and Wedgwood, upon visiting him, found him in the 'last stage of a worn-out constitution.' Darwin as

usual was sent for; but when he came he could give no hope. On November 18, 1774, John VVedgwood died

To the great grief of his father & sister & relations (as Wedgwood imparted to his friend), for who can but lament to see a young man, the only son of an aged & affectionate father, with

' Vedgwood to Bentley, December 17, 1774.
' Ibid. October 6, 1778.
428 RICHARD WEDGWOOD, SENIOR. CHAP. IX.
everything in his possession to render life agreeable & happy, cut off in the prime of life with all his unfinished plans & schemes of future life buried with him in the grave for ever? It is a melancholy consideration, but you have had your share in these distressful scenes, & I forbear to revive the remembrance of them in your mind.1

A few days later, the now solitary old man was persuaded to come to Etruria; and henceforth it was his home. By degrees he recovered his wonted cheerfulness; and venerated by his son-in-law, who always termed him 'father,' he formed a prominent feature in the domestic scene, whether abroad or at home. He was consulted in most things, for his judgment was sound and his perception clear; although occasionally he grew angry when he found no pains had been taken to make his son-in-law's merits known, or some opportunity of advancing his interests passed by.

I thank my dear friend for his good letter of the 15th (wrote VVedgwood on one occasion to Bentley), though it made my father-law ready to beat me, & you would not have escaped much better I can tell you, had you been by the fireside along with us. ' Did I not tell you—often tell you,' the old gentleman exclaimed, ' what it would come to, that other people must carry the tiding of y' improvements to Court, where you are not only permitted but commanded to carry them yourselves, & now you oblige their Majesties to send for and fetch that homage, which you ought to have carried and cheerfully paid in y" own proper Persons.2

It is evident from this that the old

man thought much more of court patronage than his son-in-law and Bentley, who had tested its value, and who were in fact too absorbed in the creation of beauty to be over-mindful of the means and methods of its dissemination. '

I Vedgwood to Bentley, November 19, 1774. 2 Ibid. May 15, 1776.
CHAP. IX. REV. WILLIAM VVILLET. 429

From this date till his death in 1782, the old man suffered from more than one exhausting illness; but when well he was habitually cheerful and industrious.

My father (VVedgwood tells Bentley) has employed himself a long time in alphabeting the initials of all the names in the London & other Directories, several ledgers &c., which enable us to make our cyphers in much better proportions for sale than before & a copy will be useful both to you & extremely so to Mr. Brownbill in taking his first assortment.1

In May 1778 Wedgwood lost his last brother, Richard.2 He had been ill for a long time, as the year previously the former had told Bentley——' My brother Richard, the only brother I have left, is in a very bad way. Extremely weak with swelled legs, &c., &c., the effects of a long-course of drinking & irregular living.' But he had soon after a keener grief in the loss of his brother-in-law, the Rev. William Willet, the Unitarian minister at Newcastle. His health had declined from 1776, and his little congregation had to obtain another preacher. He temporarily recovered, and employed his leisure time, as heretofore, in scientific investigation and controversial theology. Wedgwood, who perceived his decline, had his portrait modelled. ' I send you,' he said, writing to Bentley, ' this head of Mr. Willet as a specimen of Hackw0od's portrait modelling. A stronger likeness can scarcely be conceived. You may keep it as the shadow of a good man who is marching with hasty strides to the Land of Forgetfulness.'3 He lingered till the spring of 1778, when he died.
1 Wedgwood to Bentley, December this Richard to whom Priestley was 11,

1777. almoner on Vedgwood's account 1 'Richard Wedgwood senr., buried during a sojourn at Scarborough. May 30, 177.'—Register, St. John's, ' Wedgwood to Bentley, July

Burslem. It is probably a son of 1776. 430 HIS DEATH. CRAP. IX.

' This truly good man's death was of a piece with his life (wrote Wedgwood in telling Bentley of this grief) calm, serene, and sensible to the last moment. A little after nine this morning I assisted him to drink a dish of tea, as he sat in his chair, & a few moments after he expired in one single sigh. He had no pulse this morning, gasped for every breath, yet after thanking his wife for all her goodness to him, & telling her he knew he was dying, & believed he should go off in a slumber, he still talked of coming down to take that breakfast with the family, which was scarcely out of his lips before the lamp of life went out, merely through the want of a single drop of oil to sustain it another moment, & thus ended a well-spent life, with an easy & perfectly natural death, such a one as I suppose would be the general lot of all, if accident of various kinds did not interrupt the gentle hand of Nature in preparing us to take our final rest. Poor Mrs. Willet is quite wearied out. I hope we shall be able to comfort & restore her, for the sake of her young family & friends, as well as herself.'

Bentley, who it is evident had already tendered the hand of generous help, had been himself very ill; and thus Wedgwood concludes his pathetic letter from the house of mourning: ' I am greatly comforted with the good account you give me of your recovery. Pray God preserve you many many years. Take care of your precious health for all our sakes, & believe me with the truest affection & ever yours, J os. Wedgwood. ' 1 And yet whilst he wrote thus, this keenest grief of all was approaching with hasty strides.

The Bank-House at N ewcastle-under-Lyme, where this good man lived so many years, and wherein he indoctrinated Priestley in the science of optics and natural philosophy generally speaking, is still standing; a large, roomy, comfortable house, so built as to form an angle. It stands literally on a bank, overlooking the town; but the trees

' VVedgwood to Bentley, May 12, 1778.

Can. IX. THE BANK-HOUSE, NEWCASTLE. 431 which once shadowed it are gone; the garden which lay nearis almost built over; the pool which, clear and full of fish,1 lay at the bottom of the green and sloping bank is now a receptacle of rubbish and brickbats, and as dry as a drained moat; and the atmosphere around is smoke-laden in the extreme. But happily good fame sometimes, if not always, survives the perishable works of human hands. The chapel too Where he preached still remains, and is in much the same condition as in his day. It is doubly interesting, for to the left of the pulpit is yet the old family pew in which Josiah Wedgwood and his family worshipped for so many years and his descendants still occupy. The structure itself is the plainest of Nonconformist chapels, and covers, it is said, the site of one of the old Presbyterian meeting-houses which sprung up so rapidly during the brief existence of the Act of Toleration in the reign of Charles II. Whilst Mr. Willet was in the prime of life, his ministry was much frequented by persons of far different creeds; for he was an animated preacher, and to the last his sacramental exercises were singularly impressive?

Whatever might be his other engagements, Wedgwood went always to and fro with his children to school, his two eldest boys to Bolton, his daughter to Manchester; though after a period the latter went also to Bolton for a short time. The summer of 1775 was spent by her at home, and these holidays were made doubly delightful to all the children by a present sent down from London by Bentley of a large play-house; which, spread out upon the lawn before the Hall, was their unfailing rendezvous. Dr.

' John Wedgwood it may be re-and Biographical Notices of some of collected, was invitedto the Bank-his Contemporaries, by Joshua Toul

Darwin's boys came from Lichfield to spend some days and see the play-house; and the host of little cousins near at hand made up the merriest of companies. Wedgwood was in his glory. A little later in the season Bentley and his wife paid a visit; and we can fancy how a portion of it was spent by the partners when the one had lured the other thus—

I am pleased with the thought of our interview at Etruria growing nearer and nearer, & hope this hot weather will make you as impatient to leave the town as I am to see you here, & pray do not forget to bring with you some of the Books we are to read together, & I will order a portable Bench, where retired from the bustling world, we will enjoy a few of those quiet hours which it has hitherto seem'd impossible for us to find.'

In October Sukey accompanied Bentley and his wife to London, and soon the little maid won as tender a place in the heart of the former as she had in that of her father. Hitherto she had been very poorly taught; the schools had been mere places for the needle and backboard; so when she writes a loving little letter in December, which she addresses to her ' Dear and honoured papa,' she bids him tell her mamma to take her 'curiositys' out of her ' Chester drawers,' or else they will be spoiled. She then proceeds to tell him of her schoolfellow Miss Fothergill, and to express her sorrow that he has got ' a navigation cold.' ' Papa Bentley ' soon put his little favourite in her right place. Occasionally he instructed her himself; but in January 1776 she was sent to a school known as Blackland's, Chelsea. Here she soon improved, and laid the foundation of that excellent scholarship which was so useful to her busy husband, Dr. Darwin of Shrewsbury, in after years. AlreadyWedgwood had tendered his thanks 1 Wedgwood to Bentley, July 28, 1775.

CRAP. IX. BE.'TLEY'S VISIT TO FRANCE. 433 to Bentley 'for your kindness to our dear girl. I hope she will be good and grateful—at present, indeed, she cannot know the extent of her obligations_but I trust she will love and honour you & your good lady with a childlike aflection the longest day of her life.' 1

In May 1776 Bentley went to France, his business being, as it seems, partlyto buy various specimens of Sevres and other porcelain, and partly to see if his friend M. Sayde would like to undertake a commission for the sale of his and Wedgwood's ornamental goods. He was much struck with the state of the country, and the exceeding misery of the people,2 and seems to have had prophetic instinct of that Revolution which he did not live to see, but in which he would have rejoiced as others of his contemporaries; and this for the sake of the truth political tyrants had then to learn, that the forces of the moral world are no more to be repressed beyond a certain point than those of the physical. He was absent seven weeks, five of which he spent in Paris, exploring cabinets, galleries, libraries and public buildings. His route was by St. Omers, through French Flanders; and he returned by Amiens and Abbeville to Calais.3.

Just prior to this French visit he had entered into treaty to buy an estate or house; Wedgwood earnestly entreating him to avoid a cold wet soil, and to look around him well before he decided. But Bentley was a man of social tastes; he probably thought more of his Club and his Review, than gardens, fields, or picturesque scenery; and this perhaps made him decide in the spring

' Vedgwood toBentley, December He wrote soon after his return a 80, 1776. most graphic letter to his Liverpool

' Ibid. August 12, 1776. Whilst 'correspondent, Boardman, on the at Paris, the English Ambassador subject of his jmrne_v.-Bentleyans, honoured him with a call.. p. 20.

VOL. II. F F 434 I TURNHAM GREEN. CRAP. IX.
of the following year in favour of a house and grounds at Turnham Green. The soil was London clay, the site and neighbourhood fiat, the Thames too" far off to lend any of its charms to the scenery, the highway from London notoriously infested with highwaymen and footpads,1 and the hamlet itself of ill-re-

pute as the lurking-place of bad characters; but Ralph Grifiith lived here, and the printing of the Review was carried on a stone's throw from his door. In residing away from town Bentley must have substitutes for his Club at Slaughter's, his chapel in Margaret Street, if he only missed them occasionally, and for the conveniences of the houses in Greek Street where so many of the appliances of modern days were anticipated, even to that one of speaking-tubes from floor to floor, to save the time and steps of clerks and servants.-Wedgwood never liked Turnham Green, and before Bentley had concluded his purchase he thus wrote:

Ve are sorry you dare not take so many pleasurable appendages to a country house near London as would be desirable, & though we are convinced of your knowing much better than we do what part of the country is most commodious in every respect for you, yet notwithstanding this correction we did not feel right and satisfied with your taking of a house near Turnham Green, having heard so many terrible things from the papers of robbing & murdering in that line. Besides if our friend Mr. Grifiiths stays an hour later than ordinary at the Club he always professes it to be at the hazard of his life. These circumstances will make us uneasy upon this subject till you explain them more fully to us, as we heartily Wish when you do move it may be entirely to our satisfa.ction.2 '

' Numherless instances might be conch, September 8, 1774.' Hougiven from the newspapers and ma-i slow Heath abutted upon Turnham gazlnes of the day. In the parish j green. books of Chiswick is the following; 2 Vedgwood to Bentley, March entry: 'Vm. Tuck, supposed high-' 12, 1777. wayman, shot by guard of Exeter.

CIIAP. IX. BEN'TLEY'S HOUSE AND HOSPITALITY. 435
In spite of these drawbacks the purchase was made, and the letter which took this news to Etruria also conveyed the warmest invitation to both Vedgwood and his Wife. ' Mrs. Viledgwood,' writes the former, ' joins me in

thanking you for your friendly invitation to (pray give it a name if it has none) & we shall not need of a second. Do not be in haste to set your second garden. I will come and help you dig & weed, & sow & gather, and we will be joint Gardeners as well as joint Potters. '1' In

July Bentley removed to his new house; and in August the Wedgwoods, the Boardmans and others inaugurated that scarcely ceasing round of hospitality which, to the close of Bentley's life, rendered the place so cheery and pleasant. Of this visit Wedgwood wrote upon his return . home:

I have so many things to be thankful for, my Dear Friend,' that I should not know where to begin if the pleasure I received in the dear family at Turnham Green did not make the first & most lively impression. I often lament the necessity of our being so often & so far separated from each other, & if wishes would avail we should not often smoke our pipes asunder. Perhaps when Mr. Brock is better acquainted with the business in Greek Street, you may be better able to spend a little time with us at Etruria. I need not tell you how happy it would make us & I believe it would be no small advantage to us in respect to our business if we could manage to be a little more together. Besides I could teach you to bowl & love riding on horseback. To think less & play more, all of which will be of great service to you & of some to myself.2

Bentley's house is said by those acquainted with the neighbourhood to be one with that now known as Linden

House, lying eastward of Turnham Green on the south side of the high road to London. Attached to it was a

' 'edgwood to Bentley, April 22, 1777. ' Ibid. Uctnhnr 4, lTT7.
5'1-'2 436 HOUSEHOLD SCENES. Cusr. IX. considerable extent of ground; the far larger portion to the rear, a comparative strip towards the highway; for the trafiic in those days of mail coaches and flying waggons was very great, and the dust and noise were probably extreme. Wedgwood evidently alluded to-this when he said he should come and

enjoy his friends garden, but not that part of it on the side towards Turnham Green. To the house itself Bentley seems to have made additions and alterations, and others have been effected in quite recent years. The bas-reliefs inserted in the walls, and the niches for busts and figures still remaining in the lower rooms, evince the hand of taste which consecrated this dwelling, as it was hoped, to long days of peace and love. Here we can fancy, for such things were, those precious jasper tablets Wedgwood had hidden him keep and hide _ in a napkin, that cabinet of gems gathered for him, those beautiful vases, black or Greek encaustic painted, those marvellous busts, those fine medallions, those exquisite things of so many forms and kind. Here we can see him smoking his favourite evening pipe after tea, his wife and sister-in-law beside him, his little Sukey near playing with her doll, or on the fine harpsichord he bought for her to practise on. These were happy hours, and Wedgwood tells us of them:—

Mrs. Wedgwood (he writes) unites with me in love & every good wish to the Bentleys & Stamfords & Wedgwoods. What a happy man are you with all your friends about you. Methinks I see you with your evening pipe in your mouth & your soul peeping out at your eyes, as happy in the circle of your favourite females, I will not say as a king, but as a good man ought to be. May you ever remain so, & so long believe me your truly grateful & affectionate J os. Wedgwood.'

'Wedgwood to Bentley, March 26, 1778.

Cnsr. IX. RALPH GRIFFITHS. 487
The identity of the house occupied by Ralph Grifliths is not so certain as that of Bentley's. It was either What is now known as Campden House on the east side of Turnham Green, or Bolton House on the west. He had married a second time, as we have already seen, in 1767;1 and now a family of young children were around him. It is therefore to be hoped that these amenities of domestic life had softened his temper, and made his dealings more generous with

that authorcraft by whose toil he lived. He was in all respects a far inferior man to Bentley, and probably gained more from him than Bentley did in turn. But tastes in friendship, as in love, are often inexplicable; and Ralph Griffiths must have had some of the finer touches of our common nature to have secured and kept two such friends as Wedgwood and Bentley. He outlived them both.2 _

Wedgwood's little daughter passed the Midsummer holidays of 1777 at Etruria, her Christmas holidays at New Church with Edgeworth and his wife— both of whom formed a high opinion of her character. In the spring of 1778 she was ill, and for some time Bentley and his wife watched her with sedulous care; Sir Richard J ebb being her physician. 1/Vhen able to travel, Mr. Byerley fetched her home by slow stages.

How shall I thank you (Wedgwood wrote to Bentley) & your good lady, for our dear girl? It is impossible. I can only return you our warmest affection & gratitude which will end with our lives & not before when I must refer you to the next 'world for a more complete recompense for y" goodness in this.3

' R. Grifiiths married to Eliza l particulars relativet0Bentle_v'sh0use, Clark, 1767. ' to the kindness of the Rev. Lawford
' Hal 1: Grifliths died October 3, T. Dale, Vicar of Chiswick. 1803.—. arriage and Burial Registers ' Wedgwood to Bentley, April 6, of the Parish of Chiswicl-r. I am 1778. indebted for these entries, and the l438 PLEASURES AND STUDIES. CRAP. LY

Sukey soon recovered, and when the Midsummer ho1i- days came again, and his boys were home from their school at Bolton, Wedgwoocl gives us this picture of how the days were spent. He has been telling Bentley to go from home, to ride, to make a change in his daily life— for though ' you have everything, We well know, in your delightful habitation to make you abundantly happy, yet it is not well for a man to continue long in a place.' And he adds:

Sukey is now very well, & is pretty strong, which I attribute to riding on horseback. We sally forth half-a-dozen

of us by 5 or 6 o'clock in the morning & return with appetites scarcely to be appeased. Then we are very busy in our hay, & have just made a new garden. Sometimes we try experiments, then read & draw a little, that altogether we are very busy folks, & the holidays will be over much sooner than we could expect them to be. Poor Sukey is quite out of patience with her old spinet, & often asks me when her new one will come.1

A fine one by Kirkham was selected, and its arrival is thus recorded:

We have great rejoicings here upon the news of the'—the defeat of the French fleet? But the more important news of the arrival of our new harpsichord at Newcastle, & we can hardly wait till_ Monday without a sight of the instrument. Long may this disposition continue, & then you shall hear what music we can make the next time you deign to visit our humble plains.2

In this year, 1778, Wedgwood commenced his study of shells. He formed a collection," and begged Bentley to look out for sea-anemones during a sojourn the latter made at Margate. Soon after Christmas Bentley and his Wife were at Etruria, where some weeks were spent most

' Wedgwood to Bentley, July 17, lection bought in 1777 of Mr. John 1773-_ Goswill, Mill Street, Southwark.-' Ibid. August 9, 1778. Mayer MSS.
3 The nucleus of this was a col

CHAP. IX. 7 BENTLEY'S LETTER. 439 happily. Just prior to this he was ill, and suffering mentally from the basest ingratitude of a person he had generously aided; and in one of his letters to Wedgwood he thus gives expression to what he feels on this account, as also to his deep affection for his friend. It is the more interesting, as scarcely a letter of Bentley's is preserved. My head is better or worse, as I think more properly or weakly about the ill usage I have met with.... A full discussion, or one good conversation upon it with my dear Friend would probably do me more good than any other application, for I have not any Friend here by whose side I have been accustomed to engage & conquer, & who has the same Energy that you constantly possess when there is occasion for it, either to promote the public good, assist your Friends, or support your own rights. I fancy I can do anything with your help; & I have been so much used to it, that when you are not with me on these occasions, I seem to have lost my right arm.... If we should come, we hope you & good Mrs. Wedgwood will return with us & favour us with your Company, as long as you can find in your Hearts to stay at Turnham Green.1

With age Wedgwood's scientific tastes became more absolute. At his desire, Warltire, a well known chemist, resident in Birmingham, and the friend and correspondent of both Watt and Priestley, came to Newcastle to give a course of lectures on the principles of chemistry. These were regularly attended by young John Wedgwood, who was sent for in February from school to attend them, and by young Robert Darwin. Warltire also gave them private instruction at Etruria, and Wedgwood increased their interest in the subject by making experiments with them. Whilst thus occupied, it occurred to him to render the chemical afinities, composition, decomposition, and recomposition, &c., visible, by assigning to each change

' Bentley to Vedgwood, dated from Turnham Green, December 18, 1778., 440 WARLTIRES LECTURES. CRAP. IX.

a definite colour; and where bodies were composed of two or more parts, such should be expressed by a like number of colours. Darwin and W'arltire gave their sanction to this idea, which in a later day was more effectively carried out by Dalton in relation to his atomic theory; symbols being substituted for colours. Darwin was a believer in this theory, and seems to have preceded Dalton in his estimate of it as a principle in nature.

Warltire was an admirable lecturer, and a good chemist. His experiments on the combustion of gases, ayear or two after this date, was one of the steps which led to the discovery of the composition of water by Watt, whose claim to this is undoubted. During these lec-

tures Bentley supplied Warltire with data relative to Priestley's most recent discoveries, as from the time the latter had become Lord Shelburne's librarian, they often corresponded; and when Priestley was in town Bentley frequently visited him at Lansdowne House. One of Warltire's Newcastle lectures was upon light and colour; and during it he introduced a solar microscope to show opaque objects, and of this Wedgwood made most interesting use. It occurred to him to show some of his finest cameos by its aid, and the result, for exquisite detail, finish and perfection as a whole, was beyond all expectation, and led Priestley, when the experiment was reported to him, to order a set of cameos for Lord Shelburne's microscope. Warltire's audience were so pleased with this lecture, that they requested one or more in addition, during which were examined crystallizations, animalcules, the circulation of the blood, the solution and precipitation of nitrates, and other like natural phenomena.

These lectures ended in March; in April Wedgwood paid a visit to London and Turnham Green; and in May

CRAP. IX. THE FAMILY PICTURE. 441 we hear of Stubbs and the family piece he was to paint. Its idea was thus originally sketched out by VVedgwood, though when Stubbs set actually to work, a year or so after, the engraving shows that one picture took the place of two, that details were altered, and that as accessories horses were substituted for chemical apparatus. ' There would have been much less formality in Wedgwood's grouping than in motionless equestrians set in a row, merely because Stubbs was a painter of horses. But as a family piece the engraving, which is a reduced but admirable copy of the original picture, is of exceeding interest as it places us face to face with a great man, and those whom in his tender love he sought to make good and intelligent men and women. '

The two family pieces I have hinted at (he tells Bentley) I mean to contain the children only, & grouped perhaps in some such manner as this—-Sukey

playing upon her harpsichord with Kitty singing to her as she often does, & Sally & Mary Ann upon the carpet in some employment suitable to their ages. This to be one picture. The pendant to be Jack standing at a. table making fixable air with the glass apparatus &c., & his two brothers accompanying him, Tom jumping up & clapping his hands in joy, & surprised at seeing the stream of bubbles rise up just as Jack has put in a little chalk to the acid. J os with the chemical dictionary before him in a thoughtful mood; which actions will be exactly descriptive of their respective characters.

' Stubbs' account with Vedgwood,. also 'on horseback. The latter, an in his own handwriting. 1 extremely valuable icture, is in the £ s. d. ossession of I) C. l arjorihanks,Esq.,

My first thought was to put these two pictures into Mr. Wright's hands; but other ideas took place & remembering the Labourers & Cart in the Exhibition, with paying for tablets &c., I ultimately determined in favour of Mr. Stubbs, & have mentioned a fire piece to Mr. Wright in a. letter I wrote him the last week to tell him I should be glad to see him here in a fortnight or 3 weeks. But what shall I do about having Mr. S. & Mr. VV. here at the same time--will they draw together kindly think you? '

Wedgwoodin the previous year had bespoken a picture of Wright of Derby, who, neglected by his countrymen, ' would,' as Wedgwood said, 'starve as a painter if the Empress of Russia had not some taste & sense to buy these pictures now, which we may wish the next century to purchase again at treble the price she now pays for them." Soon after this VVright tried enamel-painting, and towards the close of 1779 he promised to visit Etruria and ' catch any help from its fires; ' but it is not till subsequently that we hear of the fine picture he painted for Wedgwood.

During the summer of 1779,we have another charming sketch of Wedgwood amongst his children.

We have all our little folks about us now (he tells Bentley), & I am travelling through England with Mr. Byerley & take the young men along with me.

VVe examine what orders are taken & business done as we go along, which makes the route edifying to us all. I shall lead them through my cabinet of fossils as time & opportunities will permit, & mean to class them as we proceed.a

Three months later young Jos. Wedgwood was taken ill at school at Bolton, and his parents hastened thither. Travelling was dangerous just then, for the roads of

CRAP. IX. DIFFICULTIES IN EDUCATION. 443

Lancashire and Cheshire swarmed with mobs of machine breakers. These principally consisted of workmen who had been turned of from a want of demand for English woven goods in the foreign markets; whilst the nonimportation agreements the Irish had adopted had also had a disastrous effect on trade. Wedgwood describes these scenes most graphically. The two youngest boys returned home with their parents, for both were ill.

The truth is (he writes to Bentley) that they have more business, confinement & phlogisticated air than their machinery can dispense with, & how to remedy this evil & give them such an education as the fashion of the times requires, I am utterly at a loss to determine. I am convinced that if they are confin'd again to school air, & rigid confinement with school discipline, their health & bodily strength must be diminish'd very considerably, if not totally lost. What I now advance is upon some years' observation of their constitutions, 8: not a hasty conclusion from their present indisposition. I believe early confinement & severe application are too unnatural not to have bad consequences in a greater or less degree upon most constitutions, but my boys, I am very certain, cannot suffer it without great injury, & I am really distress'd to find out a sort of compromise between the body & the mind that shall do the least injury to either, in this business of education. You are an adapt in this service, & if you will have the goodness some time, at your leisure, to communicate a. few hints to me I shall be thankful for them.'

Whatever it was that Bentley advised, Wedgwood in some measure hit upon the true remedy, though but tested for a brief season. He resolved to have masters and educate his boys at home. But he did not see the physical and philosophical truth to the full. He did not see that men of genius very rarely reproduce their own intellect; or that minds' and bodies sprung from those 1 Wedgwood to Bentley, October 9, 1779.

444 WEDG WOOD AT FAULT. CHAD. IX. exhausted by the labours which declare genius, show few signs of inheritance. If the characteristics of mental vigour and originality do reappear, it is in an entirely new direction, as has been markedly the case in his own descendants. Here and there are instances to the contrary, for physical laws are strengthened and confirmed by occasional aberrations-a Hallam or a Herschel for instance. But then we must recollect that Hallam wrote amidst the philosophical ease of comparative afliuence; and Herschel studied science amidst the amenities which science begets.

In Wedgwood the ability of generations had culminated in genius; but this he had only made visible by a persistent drudgery that wore body and mind to the full. It was perhaps therefore a mistake to suppose his boys would have the same scientific tastes as himself, or the same business capabilities. He had won, and was then winning, great wealth for them; and he was surrounding them with all the appliances of aristocratic life. He should have trained them for this life; for aristocrats they really became when the pressure of his example had passed away. They could have had the usufruct in perpetuity of his great trade; but its labours might have been deputed to men willing to accept them and do by them as he had done. He had one really clever pupil in Adams. Bentley told him he spoilt his boys. But his mistake in this respect will be again and again made, till men, regarding their work for its own sake, will depute their vocations to the most able; as they shall also in that greater day of a higher and more philosophic conception of art, not

collect its riches for the use of themselves and the few, but gather them into public collections for the use and advantage of the universal eye. This non-inheritance of great talents, except differently and remotely, is not to be deplored; or else the evils We so often see in inherited rank would be alike perpetuated in the inheritance of genius.

Other matters, besides this of education occupied Wedgwood.

I have begun (he tells Bentley) upon a great undertaking. The arrangement of my fossils & making a Catalogue of them. As a potter I make clays my first article, after which stones vitmzfiable will follow, but I cannot draw the line betwixt clays & some of the stones. In steatites for instance I have specimens of every degree of induration from the hardness of soap to the most compact polished jasper, & they illustrate the fact of jaspers being indurated steatites so evenly and fully that I cannot find in my heart to keep them asunder.'

But these calm and philosophic speculations were disturbed by the discovery that his farming men had been robbing him to a serious extent, and by the illness of his little child Mary Ann. She suffered from convulsions produced by teething; and at periods she lost the use of her limbs and her sight. His distress was extreme when he found her blind. He joined with his wife in nursing her; chafed her limbs, lanced her gums, held her in the bath, and, instructed by Darwin, electrified her. The usual nostrums for this disease of childhood were burnt blood, a baked raven, with along etcetera. But Darwin laughed them all to scorn; he applied to science, and gave relief if he could not cure. The child recovered the use of her limbs and her sight, but died whilst yet in infancy.

What Wedgwood called his ' Etruscan school' was begun in November.

My boys (he tells Bentley) are quite stout & well & we have formed a pretty regular school, which I have at present some notion of improving & continuing instead of sending them 1 Vedgwo0d to Bentley, i'0;ei1be1' I. 1779.

446 DISCUSSIONS ON EDUCATION. CRAP. IX. from home again, un-

less by way of finish for some particular parts of their education. Before breakfast we read English together in the newspaper, or any book we happen to have in the course of reading. Ve are now reading Ferber's Travels with the globes & maps before us. After breakfast they go & write an hour with Mr. Swift & with this small portion of time & writing their French exercises, & entering some experiments which they make along with me, all which I insist upon being written in a. plain legible hand, they have improved more in writing these few weeks than they did in the last twelve months at Bolton-After writing if the weather permits, they ride or drive their hoop, or jump a cord, or use any exercise they please for an hour & the remainder of the day is filled up with the French lessons 8:. Mr. Swift attends them here an hour in the evening for accounts in which their sister joins with them; and we have agreed to add four Latin lessons a week to the above business for which Mr. Byerley & Mr. Lomas' have kindly ofi'ered their assistance. This last is only introduced to prevent their losing what they have already learnt, till I have decided upon this part of their learning.2

Darwin and Wedgwood had various discussions on this question of the utility of Latin to boys not intended for the learned professions. Wedgwood thought time was wasted in acquiring a dead language; Darwin, true to his doctrine of utility, considered that French would be more useful to boys engaged in trade; neither perceiving, as it seems, the true point, that the advantage gained by a classical or University education is that it gives a man a high standard to measure by, and prevents him from being too easily satisfied with his own efforts. Darwin won Wedgwood over, probably, to his opinion, for, in the middle of December 1779, we find the two eldest boys from Etruria had been a month at Lichfield, and were learning French with the Doctor's youngest son Robert. Their

' The Unitarian minister at Newcastle.
' Vedgw00d to Bentley, November 23,

177-.

CHAP. IX. LESSONS IN FRENCH. 447 instructor was a young Frenchman named Potet, who was surgeon on board a merchantman when it was taken by ' an English privateer. He taught his language, as also drawing, well; his character and antecedents were found to be good, and after a satisfactory interview, it was settled by Wedgwood that he should become tutor at Etruria for a year _his pupils to include some of Mr. Thomas Wedgwood's children. With these arrangements the year closed. How long they lasted is unknown. The eldest son John went back to the Rev. Mr. Holland of Bolton, for a time. In 1782 he became a resident pupil of Dr. Enfield's at Warrington Academy; and in the February of the same year Josiah Wedgwood the younger was at school in Edinburgh.

Dr. Darwin lost his first wife in 1770. He remarried in 1781 1 and removed to Derby. In this interval his house was kept by his sister, Miss Darwin, between whom and the Wedgwoods existed the most friendly relations. The children of both families were, as we have seen, much together; and to the chiefs, science was always lending some point of interest. In 1778 the Doctor's windmill project was again resuscitated. Watt, whose visit had been more than once deferred by a fit of hypochondriacisin, came over to Lichfield to see it. He gave his opinion, which Darwin and Wedgwood by turns criticiscd; and after some new suggestions of the Doctor's, Edgeworth made a model. From this the mill was built at Etruria, and it continued working till the introduction of one of Boulton and Watt's Sun-and-Planet-engines in 1792.

In their many visits to Lichfield, sometimes when
' Miss Seward gives this date, but it was earlier, as Mrs. Darwin is referred to in letters of 1779.—Dnrwin Correspondence.
448 DR. JOHNSON. Can. IX. merely passing through, staying at the chief inn and inviting Dr. Darwin to their table, it is unknown if Wedgwood and his wife ever saw Dr. Johnson. They were not

likely to meet him at the houses of their friends, for Johnson in his rude dogmatic way despised the literary coterie of which the Sewards were the head. Still his fame was great, and, at a later date, Wedgwood added his name to those of other illustrious men. In 1784 Flaxman modelled his portrait in wax, and the cameo medallion made therefrom, as we give it here, (fig. 83), is one of the finest ever perfected by VVedgwood. '

CRAP. IX. ADMIRAL KEPPEL. 449

Two other medallion portraits of great interest were produced about the 'same date. ' We sent a box by the coach last night containing,' writes Wedgwood, '.... a head of one Mr. Bentley al antique, & another which you are to find out, if your memory or Hackwood's skill -is not deficient.'1 Another portrait, both as a bust and medallion, which was very popular at this date, was that of Admiral Keppel. His merits were over-rated, and public enthusiasm arose more from a general feeling of opposition to the measures of the government against him, than directly from an admiration of Keppcl, either as a seaman or a public character. ButMr. Byerley sold thousands of

VOL. II. G G 450 PRINCE 'ILLIAM HENRY. CRAP. IX.

his portrait during his journeys in 1779, in the form of a cameo medallion, as here given, and also in seals and busts. During his autumnal journey through the southern counties, including the seaports, he saw much of naval life. The fleet was at Spithead, and dining on board the Terrible man of war, with his friend the chaplain, the conduct of Sir Charles Hardy, in declining to offer battle to the combined fleet, was warmly canvassed.

I can't say (he adds further in his letter to Brock, then manager in Greek Street) Sir Charles Hardy is a favourite in the Fleet, but I don't hear one person impeach his late cOnduct—For my part I think the madman that would have fought under ' such circumstances ought to be executed as a monster-3' of cruelty. The bravery of Englishmen can do much— but not impossibilities.

... When an engagement was expected the young Prince was, much against his will, as 'tis said—put on board a small vessel provided for the purpose, and ordered him a view of the action and to be out of danger—They say he enters with great facility into the manners of the sailors and is as great a Blackguard as the best of them.'

This letter, as the rest, was sent down to Etruria, and its anecdote of the young prince probably led to his me

'Byerley to Brock, dated from The prince here alluded to was Gosport and Chicliester, September afterwards 'illiam IV. Miss Burl3, 1779. Mayer MRS. ne_v's sketch of him is very similar.

Onsr. IX. " nu. PRIESTLEY. 451 dallion being made, which in a cheap form, in the black body, became soon after almost as popular in the seaports as that of Keppel.

In one form or another, and in various bodies, Priestley's likeness was being incessantly reproduced. In the houses of Dissenters it was a conspicuous ornament; and after he had given to the world his discovery of oxygen, the resemblance of this great man, either as a full size medallion or as a bust, was largely bought by continental savans. A life-size bust was modelled in May 1779 to match with those of Franklin and Newton. Till Priestley's removal to Birmingham in 1780, his visits to Etruria were very rare, although he and Wedgwood frequently corresponded on scientific points. The latter supplied Priestley, gratis, with every kind of philosophical apparatus which could be made in earthenware; and of these a catalogue was issued in 1772 to inform the scientific world of the size, forms, purposes, and prices of such articles as might be useful to them in the course of their experiments. Priestley's appointment with Lord Shelburne was a source of congratulation to his friend, though with a proviso. 'I am glad,' writes Wedgwood to Bentley, ' to hear of Dr. Priestley's noble appointment, taking it for granted, that he is to go on writing and publishing with the same freedom he now does, otherwise I had much

rather he still remained in Yorkshire.' 1 Priestley's discoveries and scientific writings during his residence with Lord Shelburne were amongst his greatest; whilst there can be no question that either his political or religious opinions were the cause of their ultimate separation. Another of Wedgwood's correspondents in 1773-5 was

' 'edgwood to Bentley, October 4,1772.

452 DR. PERCIVAL. CRAP. IX.

Dr. Percival of Manchester. The Doctor issued a pamphlet upon poisoning by lead, and asserted that this mineral was employed in all the glazes used on earthenware; that salts, as well as certain acids, acted as solvents, and exposed the users of this class of pottery to the slow effects of lead poisoning. Wedgrvood had to combat this opinion with Percival; but all the latter would concede was, that Wedgwood's cream ware glaze was the best of its kind, though the tests be had used were not sufficient solvents. But Percival's pamphlet lived its day and no more, and did ultimately no harm to the sale of this fine body.

During his early experiments for a fine porcellaneous body, and which ended at length in the perfection of that known as jasper, Wedgwood was greatly assisted by a gentleman of the name of John Bradley Blake, one of the English East India Company's resident supercargoes at Canton,who procured him true specimens of the kaolin and petunse used by the Chinese ceramists. Of these Wedgwvood made some exquisite trials of porcelain; and Mr. Blake was proceeding much further in researches for his friend, when he-died suddenly from the effects of climate at Canton, in November 1773.1 A portrait of him was brought to England, and from this Hackwood modelled a medallion likeness in 1776.

Another portrait of still greater interest in relation to English pottery, and its improvement at an early date, was introduced to Wedgwood's notice in October 1776, by its possessor Paul Elers, the father of Richard Lovell Edgeworth's first wife. Wedgwood seems to have known nothing further of this gen-

tleman, either personally or by

CRAP. IX. PAUL ELERS. 453 report, other than that he was the son of one of the brothers Elers, who came into Stafibrdshire at the close of the seventeenth century. He therefore gracefully accepted Mr. Elers's courtesy by a letter in which he offered to have it copied, and a model taken from it in clay.1 A correspondence thus opened, an enquiry followed as to the then annual amount of earthenware produced in the Potteries; and, in addition, Wedgwood was recommended to make medallion likenesses of distinguished men. In those days of high tariffs and readily-imposed taxes, an answer to such a question required great circumspection; and Wedgwood consulted Sparrow, stating his scruples, and enquiring if they had given out any amount of that kind, in their printed papers, when soliciting Navigation and Turnpike Roads. Sparrow advised something more than caution, and gave Wedgwood no very flattering account of his correspondent.' Unwilling as it seems to accept all that Sparrow said on this latter point, Wedgwood sent a polite but guarded answer;8 and in respect to the recommendation to do what he had already done in a manner so eminent, he, with great dignity, enclosed a catalogue and some fine specimens of medallion portraits. In the January of the year succeeding, 1777, we hear more of the portrait.

I hope (Wedgwood tells Bentley) you have read Mr. Elers's fine letter, & and are preparing to send down the Heads of all the Illustrious men in all the Courts & Countries of Europe to be immortalised in our artificial jasper. There is one however we must send for & copy, or ofi'end this good Gentleman. I

' Draft of a letter from Vedg-the annual amount of the whole wood to Paul Elers, October 17,1776. manufacture of earthenware, in the " Vedg'wood to Bentley, Novem-Potteries in about 1725, was under ber 23, 1776. £15,000. The increase at the eriod 3 In this re ly, of which there is a he wrote was fourfold or fivefo d.

rough draft, 'edgw0od states that l 4-34 HIS FATHER'S PORTRAIT. CRAP.

IX. mean his Fathers from his sons in Ormond St., where it is waiting for that purpose. I shall be glad to have it copied by Mr. Day or Rh. Unwin—which you think proper, & from that copy Haekwood shall model it——s0metin1e.'

Other 'fine letters' followed, 'of which,' said Wedgwvood, ' I am sick and surfeited.' Upon the appearance of the cameo medallion in the summer of the same year, Wedgwood writes again:—

My last letter from Mr. Elers is without a date, but it is about ten days since I receiv'd it-. He returns thanks for the Heads, & asks if he could properly be indulged with about half a doz" of these Portraits, for his friends are pretty numerous. How (fnar. IX. ELERS' IMPROVEMENTS. 455 far must we indulge this good Gentleman in his wants & wishes?... He further acquaints me, that he has in order that these representations of his father may be more cheaply extended & diffused, desired Mr. Bentley to send one of the heads to an engraver, to have an engravement for a print to be made, & directed this inscription to be on the copper. 'Johannes Philipus Elers, Plastices Britannicze Inventor.' This inscription, if I understand it, conveys a falsehood & can therefore do no honour to the memory of his father who was not the inventor but the improver of the art of Pottery in Britain, if there be any dif ference between ivwenting & 2'mpr0t'ing an art.' time immemorial; & the reason for Mr. Elers fixing upon Staflbrdshire to try his experiments seems to be that the Pottery was carried on there in a much larger way, 8: in a more improved state than in any other part of Great Britain.—The improvements Mr. Elers made in our manufactory were precisely these.Glazing our common clays with salt which roduc'd Pot d'Grey or stoneware, this after they (the two Elers's) had left the countrv was improv'd into Vhite Stone _IVare by using the white Pipe Cla instead of the common clay of this.'eighbourhood, & mixing with it Flint Stones calcin'd & reduced by pounding into a fine ovder.—I'he use of Flint in our ottery is said to have proceeded from an

accident happenning to one of our Potters, a Mr.

Heath of Shelton, on his way to. London. His Horse's eves becoming l bad, he app road, who told him he would cure the Horse, & shew him what means he used. Accordingly he took a piece of black Flint Stone & put it into the fire, which to our Potters eat astonishment came out of the fire a. most beautifull white, 8: at the same time struck him with an idea that this fine material might im rove the stone ware lately intr uc'd lied to an Iiorsler on the ' amongst them. He brought some of the stones home with him, mix'd first W7u'te int Stone 7Vare.—I make no doubt but glazing with salt, by casting it amongst the were whilst it is red hot, came to us from Germany, but whether Mr. E. was the erson to whom we are indebted for t is improvement I do not know. It might have been in use at Bristol, or about London, from whence Mr. E. might bring it to us; but of this fact our old Painter may perha. s obtain some intelligence amongst t e Potters near London, & I wish you would ask him to learn how long Glazing with salt has been in use there, or at Bristol, & if they have any tradition of its introduction amongst themThe next improvement int!-oduc'd by Mr. E. was the refining our common red clay by m'fting, & making it into Tea & Coffee were in imitation of the Chinese Red Porcelain, by casting it in plaister moulds, & turning it on the outside upon Lathes, & ornamenting it with the tea branch in relief, in imitation of the Chinese manner of ornamenting this ware-For these improvements & very great ones they were for the time, we are indebted to the very ingenious Mess" Elers's, 8:. I shall gladly contribute all in my power to honor their memories, & transmit to posterity the knowledge of the obligations we owe them, but the sum total certainly does not amount To inventing the Art of Pof(er_r/ in 3rr'lar'n. And I think 456 RICHARD LOVELL EDGEVVORTH. CHAP. IX;

During a visit to Etruria by Edgeworth and his second wife, Wedgwfood was amused by many further particulars

of Mr. Elers and his family, and of which the former made no secret, as they are given in much the same way in his autobiography. 1 Yet the correspondence dragged on wearily?

I have just wrote to Hr. Elers in the way you advis'd me (says Wedgwood to Bentley) & I wish it may have a proper effect, at all events I am determin'd either to drop, or very much abridge our correspondence for I have no time to spare, I may say throw away upon such employments, besides he favours me with so many hints and instructions, that I shall be as much indebted to him soon, as the country in general is to his father. I ask the good gentleman's pardon for he may mean very well, but when he advises to ' apply our composition 3 to the making Reservoirs in fortifications, the whole of one solid mass, for the preservation of records, magazines &c. so as to be Bomb-proof ' & when one is oblig'd to reply to such extravagancies it is teizing it would be injuring their memories taken notice of by Lady Barrington to assert so much, for which I ma note the old adage—Grasp at, lose all. But how these things may be said to Mr. Elers, our present correspondent, without offending him is the dificulty, especially as he evidently & professedly means to make some bmu;/icial use of his fathers merit in this respect—I must write to him, but as he only tells me——I1e has given directions to have the plate e1_1g1-av'd &c. without asking my opi_-.

nion concerninw the inscription, it would perhaps be impertinent in me to interfere, or give my opinion u n the subject my intention there ore at present is to say nothing u on that subject (the inscriptiog) ess _my opinion is asked.' edgwood to Bentley, July 19, I77 7. 1 Memoirs of Richard Lovell Edgeworth, vol. i. p. 108 at supra. 2From the particulars given by Edgeworth to Ved ood we learn that John Philip 'lets ' had been in distress'd circumstances 8: was

' a. whimsical good sort of Lady, 8: by ' her set up in a Glass & China shop in Dublin &: were ver successfull in business—which ena led them to send their son Paul to the Temple in London, where he made a great proficiency in his studies, 8: became a first rate counsel.' After a long narration, in substance the same as that wen by Edgeworth in his Memoirs, edgwood adds:—' But not:wit.hstanding this great error of his life, & all he has done to serve great men, Mr. Edgeworth adds he has so much real learning, such gentleness of nature & true politeness, that he would if he possibly could, think him a realy good man.' Vedgwood to Bentley. VVithout date. Previous to his residence in Dublin John Philli Elers was for some time with piermont at Chelsea. So it is handed down.

-" The ingredients of thejasper body were expensive.

CHAP. IX. ELERS' EXTRAVAGANT PROPOSITIONS. 457 at least, and which one would wish to be excus'd from if it might be.'

What correspondence followed upon this we know not; but, at a later date, a fresh extravaganza is heard of.

I have a fine letter (Wedgwood tells Bentley) to answer by this post from my good old friend Paul Elers Esq, who has cut out a trifling job for me, which when I engage in will lift me far above all Intaglios, cameos, and such trifling trinkets... But I will not detain you upon the rack of expectation any longer. The business then, is no less than making earthen water pipes for London first, and then for all the world. I have a mind to furnish London and Vestminster first on my own account by way of experiment,& then, if you will accept of a partnership for supplying the rest of the world, I now make the offer & will finish the bargain over our next pipe?

It is very evident from this, from whence arose the assertion stated gravely in modern times, that John Philip Elers taught the Wedgwoods the art of mixing clay if not of pottery. Mr.Wedgwood, who lived a century nearer to the Elers epoch than ourselves, gives, as we have seen in his own valuable words, the precise amount of improvement carried out by the brothers Elers. It was much for the time, and as such is acknowledged; but beyond this it did not go is very clear. A man who wearied

out others with useless letters, and who Wasted his time in making impossible and often impertinent suggestions to men of acknowledged capacity, even whilst neglecting his own affairs to a ruinous extent, was precisely the one to draw upon his imagination for the efficiency and importance of his ancestors. The Wedgwoods were the most accomplished potters of 'their time, even at the close of 458 TRENT AND MERSEY NAVIGATION. CRAP. IX.

the seventeenth century, and to them, as to other able men who were their contemporaries, is really due that succession of improvements which slowly ushered in the great artistic and commercial changes wrought by the genius and skill of Josiah Wedgwood. Englishmen owe something to foreigners, and they have been ever ready to acknowledge it; but the Staflbrdshire potters, like others of their race, owe more to mother-wit and steady industry.

In May 1777, Wedgwood had had the delight of witnessing the completion of the Grand Trunk Navigation. Prior to this, and after, various schemes were afloat for intersecting Staflordshire, as well as the adjacent counties, with a network of branches of more or less importance. In the progress of many of these he took an active interest, and even in 1785 we find him still full of business for the Trent and Mersey Navigation. His duties as treasurer of this, and as patron of others, brought him into incessant intercourse with various classes. By the trading part of the community he was greatly regarded as having been one of the direct agents through whicn inland transport was reduced one fourth in cost; and by a higher class, not only for his great artistic merits but as one who, through keen insight and indomitable energy, had increased the value of their estates by several years' purchase. How he was honoured by the aristocracy we have already had some glimpses: another we must give. After visiting Sir Roger Newdigate at his seat in Warwickshire, he tells Bentley:—

I dined with Ld Denbeigh yesterday.. . He was extremely civil to me. He sent a. servant to waylay me on the road to

Newnham, & bring me through his fine rides. Show'd me the whole house himself & and intended the same civility to me in the pleasure grounds & gardens, but we unfortunately missed each other in our walks. The House his Lordship told

CRAP. IX. DEATH OF BENTLEY. 459 me is Mr. Brown's first essay as an architect. It is a. very convenient house in the distribution of the rooms, & one, the Grand Drawing room, is very magnificent. It is full of family pieces by Vandyke, & the chimney-piece elegantly finish'd with a fine set of vases by Wedgwood & Bentley.I

But the days so long brightened by the aid, faith, and affection of a friend as dear to Wedgwood as Bentley was, had drawn to a close. No letters or papers of the year 1780 remain to tell us when they last met, or any of the circumstances of Bentley's death.' His health had been for a long time waning; but we may infer that the end came suddenly at last, for if otherwise Wedgwood would have been by his dying bed. He may have died from pleurisy, as the season was cold, from gout or from apoplexy, as he had evidently suffered from determination of blood to the head. All we know is, that he died on Sunday, November 26, 1780, and on Thursday, November 29, we find, from one of Dr. Darwin's letters, that Wedgwood was already on his way to Turnham Green. What must have been the household grief at Etruria when the dread news came; What must have been Wedgwood's feelings on that wintery road! Darwin advises him to read the letter of Sulpicius to Cicero on the death of his daughter, but more immortal truths lent their consolation. Bentley was buried on Saturday, December 2, in a vault within the church at Chiswick.a

The loss to Wedgwood must have been for a time overwhelming, particularly if it came Without forewarning.

' Vedgwood to Bentley, June 20, this:—' Thos. Bentley aged 49 years. 1776. In a. new family vault 6ft by 7ft 2 By a singular coincidence the in the clear, the mouth of which is Vedgwood & Mayer collections are close to the west door of the new Isle.' alike destitute of any record of The entry in the Burial Register is Bentley's death. as follows:—1780. Dec. 2 Buried 3 The entry in the parish books is Thomas Bentley in the Church.

460 ITS EFFECT ON WEDGWOOD. CHAP. IX.

He had probably never had a grief so great, if we except that connected with the death of the brother who was drowned. That it affected him in some senses physically, it again in 1781 its vigour is gone; and his portrait, taken the year following by Sir Joshua Reynolds, is that of a man much older than his real age of 52. There is an expression in the face, the eyes especially, that speaks of suffering mastered but not obliterated. There are griefs no time can cure.

Wedgwood raised a tablet to his memory in Chiswiek church, with which their mutual friend Athenian Stuart, aided by Scheemakers, took unwonted pains. There it remains as fresh and as bright as on the day of its erection, in memory of a good man, whose fame it is that he was the dearest friend of Josiah Wedgwood, and a partner in many of his greatest works. There his dust lies in as fair a spot by the Thames as that in which it was endowed with life by the Dove. Just two years before his death Wedgwood had written to him from Tutbury in Staflbrdshire: ' I have been enjoying a view on Castle Hill, where I had doubtless the place of your nativity before my eyes, though I wanted a guide to point out the rural spot to me, and say, there your Bentley first saw the light.'

CHAPTER X.

PHILOSOPHY AND ART.

HE death of Bentley led to changes of various kinds. In the spring succeeding it Wedgwood secured the able services of Alexander Chisholmas his secretary and chemical assistant; and the summer after, July 2, 17_82, Henry Webber, a modeller of uncommon ability, recommended to him by Sir Wm. Chambers and Sir Joshua Reynolds, became the head of the ornamental department at Etruria at a salary of 252i. per annum, a

sum afterwards increased.1 Wedgwood was thus freed from many anxieties, and much personal drudgery. In the one case his correspondence was carried on with a business-like accuracy hitherto unknown at Etruria, in many chemical matters he' had but to direct, and the analysis or experiment was laid perfected before him; in the other the ornamental department and its countless details were kept in working and progressive order, without the necessity of that incessant personal supervision, which for many years had been the most irksome that art, and one of them, who was Wm. Hamilton, June 24, 1786.

VOL. II. II II 466 ALEXANDER CHISHOLM. Cm. X.

portion of his labours. In Chisholm, as might be expected, he found a faithful friend and servant; and his good fortune may be considered great, in thus securing at such a time his valuable services. Chisholm had filled a like post for thirty years with Dr. Lewis of Kingstonupon-Thames, the author of the ' Commercium Philosophico-Technicum,' and other able scientific works; and at the time he thus settled down for the rest of his life at Etruria he was more than fifty years old. His education was good; his taste for science only less than that of Wedgwood's. He wrote with the ease and precision of a scholar; and he was practical, even amidst the abstractions of science. Hitherto, it is probable, that Wedgwood's experiments had been made, so far as possible, in the.quietude of his study, orin the little crypts underground which led therefrom; but henceforth the laboratory at the Works became, as Chisholm's head-quarters, a place of the greatest scientific interest. Here amidst fossils, earths, alkalies, acids, colours, chemical ingredients, and chemical vessels of every description, amidst trials and mixtures, amidst books, papers, and the correspondence of the chief savans of the time, the master and his faithful servant pursued their labours. The serenities of science were tasteful and akin to both; and at no period of his life was Wedgwood more congenially employed. Here, if anywhere, he forgot his silent sorrow for his part-

ner and friend—and in thus following out the more abstract portions of his art—he knew full well, he ministered, if indirectly, to ultimate perfection and ideal truth.

At no late date the fruit of these experiments and labours was shown. In May 1782, Wedgwood communicated to the Royal Society, his paper on the ' Pyro meter or heat-measuring instrument; 1 two years later an additional paper was read on the ' Attempt to Compare and Combine with it the Common Mercurial Thermometer;' 2 and in 1786, a third paper was contributed on ' Observations ' 3 connected with the same subject; the experiments thus extending through a period of six years. The subject of course was one which in practice had been before Wedgwood his whole life..His many improvements and discoveries both in relation to bodies, glazes, and colours, had greatly depended on the application of specific degrees of heat, and therefore, these papers were rather the philosophical embodiment of a long sequence of it priori results, than discoveries in themselves essentially new; although the experiments made thus specially to a given end, and not during the hurry of everyday practice, led to certain observations of a highly scientific kind, as that of the relation of form to resistance to heat.

His cousins, Thomas and John Wedgwood of the Big House had, as we have seen, been amongst the first to observe the changes in colour made by progressive degrees of heat; by these signs they regulated their own firings; and for a period Josiah Wedgwood guided himself by similar indications. But he found them too uncertain to serve any general purpose, and that their use was confined to a particular structure of furnace and mode of_ firing. It then occurred to him that the diminution of bulk by fire of argillaceous bodies was a more certain and extensive measure of heat, as he found that this diminution proceeded regularly as the heat increased; the difiiculties principally consisting in the 1 Philoso hical Transactions, vol. lxxii. _305. _

" Ibid. vo. lxxiv. p. 358. ' bid. VOL

1XX'1-P-390-
468 DESCRIPTION OF THE IN-STRUMENT. Cmr. X ever varying qualities of these bodies, and of procuring one specimen precisely like another. During the necessary experiments he made some interesting observations on the pottery of ancient and modern times; and he found that all antique ware had been subjected to far less degrees of heat than those found requisite in the present day.

The construction of his Pyrometer thus rests on the principle of a diminution of bulk by heat. It consists of small cylinders formed of prepared clay and earth of alum, placed between cylindrical rods, which are wider apart at one end than the other. On these rods degrees of heat are marked, and as the cylinders, which are put in at the Wider end shrink by the action of the fire, their progress along the graduated scale, marks the degrees of heat to which they are exposed, and consequently that of the furnace into which they are introduced. The pyrometer is still used at Etruria and extensively throughout the English and foreign potteries; though it is universally admitted by scientific men, as it was also by its inventor, that it is essentially an imperfect i11strument, and that one which shall mark the relative degrees of heat with a precision worthy of science, is a want, the void of which has yet to be filled. It is probable that by methods and agents, wholly new and as yet unsuspected, the laws of these necessary truths will be evolved.

As a result of these valuable labours, Wedgwood was elected aFell0w of the Royal Society in 1783; his election being simultaneous with that of Priestley. His next series of experiments related to an attempt to connect the pyromet-er with the common mercurial thermometer; this by continuing the scale of the latter indefinitely upwards

OIIAP. X. EXPERIMENTS AND THEIR RESULTS. 469 as a standard, and by reducing the divisions of the former to the same scale, the whole range of the degrees of heat might be brought into one uniform series. And this attempt was founded on the application of an intermediate measure which takes in both the heats that are measurable by the mercurial thermometer, and a sufficient number of those of the other to connect the two together.

The experiments necessary to this connection led him into an analysis of the expansion of metals, and to the theory of freezing. In this direction his curiosity was stimulated by some observations recorded by Lavoisier and La Place, and also by some curious results of his own experiments. He found that the seemingly opposite processes of congelation and liquefaction went on together under certain circumstances; and that water highly attenuated, as in the instance of vapour, would congeal with a less degree of heat, than water in the mass.

Whilst this was the train of speculation and experiment, Dr. Darwin was as usual in correspondence with his friend. He agreed with Wedgwood, in Dr. Black's opinion, that water after being boiled, will freeze sooner. ' I suppose ' he says ' by the expulsion of the air in the water, the particles are already got nearer together, which vicinity I suppose to be the proximate cause of freezing.' He considered that there was great analogy between the laws of the propagation of heat and electricity, and that atmospheres of heat of different densities like atmospheres of electricity, repel each other at certain distances, in a manner analogous to that of globules of quicksilver when pressed against each other; and that hence by applying a heated body near one end of a cold body, the more distant end might immediately become 470 DARWIN'S THEORY OF CONGELATION. CHAD. X. warmer than the end nearest to the heated body. Darwin difiered with Wedgwood in thinking that vapour freezes with a less degree of cold than water in the mass. He thought more cold was necessary to turn it into ice, and that the phenomena Wedgwood had observed depended on a circumstance which had not been attended to.

When water is cooled down to the freezing point (he says) its particles come so near together, as to be within the sphere of their reciprocal attractions, what then happens? they aceed with violence to each other & become a solid, at the same time pressing out from between them air which is seen to form bubbles in ice & renders the whole mass lighter than water by this air having regained its elasticity & pressing out any saline matters, & lastly by thus forceably acceding together, the particles of water press out also some more heat, as is seen by the thermoxneter immersed in such freezing water. This last circumstance demands your nice attention as it explains the curious fact you have observed. When the heat is so far taken away from water that the particles attract each other, they run together with violence & press out some remaining heat which existed in their interstices. Then the contrary must also take place when you add heat to ice so as to remove the particles into their reciprocal spheres of repulsion; they recede from each other violently, and thence attract more heat into their interstices.... Thus ice in freezing give; out heat suddenly— and in thawing gives out cold suddenly; but this last fact had not been observed (except in chemical mixtures) because when heat has been applied to thaw ice, it has been applied in too great quantities.' '

These and other most original points in connection with the theory of congelation, Darwin discussed with 1 Darwin to 'Wedgwood, March attributedto the waterfrom thawing 11, 13, 23, and April 1, 1784. One ice in the daytime, filling valleys in of Darwin's opinions bears upon the the remaining ice, & by its freezing lacial theory of the present day. there cracking the old ice by its ex e says, 'The detension or expulsion pansion at freezing, & not b its of parts of icy mountains I always expansion by an increase of col.'

CRAP. X. DISTURBED CONDITION OF THE POTTERIES. 471 his friend, and their relative experiments appear to have extended over a considerable period.

Wedgwood's final paper on the Pyrometer related to its improvement, by a greater care in the preparation of the clay, and by mixing it with earth of alum or pure alumini. During the course of these experiments he found that clay made the stitfest in pressing, shrunk the least in firing, and that the nearer the pieces came to a circular form, the less was the inequality of their contraction in the fire; and by making them entirely circular the imperfection appeared to be obviated altogether. He chose this last form for his pyrometrical pieces, leaving only one narrow flat side as a bottom for the pieces to rest on, and to distinguish the position in which they were to be measured in the gauge.

For several years Newcastle and the Potteries appear to have been in a disturbed condition. A lawless set of fellows took to the road as highwaymen and footpads, and during the spring of 1778 they committed many outrages. Life was for a time so much in danger, that the peaceable inhabitants had to travel in bands at night; and the people employed at Etruria dare not quit the works unarmed or singly. The magistrates and inhabi

‘ tants of the several districts took up the matter; and

Wedgwood and his neighbours for his. Men were sent in pursuit, some highwaymen were arrested, committed, and tried at Stafford.1 For a time better order prevailed. But disaifection and disorder were then the chronic state of the manufacturing districts, and the idle and dissolute were always wandering from place to place, and inciting those who, out of work, or as worthless as themselves, were ripe for revolt and riot.

‘ Wedgwood to Bentley, March 19 and 26, 1778.

472 RIOT AT ETRURLA. Cnar. X.

In this year, 1783, the condition of the country was lamentable. The long struggle with America had crippled and exhausted its financial resources; trade was stagnant, and a bad harvest completed this ruinous state of public and social affairs. The working classes of those days, untaught by the clergy or the schoolmaster, saw in revolt the only remedy for dear bread and want of employment; and even when better taught,

they were too often the mere tools of the designing. Thus where discontent prevailed, riot was almost always sure to follow. The Potteries were not exempt from these evils. Many of the manufacturers had turned off their men soon after the beginning of the American War, and thus the towns of the district, like those of Lancashire and Cheshire, were the centres of a feverish state of things; to appearance orderly, but in reality ripe and ready for mischief. The flame broke out at Etruria. A boat laden with provisions stayed at the wharf there, and the goods, as it was supposed, were for use in the Potteries. But as soon as it was found they were destined for the Manchester market, this simple fact was interpreted into a design of the owners to enhance the price and scarcity of provisions. I/Vord of this was conveyed to Shelton and Henley; and the result was the collection of avast mob which hastened to the scene of action. The boat meanwhile had gone on its way, but it was followed to Longport, seized, brought back to Etruria, and with another boat which had just come up to the locks, was rifled of its contents. These were sold at such prices as the mob pleased. An endeavour was made to give an air of justice to this daring act, by handing over the proceeds to the captains of the boats; but the real spirit of the rioters was shown in the attempt made to rifle and fire several houses and to do other mischief. For a time‘ the Works seemed threatened; but Mr. Wedgwood, who was fortunately at home, despatched messengers to Newcastle, and the result was the speedy arrival of a company of the Welsh Fusileers, and a detachment of the Staflbrdshire militia under the command of Major Sneyd. Two magistrates also hastened to the spot, the riot act was read, and the order given to charge—but the mob, as cowardly as it was ignorant, fled in all directions. 1 Two men were subsequently arrested who seem to have been rather the victims of others than the worst of the aggressors. Both were tried and convicted; and one named Stephen Barlow was executed. Great etforts-were made to save

his life, as he was not a native of the district, and of respectable family; but mercy was refused, for the government which had done so much towards bringing the country into the deplorable condition it then was, were alarmed at the disposition of the people to take redress into their own hands. There can be no doubt that this wise show of resistance at Etruria saved the adjacent towns from widespread ruin. The only damage done at Etruria was the burning the crateshop, as also some breakage or other injury to the house of a.person named Lounds. In both cases the damage was made good by the Committee of the Trent and Mersey N avigation.2 _

As soon as tranquillity was restored to the district, Mr. Wedgwood wrote and published a small pamphlet, in which he endeavoured to enlighten the generation rising

‘ Vard’s Stoke-upon-Trent, p. the Straw for Thatch of which no 445. charge is made, and sent into the 1 The Proprietors of the Naviga-office at Stone £1 5a. 911. A further tion from the Trent to ye Mersev, sum of £2 14s. was paid to Lounds 1783. To Josiah Vedgwood. To for damage to his premises.-Mayer Repairs of the Crate Shop at Etruria MSS. damaged by the Riot exclusive of 474 WEDGWOOD’S PAMPHLET. CHAP. X.

around him, as to the folly of looking to such outbreaks for a redress of social wrongs. It is entitled ‘ An Address to the young Inhabitants of the Pottery.’ In the simplest and clearest language, it answers the complaints common with the labouring classes of those days, and shows the true causes of the evils complained of-‘ As the Dearness of provisions; The great number of Dealers in those provisions,’ and ‘ That no relief is given to the Poor by their rich neighbours, unless the former rise to demand it.’ After disposing of these questions by answers that show a keen insight into the nature of social wrongs, as also of economical laws, he adds:

Let me now beg of you who are approaching to manhood, and who by your future behaviour must stamp the character of the potters of the rising generation; let me intreat you, as you value your own reputation and happiness, and the welfare of your country, never to harbour a thought of following the fatal example which has been set you by men who have so greatly mistaken their own and your real interests; but when you labour under any real grievances make your case known in apeaceable manner to some magistrate near you, or to your employers, who are best acquainted with your situation, and I have not a doubt of your meeting in this way with speedy and effectual redress, which it would be impossible for you to procure for yourselves by the measures you have lately seen pursued, or any illegal ones wha.tever.—'Before I take my leave I would request you to ask your parents for a description of the country we inhabit when they first knew it; and they will tell you, that the inhabitants bore all the signs of poverty to a much greater degree than they do now. Their houses were miserable huts; the lands poorly cultivated, and yielded little of value for the food of man or beast, and these disadvantages,'with roads almost impassable, might be said to have cut off our part of the country from the rest of the world, besides not rendering it very comfortable to ourselves. Compare this picture, which I know to be a true one, with the present state of the same country. The workmen earning nearly double their former wages—their

Cmr. X. EMIGRATION OF WORKMEN. 475 houses mostly new and comfortable, and the lands, roads, and every other circumstance bearing evident marks of the most pleasing and rapid improvements. From whence and from what cause has this happy change taken place? You will be beforehand with me in acknowledging a truth too evident to be denied by any one. Industry has been the parent of this happy change—A well directed and long continued series of industrious exertions, both in masters and servants, has so changed for the better the face of our country, its buildings, lands, roads, and notwithstanding the present unfavourable appearances, I must say the manner and deportment of its inhabitants too, as to attract the no-

tice and admiration of countries which had scarcely heard of us before; and how far these improvements may still be carried by the same laudable means which have brought us thus far, has been one of the most pleasing contemplations of my life. How mortifying then is it to have this fair prospect endangered by one rash act!... But I place my hopes, with some good degree of confidence, in the rising generation, being persuaded that they will, by their better conduct, make atonement for this unhappy, this unwise slip of their fathers.

A publication of a similar character marked this year of great literary industry. From time to time, through a considerable period, attempts had been made to lure workmen from the Potteries with a view to the establishment of earthenware manufactories in other countries. As early as 1766, a Mr. Bartlem, a Stafibrdshire potter, who had been unsuccessful in his own country, emigrated to South Carolina, and commencing his trade there, induced various workmen to follow him. Disaster and deathwere the results, as also in an attempt made to establish a china Work in Pennsylvania. Somewhat later, it was sought to turn this tide of emigration towards France. A man named Shaw-probably a son of the Ralph Shaw who had gone thither after a legal contest with his brother potters relative to a patent--tried by every means to induce 476 AN ADDRESS. CRAP. X.

workmen to leave their masters for service in various parts of France. Some went-only to find the promises which had lured them thither worse than a fallacy; for, discovering their wish to return, various pretences were made to detain them-and the majority died in prison or elsewhere, for they never saw their country again. The next attempt was on a plan more bold and organized. Finding the vast increase of the English trade in earthenware, several German and French masters combined to send spies into this country with a view to discover all the processes of manufacture, as also to bribe workmen to emigrate. The head quarters of these mas-

ters' agents was at Douay in Flanders, and thence under the soubriquet of 'Jones ' they carried on a correspondence with the spies engaged in this country. Some of their letters seem to have fallen into Wedgwood's hands. To neutralise the effects of these, as also the false statements made verbally, he wrote and published ' An Address to the Workmen in the Pottery on the Subject of Entering into the Service of Foreign Manufacturers.' After pointing out the fallacy of the bribes held out to them, and the miseries and misfortunes of those who had thus been tempted to leave their native country, he thus concludes:

You must by this time be fully convinced how delusive the offers held out to you are, and how contrary it would be to your own interest to accept of them. But supposing for a moment, that with regard to your own particular persons there was a real and lasting advantage, would it have no weight with you to think, that you were ruining a trade which had taken the united efforts of some thousands of people for more than an age to bring to the perfection it has now attained? a perfection no where else to be found—an object exciting at once the envy and emulation of all Europe l but they will both ever be harm CIIAP. X. ITS PATRIOTIC SPIRIT. 477 less to us whilst we are true to ourselves; for Englishmen, in arts and manufactures as well as in arms, can only be conquered by Englishmen: the enemy must first gain over some traitors and renegadoes from among ourselves, before they can obtain any decisive advantage. Is there a man among you then who will stand forth, and acknowledge himself to be that traitor to his country and fellow workmen? who will openly avow, that for the sake of a paltry addition to his own wages for a few years, he would betray their interests, and wantonly throw away into the hands of foreigners, perhaps of enemies, the superiority we have thus laboured for and obtained l I wish to entertain a better opinion of my countrymen than to suspect that there is a single man, who could be so base; and am willing to persuade myself it has been owing to want of t-hought, or of proper information that any have thus deserted the cause of their country.

To this spirited conclusion to the pamphlet several clauses were added from the Acts of Parliament passed in that reign to prevent the emigration of workmen; and we shall see that he subsequently moved a resolution in the Chamber of Commerce, to prevent by means still more stringent the seduction of artisans from their employment and country for the mere purpose of obtaining the methods of their respective trades. According to the narrow social and political opinions of those days, this restriction on the liberty of the workman was considered not only laudable but right; though we much question, apart from any exceptional expediency necessitated by the relation of one country to another, as Great Britain to continental states at that period, if such restriction is either just or founded on true economic laws. If the masters had freedom to carry their trades out of the kingdom, and pursue them for their own profit elsewhere, so also should the workmen. The natural laws of supply and dcmand—— the difficulty of establishing 478 DERBYSHIRE BLACK WADD. Cnsr. X. manufactures resulting from skilled labour in newlysettled, thinly-peopled, or poor countries, and the moral force of self-interest, would have proved, then, as now, a surer controlling power than laws purely restrictive. But the monopoly of both labour and material was at that period considered necessary, as much to the existence of a manufacture, as to the well-being of the manufacturer and those he employed.

In the midst of the discussion of these grave social topics, philosophy was not forgotten. Wedgwood in the same year, 1783, contributed a brief paper to the Transactions of the Royal Society. It related to the 'Ochra friabilis nigro fusca' of Da Costa, or the Black Wadd of the Derbyshire miners. This was one of those oily or bituminous substances frequently found in certain strata of the Midland counties. Analysis proved it to contain, lead, iron, manganese, and

earthy particles; it gave, when mixed with the body, darker and lighter shades to pottery, and, mixed with oil, was found to be serviceable in ship and house painting

From the date of the settlement of the question relative to Champion's patent, Wedgwood had become lessee, in conjunction with a Mr. Carthew, of certain clay mines near St. Austle in Cornwall; and as his knowledge of the mineral resources of the county extended_both through

' Philosophical Transactions, vol. 1774. Da Costa who had been lxxiii. p. 284. 'Vedp,wood knew secretary to the Royal Society, left

Da Costa personally. Of their first acquaintance the former writes to Bentley:—' Dr. Percival has sent me the famous naturalist Da. Costs, with injunctions to be very civil to him. I gained a little relief by sending him two miles to see a flint mill. But that is over and I am obliged to it under a cloud, for there were mistakes in his accounts which were never made clear. But according to Dr. Percival, he was much esteemed. Vedgwood, after telling Bentley this, adds: ' I thought him the most disagreeable mortal who bore the name of a hiloso her, I had ever be rude to him whilst I write.'—— I known, or shou d not have left Vedgwood to Bentley, August 6, i him sosoon.'—Ihid. Augustlfi, 1774.

his own agents, and from information derived from Boulton and Watt, whose mining business was at this period on an extensive scale_he seems to have entered into arrangements for working others, of which the products were not entirely clay. To look after his interests in this direction he again visited Cornwall in the spring of 1782, this time accompanied by Baron Beda. Of the products of one mine he was about to visit, Watt had given him intimation, and when about to set out on his journey, the latter wrote and asked to share in them. He cheerfully promised 'half the produce of the mine or vein on the terms mention'd & whenever you shall make the claim '.... ' for it would be unreasonable indeed in me to wish to pre-

clude you from a share of the materials of which I should have been ignorant without your information.' It was also at this date that he wanted ' a mine captain to look after some workmen, to pay my rents, & other matters.' 1 And he asked Watt if he could think of such a person on the spot. About the same date Y/Vedgwood became a shareholder in the Polgooth mine and somewhat later in the Cornish Metal Company, by both of which he was unfortunately a considerable loser..

Wedgwood's foreign trade had by this time vastly increased, though its greatest developement, as we shall see, took place after the signing of the Commercial Treaty with France in September 1786. His earliest consignments _were to North America and the West Indies; 1 Wedgwood to Watt, May 15, congratulate you and your worthy 1782. partner & the public on having so

' Boulton transferred a 10001. many of your valuable engines at share to Wed wood in October 1' work, & I most heartily wish you 17B2.—Boulton onespondence.Two ' both many years enjoyment of the months later Vedgvood adds to a ' fruits of your important & merileter relative to the same mine, 'I torious labours.' 480 FOREIGN TRADE. CRAP. X.

but his first foreign patrons were the Russians. As early as 1768, a very large amount of cream-colour and black and yellow enamelled ware was sent to St. Petersburgh through the agency of Boulton; and by degrees Russia became one of the best markets for ornamental goods. Boulton's agency also opened a trade with Cadiz. In 1769, we hear of Du Burk and his warehouse for pottery in Amsterdam. For a period sufficient to win the confidence of Wedgwood and his partner, his orders for highclass goods were extensive, and his payments prompt. But he soon showed himself to be, what he really was, a cunning knave without conscience or principle. His stock of goods drawn from Wedgwood and Bentley became enormous, his payments rare, his accounts disordered, his statements contradictory. He lived extravagantly, made visits of pleasure rather than business to London; and his wife, whom Wedgwood had good reason to call 'a diable of a woman,' aided him in all his nefarious transactions. At length the state of things became alarming. In 1773-4 Cooper, the printer already spoken of, 'was induced to go over to Amsterdam and join Du Burk. But the former, though a most worthy man, had no real aptitude for business, as his own failure in life showed. The sales declined, the accounts, if more open, became more complicated. Mr. Mather was then despatched to look over them and wind up affairs. The result even of this was not satisfactory: and the end was that Du Burk was thrown into_ prison by some of his other creditors. Here he remained a long time, and was only at length released by the forbearance and charity of his greatest creditors, Wedgwood and Bentley, who upon principle never signed a schedule of bankruptcy. He plotted, prevaricated, and was a rogue

CRAP. X. ITS CONTINUOUS INCREASE. 481 to the last. What he lost by knavery and dishonesty was soon seen. After a treaty for, or a short trial of the business, by Mr. Nicholson, the secretary subsequently of the Chamber of Manufacturers, Wedgwood and Bentley's Amsterdam agency passed into the hands of Vcldhuysen and son. The business sprung into new life like a phoenix from its ashes. The sales became remarkable, depots were opened in other parts of Holland and the Netherlands, and these worthy gentlemen, capable, energetic, and honest, had the pleasure and advantage of dispersing Wedgwood's beautiful productions over a wide extent of country, and adding substantially to his fame. In 1774, large consignments were made to Narva, Revel, and Moscow; and orders came in from various parts of Italy. In the next year we hear of Jerome Ippoliti of Venice, a man as it seems of extrordinary cultivation, parts, and character: a true Venetian merchant, worthy of his city in her greatest days of art and freedom. Then we have Du Rovery in Dunkirk giving great orders; and, in 1776 and 1777, we hear of merchants

and correspondents in Valentia, Leipsic, Leghorn, Hamburgh and

Riga; the last the great merchant-house' of Welpert and _

Co. So the vast tide of commerce grows year by year; till in 1783, 1784, 1785, and 1786, the whole continent, and something more is embraced; and yet this tide is not at its full. We hear of Giacinto and Fratelli of Genoa, Guiseppe Riva of Lisbon, Micali and Son of Leghorn, and of other merchants and traders in Hamburgh, Leipsic, Ratisbon, Naples, Leghorn, Boston in New England, Versailles, Turin and St. Petersburgh; Capper, a Birmingham merchant having a great establishment in the latter place, and giving his orders for cream-ware and other useful goods by thousands of dozens. It was this sale of VOL. II. I I ordinary ware which enabled Wedgwood to spend so much in ornamental art. Had he had to live upon the fruits of his cameos and his bas-reliefs, he would have died a poor, if not an insolvent man; and it must be ever recollected, that what he threw into the scale of beauty was for the advance of the arts of his country and not for himself. Utility and beauty were thus indeed one, for the finest bas-relief or vase he ever made could have had no existence but for the homely plate and dish.

Micali and Son of Leghorn, Rostof Leipsic, Ippoliti of Venice, Welpert and Co. of Riga, Schilling of Bayreuth, the brothers Centini of Lisbon, and Giacinto and Fratelli of Genoa were amongst the most valuable of Wedgwood's agents and correspondents. They were all gentlemen: many of them artists. What beautiful articles Rost of Leipsic orders year by year for the great Fair held in his city! Ippoliti sends his own sketches, often his own models; and corners and spaces in the quaintly-worded letters and orders of most of them are filled with little drawings of vases, ornaments, or useful ware required. To these old mouldering documents, the reader is indebted for most of the border edgings already given. I But generally when sketches were necessary they were made on a larger scale on tissue paper, and upon reaching Etruria,

were pasted and numbered in order books. An (Fig.:58.) TUREEN. PEARL-WHI'I'E w,n1-:, Italian Ol"(lGI' fllI'DlSllS the accompanying tureen and plate in pearl-white ware (figs. 88 and 89).

The form of the first is exquisite, and the overlapping garniture, as though of a leaf or a shell, is delicate in the extreme. The plate which matches it is somewhat similar in its form and ornament to those made in the old tortoise-shell body. _ _ Besides these pen-and-ink illus-If trations, which render many of the foreign letters and orders so full of interest, we have descriptions and facts which are more so. VVe 'F"' ',','Qm_':_';;';:'",m_ read of fine services of enamelled mu" """" ware, that were never unpacked by human hand, but went down in the depths of the Adriatic, the Bay of Biscay, the Atlantic, the North Sea, or the English or Irish Channels, and may lie there still amidst the wracks and ruins which are building up the continents of future ages; we read of exquisite forms for utility on which the enameller had laid the leaf, the flower, the shell, the Grecian convolute, or honeysuckle, so left on the shores of stormy seas, by the carelessness of captains, seamen, or pilots, till they were chipped and defaced into ugliness, or shattered in a thousand pieces by the incessant beating of the waves on the barrels in which they had been packed. We read of monstrous thefts, and the exchange of base articles for fine ones; and of the carelessness or dishonesty of packers and servants, by the substitution of thirds for firsts, or damaged articles for perfect ones. But we read more frequently of honest admiration, of offers of service, and of efforts made to procure works of art, or to secure the consignors against the trickery of the fraudulent. We have national characteristics and national tastes. Vc find that princes may love 484 MERCHANT PRINCES. CRAP. X.

works of art, but can forget to pay for them. Insolvency was the rule rather than the exception of royal and ducal houses in those days; in Germany more than elsewhere: but the princes of

Mecklenburgh-Strelitz and Saxe Coburg, with one or two others of ducal rank, were gentlemen as well as patrons. In the merchant class were princes too. The Micalis, the Ippolitis, the R-osts, the Veldhuysens, and the Schillings, could return the hospitality shown at Etruria to members of their respective firms by an equal hospitality in their own houses and cities. We read these facts of a great and everwidening commerce, and then recollect that they had their beginning in a certain thatched cottage on the Staffordshire moorlands; and were the growth not of advantageous fortune, but of a just application and a wise pursuit of, those moral and social laws, on which depend not only the well-being of the individual, but aggregately of communities.

We have seen that Wedgwood and Bentley's partnership referred solely to the manufacture and sale of ornamental goods. In 1781, soon after the death of the latter, and in order to a final settlement of affairs in connexion therewith, all the ornamental ware in stock was sold by auction at Christie's Rooms.1 The sale lasted twelve days, and the results were satisfactory. At this date Mr. Byerley took up his residence in Greek Street, and shortly afterwards married Miss Frances Bruckfield, of Derby; nothing else was changed. A Mr. Howarth joined Mr. Brock in the duties of the head-clerkship, and a Mr. Le Riche became interpreter and translator; but 1 The Catalogues of this sale are ' our hands, and from which we shall now extremely rare. But ata sub-I be able to draw some interesting sequent period, one will pass into ' particulars. the artists employed were the same, and Flaxman still occasionally rendered important services. The subjoined bills show upon what works he was engaged for Mr. Wedgwood during various parts of the years1 1781, 1782, 1731-.4' s. a'.

March 7. A Shell Venus 1 5 0
A Bacchante. 1 6 0
Cupid 8: Psyche... 1 4 0
Two busts of Rosseau & Sterne O 16 O
A Sitting Flora.... 1 5 0
May 20. Moulding a bust of Dr. Fothergale 1 4 0

£6 19 0
Received in full of all demands by John Flaxman.
Mayer MSS.
Mr 'edgwood to J. Flaxman.
1782.:8 a. (1.
April 28. Moulding a Turin..... 0 18 0
83. Moulding a Bust of Mrs. Siddons... 1 11 6
Sept. 6. A cast oiP a fragment by Phidias... 10 6
£5 0 0
Received in full by John Flaxman.
1783. Mr. Vedgwood,
to J. Flaxman Jun'.
July 11. £ 8. d.
Two drawings of Crests an Owl & a Griflins head....... 3 0
A portrait of Mr. Herschel. 2 2 0
A d" of Dr. Buchan..... 2 2 O
Oct. 12"'. A portrait of an Officer from a print for a ring.......2l26
A drawing of a Crest, Cap of Liberty 8: a flame....... 1 0
30"'. A figure of a Fool for Chess... 1 5 0
I)ec. 13"'. A drawing of the Shield, crest & arms of Sir
N. Nugent...... 2 6
18"'. Grinding the Ed s of 6 Snuff-boxes for the
Spanish Am assador.. 15 O
1784.
J an' 24. A model in wax of Capt. Cook. 2 2 0
Feb, 3". A d of Dr. Johnson..... 2 2 0
A rint of the D' for assistance in the model 2 6
March 21". A as-releif of boys in wax... ll 0 6
A portrait of C. J enkinson Esq"... 2 2 0
Two drawings for the Manufacturers' Arms 15 0
A third drawing for the Manufacturers' ' Arms....... 5 0
Dec. 1". Three days employed in drawing bas-reliefs vases, Chess-men, &c.... 3 8 0
Carried forward £30 15 0
486 SUBJECTS AND PRICE. CRAP. X. 1783, 1784 and 1787. Manyother bills have undoubtedly perished, as there exist clues to much more modelling
Brought forward.. £30 15 0 Dec. 12". A

has relief in wax of Veturia 8.: Volumnia entreating Coriolanus.... 9 9 0 Jan1 14"' A portrait of Gov'. Hastings... 3 3 0 March 8. A drawing of Chess-men.... 6 6 0 An outline for a. Lam 8: stand... 10 6 Cutting the curved si es of two Omamental freizes parallel, 3 days & half 9 TQ April 9. A drawing of a Chimneviece... 10 6 July 22-'. A d" from that in Mr. e1gwd'B Shawroom, & several mouldings drawn at large....... 1 1 0 Aug'. 8"'. A Mason's time taking down a Chimneypiece....... 2 0 A Labourer at do..... 1 3 A drawing of an Arm and olive branch. 2 O A drawing of an Oak branch for the border of a plate...... 3 0 Nov. 23. A model of the King of Sweden. 2 2 0 Dec'. Mr. & Mrs. Meerman's portraits. 5 5 0 Dec. 18"'. Four patterns for Steel frogs 10 0 1787. J an'. 16"'. A model of eace preventing Mars from » bursting t e door of Ja.nus's Temple. 15 15 0 A packing Case...... 1 0 March 26. A model of Mercury uniting the hands of England & France.... 13 13 O A acking Case...... 1 6 A rawing of a Cypher R. H. &: Bloody hand 2 0 June 1". A model of the Queen of Portugal.. 3 3 0 J une 11"'. A Marble Chimney-iece, containing 5 feet 11 inches at £1 8:. p' foot... 11 4 (1 Masonry & polishing..... 18 0 Carving....... 6 0 A Marble Chimney-piece containing 5-feet 3 inches..... . 9 19 6 Masonry & polishing..... 21 4 0 Twenty-four tinned Cram... 12 0 Seven packing Cases, 7s. 6., 7:. lll1., Tn. 211. , 2 8,. 68. o¢1.,5». 6d., 7; 04., 8s. 1d.. " Nails........ 2 10 Packing three days..... 10 6 Cart to the Inn...... 6 0 Toll Porter 8: booking.... 1 9 103 14 4; taking down a Uhimliey-piece... 5 3 Cuttin Tiles...... 5 0 Cases or the Chimney-piece... 19 6Q Aug. 10"'. A has-relief of_ Hercules in the Ilesperian Garden... 23 O 0 £188 4 2 Cr. V 116 11 9

CRAP. X. GROUPS OF CHILDREN. 487 than is here indicated. From one brief note addressed by Flaxman to Wedgwood in the autumn of 1782, we find that the jasper ware was being rapidly adapted in a highly ornamented form to useful purposes:

According to the desire you expressed in the last letter you favoured me with I have designed some Groups of Children proper for bas-reliefs to decorate the sides of teapots. No. 1 & each side, the 1st is Blind 2 are intended to go intirely round a Teapot of a. Flat shape except where the handle & spout interrupt them, I have therefore made seperate stories for man's buff, the 2nd is the game of marbles, 3 & 4 are the Triumph Cupid, to be disposed in a similar manner on the sides of round and upright Teapots, when you return the sketches to _ be modeled from, be pleased to give instructions con cerning the Size and other (Fig. 90.) ens-nsunr. numr u.."s BUFF.

necessary particulars.'

FLOWER POT. I-'AIXJKE COLLDCKTON.

Flaxman excelled as much in the delineation of child

Mr. F iervill'e,

No. 12 Edward Street, 1784.

Portman Square.

to J. Flaxman J un'.

J une 12. A Tomb to the memory of Rosseau in Port-£ 0. rl.

land Stone, erected on Mr. Fiervilla's estate near Stanmore

Mayer MSS.

This bill is connected with YVedgwood's name, inasmuch as Mr. Fierville became a bankrupt, and Flaxman had to wait some years for a balance left unpaid. He had commenced the tomb in 1783, and from that date various sums were paid on account. A balance of 331. 6a. 81!. remained unpaid in 1787, .105 0' 0 when he went to Rome, and Mr. Vedgwood, or rather Mr. Byerley, received the final dividend on Fierville's estate for Flaxmnn.

1 Flaxman to Vlledgwood, October 28, 1782. This letter, with two of the subjoined bills I owe to the courtesy of Francis Vedgwood of Etruria. 488 SALTCELLAR AND TEAPOT. CRAP. X. hood, as he did in more classical a11d finished subjects; and from this date his games of marbles, and blindman's bull', and infant Cupids engaged in various kinds of play became favourite decorations in relief for cameos, vases, teapots, cream-jugs, flowerpots, saltcellars, teacups and saucers, and countless other articles in

jasper ware. On the subjoined flowerpot (fig. 90) from Mr. Falcke's collection, we have blind man's bull'. On the saltcellar (fig. 91), Cupids

CRAP. X. CURVED AND OTHER CAMEOS. 489 playing; and on the teapot (fig. 92) and three cameos, (figs. 93, 94 and 95) other exquisite examples of childhood and maternity._ The teapot from the ornamentation of the foot, is probably of an early stage of the jasper body in its application to ornamented, but useful purposes. Lady Templeton also contributed in the succeeding year some charming groups of little figures, which were copied in small bas-relief with so much success, that Wedgwood solicited other groups from her Ladyship's pencil.1 We owe to Flaxman, as we see, a bust of Mrs. Siddons, and about the same period he probably modelled this exquisite cameo medallion of the great actress (fig. 96). In beauty, force, and expression, it even surpasses that of Dr. Johnson, given in a previous page. She is represented in the character of Lady Macbeth, and probably at the moment when she exclaims ' Give me the dagger! '

' Wedgwood to Lady Templeton, June 27, 1783.

490 VVEDGVVOOUS PORTRAIT. CHA P. X. as, though the weapon is absent, the position of the right hand and arm suggests the action of holding one ready to strike with. We also find from the bills that Flaxman modelled ' Cupid and Physche,' but whether it was a remodel of the Duke of Marlborough's famous cameo as modelled by Hackwood, or the same figures in another manner and attitude, is not apparent. (m _95_) mm The cameo medallion of Sir "mm" "'""'-Joshua Reynolds, was another of Flaxman's works, though the date is uncertain. In 1783 Wedgwood and his wife sat to the great master, and it is not improbable that his success with their portraits led to the modelling of his likeness. It is thus given (fig. 97). After the death of Reynolds in 1792 it became very popular amongst his numerous sitters and friends. Wedgwood's portrait by Sir Joshua is said to be characteristic and like the original. Two dif-

ferent engravings have been made from it, but neither fully convey the grace nor expression of the original painting. Wedgwood is dressed in a mulberry-coloured velvet coat, his hair is covered by a small wig, and a singularly ruddy hue extends over the face and forehead. This is probably a defect arising from time or injury to the painting. The eyes are large and have great originality of expression; keenness, benevolence, humour, melancholy, deep meditation are all there; and the eyebrows are such as generally belong to the true artistic type of countenance. It has been said that Reynolds gave to all his sitters an air of refinement, and it is not absent here. But it is too lifelike, too much an introspection to be the effect of art

CRAP. X. PORTRAIT BY STUBBS. 491 alone. It is the expression of the truest of all refinement, that begot by intellectual pursuits, the practice of the kindliest emotions of our being, and by association with those equal to or superior to ourselves, morally or intellectually. In the face, the form, the air, is a look of weariness, overwork, and premature decay, which lends, if possible, a more touching and serene expression. Stubbs painted a portrait of Wedgwood, and it was engraved by George Townley Stubbs, an illegitimate son of the artist, who was brought up as an engraver. It is not very life like, and a wig in the stiffest buckle, with a knitted jacket fitting tight to the body, convey to us the idea of a common-place workman, rather than the greatest English potter. A reduced copy of Wedgwood's portrait by Reynolds was also made in oils, and a miniature of him was painted by Montstephen.

In December 1784, and March 1785 Flaxman was employed upon his celebrated Chessmen. His custom in many cases seems to have been to send Wedgwood a rapid sketch of a proposed work, and when approved of, a more elaborate drawing was made. It was probably cm». x. THE CHESSMEN. 492 so in this instance. The drawing sent to Etruria. in March 1785, and charged 6l. 6.5-. in the bill, was that from which the figures were modelled.

At a later date Herbert Crofts a resident at Oxford, and the author of a grammar, and some other literary works, sought to obtain this drawing. After ordering a suite of English medals, a set of Chessmen, and 'the head of his old friend Dr. Johnson' he thus wrote: 'Provided you do not hang up Flaxman's drawing of your chessmen, I shall be very glad to give it houseroom amongst my prints and drawings, and he, I'll answer for it, would not be sorry.'1 Happily this request was not listened to. Wedgwood had become one of the greatest admirers of Flaxman's genius. The drawing was carefully preserved, and still remains one of the treasures of the manufactory at Etruria.

True to that keeping which was one of the minor canons of his art, and one to be found in alliance with all his best works, Flaxman recollected that Chess was essentially a game of the Gothic, Frankish, and Mediaaval periods, and that any art in connection with its representative signs must relate thereto. Hence instead of having recourse to classical types, as an inferior artist might have done, he evidently made the efiigies and tombs, as also the painted glass in our abbeys, cathedrals, and churches, the models from which he drew his king and queen, his knights and ladies, his archer and horseman. He was of opinion that when a story had to be told, no clue to its real history should be forgotten'hence we can fancy him reading old ballads, and chronicles, for the adventures of St. George and the Dragon, and the stories of the Faithful Knight and Virtuous Lady. He may have gone to Shakespeare for the fool, and to the ballads of Robin Hood and Chevy Chase for the type of his bowman or archer. His study of

' H. Crofts to Wedgwood, dated Holywell, Oxford, September 26, 1T06. — Mayer MSS. ' Lectures, p. 170, wt supra.

Cant. X. MANUFACTURERS' ARMS. 496

Grecian models, and his habit of delineating the human form under its most beautiful and perfect aspects necessarily served him as much in the figure of a mediaaval knight, as in that of a Roman legionary, or a Grecian warrior. Yet something more than this was required; and Flaxman had ability to give it. It was necessary to convey the attitudes and expression incident to the habits and trains of thought of a rude but chivalrous period. And this we have; for the knight is knightly, and the queen is queenly-even after the manner in which they live to us in the old chronicles and ballads.

The figures were generally made in the white jasper body; but occasionally they were blue or black, the pediment remaining white. They were largely exported to the continent, especially to Germany and Russia.

Three drawings for the arms of the ' General Chamber of Manufactures ' were, as the bills show, amongst Flaxn1an's labours for Wedgwood in 1784. N 0 use was ever made of them. All three are in outline—the first two filled in with Indian ink. In the centre of each is a shield or circular tablet; on the top of this sits Britannia, the supporters on either side being Neptune with his trident, and Plenty with her cornucopia. The principal variation is on the table of the shields. On the first is the fasces, a reaping hook, three bee-hives, and a ship; round the edge is lettered, 'The General Chambers of Manufactures of Great Britain,' and on labels at the foot ' Union and Security '-' We know not men but measures.' The inscriptions on the second sketch are the same, and only differ in the emblems on the shield _and in the substitution of joined hands for the central bee-hive. In the third sketch, Neptune is made the left instead of the right hand supporter. Britannia is more distinctly 496 IMPROVE-MENTS,IN JASPER ORNAMENTS. CRAP. X. drawn, the edge of the shield is without inscription and the decorations of the field are a reaping hook, the fasces, and three instead of two joined hands; and the words 'Success follows Unanimity' are substituted for ' Union and Security. ' 1

A great variety of articles were now made in the jasper body; though un-questionably vases with simple decorations, and useful ware of the same character, preceded those with more costly and elaborate orna— ments. As early as 1775 Wedgwood had thrown out the idea of jasper vases decorated with white bas-reliefs in the same body; 2 but so slow was the progress in this direction at first—that prior to the death of Bentley it is very evident, that their ornamentation had not extended beyond medallions, trophies and festoons. Candlesticks were also made in this body though simply decorated. But as soon as Wedgwood was able to put his heart again into his ornamental work,-and Flaxman, Webber, and other artists were employed in the modelling and preparation of appropriate bas-reliefs, ornaments, and borderings, the art of adorning articles in this exquisite body made extraordinary progress. In 1782 Flaxman, as we have seen, was preparing bas-reliefs of a simple character for teapots and other useful articles; in 1784 he had advanced to bas-reliefs for vases; and two years later, such was the progress made, that Wedgwood thus wrote to Sir William Hamilton:

I have just now executed an order by the direction of a. merchant in Manchester for an assortment of my jasper ornaments with blue grounds & white figures which he tells me are 1 All three sketches are included graceful woodcut. in Mr. Mayer-'s collection of VVedg-" Wedgwood to Bentley, January wood's papers, but the artist con-15,1775. sidered them too rude to make a for the King of Naples. If so, you will perhaps see them in a. short time, and I mention this to beg the favour of your correction if you think any of them worth so much of your notice. One thing I persuade myself you will observe that they have been objects of very great care, every ornament and leaf being first made in a seperate mould then laid upon the vase with great care & accuracy, & afterwards wrought over again upon the vase itself by an artist equal to the work; for from the beginning I determined to spare neither time nor expence in modelling and finishing my ornaments, and I have the satisfaction to find that my plan has hitherto met with the approbation of my friends, for the purchasers of every nation declare them to be the highest finished & cheapest ornaments now made in Europe. I lamented much that I could not obtain liberty of the merch' to send a vase, the finest and most perfect I have ever made, & which I have since presented to the British Museum. I enclose a rough sketch of it: it is 18 inches high & the price 20 guineas, Mr. Cha' Greville saw it, & wished it was in his Majesty's Cabinet at Naples.'

We thus learn that from the close of 1785 we may date all the finest and most elaborate of the ornamented articles in jasper; as also probably many of the choicest bas-reliefs. Another change, analogous to that which had taken place with respect to the body of the cameos took place about the same period in regard to the jasper ware generally considered. A jasper dip or wash was substituted for colouring in the mass, or for a body wholly jasper; Wedgwood having by experience and a series of special experiments, perfected this easier, and probably less costly method. At the same date, 1786, another im

' provement was introduced; the jasper ornamental ware, as tea-things, were polished within in the manner in which agate and other stones are polished. The first

' P.S. The sketch of the vase Apotheosis of Homer. Wedgwood could not be got ready for this post to Sir William Hamilton, June 24, but shall be sent soon. Subject, the, 1786.

VOL. II. K K -198 PEDESTAL UR ALTAR. CRAP. X specimens, and differently ornamented to any made before, were sent to Mrs. Eden.

Guided by information thus derived—we give a place first to specimens in jasper of simple ornament, leaving to the next chapter those superb vases, articles of jewellery, exquisite cups and saucers, and other productions which proved Wedgwood's greatness as an artistic potter. I In this pedestal or altar (fig. 99), with white ornaments on a blue ground, from Mr. Maycr's collec-

tion, we see an exquisite adaptation of trophies, masks, ribbons, and

CRAP. X. PLATE: INFANT ACADEMY. 499 fruit-wreaths as ornaments. The border beneath the entablature is truly Grecian in its type, as is also the scale ornament round the foot. In the next illustration (fig. 100) we have a dessert plate or dish from the De La Rue collection. The exceeding beauty and delicacy of its decoration led to its 'being framed as a precious relic. The leafage round the central field is very graceful; and the little group in the midst is a reduced copy of a picture by Sir Joshua Reynolds-known as the Infant Academy. The three little sitters are familiar to us, in a plaster medallion yet sold about the streets. The third specimen (fig. 101) is a tripod and flower-vase, blue ground and white ornaments. Examples are common in all collections; though of these the ornamentation is very varied, both in form and colour. Every part of its beautiful workmanship will bear inspection; although the example 500 TRIPOD AND FLOWER VASE. CHAP. X.

given is by no means unique.

One in the Sibson collec tion is worthy of particular mention, as the vase within the tripod escapes the very ordinary fault of this class of ornaments, of not hanging clear to the perpendicular. The succeeding cuts (figs. 102, 103 and 104) give five very ex quisite specimens of tea and coffee ware. The rayed saucer and its cup, with one of Flaxman's' or Lady Templeton's groups of children encircling the outside, is worthy of notice, and it will be observed that it. forms a portion of that on the saltcellar. The ornaments are white on a delicate lilac ground. Both cup and saucer are in the South Kensington Museum, as are also the succeeding coffee-cup, saucer, and slop-basin (figs. 103 and 104). The ornamentation on all three is charming. Of these the ground is blue, the ornamentation white. The border springing from the bottom of the basin, and the edging above it, are 'orlh _v of especial OI)SC'l''lllOl1; as is

C-HAP. X. CUP AND SAUCER. 501 also the bottom and top bordering

on the cup. I The next example (fig. 105) of a sugar-dish or basin evidently matches the slop-basin and coffee-cup, although it is from the Falcke collection. The form of both basins deserves notice, particularly that for sugar, as also the accuracy with which the cover fits the body; for together they look one. In the two succeeding cuts (figs. 106 and 107), We have a tureeu, and a wine cooler of great originality, from the De La Rue collection. On the last we see the vine-wreaths again, and an infant Bacchus or satyr, and in the ornamentation of the other we have in the lower border, an instance of feather or grass edging.

502 SLOP BASIN. Can. X.

The form of this first example is exquisite and the ornamentation of the ridge both rare and curious. The next cut (fig. 108) shows Mr. Gladstone's celebrated déjefiner service. It was made probably at a later date than the foregoing, from the fact of the ribbon-border being first used upon articles for personal decoration or use as snuff boxes, etui cases, and similar articles. The quatrefoil pattern also betrays a medium if not a late period of workmanship. The ground is a slaty-coloured blue; the ornaments white. This became a very usual style of ornament, the quatrefoils being simply varied in colour. In Mr. Mayer's Museum are many very exquisite specimens of this pattern; Mr. Falcke and Mr. Barlow have also some fine examples. From the invoices we find that déjefmer services of the quatrefoil pattern were very popular; and one precisely similar to this of Mr. Gladstone's was made for and used, _. ,. by Lady Auckland. (Fig. 105.) SUGAR nAsr.'. mu:..-n warm "span. With the exception of "ME Cm"mN' that of Octavia and Volumnia entreating Coriolanus, and the two tablets connected with the settlement of the Commercial Treaty with France—it is not exactly (Fig. 106.) 1'L'REE.'. mu; AND wn-rn»: JABPEII. vs LA nus common.

known what were the subjects of the larger bas-reliefs modelled by Flaxman for Wedgwood in the period between the death of Bentley, and his departure for Rome in the autumn of 1787. He was otherwise 504 VVINE COOLER. CHAP. X abundantly employed, for work flowed in as his fame increased; but without doubt his labours for Wedgwood were more or less continuous, as still existing cheques and receipts show he frequently drew money on account throughout the whole period.1 It is also known that Vedgwood advanced him a part, if not the whole, of the funds necessary to his journey. Mr. §lVedg'ood likewise gave him letters to various people, amongst others to his agent Sykes in Paris, and to Micali and Son of Leghorn.2 The latter were commissioned to take

' Flaxman's brother William was, the property of Mr. Flaxman, an aralso much employed by Vedgvood i tist of this country, and a. much and his family. lie framed sketches valued friend of mine, who is going for Miss "edgwood and her sisters, to make some residence in Italy. I as also the numerous designs and have not hesitated to apprize him drawings presented to Vedgwo0d that you would have the goodness by such artist friends as Miss Crewe, to fulfill all his wishes in res ct to Lady Templeton, and Lady Diana this chest and box, which e has Beauclerk. expressed in the annexed paper,' and whatever expenses may be increased 2 Mess Micali & Son. you will please charge to mv acLeghorn. count, and favour me with a line of

London August 17, 1787. Gentlemen, I have the pleasure to enclose you Bill of Lading of a Chest I F, and a box directed for Mr. Thomas Jenkins in Rome. The former is advice.

'Whatever civilities you may show to my friend Mr. Flaxman, ll shall be very thankful for, and consider as done to him who has the honour to be with real respect.

' The Inventory.

CRAP. X. DEJEUNER snnvrca. 505 particular care of a chest containing the personal effects of Flaxman and his wife, of which we give, in the next page, a reduced copy. It is in Flaxman's own handwriting. Flaxman stayed some days en route in Paris, taking up (Fig. 108.

) I'l.4'l'E COl.l)l'l AND WHITE. hlil"F3IL

GLADSTONE (.'(1L.E(.'l'l0N-

his residence at the Hotel d'Alique, Rue d'Orleans, St. Honoré, where he was visited by the Due de Bouillon, who had previously employed him, and made him agent for various commissions for Wedgwood. Flaxman whilst

The letter is unsigned, being merely a rough draft dictated by VVed wood to Byerley. In addition, laxman directs Messrs. Mieali to forward his chest to the care of Mr. Gavin Hamilton at Rome, free of expense; and if possible to put it on board a vessel for Civita

Vecchia, to proceed from thence immediatel to Rome. But if it is absolute y nece for the box to be 0 ned at the ustom House at Leg orn, Mr. Micali is earnestly requested to let a careful person attend to the impacking of the . things.-IIa _ver MSS.

here was joined by Mr. Byerley, to whom previously writing to give his address, he says:—'The Duke de Bouillon made kind enquiries after you, and desired me to tell you he wishes to see you at the Castle of Navarre on matters of business.'

Webber, as we have seen, had settled down earnestly to his work at Etruria in May 1782. His first essays in modelling were ' A Triumph of Mars, ' ' A boy leaning on his quiver, with doves,' ' A Cupid drawing his dart,' 'Hebe, its companion,' ' Apollo and Daphne as a beaupot,' 'Cupid, a model,' 'A Sacrifice to Hymen ' a model in basso-relievo for which the charge was 3l. 3 8. and 'A Sacrifice to Concordia, its companion,' at the same.

Curr. X. HENRY WEBBER. 507 price. He also modelled vases, cups, chimney-pieces, and a variety of other articles. According to an agreement made with Mr. Wedgwood in July 1787, Webber shortly afterwards proceeded to Rome, where in March 17 88 he was at work in the Museum Capitolinum. Wedgwood's eldest son was at this date also in Rome. In the following year he travelled through Italy accompanied by Webber. They took their way home by Switzerland, of which country the latter

was either a native or had friends settled there, and after visiting Paris reached Etruria at the close of November. From this date Webber was engaged upon the Barberini Vase, as also in modelling bas-reliefs and other works of art from sketches he had made whilst in Italy. He continued his employment at Etruria, till Wedgwood's death, or shortly before it. He appears to have been an able and industrious artist, as well as an economist. He allowed his salary to accumulate at interest in his great master's hands; and he appears to have rendered incessant and praiseworthy assistance through the whole anxious period connected.

with the copying of the Barberini Vase.

Lochee was another artist employed by Wedgwood at this period. He was an exquisite modeller of small things, and we find him at work at Stowe in December 1787. In the March following be was again there, this time accompanied by an assistant named Peart,1 and thus obtained copies of the finest gems in the Duke of Buckingll1a1n's possession. In fact this was a golden period for artists of all kinds. Even Westmacott and Wyatt, then very young men, seem to have done some modelling for Wedgwood, and were also purchasers of various ex WRIGHT OF DERBY. CHAP. X. 508 quisite specimens of ornamental ware.I In 1784, Wright of Derby painted for Wedgwood, his celebrated picture of the Maid of Corinth, as also a portrait, which was probably that of the very friend who had as far as possible replaced Bentley in his heart, Erasmus Darwin. After some critical ' remarks on female drapery, Wedgwood in writing to the painter, said of his Maid of Corinth:

I do not say I am satisfied with the lover, but that I think it excellent, I had almost said inimitable, & I should quake for any future touch of your pencil there. It is unfortunate in my opinion that the maid shows so much of her back; but I give my opinion only, with great difiidence and submission to your better judgment. In one word, you have been so happy in your figure of the lover, that almost any other must appear to disadvantage in so near a comparison. Make her to please yourself, and I shall be perfectly satisfied.2

' Wyatt the sculptor's accounts, 1784 to 1793.—Ma 'er MSS.

Wedgwood to Vri ht of Derby, April 29 1784. In 1%86, VVi-ight painted for Mr. Ved ood one of me than the Alchymist, though my principal reason for having this subject would be a sin against the costume—I mean the introduction of our vases into the iece, for how his finest pictures, ' he taktin of Gibraltar.' Darwin considers it 'sublime.'

Six years previously, Wright had painted for Mr. Wedgwood one of his most celebrated pictures. Writing to Bentley the latter says, ' I am glad to hear Mr. YVright is in the land of the living I should like to have a piece of this gent1ema.n's art, but think Debutades' daughter would be a more apropos subject for could such fine things e supposed to exist in the earliest infancy of the Potter's Art? You know what I want, & when you see Mr. IV:-ight again I wish you would consult with him upon the subject. Mr. Vright once egan a piece in which our vases might be introduced with the greatest propriety. I mean the andwriting upon the 'Vail in the Palace of Nebucadnazzer. '—Wedgwood to Bentley, May 5, 1778.

LECTION—BRIDAL VASE—VASE, CONVOLUTED ORNAMENTS—VASE, BAS-RELIEF THE DANCING IIOURS—VASE, QUATREFOIL OBNAMENTS

WOOD—I'ROPOSALS TO REMODEL THE CHAMBER—VITALITY OF THE TRADE WITH FRANCE—SYKES AND DAGUERBE—FLAXMAN'S BASRELIEFS—COIlMBIlORATION OF THE TREATY—ABOLITION OF THE SLAVE TRADE—COPIES SENT TO FRANKLIN—LAST CONTRIBUTION TO THE PHILOSOPHICAL TRANSACTIONS—SETTLEMENT AT SYDNEY COVE —'WEBBER'S IlEDALLION—D.RWIN'S VERSIB—WEDGWOOD AGAIN ILL—IS ASSISTED BY HIS SONS—HIS CEASELESS ENTIIUSIASM FOR

HIS ART.
CHAPTER XI.
THE PERIOD OF ARTISTIC PERFECTION.

HE jasper vases, as we have seen from Mr. Wedgwood's letter to Sir William Hamilton, had, by the summer of 1786, been brought to a great degree of perfection. The period, therefore, from this date to the close of his life—indeed, to a point beyond-is certainly that to which may be assigned all the more splendid examples of these beautiful ornaments; and which, generally speaking, we may consider as absolutely perfect works of art, whether we regard their form, colour, decoration, or combined effects. To assign any exact date to the specimens selected for illustration, except in one case, is of course impossible, as they have probably passed through many hands since the period of their manufacture; but ten or twelve years is, without doubt, (Fm M) um um "D mm mm" their correct limit, and are suf-""""""""S ''-"""-"ficient to answer every purpose of the connoisseur and the collector. The vase (fig. 110) which thus heads the illustrations of these beautiful specimens of fictile art belongs to the collection of D. C. Marjoribanks, Esq., M.P. Its height is 19% inches, and, when mounted upon its pedestal, is a truly superb ornament. l The ground is a pale blue, the basrelief and other decorative portions white. The form is not only truly antique but very beautiful, and the place and annexation of the handles most graceful, as their upper curve, meeting the true line of the vase above the entablature, takes from it any appearance of overweight or disproportion. The encircling bas-relief is Flaxman's Apollo and the Nine Muses, and on the flanged rim we have the egg-and-tongue border so often seen on the Arretine ware. The cord or beading above is a graceful finish, and the rayed leaves are surmounted by a pine cone as a knob or handle. Beneath the flanged rim we have the fruits and leaf festoon and ribbon border of which we have already had examples. The beading, the bordering, and the rayed ornaments of the foot and plinth, are equally

beautiful, and add by their simplicity a new grace to the more richly-decorated portions. This vase is altogether one of Wedgwood's chef d'auvres in his art. The next example (fig. 111) is equally fine. It is the gem of Mr. Falcke's collection, and probably belongs to the period of the fabrication of the Barberini Vase, as at that date Wedgwood was making trials of black as a groundwork in the jasper body. The rams' horns pedestal on which it stands does not really belong to it as a work of art; their juxtaposition was temporarily made on account of colour. This example of a pedestal is rare, though less perhaps in keeping, artistically considered, than the vase it supports, which in both form and decoration is 1 The pedestal was unfortunatel at Mr. Marjoribanks' seat in Invernessshire, a district too remote for a p otographist to be easily met with.

CRAP. XI. VASE most masterly. In the bas-relief We have another section of Apollo and the Nine Muses. Every portion of this lovely vase will bear _inspection, Whether it be the masks, the festoon ornaments, the beading, the bordering, or the plinth. The height of the vase is 12 inches; of the pedestal, 9 inches. In the latter We have one of those incongruities which occasionally disfigures Wedgwood's more classic specimens,theblending of the modern and antique; as, though the upper moulding, and perhaps the rams'horns, may be referred to a classical model, the female figure, the grifiins, and the border round VOL. II.

: FALCKE COLLECTION. the plinth, are purely mediaaval in character and style.

The succeeding woodcuts give two other fine and most original specimens of black and white jasper. The first (fiv. 112), known as the ' Bridal Vase,' is in Mr. Barlo"s collection. The' hymeneal torches, their interlacing cords, the flange, the border beneath, and the exquisite decorative border round the crown of the plinth, are all worthy of minute examination. In the next choice example we have perhaps excess of ornament, though really deadened in effect by the shadows of the grounds. The

Grecian eonvoluted ornament of the centre is well carried out by those of the plinth, the section above the pedestal, and the upper portion, though the critical eye perhaps sees in the child

CHAP. XI. VASE: BAS-RELIEF. THE DANCING HOURS. 615 like figure which crowns the whole, another blending of the modern with the classical in style. A Cupid would have better borne out the relations suggested by other portions of the ornaments. This exquisite specimen belongs to Mr. Tulk of Firfield, Addlestone, Surrey. The next most lovely vase (fig. ' 114) strikes the eye at once by its simplicity, perfection, and the entire keeping of all its details. It is said to be the last made by VVedgwood, and in conjunction (Fi"',',..'.3;§_,._:',?§1..-'§.fi§,¢'§:.'§,-' _i'm with his pupil, William Adams. Being brought into the room where the great potter lay upon the sick-bed from which he never rose again, the master bestowed it upon his friend and favourite pupil, by whom it was gratefully and reverently preserved. Ultimately it passed into the hands of Adams's granddaughter,' and now adorns, with other choice specimens of Wedgwoodware, a quiet parsonage in Cornwall. Adams afterwards settled at Tunstall, and vied with Turner of Hanley in the production of 1 The wife of the Rev. '111. writerisindebted for the photograph.ver_v, of St. Goran, legavisse_v, of which the woodcut is an exact Cornwall, to whose kindness the copy.

the finest specimens of jasper ware; for the secret of its chief ingredient, the sulphate of baryta, was spread far and wide for some time previous to Wedgwood's death. Adams acquired a good trade, and his show-rooms at his works were on a truly splendid scale; 1 but he died suddenly in the prime of life, and now it is unknown if his only surviving and youngest son Benjamin succeeded him in his business?

The colour of this vase is of extraordinary beauty, and is due to a discovery made by Adams_but now, it is said, lost-of the liberal use of the purest gold filings in the composition of the

body. When the pupil made the success of his experiments first known to his great master, VVedgwo0d remarked, 'I have hitherto put too much butter in my paste,' probably meaning that the use of this finer metallic oxide made cobalt less a necessity than heretofore.8 This beautiful example of jasper ware is 16 inches high, and the subject of its bas-relief Flaxman's Dancing Hours. The stem and plinth are alike most exquisite, and the handles faultless in their annexation. It will be observed that both the decoration of the neck and 1 From Mrs. Boote, an aged lady, and another descendant of Adams, we have the following interesting particulars: ' Mr. Adams was himself the true type of the English gentleman; with a benevolence of nature, and generosity of heart that made him a singularly attractive person. His wife too was a loveable character; and his four children all growing up to man orwomanhood, were examples of all that tended to make a home harmonious. But this domestic bliss was not destined to last long; for consumption swe t of? in rapid succession one son the e dest, attheage of 21, and then the youngest daughter. As nearly as I can task ' my memory Mr. Adams himself died about the year 1804 or 1805, and picture of ' as it appears somewhat suddenly. He occupied an elegantly furnished house standing in its own grounds at Tunstall. In each room were many and most exquisite s ecimens of jasper. I know not ow Mr. Adams acquired the privile e of manufacturing this ware,but recollect its being said that it was a privilege which would die with him: and which I imagine it did, as the works were shut up after his death.'

' Shaw, with his usunlinaccurac, says that Benjamin Adams m e Esper ware at Tunstall in 1800.— ist. of Staflbrdshire Potteries, p. 221.

5 Communication from the Rev. Vm. Avery.

CRAP. XI. VASE: BOHN COLLEC-TION. 517 the entwining serpents had been used by Wedgwood long before in the decoration of his fine crystalline jasper vases. The three woodcuts which follow illustrate vases of other forms

and styles of ornament, the ground being blue and the decorative' portions white. In the first (fig. 115)-from Mr. Bohn's rich collection_we have the quatrefoil or cheque pattern, already seen in Mr. Gladstone's dejefmer service, with small bas-reliefs of a somewhat unusual character. Gilding was rarely introduced upon the jasper vases; but in this case the crowning bunch of grapes is so decorated. The pattern on the foot is also elegantly in keeping with that of the body. The bas-relief on the next example (fig. 116) gives us again Apollo and the Nine Muses; wreaths and musical instruments forming the underlying border. The upper portion of this vase bears the minutest inspection, crowned as it is by Pegasus, and adorned with P's-Ivlflgfl;-Lfl;; _Gf:::m'f:o§§;g0;wPmleafage ornament of an elegant character. The octagonal base is however in objectionable taste. The goblet-shaped vase (fig. 117) which follows—white, on a pale sea-green gr0und—is one 518 VASE: MAYER COLLECTION. CHAP. XI. of a pair in Mr. Falcke's collection. The scroll ornamentation is, as it will be observed, a repetition of that on Mr. Tulk's fine vase. Anything more beautiful than the form, colour, and ornamentation of this lovely cup cannot well be conceived as seen in a woodcut, for half of the finest effects of the ornamentation is lost in this, as in other instances, through the absence of the necessary contrast in colour.l Did our space permit, a lustre candlestick would be 1 The ordinary jasper vases rangiediin price —l;I"(_);l 1'.-£2 12 6 to £1 11 6. Vases 11% inches high were charged £3 3 each; those of 10 inches £2 2 given, but a specimen of a hand-lamp (fig. 118) of antique form must suffice. This is white on blue, and the small bas-relief representing Bellerophon watering Pegasus at the Sacred Spring is one common to countless cameos; and the oak-border, though, perhaps, critically speaking, not in keeping with the antique subject of the hasrelief, is truly elegant. The jasper body was, as already seen, early applied to the purposes of personal (Fig.ll7.) uuuwr. r.u.s oimxx..

'n wurru

Thosc of course which were richly ornamented with the finest has-relii-l'. =, as that of Apollo and the Nine.luses, or the Dancing Ilours, were clmrgod much highel'.

520 PERSONAL ORNAMENTS. CHAP. XI_ cases of every shape and kind, were articles set with, or formed wholly of the most exquisite cameos and intaglios_the setting being gold, silver, but more commonly steel. From the date of Bentley's death, or shortly after, to the close of Wedgwood's life_Which may be said to form the true period of this exquisite work in its highest degree—the number and beauty of the ornaments thus produced can hardly be conceived. Birmingham was still the great workshop for those set in steel, but much of the finest gold work was done in London by an engraver and setter named Darling. Some of the small bas-reliefs and cameos thus enshrined, seem in their groups and figures to breathe and live; an intense vitality denoting the conceptions and work of true artists, and standing out antique-like and in infinitely marked contrast to their dead and earthy representations in modern days, though struck from the old moulds or copied from the old models.

To exemplify these beautiful objects, we give a brooch (fig. 119), a snuff-box (fig. 120), a locket (fig. 121), a watchcase (fig. 122), a pair of earrings (fig. 123), an opera-glass (fig. 124), a girdlebuckle (fig. 125), a ring (fig. 126), and a pair of smellingbottles (fig. 127). The little bas-reliefs on the brooch, snuffbox, rings, seem in their figures to live. Flaxman's Cupids making their sacrifice to Hymen speak to one another and move, even whilst we look; and the Muses watering Pegasus in Helicon is still more expressive of intense vitality. This small bas-relief is one of Flaxman's masterpieces. The horse is' so instinct with life that it seems to snort and move; and the Muse standing beside it looks as though she lifted her water-bearing vessel to its lips. The lifelike attitude of the Muse who seeks to wash the foot of the immortal steed, and of the one who caresses it, are equally

remarkable. Even the water breaks into waves. The ornamental setting of this most perfect and exquisite example of Wedgwood's and Flaxman's art in combination, shows in masterly detail one of the finest borderings peculiar to the jasper ware. The nosegay cameo, framed in gold as a locket, charms by its simplicity, and on the 5:22 EARRINGS AND OPERA-GLASS. CHAD. Kl.

watch back we have the Three Graces as derived probably from an antique gem.

The ear-rings (fig. 123) are a study. The chief bas-reliefs represent Night and Morning,1 and the small figures in the """"" u.ppersections are derived from antique gems. The setting is steel. The opera-glass was that used by Queen Charlotte; the chief moulding, as also those faceted, give a rich effect, and the floral festoons add a beauty to the whole; but the female figure, though probably derived from an antique source, is elumsy and illproportioned. In the buckle still attached to the gold lace band which formed the girdle, we have another of those ornaments favoured by our great grandmothers. The setting is steel, and the little bas-reliefs 1 The latter, Aurora. meeting the Dawn. The whole subject is seen in the exquisite czuuco given in ol. I. p. 252. sents Sterne's Maria; the other a Bourbonnais Shepherd. Both are minute copies of large bas-reliefs. The next example (fig. 126) is a ring of great beauty; the subject, Jupiter.

The two smelling-bottles (fig. 127) represent a class of useful ornaments which were-very popular. In decoration they are much the same; the chief difference being in their forms and bas-reliefs.

Much has been already said and shown relative to the cameos.

BUCKLE AND RING.

The intaglios, as _regards illustration, we 524 INTAGLIUS AND CAMEOS. Cnar. XI.

have necessarily passed over; the dificulty of representing their sunk portions being insuperable to the artist, at least so far as to do them justice. Two examples we however give: one, the

tail-piece, Health is Rest;1 the other-at a later page—represents as a seal the Slave, cameo and intaglio, for the Society for the Abolition of Slavery. Speaking of the originality of his labours in this direction, Wedgwood writes to Darwin, 'I only pretend to have attempted to copy the antique forms, but not with absolute servility. I have endeavoured to preserve the style and spirit, or if you please the elegant simplicity of antique forms, & so doing to introduce all the variety I was able, & this Sir

I Vol. 11. P. 103.

Wm. Hamilton assures me I may venture to do, & that it is the true way of copying the antique. You ask ' Was any thing of consequence done in the cameo or medallion kind before you? In real stones, & in imitation of real stones in paste, or soft coloured glass, much has formerly been done, witness the Portland Vase and numberless pieces of inferior note. Bassorelievos of various been made of a warm brown earth of one colour. But of the improved kind of two or more colours, and a true porcelain texture, none were made by the ancients or attempted by the inoderns that I ever heard of till some of them began to copy my jasper cameos.'1 Such is Wedgwood's own testiniony to the truth and originality of this branch of his art, and of which, considering the vehicles he employed, the ancients had not even a conception.

Elongated picture cameos were used for a great variety of purposes. One already given (fig. 94) is full of vitality. The Cupid chasing the butterfly, the one blowing a pipe or horn, the two sporting on the ground, are no dead 1 ''edgwood to Darwin, dated from Blackpool, Lancashire, June 28, 1789.

pieces of clay, but children instinct with the artlessness and gaiety of their years. 1 The cameo on page 525 (fig. 128)-a Cupid with a floral wreath-throws his flowers in the air as though the very spirit of spring, youth, and sunshine animated his whole being. How graceful and inimitable is the whole! How typical of innocence and of a golden age! In the two cameos which succeed (figs. 129, 130) we have other specimens of these beautiful gems. The subjects, Neptune borne on the ocean on a shell, and a Watergod pouring out a river from his pitcher, are particularly worthy of attention. In another illustration already given (fig. mg' '"';.1,,,f§§.','K__"""'"' 93) we have one of those curved cameos used for insertion in articles of furniture, in boxes of all kinds, and for mounting as buckles. The design is probably one of those supplied by the three ladies of rank, Lady Diana Beauclerk, Lady Temmg 1%) mxo__smm pleton, and Miss Crew, whose fame ""'"'" it now is, that they employed their pencils in the service of their great countryman. The figure of the girl reading reminds one of a design of Stothard in its simplicity and innocence, but the child who listens is far less perfect. We also include in this section the jasper bas-relief, the Apotheosis of Virgil (fig. 131). Its date of production is uncertain, for though the chimney-piece at Longton Hall—of which it forms 1 These picture cameos, encased! Their price,as given in one of the in c 'stal, were much used as lids to foreign invoices, is £3 3 each box. smal boxes. A toothpick ease of this One would now realize twice or character is in the possession of Mr. three times that sum. Barlow. Its beauty is extraordinary. (IHAP. XI. APOTHEOSIS OF VIRGIL. 527 a part——--is referred to in 1777, there is reason to think it was not completed till some time after, as this basrelief is not named in the last Catalogue, that of 1779, published prior to Bentley's death.

Again weturn to the ornamental useful ware to give six more examples of the elaborate pains VVedgwood bestowed in this direction. This exquisite cup and saucer (figs. 132, 133), from Mr. Bohn's collection—-blue ground and white ornaments_is one of the finest specimens of decorated jasper extant.1 Every detail will bear examina 528 CUP AND SAUCER. BOHN COLLECTION. CHAP. XI.

tion. The trophies, the rams' heads, the fillets or ribbons, the floral festoons, and the medallions, all deserve the minutest inspection. The latter are in pairs;

the first represents, apparently, Bacchus in his chariot drawn by pards; the other, Orion on the dolphin. The difference in the medallions on the cup, and H _, the unique character of (Fig. la-1.) Cur. m. u1-: A::L:::::;lsrnn.-sons the ground border, be_ speak the lavish pains bestowed on this class of ornamental ware. Such cups and saucers must have been intended for preservation in a cabinet, for they are articles to contemplate, not to use.

CHAP. XI. EXAMPLES: FALCKE AND TULK COLLECTIONS. 529

The next examples (fig. 134) are of a character still more rare. The ornaments are blue, the ground white. The floral wreath round the saucer, the pensile leaves and flowers about the cup, the edging of the lid, and the flower of the water-lily crowniiig it, are most lovely. A cream cup of unusual form and decoration is the subject of the next woodcut (fig. 135). The ground is white, the floral festoon green; whilst the small bas-relief medallion is white on a blue ground. The cut succeeding shows a cup of the VOL. II. M M 530 FINAL SPECIMENS. CRAP. XI. choicest beauty (fig. 136). The bas-relief is a triumphal procession of Cupids, from a design by Flaxman. The ground is a blue of the rarest tint, and brings to the recollection the fine colouring of Dresden and Sevres. It is figured in the last edition of the Catalogue published during (m_'36_) cm am AND "M VVedgwood's lifetime. The last ¢M" =R——'"""=-F-"-"81 and final example (fig. 137) of these beautiful productions—white on blue—has some features in common with specimens already given.

It will be observed that the borderings of the jasper

Cnsr. XI. JASPER BORDERINGS. 531

ware are almost as varied as those on the enamelled; but there is this difference, the former are more reticulated in their character, in order A to show the colour of the ground beneath; whereas the latter are rather the superinduction of hightoned tints upon lower ones,_ for the purpose of contrast. The most beautiful and original amongst i the jasper

borders is that of the ribbon,which is said to have been taken from a sketch by Flaxman. We givehere a sectional example (fig. 138), in order that the exceeding beauty of thisborderingmay be more distinctly seen. The one which precedes it is of still greater rarity, it forming theborder of apair of fruit baskets.1 Many other examples might be given, but these (Fig. 138.) JASPER nonuna nuumus.

_' In the possession of the writer. The ground is dark blue, with an elegant. outer basket-work of white and yellow. 532 MERCURY AND SHAKESPEARE. CHAP. XI.

To the same period, 1786-1795, may also be assigned the highest productions i11 many other classes of ornamental ware. The crystalline jasper vases and other articles in that body had dropped apparently much into abeyance, but the Etruscan painted vases were still sought for as masterpieces of their kind. In the black Egyptian or basaltes, the busts, plaques, and some of the bas-reliefs, were become, for size and perfection, absolute. This bust of Mercury (fig. 139) from Mr. Faleke's collection, and the plaque or large medallion of Shakespeare (fig. 140) from that of Mr. De la Rue, justify this high encomium. Anything more perfect or full of expression than either

CHAP. XI. FURTHER IMPROVEMENTS. 638

was never produced. The Mercury is from a model by Flaxman, and was probably one of the many sent by him from Rome. The large medallion of Shakespeare is equally a lTll..terpiece; for, if idealised, we at least feel that we have before us a countenance worthy of our king of poets. The improvements in the cane-ware, strawcolour ware, and black ware_-decorated with red ornaments--were by this period also marked; as this straw-(Fig-14' "WY Cvwmw W-E, RH» "M1

' In this section, in which' con-I very beautiful open-worked and tiiiuous improvements in ornamental i highly glazed cruet-stand, as also a ware have been referred to, many, red teapot of palm-leaf form, with articles of a distinctly useful chara.c-i white flowers in relief, both the proter might have been specified had; petty of H. G. Bohn, F,sq. , the SPILCC permitted. Amongst others. a eminent connoisseur. They are re 534 FOREIGN IMPOSTS. CRAP. XI.

From a very early period, Wedgwood had naturally taken the deepest interest in all those questions which bore a political or commercial relation to the manufacture and trade in pottery. At various periods throughout 1772 and 1773, we find him and Bentley in negotiation, through Lord Gower, with the Lords of Trade. as to the prohibition of, and duty upon, ware imported to France. Their representation of the injury efiected by these restrictions was courteously listened to, and hopes were for a time entertained that by their means redress would be afforded; but the war with that country, consequent on our quarrel with America, intervened, and the restrictions, so far as the majority of the continental states could enforce them, became more grievous than ever. In 1775, Lord Gower greatly aided the potters in their contest with Champion; and in the succeeding year he rendered essential service in respect to lower duties on Saxonporcelain. At the beginning of the year, Lord North had consulted the chief manufacturers in Staffordshire on the question of a freer trade to continental states. ' We are much obliged to L"l North for his attention to our manufactory & for his condescendtion in asking our opinion,' wrote Wedgwood to Bentley.

My sentiments perfectly coincide with those you have delivered to the Treasury, & I hope the rest of our brethren will agree with us. I should be a.sham'd to feel anything like a fear in having a. freer intercourse open'd between Great Britain & all the Potteries in the World—we enjoying a. like liberty of exporting our manufactures to continental states.'

But the wishes of the minister and the manufacturers were one thing; realisation another. The rulers of most of niarkable examples of Wedgwood's (Mr. Bohn an engraving of the emetpgrsistent efforts to improve and y stand will subsequently appear.

autify the commonest articles for ' VedgwoodtoBent-ley, February daily use. Through the kindness of 3, 1776. _ _'_-A

CHAP. XI. DEMAND IN FOREIGN MARKETS. 535 the continental states were dazzled by the fallacious principle of forcing home-manufactures by premiums, and by imposing duties on those of other countries, and concessions were rarely made.1 Yet, in spite of these retarding circumstances, the exports of earthenware steadily increased.

In a conversation with Lti Gower as to improvements in trade (again wrote Wedgwood to Bentley) I told his Lordship that the sale of our manufacture had greatly increased of late in Germany, Russia, &c., 8.? our own business continued good notwithstanding so many prohibitions & high duties had been laid upon it abroad, & believed the demand for it in foreign markets under all these disadvantages was owing to its being the best & cheapest pottery ware in Europe, & that we had no objection as potters to a free trade with all the world except the East Indies.2 were prohibited, and ten per cent. 1 was laid by the King of Prussia upon their going into Dantzic; besides another very high duty on the same duty in their way to Poland. In the Austrian Netherlands English manufacturers paid fourpence per pound weight inc uding the packages, which was nearly three times the value of the goods. The Germans were also at this date establishing manufactories of earthenware in order to compete with us in the English markets. In Russia the duty was forty per cent., in spite of which the exports of English ware were very large. In Holland the demand was large thouvh the duty was high. In Spain the duty from the period of the war was high, yet imports from England were considerable, and a large demand for goods, includin those highlv finished, existed in urkev, the East Indies, and Italy. In Sweden and Denmark they, as also in Portugal, were rohibited; in France likewise, t ough useful earthenware as well as porcelain of French manufacture might be imported into this country upon pay. ment of a certain du-

ty.

" 'edgwood to Bentley, August 22, 1777.

From Wedgwood's answer to one question—that relative to the then existing superiority of British earthenware—there seemstobe truth after all in the old tradition that he was made Her Majesty's potter in 1763, and this after the resentation of a service of some kin in his improved cream ware. The occasion was probably the birth of Prince Frederick, afterwards Dukeof York, June 17, 1763. 'The Revolution in our favour was brought about by the invention of several new species of earthenware, never made before in this or any other country, and is greatly promoted since by the skill and ingenuity of those concerned in this business cooperating with the cheapness and excellence of the useful sorts and by the encouragement received since the year 1763 from the patronage of their Majesties and the public.' In another pp, er en-. dorsed 'Answers from the i iinufao turers of earthenware in Stafford 536 TRADE YVITH IRELAND. CRAP. XI.

Such, generally speaking, were the opinions of the Staffordshire potters in relation to continental states, because they well knew that, in order to secure the export on a sufficiently remunerative scale of their own productions, they must make like concessions in relation to the manufacturing products of those they Wished to secure. as customers. Even with respect to Ireland, they desired the same freedom of interchange, provided the fiscal burdens in either country were equalised; for it had to be considered that the English manufacturer was heavily taxed, and the manufacturer in Ireland hardly at all.

It is not known what part the master Potters took in the concessions made in 1780 by the English Government, in respect to the foreign and colonial tradejof Ireland, or if they joined with those who treated the removal of certain prohibitory duties upon some of the staple articles of Irish manufacture as an invasion of their vested rights. We are only certain that the general opposition brought to bear against the Act passed at that date rendered it in fact a dead letter; and when, five years later, Pitt, with enlightened judgment, sought—though prematurely—to adjust the commercial relations of the two countries on an equitable footing, the old antagonism sprung _ anew into life and the manufacturers of northern Staffordshire renewed with vigour their former contest, and armed with their old plea-inequality of taxation—and consequently a higher rate of productive cost. Abstractedly considered, shire': 'To this manufacture (the comparatively barren one, and Her cream ware) on its first a pearance Majesty's Potter held in little rethe Queen graciously con escended membrance, for Miss Chetwynd in to give her name and atronage, 1767 to have applied, as we have commanding it to be calle Queen s-seen she did, to a. stranger in Newware, and at the same time rewarded castle for a Roval tea.-service, in the inventor with the honourable stead of giving 'the order direct to distinction of Her Majesty's Potter. ' 'edgwood. This distinction must have been a I

O om». XI. POPULAR IGNORANCE. 531

Pitt's views of commercial policy were just and sound; but they were far in advance of general opinion, and hope lessly impracticable in the face of two hostile legislatures, and two nationalities opposed to each other through the force of bad laws and years of misgovernment. On the other hand, the manufacturers, though patriotic and pains taking, were almost to a man as ignorant of the true principles of commercial freedom, as of those which govern the rise and continuance of great staples of industry. The wiser of them saw in the union of the two countries and the rule of one legislature, the first step to the solution of these great difliculties; but they were scared by a phantom of their own creating, when they fancied that the manufacture of iron or earthenware or like staples would be transported, through the agency of commercial treaties, from one country to the other.

In these mixed opinions Wedgwood, Boulton, Watt, and many others shared;

and the former, in spite of his visibly declining health, threw himself into the contest with an energy and ability that it is astonishing to contemplate, even at this day. He was in fact the life and soul of the great commercial movement against the Irish Propositions. Viewed by the light of experience, and a sounder knowledge of the natural laws which govern production and commercial exchanges, we can but admire his energetic patriotism, though utterly dissenting from the principles on which it rested. Restriction had been the creed of Englishmen for generations; and thus even the man whose opinions relative to art had all the freedom of nature, shared, with nine-tenths of his countrymen, in errors yet unexploded.

As early as 1784, Pitt had under consideration his scheme for giving to Ireland unlimited commercial advantages; and, in January 1785, the Eleven Resolutions framed by himself and his colleagues were transmitted to Dublin. Early in February they were laid before the Irish Parliament, and on the 22nd of the same month before that of England. But, prior to this, Wedgwood, ever watchful where the interests of his country and its manufactures were concerned, had conferred with his friends in Manchester, Birmingham, Bristol, and elsewhere. He visited town, accompanied by one of his sons and Chisholm, and took spacious and handsome rooms at 10 Great George Street, Westminster; and, two days previous to the Resolutions being laid before the House, he gave evidence to a Committee of the Privy Council, to which the duties and powers of the Lords Commissioners of Trade and Plantations had been transferred in 1782. After stating that the export of earthenware to Ireland had steadily increased; that the cost of sending it thither from the Stafibrdshire potteries was 792-per eent.; that the duty upon ware exported to Ireland was 15 per cent.; and that a pottery for making cream-ware had been established in Dublin in 1774, though soon given up, he came to the chief point of his evidence, that in answer to the question— If British Potteries would have reason

to fear a competition from Irish Potteries, were such established? ' I certainly apprehend,' was his answer, ' that there might be danger of a competition in time, in their own and every foreign market. I should think we were safer if earthenware was allowed to be imported free of all duties into both countries, because the Irish would not have then so much encouragement to begin to set up Potteries, or to establish them to any

CRAP. XI. RESTRICTION AND FREE TRADE. 539 extent." In this reply lay the whole weight of the argument, so far as the earthenware trade was concerned. The Potters were willing to compete with Ireland on the principles of free trade. But, fettered by heavy fiscal burdens, and fearful as they were of further imposts, they were unwilling to trust to the chance of the establishment or non-establishment of Potteries in a country where taxation scarcely existed and labour was cheap. They presumed that, because glass houses had been established and were flourishing since a duty had been laid on English glass, so also the same process would follow with respect to pottery; but the experience of near a century has proved the fallacy of these opinions. ' The two cases were wholly different. Glass can be made almost anywhere, but the production of pottery depends upon immediate sources of coal, if not of clay; and, though possessing some of the materials within her area, Ireland even at this day has but one pottery, and that recently established for small ornamental articles.

Two days after this examination, we find Wedgwood hurrying down again into Staflbrdshire, and on the way we hear first of the Chamber of Manufactures. He writes thus to Boulton, who, also probably examined by the Committee of the Privy Council, stays in London:—

I go by Birmingham as your desired & will endeavour to see Mr. Garbett & one or two more at the Hotel. I mean to recommend to them the measure of a Committee of Delegates from all the manufacturing places in England & Scotland to

' Evidence inthe CouncilChamber, ' According to Mr. YVedgwood it was Whitehall February 19, 1785. Mr. re rinted in the General Advertiser. Josiah Vviedgwood, Dele ate from T c files we have been able to conthe Staffordshire Potters. nprinted I suit are imperfect, the only evidence Mayer MSS. This evidence 18 most extant being that of Mr. Robert Peel dillicult to procure. Not a notice of on the cotton trade. it appears in the Lords' Journals., 540 CHAMBER OF MANUFACTURERS. CRAP. XI.

meet & sit in London all the time the Irish commercial affairs _ are pending. This strikes me as a measure which may be productive of very beneficial affects, principally in forming and cementing a commercial band which may be of great use upon others as well as the present occasion. If this is approved of, I submit it to you Gentlemen who are already upon the spot, whether it would not be proper to apply to the various country connections in town for them to write to their friends. Perhaps a printed letter from the delegates already in town recommending such a measure after stating the necessity, & might be proper.... Consult L'1 Sheffield, he will give you able advice & assistance.'

From this proposal sprung the celebrated Chamber of Manufacturers, which formed so important a feature in the great commercial contests of that period; and for this it was that Flaxman made a drawing of arms. The idea of an institution of this character could have been no new one to men like Wedgwood, Boulton, Thomas Walker of Manchester, John Wilkinson the ironmaster, and many others; for, to say nothing of the old Chambers of Commerce, of which-they must have heard, they had been accustomed to occasionally meet in their respective centres of industry for the purpose of deliberation on important commercial questions. The idea was therefore at once realised. The delegates then in London met at the George and Vulture Tavern, Cornhill; rules were proposed and drawn up by Chisholm; a large room was hired at 38 Fenchurch Street. Mr. Nicholson,

who had been previously employed by Mr. Wedgwood in Amsterdam, was appointed secretary. The Chamber was to consist of president, vice-presidents, chairman of committees, delegates, and members. The subscriptions, £1 1 a year, or

I ' Wledgwood to Boulton, dated from Maidenhead, February:21. 1785. Soho MSi.

Cnsr. XI. ITS CONSTITUTION. 541 a donation of £10, gave a vote. Sir Herbert Mackworth, M.P., was induced to become president, and the chairman of committee was the most important delegate upon the spot-—Wedgwood, Boulton, Walker, or Wilkinson, as the case might be. Thus, with a central point of action, the movement increased in force; and, through the medium of the Chamber, public meetings were held at the London Tavern, the Crown and Anchor, and elsewhere; papers and resolutions were printed and circulated, delegates were summoned, witnesses examined, and the chiefs of Opposition were appealed to. But the constitution of a General Chamber in no way relieved Wedgwood of the dead weight of business and responsibility. Many of the delegates were unpractical, sluggish, or soon wearied; and he had to appeal to their patriotism again and again. He had to discover and open new sources of information, to overlook ill-digested statements, or alter those which were not rigidly true. He had to bear censure, and he did not escape calumny.1 He had to confer with ministers, and consult the members of Opposition. Ve find Dr.

' "Wedgwood and other of the ' whole, and they had waited with no del-egateswere censuredbecause they small anxiety for alteration of the did not petition againsl: thebReso-, objectio'rln;lbledplarts of atlhe liesolip lutions as soon as t ey ecame tions. ' e e egat/as so t oug t known; as also because they did not J that when the Resolutions were so upon their examination before the ' modified they would be held forth Committee of the Pnvy Council. for their consideration and approba-make known all those facts and 1 tion or the contrary/—Abstract of reasons

which they afterwards paper, March 19, 1785. Mayer MSS. brought in evidence against the Irish i n a public appeal made at a later Resolutions. It was also said that date, the Committee of the Chamber the delegates joined with the oppo-. of Manufactures spoke of the nesition more upon factions rinciples. glc-ct of their private affairs, and of than from apprehension 0 any real. injury to their health incurred by danger of the Irish Resolutions pass-' their public labours. The public ing into a law. Vedgwood replied i had not treated the Chamber well; generally to these charges by saying and _in Ireland they were accused of 'That the delegates thought the unkindness to the sister kingdom, Resolutions were so far binding u n and of undue partiality to their own the British House of Commons, 1; at interests. they could not alter one without the served and pre-occupied minister, not a word on art even closing those on politics; but there were times and seasons when Pitt's simple and unostentatious orders were sent to

' The result of one of Vedgwuod's interviews with Dr. Pretyman in the absence of Pitt led to misstatements which greatly annoyed him. His conduct was marked with great.

dignity, and I'ret_vman's much' the contrary. An account of the matter, written by Vedgwood himself, was published by his friend Almon in the columns of the General Advertiser.

CRAP. XI. MEMBERS OF THE OPPOSITION. 543

Greek Street. From his childhood, Wedgwood's works had been before him—for his mother, Lady Chatham, was one of the great potter's earliest patrons_and we have seen how beautiful was the dessert-service he had had enamelled for her-the grape pattern _with frui_t blushing purple, the tendrils and leaves dressed in green and gold. The adornment of this exquisite service had been a labour of taste and inclination; for Wedgwood profoundly venerated Chatham, knowing as he did-as all Englishmen do-what the great statesman had been to England in her hour of peril. There were interviews, too, with the Duke of Portland, his Grace occasionally calling upon Wedgwood in Great George Street. By the chiefs of Opposition he was still better known-Fox, Lord Shefiield, Mr. Eden, Sir Charles Grey, Sheridan, and many others visiting him or inviting him to dinner. Ever ready to mingle the graces with the graver duties of life, Fox on one occasion introduces Lady Diana Beauclerk to Wedgwood by sending some of her beautiful drawings, Of these the latter writes, with compliments:_

A thousand thanks for the beautiful drawings he has received, & will be much obliged to Mr. Fox, if he will be so good to signify to Lady Diana Beauclerk how much he esteems himself indebted for this flattering mark of her Ladyship's notice. He has sent a few bas-reliefs, which were modelled from some beautiful cut Indian paper which Lady Templeton favoured him with— jnst to shew the manner in which he will attempt to copy the drawings he is now honoured with——Mr. Fox is desired to dispose of the bas-reliefs ashe thinks proper——Mr. V. has other obligations to Mr. Fox's kind partiality which he will ever remember with grafitude—Nor can the manufacturers of G. Britain ever forget what they owe to his very able & spirited exertions in their favour.' '

' Wedgwood to the Right. Hon. C. J. Fox, dated Great George Street, July 23, I785. Mayer MSS.

544 MR. EDEN. CHAP. XI.

The letters to Lord Carlisle which Mr.Eden had published in November 1779, first made his name familiar to Wedgwood; and subsequent commissions for earthenware and cameos led to correspondence, and this to personal knowledge. As chairman of the Committee appointed in 1784 to enquire into the illicit practices used in defrauding the revenue, Mr. Eden had several conferences with Wedgwood; and now the Irish Propositions were laid before Parliament, the former, as a member of the Opposition, took active measures in support of the views held by the delegates. His opinions were in unison. He

writes in one of his numerous letters to Wedgwood:

You observe it is now admitted by Mr. Pitt, that the countervailing duty described in the fifth Proposition is not to be the sum of the original dut-y estimated by weight or by measure—— but a sum adequate to the duties paid on the material of manufacture-I think it appeared yesterday, but I am sure it may be shewn by able men in different branches of manufacture, that the notion of an adequate couvztervttiliizg duty is impossible to be reduced to practice in many articles of manufacture, and the result will be what appears in other parts and views of the business, that it is idle and visionary to place on the same commercial ground two neighbouring nations, when the one is highly taxed, and the other comparatively without taxes. It , might be happy enough for both the nations to form a national union of Government and Taxation; but this union of advantages without any union of burthen is stark nonsense—-And the worst part of it is, that at the same time you establish so silly a system, you for ever preclude the establishment of the wise and beneticial system.'

On the grounds thus explained by Mr. Eden, as also on others, the General Chamber of Manufacturers had commenced their opposition to the Government measure.

1 Mr. Eden to Vedgwood, dated Parliament Street, April 16, 1785. Mayer MSS.

CHAP. XI. MEETINGS, PETITIONS, AND DELEGATES. 54-5

Their principle was still to retain Ireland invcommercial subordination to this country; nor would they allow that the Propositions at least intended a participation and community of benefits, and the aggregate interests of the empire. Meetings were held, petitions were presentedthe first being those from Manchester, Birmingham, and the Potteries_witnesses were examined, and counsel heard, at the bar of the House of Commons.1 It was a party question, a great Whig question; and as such it was warmly supported by the Opposition. But, generally speaking, the pub-

lic, and indeed some of the great traders and manufacturers, were indifferent to the outcry. Many of the ironmasters, soapmakers, t-anners, sugarboilers, and others, would not trouble themselves to send delegates: this, numerically speaking, not from enlightened motives, but because they were ignorant and selfish. Wedgwood was constantly urging Boulton to rouse the ironmasters to a sense of their duty. The Government wished to settle the matter; the General Chamber of Manufacturers to gain time. Two months were thus passed. Every resolution was contested; some more vehemently than others. Amendment succeeded amendment. The second and most important Proposition, by which Ireland was to be admitted to a participation on equal terms with Great Britain in the commerce of the world, was now qualified by excepting the trade with India; and the fourth Resolution, relative to duties on the manufacture of either country, was amended by the introduction of a new term into the compact, which provided that the laws for regulating trade and navigation should be the same in both kingdoms; and that such laws and regulations should be 1 The celebrated Erskine was their leader. VOL. II. N X 546 DEBATES ON THE IRISH PROPOSITION. CRAP. XI.

framed by the Parliament of Great Britain, and be ratified by the Parliament of Ireland. Both these amendments were adverse to the interests of Ireland. By the one she was excluded from the most lucrative branch of British commerce; by the second her independence was compromised, for her Parliament was denied the initiative of any laws affecting trade and commerce. The eleven original Resolutions became in their amended form twenty. Yet the commercial interest was still unsatisfied. It was not to be propitiated with a less concession than legislative supremacy to Great Britain in matters of trade and commerce. The amended Resolutions were submitted to the British House. of Commons on the 12th of May, but before this many of the delegates had returned home, or were away on their own business-Boulton amongst others. Watt pressed for his return; Garbett secretly urged it. Watt grew testy. When asked merely to attend a meeting in Birmingham, he would promise, though, as Garbett said, in a manner ' extremely out of temper.' Yet he loved to grumble about the supineness of manufacturers and the heaviness of taxation. ' The only prospect of relief,' he Writes to Wedgwood, after saying that people ought to go without luxuries in order to compel a withdrawal of taxes, ' seems to lie in this, that as everything has its climax, or maximum, we seem to be fast approaching first to the maximum of taxes, & I hope still faster to the maximum of national patience; when matters are at the worst they must mend. ' 1

Ifa thousand matters awaited Boulton's return,his steamengines at Soho and his mining business at Chacewater, so

' Watt to Wedgwood, July 14, 1785. Mayer MSS. ""9 learn from this letter that Boulton was about to set out for Cornwall and stay six weeks. '

CRAP. XI. WEDGWOOD'S UNTIRING ENERGY. 547 also did Etruria want its master; but Wedgwood stood foremost and faithful to the end. 'VVe all know,' he writes to Boulton, 'that any house may be brought to remove, if those who made it will come forward as they ought to do. For myself I have only one plain simple line of conduct to pursue. I have promised those who sent me hither to do my best to prevent the Irish Resolutions passing into a law. I have done so hitherto & will continue in the same, though I am even left to do alone. The loss our cause sustained when you left us will not easily be retrieved.' 1 Again and again he urged the iron-masters to shake off their supineness. He himself appealed to many of the traders in London, yet they sent no delegates. 'The principal glover,' he says, 'has a contract under government and does not appear. The button-maker makes buttons for his Majesty & therefore he is tied fast to his Majesty's minister's button-hole. In short the minister has found so many button and loop holes to fasten them to himself, that few of the prin-

ciple manufacturers are left at liberty to serve their country.' Garbett, as usual, was lukewarm. Crawshay, the great iron-master, favoured the Resolutions. Pitt, as Wedgwood said, was hurrying on the business. No time was to be lost. He sent an express for his friend John Wilkinson —' for if the Resolutions have passed by the time you arrive '_is his message-' you will catch the Bill in the House of Lords.' The General Chamber redoubled its exertions. It took the opinion of Mr. Sergeant Hill on the question of Patents, which had been introduced into the amended Resolutions. It sought for fresh petitions. Amongst those sent was one from the Committee of 1 Vedgwood to Boulton, May 1, 1785. S0110 MSS.

548 IRISH AGENCIES. CRAP. XI.

Potters, held at the Swan, Hanley, June 7, 1785. Yet these efforts were in vain. The twenty Resolutions passed through the Commons. Then came the hope that they would not pass the House of Lords, or, doing so, would not be accepted by the Irish people. The last was the case. After fierce debates, the Bill only passed the Irish House of Commons by a majority of nineteen. Such a victory was no other than a defeat. The Government relinquished the bill, and the manufacturers of this country were free from a competition they dreaded, and so erroneously. The defeat of this measure to free Ireland from the commercial restrictions so cruelly imposed upon her since the Restoration was not without effects of a most beneficial character. The contest awakened attention to commercial rights and duties; and the result made clear to the apprehension of both the ministry and the governing classes that England and Ireland must be united for an unfettered commerce to flourish between them. Wedgwood lost largely by the part he took against the Irish Resolutions. His indirect trade may have not suffered so much; but the agencies known to be his perished literally for some years. Esau Clarke, who had succeeded Brock in the Dublin business, could sell no goods. 'Many of the people of quality that formerly dealt with me,' he wrote, ' will

buy no more on account of your opposing the Irish Propositions, and many others will not buy from me because I cannot sell as cheap as the other houses.'1 'One nobleman said that if more of Wedgwood's ware came to Ireland, if the public did not break them he would. ' Clarke then entreats his employer to take the ornamental stock ofl' his hands, it consisting of 'black 1 Clarke of Dublin to VVedgwood, August 29, 1786.

griflin candlestieks, Tripods, marble and gold vases, cameodesigns, tea pots, sugar basins, &c.'1

This period of severe mental and bodily labour was varied by artistic business and cheered by the courtesy of friends. Mr. Wedgwood visited the studios of Stubbs and Fuseli, and the uteliers of Flaxman, Wyatt, and Westmacott. He dined with Lord Sheflield and others of the nobility, and occasionally spent a day at Beckenham with Mr. Eden. He went to Hampstead to see Mrs. Barbauld, who had then a house in Well Walk; and to Turnham Green, to pay Ralph Grilfith a visit. Early in June, Dr. and Mrs. Darwin were in town, and joined him on several occasions; and, on the 23rd of the same month, he turned his face towards home. Failing to see Mr. Eden to bid him farewell, he wrote and sent some small has-reliefs ' to an amiable little group he had the pleasure of seeing at Beckenham." Upon reaching Etruria, he recruited himself with a brief tour in Wales, and by a visit to Archdeacon Clive?' His absence was short, for his children were at home. His son John had stayed at Warrington Academy but a few terms, for dissensions amongst the trustees and bad management were hastening the end of that once noble institution. He had afterwards joined his brother Josiah in Edinburgh, and studied there with him some time. But both had now returned, and Tom-at this date a lad verging upon sixteen-needed to be sent nowhere for discipline or study, for he was always poring over books or else employed in the laboratory 1 Clarke of Dublin to Vedgwood, wood's return, he received the thanks November 5, 1786.

Mayer MSS. ' of the Birmingham Commercial

' They were modelled from cut-' Committee for his ability and exertings in paper by Lady Templeton. tions in favour of the manufactures Nos. 49, 50, 51, 53. of the country.

3 A few days after Mr. Wedg 550 FOREIGN SPIES. CRAP. XI. with his father's secretary, Chisholm. His passion for abstract studies was unbounded. Even thus early he was busy with 'Playfair's Chronology,' and a little later he was absorbed in Hartley's work on 'Man' and Edwards on ' Free-will.' Chisholm at this time was not only secretary but schoolmaster.' We learn this from Wedgwood himself. Dr. Austen of Oxford had applied, through Whitehurst of Derby, for Chisholm's services for a month, in order to assist him in practical chemistry. ' I should gladly comply,' writes Vedgwood to the Oxford doctor, 'if I could do it with convenience to myself. But having six children at home & Mr. C. being their only master in some branches of their education you will be convinced at once that 1 am constrained to deny myself the pleasure of complying with this request.'1 In the month succeeding, he was in correspondence with Mr. Nicholson, the Secretary of the Chamber of Manufacturers, on business relative to the spy system on trade, then so prevalent. Watt and some other Birmingham manufacturers had informed him ' of there being three different sets of spies upon our machines and manufactures now in England, from three different nations.' More were soon afterwards discovered, and Wedgwood considered it the duty of the Chamber to put the manufacturers upon their guard against these dangerous guests; both generally by public advertisement in the papers and particularly by private letters to friends in correspondence with the Chamber.

The foreign gentry (he tells Nicholson) have some of them exhibited the greatest show of impudence ever known upon like occasions. For having been refused admittance by one clerk, they have come again when he has been absent, and almost forced their way to the machines they wanted to see.

1 'edgwood to Dr. Austen, September 23, 1785.

CHAP. XI. REMEDIES PROPOSED. ' 551

In another instance having been turned out.of one door, they have waited an opportunity of entering in under diflerent pretenees at another. Sometimes they pretend to he possessed of improvements to the machines they want to take drawings or models of. At others they procure recommendations from gentlemen who are not aware of their intentions, or even bring those gentlemen themselves with them, when they can prevail upon them so far; and in short use every possible means to accomplish the purposes they came hither for. And therefore no time should be lost, nor any dilligence spared on our part to prevent them.1

Some of these me11 were ultimately taken up; and means were used to procure the names of those foreign manufacturers who were likely to employ such agents, or encourage the emigration of workmen. Whilst, so little were the rights of labour then understood, it was proposed to the several provincial Chambers or Committees of Commerce, to introduce a clause into their respective rules to the effect that the Minister of State be applied to to grant his permission to postmasters to open the letters of such suspected persons. Four years later, a still more elaborate system of espionage was discovered. The searcher at the Custom House, London, came upon five large chests of suspicious character. Upon being opened, they were found to contain tools and raw materials in different stages of manufacture. With these was included a large bound manuscript book filled with drawings and plans of different machines and engines, with a full account of each written in the Danish or German language. One chest had special reference to the manufacture of pottery, and contained not only ware in every stage of preparation, but the substances employed for glazing and colour

' Wedgwood to Nicholson, dated from Stone, October 25, 1785.

552 LJUNGBERG THE DANE. CRAP. XI. ing it. The owner was found to be a Dane named Ljungberg, who had been in this country thirteen or fourteen years, and all that time had been employed in obtaining every available manufacturing secret he could. He had been in the Potteries some weeks; but, detected in the fact of bribing workmen to procure him drawings of the kilns, &c., he suddenly deeamped for fear of being arrested. Upon the chests seized at the Custom House being traced to their ownership, Mr. Byerley and Mr. Neale, at Mr. Wedgwood's request, inspected that containing specimens and materials of pottery, and upon their report a Meeting of Potters was held at Etruria Inn, August 24, 1789. At this it was resolved, that the manufacturers of the districts Ljungberg had visited should petition the Commissioners of Customs to have the things destroyed.- Boulton, Garbett, Walker, and other influential men, were very active in this business. A Committee of Manufacturers from the districts the Dane had visited were appointed to examine the chests; and Garbett made a report to the Government through the official channel of Mr. Rose and Mr. Stiles. On the other hand, Ljungberg had apparently powerful friends, and through them made strong appeals to have his goods restored. The result is unknown. But the whole business made.Wedgwo0d, Boulton, and many others still more ehary of showing their manufactories, especially to foreigners. Even when these came prepared with weighty letters of introduction, Wedgwood habitually declined to show his works. And in special cases of danger——as where the visitor had a ready pencil, a keen eye, and sound judgment—he would, if he had to speed them to Soho, give Boulton premonitory warning. A case in point was the visit of the President de Virley, President of the

CRAP. XI. TRADE WITH FRANCE. 553

Parliament of Dijon, who brought a letter of introduction from Sir Joseph Banks.

In December, Wedgwood was supplying, through Mr. Eden, Pitt with valuable information relative to the trade between this country and France. In the Treaty of Peace concluded between the two countries in 1783,1 it had been stipulated that commissioners should be appointed to make the necessary arrangements; and Pitt employed the Parliamentary recess in maturing this and another measure of great utility—that relating to the consolidation of various duties of excise and customs. These sound principles of unrestricted national trade, which were thus practically attempted during the first four years of his administration, had long been a. necessity, both for the increase of revenue and reciprocal international demand. It began to be seen that the 'war of material interests must cease, and that a trade with twenty-four millions of people, possessing many valuable commodities which we stood in need of—and, on the other hand, wanting many articles which we manufactured——was likely to be an object of greater importance to a manufacturing and commercial people than a trade with any nation of inferior population and opulence. Mr. Pitt's scheme therefore embraced the repeal, with some few exceptions, of prohibitory duties on the products of either country; whilst a moderate tariff, mostly for revenue purposes, was to be paid on certain commodities, as on porcelain, earthenware, and pottery, an ad valorem duty of 12 per cent. reciprocally.

1 In this year the Staflbidshire I factures taken into consideration in potters, throu h the instrumentality l the Treaties of Commerce to be negoof Wedgwood, petitioned Fox and tinted.

Sir Grey Cooper to have their manu-
' 554 PROPOSED COMMERCIAL TREATY. CRAP. XI.

Wedgwood, Boulton, Watt, and some others, whose views in relation to foreign trade were as free and enlightened as those relative to commerce nearer home were narrowed by the dread of manufacturing competition, regarded the proposed Commercial Treaty in the most favourable light; and their influence and example were, there can be

little doubt, efficacious in reconciling large numbers of manufacturers and traders to the measure. Wedgwood's cream-ware and enamelled and ornamental ware, were, in the face of prohibitive duties, well known in France; and many dealers had, since 1783, impatiently awaited the adjustment of the Treaty.1 Most of the ambassadors from the English court to that of Versailles had carried over beautiful specimens of ornamental ware; it was favoured by the Princesses, by the Cardinals, and high noblesse; and the busts and cameo medallions of the kings of France, as also of its illustrious men and Women, had added to this popularity.

Parliament met on the 24th of January, and, on the 14th of February, Wedgwood, who had been summoned to attend the Committee of the Lords of Council, set out on his way to London. At Birmingham he found the Commercial Committee of that place sitting upon the letters they had received, and that Boulton and Garbett had accepted the delegateship. Walker of Manchester refused to attend, because the Lords of Council would not first send down the purport of their questions, to be discussed in a select committee at Manchester; and other delegates were chosen. The evidence which Vi/edgwood and his friends gave on this occasion partook of much of the

' Amongst others was Charles chant, of Manchester. August 1784. Chappuis, of Versailles. He had Mayer MSS. been clerk to Mr. Radcliffe, mer

CIIAP. XI. MR. EDEN'S APPOINTMENT. 655 same character of that given in relation to the Irish Propositions, with the exception that it related to an export trade with a foreign country. A considerable degree of caution was required in answering these questions, as manufacturers, generally speaking, were averse that Government should become acquainted with the full extent of their production and trade.1 Wedgwood was in daily intercourse with Mr. Eden, who, as it is well known, had displeased his party by accepting Mr. Pitt's proposal of proceeding to France as Envoy Extraordinary and Minister

Plenipotentiary to negotiate the Treaty of Coin merce. He refers to this matter in a letter to Walker:

L'1 Sheflield invited me to his table twice, where I had the honour of meeting Ld North & L'l Loughborough, Mr. Ashley, Mr. Guttridge, & Mr. Bell. Ld North is you know very excellent company & the little time I could pass with them passed in the most agreeable manner but it was Committee night at the Chamber, & as President I thought it might be my duty to attend & therefore stole away at an early hour. Nothing was said about Mr. Eden—neither did the Duke of Portland mention him to me when I waited upon his Grace. Ld Shefield is the only one of Mr. Eden's old friends who talks of him freely to me. He tells the others that they are too violent & that he cannot give up an old friend all at once.

Yet in spite of this party feeling, Mr. Eden's appointment gave general satisfaction,''' for all were convinced

' At a later date Wedgwood, upon I not wonder if they took the summary principle, refused Lord Auckland details of this character. ' The increase in our trade,' he writes, ' may be 25 fold in the last 80 years. But this is mere conjecture & could not be well ascertained without going to the books of the respective manufacturers. If after this examination on in art any disagreeable circumstiihdias should arise betwixt government and this manufacture though they had in reality no relation the one to the other I should

Birmin ham method with me and my wor s. This is a dilemma I am sure you would not wish me to risk.' —Wedgwood to Lord Auckland, Jan. 28, 1792.

' Boulton, in one of his letters to Wedgwood, gives ex ression to this general feeling. ' Government had left the appointment of a Commission to settle a Treaty of Commerce to me, I should have fixed upon Mr. Eden, feeling myself as a member of the General Chamber as a manufacturer and a man who despises party. Great ains have been taken ylittle minde men to clothe the manufacturers with party coloured robes but I am persuaded no reflections they can make will change the 556 GENERAL BUSINESS OF THE CHAMBER. CRAP. XI. that for once the right man was in his right place. He proceeded to Paris early in April, and at once entered upon the diflicult business of the Treaty.

From the first, Wedgwood's perplexities and difiiculties with respect to the General Chamber had been great— these were now increased by dissensions amongst the delegates. Some were lukewarm and would not attend except when necessity compelled; and there was a general feeling that something was wanting to give the Chamber stability in the eyes of the public. A Charter was spoken of; next an Act of Parliament. With either it would seem to have some existence; as it stood it was a Chamber, but, as its opponents said, ' a self-delegated one.' Besides the business of the Commercial Treaty, it had at this period under consideration the smuggling of wool, and the best means of preventing it. Whilst staying at Matlock the preceding autumn, Wedgwood had had the felicity of making Arkwright and Sir Joseph Banks known to each other; and as both were interested in improvements in the spinning, as also in the general trade in wool, a correspondence ensued both with Wedgwood and the west country dealers and manufacturers.

Art, too, had its share in these multifarious duties. Wedgwood, who, as we shall see in the next chapter, had opened negotiations with respect to the Barberini Vase during the preceding autumn, had now renewed his efforts to purchase it; and a little later he and Boulton were again busy with their old business relative to the sale and improvement of buttons and cameos. By this true blue that is dyed in the grain.' Quoted in VVedgwood's letter to Mr. Eden, Janna 5, 1786. Lord Auckland's Journ s and Correspondence, Vol. I. pp. 92-93.

CRAP. XI. PIRATES AGAIN. 557 time it is evident that the secret of the sulphate of baryta as a body-ingredient in the jasper had become known, as pirates were abroad. On his way to town Wedgwood had left some cameos at So-ho; Boulton was absent, so on reaching town he thus wrote:—

I wish you would give your foreman in this branch a. caution that they are not carried out by any of the workmen, to be moulded or copied. A manufacturer of Birmingham whom you know has made a laudable attempt in this way at my warehouse in town, that is to buy a complete set of cameos for patterns; but his intention being discovered I told him I must take care not to sell him a set of models for a few shillings which had cost me besides time & labour some three times as many guineas.I

Upon leaving Lord Shelburne, in 1780, Priestley settled in Birmingham, and shortly after, Wedgwood, in order to assist in his scientific and literary pursuits, generously

I afforded him an annual allowance of twenty-five guineas.

This was continued to the period of Wedgwood's death; and after it by his son Josiah, to the close of Priestley's life. Other sums were occasionally added as extraordinary gifts; and Priestley's laboratory was profusely supplied with retorts, tubes, baths, crucibles, mortars, and other vessels necessary to chemical analysis. Wedgwood also saw more of Priestley than heretofore; and their correspondence upon scientific subjects was frequent. In 1788 they discussed the composition of air; and in 1791 had under consideration improvements in furnaces for heating metals. But, contrary to the generally received notion, Wedgwood was not, like Priestley, Watt, Boulton, Dr. Withering, and others, a recognised member of the Lunar Society. He was occasionally present at its meetings, and probably contributed at intervals sub 1 Wedgwood to Boulton,June14, 1786. Soho MSS. jects for discussion, but Etruria and Birmingham were too distant for any regular monthly attendance.1 To Darwin and himself science always afibrded something new. Bergmann, the friend of Lavoisier, lent whilst yet in MS. his work on ' Electric Attractions ' to Wedgwood; and he in turn confided it to Darwin. In mechanics the model of a steam-engine was contemporary with

that of a windmill. Even before they had discussed the scientific theory of congelation, Darwin made Wedgwood the ofl'er to share in its expenses and profits. But although the latter was pleased with his friend's proposal he declined it.

I sigh (he wrote) that I am becoming an old man, that age and infirmit-ies overtake & more than whisper in my ear that it is time to diminish rather than increase the objects of my attention The increasing cares of my family, my various concerns which cannot be delegated to others, with many notices of a fabric far passed its meridian, all concur in the unwelcome monit-ion to avoid any further addition to occupations already too extensive for my peace or content; & 10th as I am compel me to decline accepting the very flattering offer you have made me.'

Henccforward Darwin's 'steam-wheel,' as he called it, stood still, for Derby, whither he had removed, was scant of men of scientific tastes. But the inventive faculty of the philosophers was soon again busy. They had an electrical machine under consideration, and this was fol 1 Priestley tells us distinctly, 'I consider my settlement at Birmingham as the hep iest event in my life, being hig ly favourable to everv ob'ect I had in view, hilosophical or t eological. In the ormer respect I had the convenience of good workmen of every kind, and the society of persons eminent for their knowledge of chemistry, particularly Mr. VVatt, Mr. Keir, and Dr. Witheriug. These, with Mr. Boul ton and Dr. Darwin (who soon left us by removing from Lichfield to Derbv), Mr. Galton, and afterwards Mr. Johnson, of Kenilworth, and n1v-self, dined together every month, calling ourselves the Lunar Society, because the time of our meeting was near the full moon.'——Rutt's Life of Priestley, vol. i. pp. 338, 339.

' Vedgwood to Darwin, August 1782. Darwin Correspondence.

__ '_. 4'

Can. XI. SCIENCE AND FRIENDSHIP. 659 lowed by experiments in the construction of lamps. For some part of their machinery Wedgwood made bladders of goldbeaters' skin, and Darwin tried weights and springs of various kinds. These lamp-experiments extended over four years-1782-1786_and seem never to have been perfected, as the Doctor only found time for them during the long nights of winter. Meanwhile, the children of both families were becoming men and women, and their intimacy took growth accordingly. The young men at Etruria sent the Doctor's daughters-in-law valentines and Christmas presents, and Miss Wedgwood and her sisters were often at Derby. During some of her visits, Miss Wedgwood, who was a great favourite with her future father-in-law, smoothed away perhaps a little of his ruggedness, by lessons in music; at others, it was a continued whirl of festivity. On occasion of one of these visits, Darwin thus writes:_' Your medallion I have not yet seen; it is covered over with so many strata of caps & ruffles & Miss Wedgwood is whirled oil' to a card-partyseen and vanished like a shooting star.' On the other hand, the Doctor's daughter-in-law, Miss Pole, joined Miss Vedgwood in her visits to London; and the houses of either family stood reciprocally open to each other. Derby lay in the way to London, and the Wedgwoods were expected to rest there, either on their going or return. ' Mrs. Darwin,' writes the Doctor pleasantly on one of these occasions, ' says she hears your whole family are going to town in a body, like a caravan going to Mecca; & we therefore hope you will make Derby a resting-place, & recruit yourselves & your camels for a few days, after having travell'd over the burning sands of Cheadle & Uttoxeter.'1 Such were the social graces 1 Darwin to Wedgwood, March 13, 1784. Darwin Correspondence.

660 DISSENSIONS IN THE CHAMBER. CHAP. XI. which varied philosophic intercourse; and many of the choicest productions of Etruria gave further expression to a friendship so long and well founded.1

The Treaty of Commerce was signed at Versailles on September 26, although the business connected therewith de-

tained Mr. Eden in France till the middle of the following year. In the interim the convention was signed on January 23, and soon after the meeting of Parliament an address in approval of the Treaty was carried by overwhelming numbers—236 against 116.

Prior to this, the Committee of the General Chamber of Commerce had marked its approbation of the French Treaty. But soon after dissensions arose in the Chamber and amongst the local Committees; and during the absence of the chief leaders, the General Chamber presented a.

petition to Parliament objecting to the Treaty; and this was followed by innumerable pamphlets of the same tenor. The whole organisation, both metropolitan and local, was now in a blaze. The Birmingham Committee remonstrated, and refused to send further delegates till the Chamber was remodelled; whilst Wedgwood, to nullify as far as possible both the effects of these dissensions and the petition opposed to the_Government measure, called a Meeting of Potters. The result was what might

' In April 1786, Wedgwood sent

Darwin's little daughter Violette a. 'asper cup and saucer of extreme eauty; and a. few years later the Doctor thus writes:—' Mrs. Darwin has commissioned me to write to ' thank you for the very excellent Bath you have been so kind as to send her. But what was the astonishment of the family when on striking it there was heard a rattling of armour within! Some of us began to think it like the Trojan Horse, & fem-'d it might contain armed warriors _; others that like Pa.ndora's box, it might contain many evils at the top & hope at the bottom. These fears ceased on recollecting who was the kind donor, & that presents from a friend were not to be suspected like those of an enemy. So out came the straw, _ and with it the bowels of the pestiferous animal, beyond any power of numbering or naming, for each individual of which I am commanded to thank you over & over, & to add all our kindest complements to you 8:. yours.'—Dai-win to Wedgwood.

CHAD. XI. DIF FEREX CE OF OPINION. 561 be expected. The Potters again signified-as on a former occasion-their conviction that the Treaty was, in its nature and tendency, highly advantageous to the country; and this opinion further enquiry and consultation had confirmed. Wedgwood's chief opponent in these proceedings was Thomas Walker of Manchester; a good man like himself, but systematically averse to the Treaty; as indeed to any Government measure proposed by Pitt. A friend of the chief leaders of the Opposition, he seems in this one point to have cleaved to party rather than distinguished principles; and to have overlooked the advantages and noble tendencies of those great commercial and financial reforms which marked the first four years of Pitt's administration. There came days when his courageous _ opposition to the arbitrary proceedings of the Government-those days when Pitt's violation of constitutional principles involved the country in an almost inextricable web of war, debt, and taxation-proved his wisdom and unselfish patriotism; but in this business of the Commercial Treaty with France, he seems to have been as prejudiced and hasty as Wedgwood, on the other hand, was petulant and complaining. These differences separated them for a period—when necessary they corresponded stitHy—but time seems, in some measure at least, to have healed the wound; for, in 1789, we find them joined heartily--through the General Chamber-in the common cause of protecting English manufactures from the plots of foreign spies.'

' Thomas Walker holds a conspi-1 dom of his country, deserve the hand cuous place amongst the eminent Y of an able biogra her. He suffered men of Manchester. His opposition ' cruelly under t e infamous sp 'to the tax on fustians proposed by system of the eriod; and, in 1794, he Pitt, and his bold and consistent ad-; was tried at ancaster with six other vocacy of every question likely to gentlemen, upon acharge of 'medi-advance the civil and religious free-tated revolution.' He was most ho

’()l.. ll. 0 O

VVedgwood was greatly harassed by these disseusions in the Chamber, and by the unwise conduct of many of the delegates. In some cases he stopped, even whilst at press, the report of votes and speeches, which would have done _the greatest harm.

They have endeavoured to lay open our dependence upon Portugal and Spain for raw materials (he tells Boulton), and what is much more important the extent of our clandestine commerce with France, and they would have laid bare the channels of communication also, but happily the Committee did not know them..... I am just wearied out (he continues) with the nonsense of some & the pertness & abuse of others, & if I am not supported from the country soon, either by letters or by some of the members arriving at the Chamber, I must quit my post, for I have been buffeted & teased beyond human patience. Some of my friends say let the Chamber go to the Devil. I say no —we may want it hereafter. It should be new modelled (about which I shall be glad to consult my friends in Birmingham) but not demolished.‘

For a time the Chamber-as Wedgwood told Mr. Eden-‘ slept; ’ it was then probably remodelled, and continued in existence till at least the close of his life. But, from the date of the Commercial Treaty, its deliberations and acts came but little before the public.

Thus unfettered, the great natural trade between France and England was rapidly developed. Sykes, of Paris, who had already dealt in many articles in jasper ware,’ gave further orders; and, in February 1787, Josiah Wedgwood the youngcr visited the capital, and confirmed a treaty with M. Daguerre for the sale of the finest class of nourably acquitted; the informer much of his correspondence with being convicted of perjury and sen-them on business subjects, chieflv tent-ed to two years’ imprisonment. political, is still in existence, as also r. ’alker, who died in 181%), was ‘ a line portrait by Romney.

on terms of intiniat-._v with nnmy of 1 ’edgvood to Boulton,Februar’ the chief

characters of the time; and 1 23, 1787. Soho MSS. ’

CHAP. XI. SYKES AND DAGUERRE. 563 goods; and, later in the year, Wedgwood himself, accompanied by an interpreter, spent a fortnight there. . No record of this visit exists, nor of one made previously. Merchants in other parts of France-as at Brest, Dunkirk, L’Orient--also opened commissions; and Sykes, as a symbol of the Treaty, sent Mr. Wedgwood, as also Mr. Byerley-whom he had known some time— thc present each of a handsome waistcoat.

Flaxman, as we have seen, had finished his two models for bas-reliefs to commemorate. the passing of the Commercial Treaty in January and March 1787. By June, some copies were finished and included in an invoice of ornamental ware sent to London, being marked at the price of £3 each. In relation to these, and his engagements with MM. Daguerre and Sykes, Mr. Wedgwood, a few days later, wrote thus to Mr. Eden:

I have made an engagement with M. Daguerre & Mr. Sykes at Paris, & am to serve only two in that place; both these engagements are only for one year. I take a share of the risk along with M. Daguerre, & have sent a considerable assortment to Rouen which I hope will be with him in a. little time. I have also made an exclusive agreement with Mr. Sykes for the city of Bordeaux to which place also I have sent a cargo of goods. I have refused many correspondents, & I am afraid I shall not able to supply these two sutficiently in addition to my . old friends.—I have modelled t-W0 bas-reliefs representing the

Commercial Treaty with France. One of these consists of three figures. Mercury as the God of Commerce uniting the hands of England and France. On the other bas-relief is represented the Temple of Janus shut & the door bolted by two caducei; Mars in a violent rage is going to burst the door open with his spear, but Peace arrests his arm and says, or seems to say, that the door so bolted is not to be broke open. I hope you will have received the first pair I

made, which I sent by the diligence for expedition, desiring M. Daguerre to deliver them to you. When his cargo arrives, if you should see anything

The bas—relicf of Mercury here given (fig. 144) was the one most popular. A considerable number of both W01‘! dispersed in this country and on the continent; but they have now become extremely rare, and sell for ten or a dozen times their original price. The bas-relief from ’lli¢’h this copy is taken is one of the finest. in existence, and once belonged to Flaxman.2

VVedg’ood reaped little personal benefit from the

Treaty of Commerce. Sykes was a bad paymaster; disputes arose with M. Daguerre; and the breaking out of the French Revolution annulled at once the Treaty and its liberal principles of navigation and commerce. Much beautiful ware, grey jasper with white medallions, sent to the Princesses of France, brought no remuneration; and a splendid service, ordered by Phillip Howard, Esq., for the Cardinal de Rohan, seems, after many adventures and roundabout methods of conveyance, to have been seized by the mob of Strasburg, and broken in a million fragments, so hated and infamous was the name of the royal favourite.

From July 1787 till the close of his life Vi/edgwood was more or less active in the cause of the Abolition of Slavery. He formed one of the Society’s Committee, andattended it whenever he was in town. He contributed largely to its funds, and wrote long letters to those of his friends who had been led to believe that slavery was a good rather than an evil, in relation to the negro race. In some instances——as in that of Anna Seward-he had the happiness of converting them to his own views. In connection with Mr. Sneyd and others, he organised country meetings; and he was in constant correspondence with Clarkson as to pamphlets, letters, enquiries, and all the general business of the society. Under his directions Hackwood modelled a design of a seal for the society, which was laid before the Committee on October 16,1787. This (,.,g_,,_.,

_,,..,M,,,,,,_,,,_,.,. design_as seen in the illustration:f',3§_m""7""""""L"""" (fig. 1-l5)—was highly approved of; a seal was ordered to be engraved from it; and in 566 HACKVVOOD'S DESIGN FOR A SEAL. CRAP. XI. 1792, Wedgwood, at his own expense, had a block cut from the design as a frontispiece illustration for one of Clarkson's pamphlets. His own manufactory also made good use of the drawing. Seals in all the various bodies, and cameos in jasper—the ground white, the relief black._were made in large quantities, and distributed gratuitously, as well as sold. Clarkson himself received more than five hundred seals and cameos; and as the cause gained popularity, so also did the design of the Slave. As a seal, a ring, a shirt-pin, or coat-buttons, gentlemen wore it; as also ladies, in every possible form, even mounted as pins for their hair.1 Through his friend Phillips, the bookseller, Wedgwood sent some of the cameos to the illustrious Franklin, and by the hand of an amanuensis——for he was ill at the time_-wrote thus:

I enclose for the use of yourself & friends a few cameos, on a subject which I am happy to acquaint you is daily more & more taking possession of men's minds on this side of the Atlantic as well as with you. It gives me great pleasure to be embraced on this occasion in the same great & good cause with yourself, & I ardently hope for the final completion of our wishes. This will be an epoch before unknown to the world, & while relief is given to millions of our fellow-creatures immediately the object of it-, the subject of freedom will be more canvassed & better understood in the enlightened nations.2

Then, referring to his indisposition, which prevents his saying more, he begs 'to be considered, Sir, among the number of those who have the highest veneration for your virtues, & gratitude for the benefits you have conferred on society.' Wedgwood did not live to see the fruition of these hopes, as the Bill for the Abolition of

' Clarkson's History of the Abo-ary 29, 1788. Mayer MSS. This lition of the African Slave Trade, letter is sketched out in pencil on the vol. ii. p. 162. back of one from James Phillips, the

" Vedgwood to Franklin, Febrn-Quaker bookseller.

CHAP. XI. MINERAL PRODUCTS FROM SYDNEY COVE. 567 the Slave-Trade was not passed till the Parliamentary Session of 1807; but his eflbrts to advance this good cause, and to increase public sympathy in its behalf, were not amongst the least prominent of those by which he sought to leave the world better than lle_ found it.

In 1790 Wedgwood contributed his last paper to the 'Philosophical Transactions.' It related to the analysis of a mineral substance which had been sent from New South Wales in 1789. It was a mixture of fine white sand, 2. soft white earth, some colourless micaceous par . ticles, and a few black ones; resembling black mica or black lead, partly loose or detached from each other, and partly cohering together in little friable lumps. The exhaustive analysis he employed led him to the conclusion that this substance was a species of pure phimbago or black lead, not hitherto taken notice of by any writer; but the quantity he had for analysis was too small for him to determine if it-contained zinc, as found by Lavoisier in similar experiments.' With this mineral, Sir Joseph Banks had forwarded some clay from the same colony, which upon trial Wedgwood found to be of excellent quality. To give proof of this, the idea occurred to him to form from it some medallions, with a view to encourage the arts and to inspire hope, amidst many difficulties, in the breasts of those distant colonists. It was a compliment likewise to the eminent naturalist Who was with Cook when he traced the eastern shores of Australia, discovered the flowery treasures of Botany Bay, and the unrivalled harbour of Port Jackson; and who, since then, when the Government of this country saw that, with America, it had lost its penal settlements and must look elsewhere, had greatly aided in dispatching the first band of colonists. Webber, as the-fore-most artist at Etruria, modelled the medallion; and the result, as seen in the engraving, was exquisite. The figure of Hope standing on a rock, with an anchor and a cornucopia at her feet, and addressing the three typical personages before her, is delicately rendered; whilst the neighbouring ocean, and the wild country yet to subdue and till, form an appropriate background. The model inspired Darwin with poetic fervour; and, elassing with it the Slave intnglio and cameo and the Barberini Vase, he thus wrote:

Whether, 0 Friend of Art! the gem you mould
Rich with new taste, with ancient virtue bold;
From the poor fetter'd Slave on bended knee,
From Britain's sons imploring to be free;
Or with fair Hope the brightening scenes improve,
And cheer the dreary wastes at Sydney Cove; Or bid mortality rejoice and mourn
U'er the fine forms on Portland's mystic urn.
Whether, O Friend of Art! your gems derive
Fine forms from Greece, and fabled Gods revive:
Or bid from modern life the Portrait breathe,
And bind round Houour's brow the laurel-wreath;
Buoyant shall sail, with Fame's historic page,
Each fair medallion o'er the wrecks of age;
Nor Time shall mar, nor Steel, nor Fire, nor Rust
Touch the hard polish of the immortal bust.

These verses, which greatly pleased Mr. Wedgwood, were sent to him whilst staying at Blackpool for the benefit of his health; and, a little later, they met the approbation of the Queen. In November, the earliest copies of the medallion were ready, and, gracefully consigned to Sir Joseph Banks (fig. 147), were dispatched by the first ship to the far-away colony.1

In 1787 Wedgwood again suffered from spectra in the eyes, and throughout the autumn of that year he was occasionally very ill.

In the spring of the year following, during a visit to London with Miss Wedgwood, he was seized with shortness of breath; and, on recovering from this, a severe pain in his amputated limb greatly affected him. It was a nervous and imaginary affection, for it seemed to afflict the limb long before removed; and it was not till Darwin's skill was brought to bear that real alleviation came.

For some years he had suffered from this pain, the result of general decay, long-standing disease, and several more or less severe injuries to his amputated limb.

In September 1776 he had been thrown from his horse, and for some time after he moved about on crutches. ; and in 1785 two accidents, whilst in London, added injurious effects. But he had now the happiness of being aided by his sons in his multifarious business. Upon his removal from Warrington Academy, young J 01111 Wedgwood had joined his brother Josiah in Edinburgh, and together they had carried on their respective

' The medallion of Hope, as well wonders, who can liquefy the granite as the design of the Slave, were engraved for the first part of the B0tanic Gardens, ' The Economy of Vegetation.' In reference to these, Wvedgwood writes: 'The Slave comes in so well, & so extremely apropos, where on have laced it, that I should e sorry to ave it removed, & I do not see how it can be so well filled up by any other, especially as considering it as a. companion to the Ilope of b'_1/ dney Cove. But I cheerfully resign him into the hands of'' the powerful magician who can work and still harder flint, into the softest poetic numbers, & with the breath of his mouth waft their varied productions to the most distant ages. — "'edgwood to Darwin, J nl 1789. Darwin, on the other han, was charmed with the medallion:— ' I have received great pleasure from your excellent medallion of Ho e. The figures are all finely beauti

ul, & s eak for themselves.'——Darwin to 'edgwood, December 1, 1789. Darwin Correspondence.

CRAP. XI. LESLIE THE MATIEMATICIAN. 571 studies. In 1786 they returned home, and, under the guidance of Chisholm, continued certain parts of their education whilst attending business at the.works. Subsequently Mr. John Leslie, afterwards Professor of Mathematics in the University of Edinburgh, became for a time resident tutor at Etruria. But young John Wedgwood's health was indifferent, and he varied business by occasional change and travel. One season, as we have seen, he was on the Continent with Webber—at another he made a tour in Wales. Josiah and Thomas were thus the home-stayers; and, by the spring of 1788, the former was able to take a very active part in the higher details of the manufacture. We find his father writing to him with respect to some smelling-bottles, on which were small bas-reliefs or cameo-likenesses of the 'Stadtholder and Princess,' and also with respect to a fluted altar flower-pot with a patera at top. This last, he wrote, 'is very well executed & a very good thing. These two articles do you credit as a potter, & will help to give you our confidence in future orders.' He then proceeds to give some artistic hints, and adds: ' Such little touches and finishings show the master in works of art."

At this date, and subsequently, the works at Etruria were in the highest state of eiliciency. One of the productions was a medal commemorative of the recovery of the King. Some of these were sent to Lord Auckland, then Ambassador at the Court of Madrid, and with them Wedgwood wrote:

I have great pleasure to tell you that the ladies are still so good as to continue my cameos in fashion, & in order to merit this as far as I am able, I endeavour to introduce all the novelty 1 Vedgwood to Josiah Vedgvood the younger, April 16, 1788.

572 MODELS FOR CAMEOS. CRAP. XI.

& as much good work as I can procure for their subjects. I employ several

modellers constantly in Rome, & get what I can from Paris, & am very happy when I can have anything done by our own artists in England; but my vorks are too small & delicate for them, so that little assistance can be obtained in England, except what is done under my own eye at Etruria.'

Other and greater works were also on hand, the crowning fruits of a longand laborious life.

CHAPTER XII.

FINAL WORKS.

Y HE Barberini Vase was brought to this country by Sir

William Hamilton at the close of December 1784. Its fame through the flildes Barberinae, the works of Bartoli ' and Montfaucon,' the published travels of Brevil and Misson, and the reports of countless connoisseurs and men of letters, had long preceded it. It is therefore not surprising that the Duchess Dowager of Portland, whose passion for augmenting her Museum amounted to almost a monomania, and who probably knew of Sir William's purchase, should be the first to visit him upon his arrival at his hotel in King Street, St. James's. Whether she saw the vase on this occasion is unknown, but four days after we find her, through Mrs. Delany, sending her proposal to Sir William by his neice Miss Hamilton, maid of honour to the Queen. Much negotiation followed. For some reason or another it was carried on by the respective ladies in the most secret manner. By whispers, signs, confabulations in their parlours and bedchambers, and by notes." At length after two or three interviews between Sir William and the Duchess, 576 SALE OF THE PORTLAND MUSEUM. Crux'. XII.-_ the negotiation was settled, and the Barberini Vase, as also two antique gems in intaglio, Hercules slaying the Hydra, in cameo, a head of Augustus, and a mosaic ring, passed into her hands. Previous to its removal, Sir William showed the. vase to many of his artistic and literary friends; amongst whom were Miss Burney, Warton the poet, and Mrs. Carter of classical fame. But from the date of the Duchess's possession till her death in the following year, July 17, 1785, the vase was lost to all but a few tried and confidential friends, so rigidly did the Duchess keep the secret of her purchase, especially from her own family. It is evident that they had greatly dissented to the sums she had spent on her Museum, as possession or rarity more than merit or intrinsic value had been her passion; and it was well known that she had paid enormous sums for comparatively worthless articles. A glance even at this day through the sale Catalogue will show that a large number of items in the collection were simply duplicates; particularly in the class of shells. Wedgwood, who was already busy with some attempts to imitate the vase from the plate in his copy of Montfaucon, and who, as we have seen, through the business of the Irish Propositions, and the then pending Commercial Treaty with France, was in frequent communication with the Duke, opened a treaty for its possession, for Darwin writes, 'I shall be glad to hear that you have purchased at the price you wished the famous vase." But the Duke, if he wished to dispose of the Museum, was also desirous of retaining some few of its treasures; and the treaty from this cause, or some other, came to nothing. In the spring succeeding, the whole Museum was sold at the late

CRAP. XII. LOAN OF THE BARBERINI VASE. 577

Duchess's residence in Privy Gardens, Whitehall. The sale beginning April 24, ended June 7, 1786, thus extending through thirty-five days, there being 4155 lots.1 It has been said that VedgWood was present at the sale, and tried to out-bid the Duke; but one part of this tradition is incorrect, and the other may be so. The Duke of Portland was represented by Mr. Tomlinson, who bought in the vase at the price of £1029, the cameo of Jupiter Serapis at £173 58. , and that of Augustus Caesar at £236 58.2 The truth probably is, that His Grace and Mr. Wedgwood had come to the previous understanding, that the one should buy in the vase, and the other have its loan for the purpose of artistic copy; for three days after the sale

this famous antique passed into Wedgwoods care, his receipt of possession, and promise of return, being attested by Mr. Byerley.3

A fortnight later Mr. Wedgwood consulted by letter Sir William Hamilton on the difiiculties of the task before him. After speaking of the Duke of Portland's gracious kindness, and his hope that its present name of the Portland Vase would never depart from it, he continues:'—

When I first engaged in this work and had Montfaucon only to copy I proceeded with spirit and sufiicient assurance that I should be able to equal or excel if permitted, that copy of the vase; but now that I can indulge myself with full and repeated

' The Vase was the last lot. Cata-sold by auction by Messrs. Skinner logue, p. 194. the 7th day of the present month of " Gent.'s Mega, vol. lvi. part 1, p. June, 1786, & I do hereby promise 540. to deliver back the said Vase and 3 'I do hereby acknowledge to have Cameo in safety into the hands of borrowed and received from His His Grace upon demand. Grace the Duke of Portland, the Vitness my hand this 10th day of Vase described in the 4155 lot of the J une, 1786. catalogue of the Portland Museum, Jos VlzIowo0D. and also the cameomedallion of the (Signed in the presence of) head of Augustus Czcsar being the Tues BY1:BLEY.' lot of the same catalogue andiboth l VOL. II. P I' 578 ANTICIPATED DIFFICULTIES. C-HAP. XII. examinations of the original work itself, my crest is much fallen, and I should scarcely muster sufficient resolution to proceed if I had not too precipitately perhaps, pledged myself to many of my friends to attempt it in the best manner I am able. Being so pledged, I must proceed; but shall stop at certain points till I am favoured with your kind advice and assistance.

Weclgwootl then goes on to tell Sir William of the faith he has in Webber's high ability as a modeller, the capacity of the jasper body to be cut and polished at the seal engraver's lathe, and also of its property of taking a blue tint from

cobalt of any degree of strength. He then proceeds:—

It is apparent that the artist has availed himself very ably of the dark ground in producing the perspective & distance required, by cutting the white away nearer to the ground as the shades were wanted deeper, so that the white is often cut-to the thinness of paper, & in some instances quite away, & the ground itself makes a part of the bas-relief; by which means he has given to his work the effect of painting as well as sculpture; and it will be found that a bas-relief with all the figures of auniform white colour upon a dark ground will be a very faint resemblance of what this artist has had the address to produce by calling in the aid of colour to assist his relief. That hollowness of the rocks, & depth of shade in other parts, produced by cutting down to the dark ground, & to which it owes no small part of its beauty, would all be wanting, & a disgusting flatness appear in their stead. It is here that I am most sensible of my weakness, & that I must of necessity call in the engraver to my assistance, in order to produce the highest finished & closest copies we are capable of making. But in this resource difficulties arise, & I fear insurmountable ones; for how few artists have we in this branch whose touches would not carry ruin with them to these beautiful & high wrought figures l And suppose one or two could be found equal to the task, would such artists be persuaded to quit a lucrative branch of their profession, & devote half a life to a single work, for which there is little probability of their being paid half so much as they earn by their present employment; for I do not think £5,000 for the execution of such avase, sup

Cm. XII. THE ORIGINAL VASE. 579 posing our best artists capable of the work, would be at all equal to their gains from the works they are now employed in; & the taste of the present age, you well know Sir, is not awake, notwithstanding all you have done to rouse it», to works of much time and great expense. Here then I stand greatly in need of your assistance, for unless some new expedient can be happily thought of, we must submit to the loss of a beauty, which we are perhaps capable of producing if all other circumstances were capable of bringing it forward.—I suppose it is admitted that the form of the vase is not so elegant, as it might be made if the artist had not been possessed of some very good reason for contenting himself with the present form—either perhaps that he would engage the whole undivided attention of the spectator to his sculpture—the vase itself being the production of an inferior artist, the verrier — or because the material made use of under the circumstances necessary for the display of his art, that is, the body being made of one colour, and the surface covered over to a due thickness with another, was not capable of taking a form with those delicate parts on which its beauty as a simple vase would in a. great measure depend, & which might be given to a vase made of metal or any more manageable materials.—NoW though we should suppose the latter to be the case, I suppose you would still advise me to copy the form of the vase as well as the figures. But what I wish to ask you is, whether you would forbid me to apply these figures to any other form of a vase, or with the addition of any borders, or other ornaments.

Mr. Wedgwood then proceeds to discuss the question of different classes of copies, to suit the requirements of purchasers of varied means. He then adds:—

In examining the bas-reliefs upon the vase, there appear a few palpable slips of the artist's attention, both in drawing & execution, as you have no doubt yourself observed. Would it be advisable in these cases to make any deviation from the original, or to copy as close as we can its defects as well as its beauties? Most of the figures have their surfaces partially decayed by time. When we mould from these figures, may we venture to restore their original smoothness, with care to preserve the drawing &c., or let the copies pass deficient as time has left the original?
580 BARBERINI BLACK. CHAP. XII.

... Several gentlemen have urged me to make my copies of the vase by subscription, & have honoured me with their names for that purpose; but I tell them, and with great truth, that I am extremely difiident of my ability to perform the task they kindly impose upon me; and they shall be perfectly at liberty when they see the copies, to take or refuse them; and on these terms I accept of subscriptions, chiefly to regulate the time of delivering out the copies, in rotation, according to the dates on which they honour me with their names.1

We have no clue to Sir William's answer to these questions; but the result makes it probable that he advised a strict keeping to the original, except so far as to correct defects arising-from artistic lapses or decay. From this date till July 1789, a period of three years, we hear nothing further of the vase. Webber must have completed his modelling by the summer of 17 67, as in the July of that year he repaired to Rome, and was absent more than a twelve-month. But there were other dilficulties than those connected with the earlier portions of the artistic work. It took time, skill, and extraordinary patience to hit the exact tint of body colour; which, paradox as it may seem, was black and yet blue. Even as late as May 1790, they were still busy with trials for ' Barberini black."" The lathe work and polishing also required the rarest patience and ability. In July 1789 no perfect copy had yet been effected. 'The prospect however brightens upon me, ' writes Mr. Wedgwood at that date to Lord Auckland, then Ambassador at Madrid; ' and after having made several defective copies, I think I begin to see my' way to the final completion of it. '3 Three months later his hopes were rewarded. The first 1 Wedgwood to Sir VVilliam of a mixture of blue and black, and Hamilton, Janu 24, 1786. then dipped in black.
2 Mems. from ondon to Etruria, 5 VVedgwo0d to Lord Auckland, May 9, 1790. The best was made July 29, 1789. Eden MSS.

Cnsr. XII. THE BARBERINI VASE. . 581 perfect copy was accomplished,

although not so fine in all respects as the one takenabroad by Josiah Wedgwood, junior, and Mr. Byerley in the succeeding year. This first vase was sent to Derby for Dr. Darwin's inspection, but under strict injunctions not to show it except to his family. The Doctor was however too proud to be conservative. ' I have disobeyed you,' he writes, " and shown your vase to two or three, but they were philosophers, not cogniscenti. How can I possess a jewel, and not communicate the pleasure to a few Derby philosophers?' 1 1 The Barberini Vase was discovered between the years 1623 and 1644, during the pontificate of Urban VIII. (Barberini), beneath a mound of earth called Monte del Grano, about three miles from Home on the road to the ancient Tusculum. It was enclosed in a sarcophagus of excellent workmanship, and this in a sepulchral chamber. An inscription on the sarcophagus, which was otherwise covered with fine bas-reliefs, showed it to have been dedicated to the memory of the Emperor Alexander Severus and his mother Julia Mamaaa, both of whom were killed in the year 235 during a revolt in Germany. The vase, in height ten inches, was deposited in the library of the Barberini family, and the sarcophagus in the Museum of the capital. The material of which the former was composed was by Montfaucon and others conjectured to be a precious stone, but Mr. VVedgwood's examination proved it to be formed of glass; the ground being a dark blue, so nearly approaching black as to appear of that colour except when held in a strong light. The white bas-reliefs are of glass or paste; the material having been fused on in a mass, and then cut out by the 1 Darwin to Vvedgwood, October, 1789. Darwin Correspondence.
582 THE SUBJECT OF ITS BAS-RELIEFS. CRAP. XII. skill and patience of the gem engraver into the designs required. The subjects of these bas-reliefs, as also the age and place of production of the vase, are points so wholly unknown as to be still open to conjecture and criticism. With respect to the first every critic has difiered. The Italians and French first entered upon the

discussion; and the introduction of the vase into England was a signal for the critics here. Mr. Charles Greville, who published some very fine engravings by Bartolozzi of the vase, considered the bas-reliefs typified the death and resurrection of Adonis. Darwin, who consulted Warburton's Divine Legation, and many other works, thought the bas-reliefs bore reference to the Eleusinian mysteries, and this, with some trifling difierence, was the view adopted by Wedgwood in his pamphlet on the vase. Another critic, Dr. King, in entire ignorance of the arts of antiquity and their best periods, conjectured that these designs bore reference to the birth and acts of the Emperor Alexander Severus,1 Whilst a far more learned and enlightened critic of our own day considers that one of the groups represents Peleus approaching Thetis. These critical diflerences might be repeated to a wearisome extent. It is on the whole perhaps safest to conclude, that the subjects of the bas-reliefs are simply a heathen and poetised allegory on the trials of human life, and its close. Such vases, as in the case of the Greek encaustic vases prepared for the Olympian games, may have been designed with a view to a general purpose, rather than a particular one. Of the vase itself, if it does belong to the best period of Grecian art, that prior to the age of Alexander, it may have formed a portion of those

C-HAP. XII. TASSIE'S COPIES. 583 innumerable spoils which we learn from Livy, Plutarch, and other Writers were poured into Rome, as proofs of subjugation and conquest. But it is questionable if the Greeks excelled as much in the art of the verrier as in that of the potter; whilst the Alexandrians, at a date when Rome was in its glory, supplied the most matchless specimens in glass and paste the world 'had yet seen. Wedgwood discovered that the Portland vase had been broken previously and repaired, as also that' the bas-relief head which forms the bottom had belonged originally to some other vase or fragment of antiquity, and that it had been ground down and then inserted by processes far inferior to those used by

the original artist. A mould of the vase was made by Peckler the gem engraver, whilst it was in the possession of the Barberini family, and from this, on its first arrival in England, a certain number of copies were taken in plaster of Paris by Tassie, who afterwards destroyed the mould. 1

At the close of 1788 Mr. Wedgwood had to regret the loss of his able partner and cousin, Thomas Wedgwood; and fifteen months later he himself retired from the more active part of his business. From the death of Mr. Bentley to January 16, 1790, the whole concern had been exclusively his own; but from this last date to June 30, 1793, the firm consisted of Josiah Wedgwood, Sons and Byerley. The eldest and youngest sons, John and Thomas Wedgwood, then retired; and from this date till the 20th of January 1785, the partnership consisted of Josiah Wedgwood, senior, Josiah Wedgwood, junior, and Thomas Byerley? Upon his retirement from the firm in January 1 Of these,whiehare nowextremely years ago, has become of great value. rare, one is in the possession of Dr. " It had to be carried on nominally Kendrick of Warrington, and since, in Vedgwood's name for a few days the serious injury to the orginal a few subsequent to his death.

1792, Mr. John Wedgwood became a junior partner in the London and Middlesex Bank, Stratford Place, London; and the youngest, whose health began to show symptoms of decline,.quitted the details of business for the change of home and foreign travel, and the society of various literary and scientific friends. Trained in science by Chrisholm, and guided through the higher department of mathematics by John Leslie, afterwards Professor in the University of Edinburgh, we find him taking interest in the most abstract questions. During the period he was connected with the manufactory he ordinarily supplemented the duties of the day by rigorous study carried on till far into the night. On several occasions his father deplores this passion, and expresses a fear 'that Tom is hurting himself." Yet he was no-mere bookworm. Whilst health lasted he took

interest in such athletic exercises as cricket and bowling, and formedone of a body of young men known as the ' Statfordshire Bowmen.' They wore a handsome uniform, and met for regular drill and exercise with the how.2 He was also a skilful draughtsman, having received, as did the rest of Mr. Wedgwood's children, lengthened instruction from Webber. In 1788 it was proposed he should study in Rome, but Webber, who was there at the time, advised a more thorough mastery of the principles of art before repairing thither. The plan was therefore changed for a brief visit to Germany, Florence, and Venice. For a period he seems to have been most active and skilful as a potter. He sketched out new patterns of every kind, both for useful and ornamental ware; and his scientific experiments led 1'Tom is very good, he labours 5'In December 1792, Thomas too hard at his studies & the works VVed wood pays Boulton a bill of together.' Wedgwood to Josiah £51 a. for buttons for the use of Vvedgwood, junior, October 10, 1790. his corps. Soho MSS.

CRAP. XII. SILVERED YVARE.. 585 in turn to improvements. To solve some problems connected with light he used silver differently prepared, and his observations thereon led to the invention of what was termed ' silvered ware, ' namely a pattern of (lead or burnished silver upon a black earthenware body. ' We first hearof this ware in February1791 and the engraving (fig. 148) will give some idea of this unique contrast. But the love of science prevailed over all. In November 1790 he was busy with experiments on quicksilver; and in 1791 Burley, his father's Birmingham mounter, prepared him solid cylinders of silver, some highly polished, others not. Barometer tubes of peculiar construction were also made for him; and silver wire of singular fineness. Nitrate of silver was sent down from Apothecaries' Hall, and the best mathematical instrument maker of the day made '. Thomas Vedgw0od to Byerley, February 1791. Uayer MSS.

586 ' EARLY PHOTOGRAPHY. CRAP. XII. him dividers and other in-

struments of the utmost delicacy.1 His father, as early as 1774, had used the camera obscura in taking views for the Russian service; and Dr. Turner of Liverpool, as it was well known, had either invented or brought to tolerable perfection the art of copying prints upon glass by striking ofi' impressions with a coloured solution of silver, and fixing them on the glass by baking on an iron plate in a heat sufiicient to incorporate the solution with the glass. VVith knowledge thus obtained and observation directed, it amounts to absolute certainty that Thomas Wedgwood during some of his experiments on the production of light from diferent bodies by heat and attrition,2 made certain discoveries, which led practically to the first principles of photography. He advanced so far as to throw objects on paper prepared with the nitrate of silver, but neither at that date, nor in subsequent experiments with Sir Humphry Davy, could a method be discovered to fix them there with any permanence. The impressions were even at the first faint, and lapse of time has almost obliterated them. But enough remains, as in the engraving from a breakfast-table scene from one of these early pictures, to prove the truth of the tradition handed down, that Thomas Wedgwood was amongst the earliest discoverers of photography, or, as it was then called, heliotype. This and another ' silver picture ' which remains 3 are wholly different in every respect from the so-called photographs from Soho. The latter were with much probability the product of some

CRAP. XII. FLAXMAN IN ROME. 587 of Egginton's water-colour processes; whilst those from Etruria are evidently due much more to scientific or chemical manipulation than to art. Thomas Wedgwood made no secret of his discovery, though he did not advance far enough to make it serve any practical purpose; and his family, to whom the results of his experiments were well known, can still supplement, through testimony handed down, the proof derived from these specimens of his valuable skill.

Upon reaching Italy in the autumn of 1787, Flaxman and his wife, after spending some little time in viewing the country and the remains of ancient art, took a house or rooms in the Via Felice, Rome: and here the great sculptor entercd at once upon those labours of self-improvement which had brought him to Italy. VVedgwood, with his usual beneficence and enthusiasm for art, had very evidently advanced a portion of the necessary funds for this journey to Italy; and to liquidate this advance, as well as keep open a running account for necessary payments, Flaxman's arrangement with his friend seems to have been this: to execute occasionally, when time and other engagements permitted, the model of some choice hasrelief or other work for Mr. Wedgvvood, but principally to suggest, overlook, and give finishing touches to the works of such artists as, hired expressly for the purpose, should give the whole of their time and attention in modelling either in direct copy of the antique, or in compositions variously suggested from the same source. This is home out by what Flaxman says in a letter to Byerley early in the spring of 17 88.

I have seen the curiosities of Rome, Naples, and Paestum, and have now got a good study (sic) and shall continue please God uninterrupted in my pursuit and employments here, among which 588 HIS FRIEND JOHN DEVAERE. CIIAP. XII.

I have been seeking a beautiful subject which I shall begin immediately and finish in the best manner the instructions of the finest works of antiquity will enable me, and employ all the time I can for Mr. V——. When you write to Mr. Wedgwood you will be so kind to inform him Mr. Devaere has been at work with the utmost diligence ever since he has been here on the bas—relief of the Borghese Vase in which he has succeeded very well, but it will still take him some weeks to finish, and after he has done I also shall have something to do to it-. Mr. Wedgwood will easily conceive as this is new work to Mr. D—— he must needs be slow at first, especially as he takes so much pains. As a

proof he follows his studies well——he has already gained the Pope's first silver medal, for a figure modelled at night in the Roman Academy.'

The modeller here referred to had followed Flaxman to Rome. He was the sculptor's personal friend, and probably one of the French artists mentioned by Mr. Wedgwood in his letter to Lord Auckland. His engagement was at a certain yearly salary, which was to be increased if he was diligent and successful. He was eminently so, for Flaxman in the succeeding year had the pleasure of sending word to Greek Street that ' Mr. Devaere had finished the bas-relief of Proserpine in-the most beautiful manner.' His salary was not only increased, but towards the latter part of his residence in Rome, Mr. Wedgwood generously allowed him to take commissions for Work, and to employ only what time he could spare for Etruria. He came over to England prior to Wedgwood's death, and ultimately succeeded Webber at the Ornamental Works; he was known there as John De Vere. Whilst in Rome he used Flaxman's atelier, and thus his modelling was constantly open to the improvements and suggestions of the sculptor, as also to his i Flaxman to Byerley, dated Rome, March 15, 1788. Mayer MSS. finishing touches. In reference to him, Mr. Wedgwood Writes to Flaxman:

I am much obliged for your kind attention and the employment of your good taste in the choice of subjects for Mr. Devaere's modelling, and amongst them the last model of the Discovery of Achilles, I admire very much for the spirit, action, and beauty of the figures, as well as the interestingness of the story itself The history of Orestes is an excellent classic subject likewise, & its being divided into several groups might increase its usefulness, but there is one objection which I fear is insurmountable and that is the nakedness of the figures. To clothe them would not only be a great increase of labour, but would require the hand of an experienced master in the art, and besides then the piece would not be a copy from the antique. I know that the nudities might be covered with leaves, but that is not enough. The objection applies to the Judgment of Paris & other pieces; and indeed the nude is so general in the works of the ancients that it will be very difficult to avoid the introduction of naked figures. On the other hand it is absolutely necessary to do so, or to keep the pieces for our own use; for none either male or female of the present generation will take or apply them as furniture if the figures are naked.'

It does not appear if the bas-relief here referred to is that where Achilles, in order to avenge the death of Patroclus, leaps down from the wall into the ditch of Troy and shows himself suddenly to the dismayed Trojans; or to that other passage in his life where his sex is revealed in the court of king Lycomedes by his seizing the armour instead of choosing the jewels laid before him. If the latter, and it probably is, we give it in the annexed fullpage woodcut-Achilles and the daughter of Lycomedes. The figures are White on a black ground.

As already seen, Webber's visit to Italy took place at

"' Wed 00d to Flaxnmn, February11,1790. The same objection applied to a eautiful bas-relief of Bacchantes at the Villa Albam.
590 SUBORDINATE ARTISTS EMPLOYED. CRAP. XII. the same date as that of Flaxman's. The. former upon his arrival in Rome employed the services of a high-class Italian artist named Angelo Dalmazzoni, and with him and young John Wedgvood he made three lengthened excursions in search of antique subjects from which to model. Dalmazzoni's labours extended over a considerable period; namely, from the autumn of 1787, to probably, the close of Mr. Wedgwood's life. He worked independently of Flaxman's control, and employed four or five subordinate artists named Pacetti, Angelini, Manzolini, Fratoddi, Mangiarotti, and Cades. Whilst Webber remained in Rome, Dalmazzoni and his artists received payment and instructions from him; but after his departure, an English resident named Jenkins transacted all

such necessary business as could not be immediately referred to Greek Street or Etruria. Many of the models of basreliefs sent to England were named as those of the first, second, and third expeditions. Pacetti's works were very numerous. They included figures reclining over the Muses, figures from Homer, copies from Herculaneum, and copies from bas-reliefs in the Museo Oapitolino. Amongst these were Priam kneeling before Achilles begging the body of his son Hector; the fable of Prometheus, the original of which was on a small urn; the Triform Goddess, who was called Luna in heaven, Diana on earth, and Hecate in hell; Esculapius and Hygeia; the Simulacrum of Hygeia; a Faun with three Spartan Bacchantes; and Endymion sleeping on the rock Latmos. Amongst other and more original subjects were Marcus Aurelius making his son Commodus Caesar, Apotheosis of Faustina, and the Nine Muses. Pacetti's labours also included the whole life of Achilles, from his mother Thetis in childbed, to his triumph over Hector. Angelini also modelled

CIIAP. XII. SUBJECTS MODELLED. 591 largely. To him are due the subjects of Apollo with the Muse Erato; Pluto carrying ofl' Proserpine, preceded by Hercules, a Victory, and Mercury; the whole Fable of Meleager; the Apotheosis of ayoung Prince; two Fauns; two Bacchantes; and a Silenus, and several figures representing the pleasures of the Elysian fields in games, dancing and banqueting. 1

Fratoddi and Mangiarotti were cameo engravers, and to these were assigned the copying on shells of the finest antiques. Angelini also executed some of his best work __ in cameo? The models of the artists were usually laid on fine slates; the modelling wax being a composition of bees'-wax, a few drops of turpentine and a little vermilion to give colour. Of these the artists also sent casts; and after the recurrence of one or two accidents, from pressure and the admission of sea water, the models, in» accordance with Mr. Wedgwood's desire, were sent by one ship and the casts by another. With so many artists thus

employed, it may be presumed that these models were very numerous. The bills of lading give boxes by almost every ship that left Leghorn; and in some of these books, prints and cameos were transmitted, which Flaxman, Jenkins, or Dalmazzoni had purchased for Mr. Wedgwood. It will thus be seen how little of the work of this period was really Flaxman's. He had come to Rome to study, and his application for this purpose was incessant. He had also on hand as commissions a group of colossal size, the Fury of Athamas, for Lord Bristol; the Cephalus and Aurora for Mr. Hope; his designs for Homer, Eschylus and Dante, besides some others. He may have overlooked

' Accounts and letters 01' Angelo the cameos is given by Dalmazzoni, Dalmazzoni. Mayer MSS. but it is too long to quote in this " A list of many of the subjects of edition.
592 FLAXMAN'S BOOKS.

Gnu. XII.

many of these productions, and given finishing touches to those of Devaere; but the large majority of the models which are still assigned to him were in reality the work of other artists.1 Of the subj ects of his commissions for Mr. Wedgwood during his seven years' residence at Rome we have no direct evidence. That he executed some, is clearly proved by the small yet continuous sums he was always drawing upon Greek Street. He was also in frequent correspondence with Mr. Byerley, who at that date had his private house at Paddington, and who during Flaxman's absence had kindly taken charge of a chest full of books belonging to him. This was opened in July 1788, and Plato's Dialogues, Virgi1's ZEneid, Ovid's Metamorphoses, Apollo Ornus on the Egyptian Hieroglyphics, and another, were taken therefrom, and forwarded to the sculptor in Rome.'

Of Pacetti's work,3 we are enabled to give two examples, the Birth of Achilles, and Priam begging from Achilles the body of his son Hector. The latteris taken from the back of the sarcophagus of Alexander in the Museo Capitolino. The third example, the Sacrifice of Iphigenia, is also from the same source, and is, with little doubt, the work of the same artist.' The Floral Sacrifice, 1 Mr. Chaflers confirms this statement. The names of the artists were originally fixed to each model.

2 F laxman to Byerley, July 8, 1788. Mayo MSS. 5 Of this has-relief Dalmazzoni's descriptionismost ex licit. 'Priam kneeling before Ac illes, begging the body of his son Hector. The young man standing by Hector is Automedonates, his shield bearer. The first vehicle is the car of Hector, and the second the cart with presents to Achilles.' Such are Dn.1mazzoni's words. But the young man standing by Hector is not his shield bearer; but Automedon the charioteer of Achilles. As already seen this hasrelief is mentioned in the first edition of "led 00d and Bentley's Catalogue. ut this version of it must have been in either the white biscuit or basaltes body. Large jasper tablets were not brought to pe ection till 1778-9, and those with black grounds, as in the one referred to were coeval with the copies of the Portland Vase, 1790-1791. 4 Fine as this has-relief is—an undraped copy in the Barlow collection is still finer. Wedgwood was quite right in saying that it took an experi

CRAP. XII. ARTISTIC JUSTICE. 593 which accompanies the Birth of Achilles, is one of those early subjects Flaxman modelled for Wedgwood.

If these fine bas-reliefs lose somewhat of classic interest through it being thus proved on evidence not to be mistaken that they are the productions of men less famous than Flaxman, they are nevertheless works of the highest merit. If Devaere, Dalmazzoni and the rest worked thus in the spirit of truth, and, giving us copies of antique art, give also their antique grace and vitality of conception, what a moral and indefensible wrong to assign to another the worthy labour of their hands. Fictions of this character serve neither art nor truth. So far as the former is concerned, and the purposes it has to serve, it would be even well if artists were less slaves to the ideas of an obsolete past; but rather, by recurring to nature as the ancients

did, enter upon the same boundless field of freshness, power and originality. »We even think that had Wedgwood, through his artists, been less a copyist, he would have done more justice tohimself; and anticipated in a degree that newer age of ' visible presentment' which will be surely ours when artists— —whether painters or sculptors_shall seek to-create in accordance with the spirit of their time, rather than be lifeless imitators and copyists of the obsolete ideas of an irrecoverable past.

The bas-relief of the Birth of Achilles has been hitherto assigned to Flaxman, but if reliance is to be put on' Dalmazzoni's own description, it is Pacetti's. In simplicity and truth of conception, and in the grace of the female and infantile figures, it is quite worthy of the great master. ' ' It is also essentially true to that canon of his art—and of the best age of Greek art too—that one idea should» enced master to clothe the figures of antique art, and even then the result is never satisfactory.

594 FIRST FINE COPY OF THE VASE. 0111.1'. XII. govern the whole, and the field of representation be not over-crowded.

By the close of April 1791 one of the finest copies of the Portland Vase till then or subsequently made was brought to London, and after being shown to the Queen by Mr. Wedgwood's friend, M. de Luc, it was placed for some days in the rooms of the Society of Antiquaries, and whilst there, its entire similitude to the original was certified by Sir Joshua Reynolds. Upon its removal thence to Greek Street, tickets to view it were issued. Persons of the highest rank and position availed themselves of this privilege; and when the show was closed it formed the gem of a rich assortment of ornamental goods, taken abroad by Josiah Wedgwood the younger and Mr. Byerley. Their passport was signed on the 24th of June by the Duke of Leeds, and by the 2nd of July they reached their first point of destination—the Hague. Here, through the friendship of Lord Auckland, the vase was shown during a private interview to the Prince Stadtholder and the Princess of Orange,

and afterwards, at a breakfast given by Lady Auckland, again to royalty and the chief people of the Hague. The vase excited universal admiration; and men whose lives had been passed amidst the arts declared it to be a masterpiece. One, named Bost, who had been long an admirer of Wedgwood's skill, and was with his wife a collector of Wedgwood's works, considered that no other manufacture in the world could pretend to such a high degree of perfection. Lord Auckland was equally enthusiastic. He considered such a work a subject for national pride and an honour to the English Ambassador who had occasion to show it. Great as this praise was, he had that to say in sincerity which came nearer still to the great potter's heart. After referring to

Cnsr. XII. FOREIGN CRITICISM. 595

Wedgwood's pamphlet on the Vase, and gently hinting that its explanations of the bas-reliefs did not satisfy him, he added in his letter:

But I will use the two or three minutes which I can further dispose of to say a few words on a subject which with all your enthusiasm for arts and sciences probably interests you much more. I mean your son. We all agree—and in this respect the people of the Hague are not bad critics—t-hat your son is a very fine young man, with every appearance of having profitted fully by the excellent education you have given him, and I have not a. doubt he will prove a source of great happiness and credit to you.1

Afier it had given much joy to the household at Etruria, the father in his pride enclosed this letter to his son, with congratulations on the honours which had already attended his and Mr. Byerley's progress.

From the Hague the travellers proceeded to Amsterdam, and thence to Hanover, Berlin and Frankfort.2 At Berlin the vase was shown to the royal family; but in spite of generous hospitality and lavish praise, subscribers were few. N 0 price had yet been named, for Wedgwood himself could hardly fix it.

With respect to the Barberini Vase,

he writes to his son: 596 TOUR IN GERMANY. Cnar. XII.

I do not yet know what to say about the price. I have not yet been able to make another good one. I have tried five more since you left us, but not one near so good as that you have. So that unless we are more successful £50 is too little to save us from loss. Perhaps it would not be amiss to say this to some of the noblesse. However there is no appearance at present of its being at all prudent to fix the price at less than £50. What encouragement is there for the moderns to attempt 1 Lord Auckland to IVedgwood, Pottery, says this visit was madc by J uly 1790. Mayer MSS. Wedgwood, the elder, but this is a 1' Whilst in Saxony Mr. Vedg-mistake. There is no evidence that wood, junior, and Byerley visited the Josiah Vedgwood, senior, was ever Royal Porcelain works at Meissen. in Germany. Marryat, in his history of Modern the production of such works, if their patrons refuse to pay 315 part of what the ancients paid to their artists.1

Of the fine copy which thus accompanied the travellers the injunctions not to part with it were most stringent.

I do not know whether I have told you in so many words that you must not on any account part with the vase, but bring it back with you. It will be necessary to keep this identical one that I may be able to confront gainsayers with it. We have not yet made one near so fine as yours."

As early as the previous May twenty copies had been subscribed for, and this number was ultimately much increased; but from the difficulties attending the various processes and their great cost, it is probable that not more than fifty copies were made in Wedgwood's lifetime, and even these were not all of an average degree of merit. Nor were they all exactly similar; some of the vases being ' made with the white without any blue in it, and some with the yellow-white, as different people have different tastes.' 3

After visiting all the chief cities in Germany, for the purpose not only of showing the vase, but also of settling various intricate business matters.With difierent correspondents, and opening new agencies for the sale of jaspcrs, cameos and common ware, Josiah Wedgwood junior and Mr. Byerley returned to their native country 1 Wedgwood to his son Josiah, October 14, 1790. Mayer MSS.

' Ibid. September 23, 1790. Mayer MSS.

' Mems. from London to Etruria. May 9, 1790.

It is uncertain how many copies of the Portland vase are yet extant. Through the kindness of Isaac F alcke, Esq., we give the list subjoined:— British Museum, 1 copy; Museum in Dresden, 1 ditto; Museum in Rome, 1 ditto; Apsley Pellatt, Esq., 1 ditto; Jose h Mayer, Es., 1 ditto; D. G. hfarjoribanks, Mil', 2 ditto; John Augustus Tulk, Esq., 1 ditto; The Right Honourable Earl of Mansfield, 1 ditto; Henr Durlaoher, Esq., 1 ditto; Isaac alcke. Esq., 1 ditto; Museum of Practical Geology, Jermyn Street, 1 ditto; Francis Vedgwood, Esq., Barlaston Hall, 1 ditto; The late Henry Thomas Hope, E.'q., 1 ditto; J. Jones, Esq_., 1 ditto;-total, 16.

Cnnr. XII. JOSIAH WEDGVVOOD THE YOUNGER. 597 in December, where a joyful welcome awaited them, both in London and at Etruria. The vase which they brought back with them was immediately sent down to Etruria, for the purpose of comparing it with what had been done and was doing. Unfortunately, there also returned with them the larger part of the beautiful ornamental goods, chiefly cameos and medallions, which had been prepared for the fairs of Leipsio and Frankfort and the coronation of the Austrian Emperor Leopold. But the coronation was postponed; and princes and people were alike too impoverished by war, heavy taxation, bad harvests and deficient vintage to have money to spare for the embellishment of their homes or persons. Wedgwood was rejoiced to have his son near him again. He was the head of the manufactory now, and all his father's letters prove that he was not only a most skilful potter, but to him was also due much of the success which attended YVedgwood's copies of the Portland Vase. It was his experiments which brought to perfection the blue-black colour of the body, which tested the kind of clay least liable to cracking, and who mastered many of the niceties in firing. In 1793, Josiah Wedgwood the younger married,1 and the old man had the delight before his death of looking upon the faces of a newer generation.

During his son's absence, and after his return from the Continent, Mr. Wedgwood was again greatly disturbed by fresh instances of the wholesale piracy of his finest works in heads and cameos. The chief seats of this atrocious and indefensible system were Birmingham and the 1 J anuarv 1793, Josiah 'Wedgwood junior, of Iltruria,Stafl'ordshire, married Miss Allen, eldest daughter of John Bartlett Allen, Esq., of Perubrnkeshire.— Gent. 's Mag. 1793. Shortly after, John Vedgwood,, the banker, married a younger sister of the above lady. Wedgwood at his death had three grandchildren—a daughter just born to his son John, and the infant son and daughter of Josiah Wedgwood junior.

598 ORGANISED PIRACY. CHAP. XII.

Potteries, and even London was suspected. In Birmingham some of the mounters, for the sake of a small bribe, permitted casts to be taken of the heads and cameos intrusted to them; and in the Potteries the thieves had organised a perfect system. Here a room was kept and a journeyman modeller employed by some persons in London or Birmingham, who engaged to supply any manufacturer with casts of the finest things made at Etruria. Bas-reliefs and cameos were alike the same, and even casts of the Barbcrini Vase were promised, as soon as any copies were made public. In cautioning Mr. Byerley in respect to the men employed in Greek Street, Mr. Wedgwood wrote: ' As most of our bas-reliefs are undercut it will be discoverable whether casts have been ' taken from them or not for it will be almost impossible to get the plaster perfectly clean out, but then they must be very narrowly examined." Yet in spite of every precaution, the thefts of these clever rascals had in a greater or less degree a long duration.

Although his health was much impaired, and during the last five years of his life was a frequent cause of grave anxiety to his friends, Mr. Wedgwood's retirement from the active duties of his nianufactory was at first more nominal than real. He however took longer and more frequent holidays than heretofore; and now usually spent portions of the spring, summer and autumn at Weymouth, Blackpool in Lancashire, Buxton or the Lakes. Buxton and Blackpool were favourite places of sojourn. Here it was that Dr. Darwin would occasionallv join him for a day or two, and where, renewing their old scientific discussions or suggesting new on_es, the hours 1 Wedgwood to Byerley, December 12, 1790. Meyer MSS.

CRAP. XII.. ' HOLIDAYS. 599 passed quickly by; Wedgwood's sobriety of judgment tempering the daring flights of Darwin's keen and previsional intellect. From Blackpool Wedgwood usually diverged into the Lake district with his wife and daughters, there to spend some weeks in the leisurely idleness of a true holiday. VVeymouth he did not like, although he received much attention from the aristocracy who visited it. In August 1793, he made a tour in Wales, and of a portion of this a brief diary remains.' Passing by Worcester, Malvern, Ledbury, Ross, Chepstow and Pontypool, he, with those of his family who were his companions, repaired to Caerwent (the ancient Venta) to see some Roman pavements of great beauty. The one first discovered had greatly suflered from neglect and vandalism. Those uncovered for his inspection were better preserved. Their patterns were, he found, of five colours; first, a dark colour nearly black, made from a native species of slate stone; second, a. dark and light brown, made likewise from the stones of the country split into laminze; next came white formed of indurated chalk; whilst the red tessera: were simply pieces of common tile. Though these colours, with the exception of the white were far from being

bright or pure, Wedgwood was exceedingly struck with the general efl'ect. 'Brighter colours,' as he justly said, ' would have produced that harshness which in some of our carpets is so offensive to the eye.' Antiquarianism had been an occasional recreation to him for some years. Once or twice he had been the guest of Major Rooke at Mansfield Woodhouse, near Nottingham, and had met there Gough, Nicholls and other well-known characters. At home his greatest hobby in later years was his — T1T§H1—SS_.

600 WEDGWOOD IN HIS GARDEN. CRAP. XII garden. Darwin had taken the greatest pains to select a head-gardener, and Downes, as his name was, was his master's right hand. The numerous bills in existence1 for what were then rare and costly shrubs and flowers, though now common in our gardens, show what pains were lavished on this part of the adornment of Etruria. His daughters shared in this taste. They were his constant companions in greenhouse and garden, and in their great love for him, looked upon it as a privilege to test the grace and beauty of new flower-pots and vases from the Works, by variously adorning them with flowers. At that date the cultivation of fruit under glass was but yet in its infancy. Downes and his master were however most successful in the production of hothouse grapes; and an aged lady yet living, spending whilst a child an autumn afternoon at Etruria, recollects the fine and tempting branch Wedgwood cut off the vine with his own hand and handed down with a triumphant ' There!' He and his neighbour, the Rev. Mr. Sneyd, made trials of various coloured bricks for walls on which fruit was grown; and their experiments seem to have resulted in a preference for black and highly glazed surfaces. With his neighbours of every rank he lived on terms of cordiality. In June 1787 he opened a bowling-green for their use; and he divided his patronage amongst those who were in trade. Whatever could be bought good of its kind in the Potteries was always favoured. A man of great ability named Massey at New-

castle supplied the manufactory with tools of every description, even those for the modellers; and from his old friend Samuel Mayer of the 1 Mayer MSS.

Gun. XII. TASTEFUL AND GENEROUS HOSPITALITY. 601 same place he had what saddlery he needed, as well as all leather goods for the Works. 1

From his first occupation of Etruria Hall his establishment had been that of a countrygentleman of good estate; as his fame and consequently his necessary hospitality increased, his establishment was likewise added to. In 1794, seven male servants, 2 alarge proportion of maid-servants, and these headed by a housekeeper, attended on the family and its incessant round of guests. The Hall must have often borne the appearance of a first-class London hotel during the season. Guests ever coming and going, visitors from the works, neighbours and friends. Foreigners from every country were occasionally there, and distinguished Englishmen formed a large proportion. Wedgwood had a strong sense of fitness and convenience, and without wasteful expenditure or ostentation, he had made his house 'a comfortable place.' Guests might well like to come and linger. In the cheery sitting-rooms, so full of light and warmth, they found the loveliest works of art —vases, bas-reliefs, cameos, medallions, and many other treasures of choice workmanship—on the harpsichord the newest music, on the shelves the newest books,3 as bills remaining show. Each day at three o'clock the dinner table was laid for unexpected as well as expected guests, for it was never known who might arrive before or after the meal was served. By the master's desire the service of the table was often changed. This week Etruscan painted plates and dishes adorned it, next simple oor musician or author was sure 0 subscribers to his works at Etruria. And the numberless

' lIa.ssey's bills. Various dates. Ditto lIa_ver's.—Mayer MSS. ' List of male servants. Duty was

' Every paid for ten horses. VVedgwood was a good horseman, and to the last accompanied his daughters in their daily rides.

bills for picture frames paid to Flaxman's brother by Miss IVedg='ood and her sisters prove the practical interest they took in art. 602-LOVE FOR BOOKS. Can. XII. cream colour, a third the grape pattern or some other variation. To-day the salt-cellars were jasper with Flaxman's bas-reliefs, to-morrow black basaltes of exquisite form, or vessels resembling shells. The dessert would be served in dishes formed as autumnal leaves, or in those modelled from the antique. Even the cook had moulds for her puddings, her fruits and her jellies, of varied kinds. Such was the master's taste.

The collecting of books was also to the last another of Wedgwood's recreations. During Bentley's lifetime Payne's catalogues of second-hand books were sent regularly to Etruria, and those Wedgwood marked were supplied. Chest after chest found its way into Stafiordshire; but time was often wanted to unpack and arrange them, much less to read them. On one occasion he writes to Bentley, ' I thank you for the catalogues, but have not had time to read a page. My wife says I must buy no more books till I build another house, and advises me to first read some of those I have already. What nonsense she sometimes talks! '1 Yet in spite of this remonstrance the old taste still prevailed; and as his youngest son grew into manhood the library became still larger and more philosophical and scientific in character. The book bills paid by Mr. Byerley were for still larger sums, and Chisholm and his master were always sending for some fine work—-either for the artists' or their own scientific information. In this relation to his art Wedgwood's liberality was unbounded. Nothing was spared which might enrich it. ' Get books, prints, models and all you require,' was often repeated to Bentley, whose tastes in this respect were as munificent as his own. All the best artistic works which were issued from the presses 1 Wedgwood to Bentley, August 1779.

CIIAP. XII. CORRESPONDENCE. 603 of Rome, Florence, Venice, Bologna, Paris, Amsterdam and elsewhere, at the close of the seventeenth and during the first half of the eighteenth century, were purchased and laid before his modellers. In this wide range of vision, this use of collateral agents, this subservieney of means to ends, were included some of the great elements of Wedgwood's success.

His correspondence had always been extensive. Towards the close of his life it increased. Lord Dundonald wished to _enlist his aid in a scheme for extracting tar and pitch from coal, Lavoisier solicited him to contribute to the 'Annales de Chimie,' a scientific journal intended as a vehicle to the discussions and opinions of advanced chemistry. He corresponded with Arthur Young on many points relative to retorts and drainingpipes; and with Bramah on the machinery of baths and other domestic conveniences.

Generosity had always been one of his characteristics. As his life drew to its close, it merged into a thoughtful beneficence, as wise as it was genial. At the close of the American war he contributed on several occasions to the relief of the distress of British residents in that country. In 1792 his sons and himself conjointly gave £250 towards the succour of the people of Poland. He subscribed to the Philanthropic and other Benevolent Societies, and ' to that for the Abolition of the Slave Trade. In September 1793, when a public subscription was proposed for the relief of the five thousand emigrant French clergy then in this country, he would not contribute till the relief of the laity was included, considering that they were by far the greatest sufferers.' To his own workmen, and the

' Proposal to relieve Emigrant French Cler. Wedgwood's MS. remarks thereon, suggesting not to omit Laity.—lfaiver MSS.
604 PARLIAMENTARY REFORM. CHAD. XII. poor of the Potteries generally considered, he was the kindest friend. A free library and sick fund were attached to the Works,1 and for some

months previous to his death he was actively employed in an attempt to procure the erection of a House of Industry for the parish of Stoke, but his endeavours were defeated by the prejudice and alarm of the lower orders.

After the outbreak of the French Revolution various societies were formed in London and the large provincial towns, for various purposes connected with politics; but in more than one instance he refused to join them, as he considered such associations did little more than set one part of the nation against another. It was in Parlia mentary Reform he saw the true remedy for many political evils.

Speaking politically (he wrote to his son Josiah) I believe you know my sentiments, that so long as we have septennial Parliaments it is of little consequence who is chosen into them... A real Parliamentary reform is therefore wh at we most stand in need of, & for this I would willingly devote my time, the most precious thing I have, or anything else by which I could serve so noble a cause... These are the principles on which have hitherto acted, but I do not desire you to adopt them merely because they have been mine. Examine for yourself, and then act according to your honest conviction in this and every other instance, and your conduct whether it is the same as my own would have been in like circumstances will nevertheless have my ap probation.'

The truth and value of his friendship we have seen in respect to Bentley, Brindley and Darwin. We hear little of Mrs. Bentley after her husband's death, except as

IBoth were under the manage-IIistory.—Watcbman Ne a merit of Mr. Greatbach. The books November 7, 1863. wsp per' were all excellent of their kind, ' Ved ood toJosiah VVedgwood and included Essays, Lectures and junior, ay 17, 1790.
Gnu. XII. FRIENDSHIPS. 605
Wedgwood managed that part of her income which lay in canal shares and profitable mortgages. Sheresided in Grower Street, then a new and choice quarter of London, from its contiguity

to the open fields, and often sent parcels into Staflordshire, by the boxes which went from Greek Street, so that we may presume she was an occasional guest at Etruria. W'itll Boulton Wedgwood's friendship and communion stood true to the end. The generous rivalries of their prime rather strengthened than not the manly regard of their years of decline. To the last they loved art, and assisted each other in its improvement. Though Wedgwood lost considerably by Boulton's mining schemes, he yet stood by him in the hour of need. He lent Boulton £5,000, which was repaid with interest in 1792. It was at that date also that Wedgwood, yet alive to every improvement for his manufactory, opened, through his son, negotiations for the erection of a steam-engine on the principle known as the Sun-andPlanet motion.

Much as he regarded his friends, Wedgwood when necessary did not hesitate to speak with candour. After the Birmingham riots, which as Darwin said ' were a disgrace to mankind, for active ignorance delights in repressing the sciences it does not understand,' Wedgwood joined Mr. Russell in affording adequate relief to Priestley. The latter, in the confidence of friendship, sent him his 'Appeal to the Public,' whilst yet in MS. On its return, Wedgwood ventured to propose certain alterations in the preface. He thought the bitterness displayed therein would only inflame public animosity still more. He considered Priestley to be superior to such a species of resentment, and he did not wish that an idea should be promulgated, that the Dissenters were in any 606 CARE FOR HIS RELATIVES. C11AP.XII.

way inimical to the government, whilst the truth was so opposite.

Wedgwood by industry and wise investment accumulated more than half a million of money. To each of his three daughters he left a portion of £25,000, to his son Thomas £29,000, to his son John £30,000, and to his son Josiah a proportionate sum, and, with the exception of the share enjoyed by Mr. Byerley, who survived till the close of 1810,

the whole of his splendid business. Mrs. Wedgwood, who outlived her husband twenty years, had an adequate life interest in his estate. Mr. Wedgwood survived all his brothers and many of his sisters. Mrs. Willet enjoyed an ample provision, Chisholm a life annuity, and many other of his relations and servants received some token of his favour. As Dr. Darwin well said afterwards:

He never knew an instance of a man raising himself to such opulence and distinction who excited so little envy; and this in a great measure arose from his prudent and modest acquisition of riches, and also from the circumstance that he was free from the failing which frequently attends easily acquired riches of neglecting his poor relations. He kindly attended to his and was of essential service to many of them.

One of his personal peculiarities was his dislike to ac-. counts. He used to say he knew he had lost thousands by not attending to this department of his business: but he could not bring himself to enter upon the details of figures, as they so wholly interrupted those trains of thought necessary to his work. One or two old pocketbooks bear evidence to this idiosyncrasy. They contain a jumble as strange in its way as the pocket—books of Brindley. For instance, he will set off on a journey on horseback to London, and for the first few miles he will diligently record his expenses, even to the penny he gives

CHAI'. XII. PERSONAL CHARACTERISTICS. 607 a girl for opening a gate or gathering him a bunch of wayside flowers. Then he drops off into some meditation concerning mixtures, colours, or forms, and all else is forgotten. The next entry is at the distance of days, and then it will relate to some possible degree of fineness in wire sieves, or some chemical experiment. In respect to debts he would take no advantage of other creditors. In the long course of his business life he only in one instance arrested a person, and that arose from a palpable attempt to misuse his property. When any of his subordinates took proceedings of this nature without his knowledge, they were

speedily terminated by enlarging the person, and paying all the costs himself.

Simplicity, modesty, indomitable energy and industry were amongst his strongest characteristics. He could not be idle. He would not believe in the impossible. His words to his own men were, in all cases of difficulty, what they had been to the excavators of the Harecastle Tunnel-_ 'It must be done.f In his youth and days of prime, he rose in summer with the sun, in winter before it was light; and was often down and busy_in his Works before his men arrived. He would take up the thread of every man or _woman's duty from day to day and mentally review it— and this even after a month's absence from home. It was not till his means were ample that he began to indulge in simple luxuries. He then buys a diamond and ruby ring as a love-token to his wife, andtreats himself to the engraving of a seal with the family arms. From this date the majo-' rity of his letters to Bentley are sealed with it, and from two of the best im-_ _ V pressions the little engraving here annexed r15;b;L4&. wEDs£_30;)r is taken, (fig. 149).
608 INCREASING VALUE OF HIS VVORKS. CRAP. XII.

In reviewing the life of this distinguished Englishman one point is very striking, that of an entire harmony between the moral and intellectual faculties, or what painters would call ' keeping.' We have had men with still higher degrees and character of intellect; but in them perhaps the moral faculties have been weak or otherwise intelligence subordinated to morality. But here the entire harmony was as perfect as it was rare. N 0 doubt if we could see the diamond a little nearer we should discover specks and flaws, just as occasionally in his works we come upon minor incongruities_-a classical bordering allied with a group of modern figures, or a mediseval decoration in juxtaposition with a design drawn from the antique. He himself confesses to occasional infirmity of temper and other small shortcomings; but the very confession only proves the worth and modesty of the man.

As he himself well said, his ornamental works 'only wanted time and scarcity to make them worth anything.' Our day proves this. Articles which originally cost pence sell for pounds now. ' With increased knowledge and taste, with more enlarged conceptions of art, with our desire to be creators rather than imitators, this worth will grow; till at length, enshrined—as we hope they may be—nlore and more in Museums and Collections accessible to the people, they may teach their great artistic lessons, not in tile direction of servile copy, but in the direction which le_.ds on; the taking up of art in terra-cotta where the great master left it, and whose possible beauty and perfection he saw in vision, but which the low artistic culture of his time did not suffer him to realise. Through means of this character we may beautify the architecture of a newer age in a manner worthy of what has gone before. Not by weak and servile copies of the ideal grace of an

CRAP. XII. SIR VVILLIAM HOOKER'S MONUMENT. 609 effete theology, but by visible presentments of vital passages in our national history. The Greeks had Homer, we too have a Shakespeare; and the trammels of costume which our artists profess to be their hindrance, will be as nothing when men shall lend their will to vitalize the work which lies before them. Could Wedgwood rise again, he would stand amazed at the veneration and regard which cleaves to his name and his productions. Men of the highest intellectual gifts collect the latter; and we are beginning to see that we may resort to his art for the expression of sentiments at once appreciative and reverent. In the jasper body which he invented, in his manufaetory at Etruria, plaques with fern leaves in basrelief are, at this date, in the workmen's hands for the adornment of a monument in Kew Church to the memory of the late Sir William Jackson Hooker, whose name, in connection with his many valuable labours, is as great in botany as Wedgwood's is in pottery. Our illustration (fig. 150) shows this beautiful design, so far as the potter's art extends.1 Early in life

Wedgwood had directed his attention to the discovery of a soft glass which, free from any admixture of 1 From a. design by Reginald Palgrave, Esq., of the House of Commons. VOL. II. R R lead, should seem as an innoxious glaze for common pottery. His experiments were interrupted by other duties. He resumed them in 1794; but whilst his trials gave flattering hopes of ultimate success, illness again prostrated him. The symptoms were old ones—pains in his right jaw and in what Darwin quaintly called his 'no leg,' shortness of breath, and debility. He repaired, as was his wont, to Buxton; and upon his return was so much better that his son Josiah wrote cheerily of him to the doctor, and he himself indorsed this good news by a letter to his old friend. In reply to this, Darwin wrote:

Your letter gives me great pleasure in assuring me, what your son Josiah had before mention'd, that you have become free from your c0mplaint—the ceasing of the palpitation of your heart & of the intermission of your pulse is another proof of your increase of strength. In respect to your breath being less free in walking up hill I ascribe to the distant approach of age and not to Asthma. You know how unwilling we all are to grow old. As you are so well, I advise you to leave ofi' the bark & take no medicine at present.1

This letter is dated December 9, 1794; and Wedgwood folding it, indorsed it, though with an error as to date, 'Dr. Darwin, December 3, 1794.' In the writing is the visible sign of failing power. A few days after, his face swelled, and, attributing this to a decayed tooth, he sent for Mr. Bent to draw it. But, to the surgeon's consternation when he came, he discovered early symptoms of mortification. The distress of Wedgwood's family was extreme when they learnt this. From this date he grew gradually worse; his throat became inflamed, and his weakness increased. Dr. Darwin hastened over from Derby, and with two other physicians and Mr. Bent 1 Darwin Correspondence.

(Inn. XII. THE CLOSE OF A GOOD

LIFE. 611 watched sedulously by his bed. But nothing could save him. He suffered greatly from pain and fever. As these lessened, insensibility came over him; and thus in uncon Sacred to the Memory 01

JOSIAH WEDGWOOD, F.R..S. and SA.

Of Etruria in this county.

I Born, August 1730. Died January 3rd. 1795.

Vho converted a rude and inconsidenble la. 'T Manufactory into an elegant Art and _ 14 An important part of National Commerce.

(Fi;z.1»1.) wtznnwooifn M0.'l7)E."'. PARIBII Cmnwfl, STOKE-UPON-'l'RK."!'. sciousness he passed away from the scene of his labours, and his good life, on Saturday, January 3, 1795, in the sixty-fifth year of his age. His children and his devoted wife, 'whose life,' as

Byerley wrote to Boardman, 'had been so full of happiness,' were his only nurses, and kept their watch and performed their ministry with a love and devotion never surpassed.1 Throughout a wide neighbourhood and at the Works a breathless interest attended on his state; and when all was over, his old and faithful servants mourned sincerely.

From the nature of his complaint, he had to be buried speedily. Through the deep snow, which then lay over England, he was borne to his last resting-place in the porchway of the old parish church of Stoke on Tuesday, January 6. At a subsequent date, Flaxman made his monument, and it was placed in the chancel (fig. 151).2

' Byerley to Boardman, January aid for the monument £ 93 19s.— 18, 1795. —Mayer MSS. ayer MSS. 2 September 3, 1803. Flaxman was

CHAP. XII. W'EDGW'OOD'S MONUMENT AND GRAVE. 613

Upon the rebuilding of the church upon a fresh site in 1829, the monument was removed into the new chancel; and the grave thus uncovered, with that of his wife, who died January 15, 1815, now lies simply railed in, as seen in the engraving (fig. 152), amidst the other graves in the churchyard. N o more than this simplicity was needed, for his name lives in the industrial history of the country he loved so well, and so enriched by the bounties of his art and the example of his worthy life.

'I EDGrWOOD'S art, considered relative to its highest development, being in advance of the times in which he lived, it naturally followed that during the period which succeeded, the taste for his productions should be confined to a few, and that little more than vivid traditions of him as a man and as a citizen be treasured in the district to which he belonged. It was also natural that in an age of more general culture, purer taste, higher artistic conceptions, the sense of what he did for art, the potters' art especially, should be superadded to these traditions of personal veneration; and that consequently combined in fitting and vital union, appreciation should widen its bounds, and exist everywhere where culture has touched with its humanising and purifying influence. Wedgwood in his own day was the artist for the few——in ours for the many— for happily Museums and National Collections show his beautiful works; and all who know something of the artistic, social, and industrial history of their country, can in a. greater or less degree, appreciate the principle be brought so efficiently into oper-ation—that of the union of grace and utility, and the applicability of such to every possible and varied purpose of his art. Herein lies the artistic philosophy of manufactures; and as we ourselves have risen through culture to an appreciation of its necessary and vital truths, so also arose the idea— widening, extending, and at length made objective—— of erecting a MEMORIAL to him, that whilst provincial in its immediate utility should be national in its fame. Such is the Wsnawoon 1Im1on1AL BUILDING now in course of erection at Burslem in Staffordshire. It will combine in an improved form the old Free School of Burslem——will be a. Museum of Ceramic Art, 21 School of Design, a Laboratory, and a Free Public Lending Library. Its first stone was laid on October 26, 1863, by the Right Hon. W. E. Gladstone, Chancellor of the Exchequer. The permanent maintenance of the building has been provided for under the provisions of Mr. Ewart's Public Libraries and Museums Act, which entitles the Institute to the advantages of a. penny rate upon the property of the district. From the first the idea has been to make the building emblematic of the arts of the district—and illustrative of the use of terra-cotta—a.s one of the distinguishing decorative features of modern architecture. For this reason the admirable design of Mr. Robert Edgar of London was chosen, which being in the Pointed Style, based upon those types of ceramic architecture so prevalent in Northern Italy during the fifteenth and sixteenth century—-allowed of the introduction of terra.-cotta in varied ornamental forms. The windows, the doorways, the outer cornices and walls will be thus ornamented; a frieze divided into eight or more compartments, will represent as many of the industrial processes of the potter's art. Portraits of Wedgwood's distinguished friends and contemporaries, as also of celebrated potters of every age painted in Majolica colours on large plaques, will fill the spaces of the arched windowheads, and over the chief entrance panels in jasper ware will be introduced. This variety of colouring with the richly moulded and ornamental brickwork will make the building unique in its kind.

618 NATIONAL AND LOCAL DUTY.

The library, and a spacious reading-room will occupy the half of the ground floor to the lefi; of the main entrance; while to the right accommodation will be provided for the school. There will also be a. laboratory and a room for literary and scientific lectures and discussions. On the upper floor the central space will be occupied by the museum; and to the right and lefi: of this will be the School of Art with its 'class-rooms for pupils of both sexes, and in various stages of progress. This upper floor, which was designed in the most painstaking manner, by the late eminent natural architect, Captain Fowke, C.E. will be wholly top-lighted. In the museum—which may be considered the feature of the scheme most interesting to those not resident or directly connected with the locality—it is hoped will be gathered the choicest examples illustrative of the history of pottery in all countries and in all ages, but especially of our own land, and of those times which led up to the crowning glory of Wedgwood's productions.

Regarded in its national sense, those who are proud of their country, of the industrial arts which have made it what it is, and who would give higher scope and aim to ultimate results, will recollect that institutions of the kind can only fulfil their purpose when rich in those appliances and accessories which teach and examplify. Hence, whatever serves to increase their eficiency, or is gathered into them, with a view to utility, whether it be by gift or bequeathrnent, is at once an expression of admiration and sympathy, and is productive of far more powerful and lasting results than can arise from accumulation in private museums and collections. Viewed locally, the Wedgwood Institute will, if rightly understood, serve a higher purpose still. It will hold in constant recognition the fame of a good man and his admirable works. It will teach to all—— if indirectly——through the traditions and history of his life, that patience, humility, truth, persistence, and an earnest desire to perfect so far as possible, are necessary to fulfilment and success. Scholars on the very spot where he himself fought so bravely many difiiculties of his earnest life, they will learn and desire to carry on their local art with an efficiency worthy of so great a master. They will perceive that he was no mere copyist, but looked around him widely for those analogies and truths out from which freshness and originality come: and they too, if the Memorial Institute fulfil its purpose rightly,

POSSIBLE RESULTS. 619 will not rest satisfied-with productions which only hear a faroff likeness to the things and ideas of an eifete past; but so become creators in their lovely art, as to make what they create at once an evidence and a sign that they have profited directly and indirectly by the life and memory of Wedgwood, and this in a manner worthy of him and of their country.

CPSIA information can be obtained
at www.ICGtesting.com
Printed in the USA
LVOW03s1020181215

467147LV00012B/417/P